The Man
Who Ate
Everything

The Man
Who Ate
Everything

And Other Gastronomic Feats,
Disputes, and Pleasurable Pursuits

JEFFREY
STEINGARTEN

Alfred A. Knopf • New York • 1998

MOST OF THE PIECES IN THIS COLLECTION HAVE APPEARED, IN SOMEWHAT
DIFFERENT FORM, IN *VOGUE*; SEVERAL OTHERS FIRST APPEARED IN *HG*, AND
ONE APPEARED IN *SLATE*.

OWING TO LIMITATIONS OF SPACE, ACKNOWLEDGMENTS FOR PERMISSION TO
REPRINT PREVIOUSLY PUBLISHED MATERIAL MAY BE FOUND ON PAGE 515.

LIBRARY OF CONGRESS CATALOGING-IN-PUBLICATION DATA
STEINGARTEN, JEFFREY.
THE MAN WHO ATE EVERYTHING : AND OTHER GASTRONOMIC FEATS,
DISPUTES, AND PLEASURABLE PURSUITS / BY JEFFREY STEINGARTEN. —
1ST ED.
P. CM.
INCLUDES INDEX.
ISBN 0-679-43088-1 (CLOTH)
1. GASTRONOMY—HUMOR. 2. FOOD—HUMOR. I. TITLE.
TX631.S74 1997
641'.01'30207—DC21 97-2815 CIP

MANUFACTURED IN THE UNITED STATES OF AMERICA

PUBLISHED NOVEMBER 11, 1997
SECOND PRINTING, JANUARY 1998

For Caron, Anna, and Michael

Contents

CONTENTS

CONTENTS

PART FIVE   **Proof of the Pudding**

The Man
Who Ate
Everything

Introduction:
The Man Who
Ate Everything

"My first impulse was to fall upon the cook," wrote Edmondo de Amicis, a nineteenth-century traveler to Morocco. "In an instant I understood perfectly how a race who ate such food must necessarily believe in another God and hold essentially different views of human life from our own. . . . There was a suggestion of soap, wax, pomatum, of unguents, dyes, cosmetics; of everything, in short, most unsuited to enter a human mouth."

This is precisely how I felt about a whole range of foods, particularly desserts in Indian restaurants, until 1989, the year that I, then a lawyer, was appointed food critic of *Vogue* magazine. As I considered the awesome responsibilities of my new post, I grew morose. For I, like everybody I knew, suffered from a set of powerful, arbitrary, and debilitating attractions and aversions at mealtime. I feared that I could be no more objective than an art critic who detests the color yellow or suffers from red-green color blindness. At the time I was friendly with a respected and powerful editor of cookbooks who grew so nauseated by the flavor of cilantro that she brought a pair of tweezers to Mexican and Indian restaurants and pinched out every last scrap of it before she would take a bite. Imagine the dozens of potential Julia Childs and M. F. K. Fishers whose books she peevishly rejected, whose careers she snuffed in their infancy! I vowed not to follow in her footsteps.

Suddenly, intense food preferences, whether phobias or cravings, struck me as the most serious of all personal limitations. That very day I sketched out a Six-Step Program to liberate my palate and my soul. No smells or tastes are innately repulsive, I assured myself, and what's learned can be forgot.

STEP ONE was to compose an annotated list.

My Food Phobias

I. Foods I wouldn't touch even if I were starving on a desert island:

None, except maybe insects.   Many cultures find insects highly nutritious and love their crunchy texture. The pre-Hispanic Aztecs roasted worms in a variety of ways and made pressed caviar from mosquito eggs. This proves that no innate human programming keeps me from eating them, too. Objectively, I must look as foolish as those Kalahari Bushmen who face famine every few years because they refuse to eat three-quarters of the 223 animal species around them. I will deal with this phobia when I have polished off the easy ones.

2. Foods I wouldn't touch even if I were starving on a desert island until absolutely everything else runs out:

Kimchi, the national pickle of Korea.   Cabbage, ginger, garlic, and red peppers—I love them all, but not when they are fermented together for many months to become kimchi. Nearly forty-one million South Koreans eat kimchi three times a day. They say "kimchi" instead of "cheese" when someone is taking their picture. I say, "Hold the kimchi."

Anything featuring dill. What could be more benign than dill?

Swordfish. This is a favorite among the feed-to-succeed set, who like it grilled to the consistency of running shoes and believe it is good for them. A friend of mine eats swordfish five times a week and denies that he has any food phobias. Who's kidding whom? Returning obsessively to a few foods is the same as being phobic toward all the rest. This may explain the Comfort Food Craze. But the goal of the arts, culinary or otherwise, is not to increase our comfort. That is the goal of an easy chair.

During my own praline period, which lasted for three years, I would order any dessert on the menu containing caramelized hazelnuts and ignore the rest. I grew so obsessive that I almost missed out on the crème brûlée craze then sweeping the country. After my praline period had ebbed, I slid into a crème brûlée fixation, from which I forcibly wrenched myself only six months ago.

Anchovies. I met my first anchovy on a pizza in 1962, and it was seven years before I mustered the courage to go near another. I am known to cross the street whenever I see an anchovy coming. Why would anybody consciously choose to eat a tiny, oil-soaked, leathery maroon strip of rank and briny flesh?

Lard. The very word causes my throat to constrict and beads of sweat to appear on my forehead.

Desserts in Indian restaurants. The taste and texture of face creams belong in the boudoir, not on the plate. See above.

Also: miso, mocha, chutney, raw sea urchins, and falafel (those hard, dry, fried little balls of ground chickpeas unaccountably enjoyed in Middle Eastern countries).

5

3. Foods I might eat if I were starving on a desert island but only if the refrigerator were filled with nothing but chutney, sea urchins, and falafel:

Greek food. I have always considered "Greek cuisine" an oxymoron. Nations are like people. Some are good at cooking while others have a talent for music or baseball or manufacturing memory chips. The Greeks are really good at both pre-Socratic philosophy and white statues. They have not been good cooks since the fifth century B.C., when Siracusa on Sicily was the gastronomic capital of the world. Typical of modern-day Greek cuisine are feta cheese and retsina wine. Any country that pickles its national cheese in brine and adulterates its national wine with pine pitch should order dinner at the local Chinese place and save its energies for other things. The British go to Greece just for the food, which says volumes to me. You would probably think twice before buying an Algerian or Russian television set. I thought for ten years before buying my last Greek meal.

Clams. I feel a mild horror about what goes on in the wet darkness between the shells of all bivalves, but clams are the only ones I dislike. Is it their rubbery consistency or their rank subterranean taste, or is the horror deeper than I know?

Blue food (not counting plums and berries). This may be a rational aversion, because I am fairly sure that God meant the color blue mainly for food that has gone bad.

Also: cranberries, kidneys, okra, millet, coffee ice cream, refried beans, and many forms of yogurt.

This had to stop.

STEP TWO was to immerse myself in the scientific literature on human food selection.

By design and by destiny, humans are omnivores. Our teeth and digestive systems are all-purpose and ready for anything. Our genes do not dictate what foods we should find tasty or repulsive. We come into the world with a yen for sweets (newborns can even distinguish among glucose, fructose, lactose, and sucrose) and a weak aversion to bitterness, and after four months develop a fondness for salt. Some people are born particularly sensitive to one taste or odor; others have trouble digesting milk sugar or wheat gluten. A tiny fraction of adults, between 1 and 2 percent, have true (and truly dangerous) food allergies. All human cultures consider fur, paper, and hair inappropriate as food.

And that's about it. Everything else is *learned*. Newborns are not repelled even by the sight and smell of putrefied meat crawling with maggots.

The nifty thing about being omnivores is that we can take nourishment from an endless variety of flora and fauna and easily adapt to a changing world—crop failures, droughts, herd migrations, restaurant closings, and the like. Lions and tigers will starve in a salad bar, as will cows in a steak house, but not us. Unlike cows, who remain well nourished eating only grass, humans *need* a great diversity of foods to stay healthy.

Yet by the age of twelve, we all suffer from a haphazard collection of food aversions ranging from revulsion to indifference. The tricky part about being omnivores is that we are always in danger of poisoning ourselves. Catfish have taste buds on their whiskers, but we are not so lucky. Instead, we are born with a cautious ambivalence toward novel foods, a precarious balance between neophilia and neophobia. Just one bad stomach ache or attack of nausea after dinner is enough to form a potent aversion—even if the food we ate did not actually cause the problem and even if we know it didn't. Hives or rashes may lead us rationally to avoid the food that caused them, but only an upset stomach and nausea will result in a lasting, irrational, lifelong sense of disgust. Otherwise, psychologists know very little about the host of powerful likes and dislikes—let us lump them all

under the term "food phobias"—that children carry into adult-
hood.

By closing ourselves off from the bounties of nature, we
become failed omnivores. We let down the omnivore team. God
tells us in the Book of Genesis, right after Noah's flood, to eat
everything under the sun. Those who ignore his instructions are
no better than godless heathens.

The more I contemplated food phobias, the more I became
convinced that people who habitually avoid certifiably delicious
foods are at least as troubled as people who avoid sex, or take no
pleasure from it, except that the latter will probably seek psychi-
atric help, while food phobics rationalize their problem in the
name of genetic inheritance, allergy, vegetarianism, matters of
taste, nutrition, food safety, obesity, or a sensitive nature. The
varieties of neurotic food avoidance would fill several volumes,
but milk is a good place to start.

Overnight, everybody you meet has become lactose intoler-
ant. It is the chic food fear of the moment. But the truth is that
very, very few of us are so seriously afflicted that we cannot drink
even a whole glass of milk a day without ill effects. I know several people who have given up cheese to avoid lactose. But fermented cheeses contain no lactose! Lactose is the sugar found in
milk; 98 percent of it is drained off with the whey (cheese is made
from the curds), and the other 2 percent is quickly consumed by
lactic-acid bacteria in the act of fermentation.

Three more examples: People rid their diet of salt (and their
food of flavor) to avoid high blood pressure and countless imagined ills. But no more than 8 percent of the population is sensitive to salt. Only *saturated* fat, mainly from animals, has ever
been shown to cause heart disease or cancer, yet nutrition writers and Nabisco get rich pandering to the fear of eating any fat at
all. The hyperactivity syndrome supposedly caused by white
sugar has never, ever, been verified—and not for lack of trying.
In the famous New Haven study, it was the presence of the parents, not the presence of white sugar, that was causing the prob-

lem; most of the kids calmed down when their parents left the room.*

I cannot figure out why, but the atmosphere in America today rewards this sort of self-deception. Fear and suspicion of food have become the norm. Convivial dinners have nearly disappeared and with them the sense of festivity and exchange, of community and sacrament. People should be deeply ashamed of the irrational food phobias that keep them from sharing food with each other. Instead, they have become proud and isolated, arrogant and aggressively misinformed.

But not me.

STEP THREE was to choose my weapon. Food phobias can be extinguished in five ways. Which one would work best for me?

9

Brain surgery. Bilateral lesions made in the basolateral region of the amygdala seem to do the trick in rats and, I think, monkeys—eliminating old aversions, preventing the formation of new ones, and increasing the animals' acceptance of novel foods. But the literature does not report whether having a brain operation also diminishes their ability to, say, follow a recipe. If these experimental animals could talk, would they still be able to? Any volunteers?

Starvation. As Aristotle claimed and modern science has confirmed, any food tastes better the hungrier you are. But as I recently confessed to my doctor, who warned me to take some pill only on an empty stomach, the last time I had an empty stomach was in 1978. He scribbled "hyperphagia" on my chart, your doctor's name for making a spectacle of yourself at the table. He is a jogger.

*For the details, be sure to read the chapters "Salt," "Pain Without Gain," and "Murder, My Sweet," in Part Three.

Bonbons. Why not reward myself with a delectable little chocolate every time I successfully polish off an anchovy, a dish of kimchi, or a bowl of miso soup? Parents have used rewards ever since spinach was discovered. Offering children more play-time for eating dark leafy greens may temporarily work. But offering children an extra Milky Way bar in return for eating more spinach has perverse results: the spinach grows more repellent and the Milky Way more desired.

Drug dependence. Finicky laboratory animals find new foods more palatable after a dose of chlordiazepoxide. According to an old *Physicians' Desk Reference*, this is nothing but Librium, the once-popular tranquilizer, also bottled as Reposans and Sereen. The label warns you about nausea, depression, and operating heavy machinery. I just said no.

Exposure, plain and simple. Scientists tell us that aversions fade away when we eat moderate doses of the hated foods at moderate intervals, especially if the food is complex and new to us. (Don't try this with allergies, but don't cheat either: few of us have genuine food allergies.) Exposure works by overcoming our innate neophobia, the omnivore's fear of new foods that balances the biological urge to explore for them. Did you know that babies who are breast-fed will later have less trouble with novel foods than those who are given formula? The variety of flavors that make their way into breast milk from the mother's diet prepares the infant for the culinary surprises that lie ahead. Most parents give up trying novel foods on their weanlings after two or three attempts and then complain to the pediatrician; this may be the most common cause of fussy eaters and finicky adults—of omnivores manqués. *Most babies will accept nearly anything after eight or ten tries.*

Clearly, mere exposure was the only hope for me.

STEP FOUR was to make eight or ten reservations at Korean restaurants, purchase eight or ten anchovies, search the Zagat guide for eight or ten places with the names Parthenon or Olympia (which I believe are required by statute for Greek restaurants), and bring a pot of water to the boil for cooking eight or ten chickpeas. My plan was simplicity itself: every day for the next six months I would eat at least one food that I detested.

Here are some of the results:

Kimchi. After repeatedly sampling ten of the sixty varieties of kimchi, the national pickle of Korea, kimchi has become my national pickle, too.

Anchovies. I began relating to anchovies a few months ago in northern Italy, where I ordered *bagna caôda* every day—a sauce of garlic, butter, olive oil, and minced anchovies served piping hot over sweet red and yellow peppers as an antipasto in Piemonte. My phobia crumpled when I understood that the anchovies living in American pizza parlors bear no relation to the sweet, tender anchovies of Spain and Italy, cured in dry sea salt and a bit of pepper. Soon I could tell a good *bagna caôda* from a terrific one. On my next trip to Italy I will seek out those fresh charcoal grilled anchovies of the Adriatic you always hear about.

Clams. My first assault on clams was at a diner called Lunch near the end of Long Island, where I consumed an order of fried bellies and an order of fried strips. My aversion increased sharply.

Eight clams and a few weeks later it was *capellini* in white clam sauce at an excellent southern Italian restaurant around the corner from my house. As I would do so often in the future, even at the expense of my popularity, I urged my companions to cast off their food phobias by ordering at least one dish they expected to detest. If they would go along with my experiment, I would agree to order *nothing* I liked.

All but one agreed, a slim and lovely dancer who protested that her body tells her precisely what to eat and that I am the last person in the universe fit to interfere with those sacred messages. I replied that the innate wisdom of the body is a complete fiction when it comes to omnivores. Soon I had certain proof that my friend was a major closet food phobic when she spent five minutes painstakingly separating her appetizer into two piles. The pile composed of grilled peppers, fennel, and eggplant sat lonely on the plate until her mortified husband and I polished it off. She was so disoriented by either the meal or my unsparing advice that she ate a large handful of potpourri as we waited for our coats.

As for me, the evening was an unqualified success. The white clam sauce was fresh with herbs and lemon and fresh salt air, and my clam phobia was banished in the twinkling of an eye. There is a lot of banal pasta with clam sauce going around these days. If you have a clam phobia, here are two surefire solutions: Order eight to ten white clam pizzas at Frank Pepe's in New Haven, Connecticut, perhaps the single best pizza in the United States and certainly the best thing of any kind in New Haven, Connecticut. Or try the wonderful recipe for linguine with clams and *gremolata* in the *Chez Panisse Pasta, Pizza & Calzone Cookbook* (Random House) once a week for eight consecutive weeks. It is guaranteed to work miracles.

Greek food. My wife, who considers herself Greek-food-deprived, was on cloud nine when I invited her to our neighborhood Greek restaurant, widely reviewed as the best in the city. As we walked along the street, she hugged me tight like those women in the TV commercials who have just been given a large diamond "for just being you" and launched into a recitation of the only classical Greek she knows, something about the wrath of Achilles. My own mood brightened when I saw that only one retsina befouled the wine list: the other wines were made from aboriginal Greek grapes in Attica or Macedonia or Samos but fermented in the manner of France or California. The dreaded egg-and-lemon soup was nowhere to be seen, and feta was kept mainly in the closet.

We ordered a multitude of appetizers and three main courses. Only the gluey squid, a tough grape leaf that lodged between my teeth, and the Liquid Smoke with which somebody had drenched the roasted eggplant threatened to arouse my slumbering phobia. The rest, most of it simply grilled with lemon and olive oil, was delicious, and as an added bonus I was launched on what still feels like an endless journey toward the acceptance of okra.

Later that evening, my lovely wife was kept up by an upset stomach, and I was kept up by my wife. She swore never to eat Greek food again.

Lard. Paula Wolfert's magnificent *The Cooking of South-West France* (Dial Press) beguiled me into loving lard with her recipe for *confit de porc*—half-pound chunks of fresh pork shoulder flavored with thyme, garlic, cloves, and pepper, poached for three hours in a half gallon of barely simmering lard, and mellowed in crocks of congealed lard for up to four months. When you bring the pork back to life and brown it gently in its own fat, the result is completely delicious, savory and aromatic. I had never made the dish myself because, following Wolfert's advice, I had always avoided using commercial lard, those one-pound blocks of slightly rank, preservative-filled fat in your butcher's freezer.

Then, one snowy afternoon, I found myself alone in a room with four pounds of pork, an equal amount of pure white pig's fat, and a few hours to spare. Following Wolfert's simple instructions for rendering lard, I chopped up the fat, put it in a deep pot with a little water and some cloves and cinnamon sticks, popped it into a 225-degree oven, and woke up three hours later. After straining out the solids and spices, I was left with a rich, clear golden elixir that perfumed my kitchen, as it will henceforth perfume my life.

Desserts in Indian restaurants. Eight Indian dinners taught me that not every Indian dessert has the texture and taste of face cream. Far from it. Some have the texture and taste of tennis balls. These are named *gulab jamun,* which the menu described as a "light pastry made with dry milk and honey." *Rasmalai* have the texture of day-old bubble gum and refuse to yield to the action of the teeth. On the brighter side, I often finished my *kulfi,* the traditional Indian ice cream, and would love to revisit carrot *halva,* all caramelized and spicy. But I may already have traveled down this road as far as justice requires.

STEP FIVE, final exam and graduation ceremony.

1 4

In just six months, I succeeded in purging myself of nearly all repulsions and preferences, in becoming a more perfect omnivore. This became apparent one day in Paris, France—a city to which my arduous professional duties frequently take me. I was trying a nice new restaurant, and when the waiter brought the menu, I found myself in a state unlike any I had ever attained—call it Zen-like if you wish. Everything on the menu, every appetizer, hot and cold, every salad, every fish and bird and piece of meat, was terrifically alluring, but none more than the others. I had absolutely no way of choosing. Though blissful at the prospect of eating, I was unable to order dinner. I was reminded of the medieval church parable of the ass equidistant between two bales of hay, who, because animals lack free will, starves to death. A man, supposedly, would not.

The Catholic Church was dead wrong. I *would* have starved— if my companion had not saved the day by ordering for both of us. I believe I ate a composed salad with slivers of foie gras, a perfect sole meunière, and sweetbreads. Everything was delicious.

STEP SIX, relearning humility. Just because you have become a perfect omnivore does not mean that you must flaunt it. Intoxicated with my own accomplishment, I began to misbehave, especially at dinner parties. When seated next to an especially finicky eater, I would often amuse myself by going straight for the jugular. Sometimes I began slyly by staring slightly too long at the food remaining on her plate and then inquiring whether she would like to borrow my fork. Sometimes I launched a direct assault by asking how long she had had her terror of bread. Sometimes I tricked her by striking up an abstract conversation about allergies. And then I would sit back and complacently listen to her neurotic jumble of excuses and explanations: advice from a personal trainer, intolerance to wheat gluten, a pathetic faith in Dean Ornish, the exquisite—even painful—sensitivity of her taste buds, hints of childhood abuse. And then I would tell her the truth.

I believe that it is the height of compassion and generosity to practice this brand of tough love on dinner-party neighbors who are less omnivorous than oneself. But the perfect omnivore must always keep in mind that, for one to remain omnivorous, it is an absolute necessity to get invited back.

May 1989,
August 1996

PART ONE

Nothing
but the
Truth

Primal Bread

*Wherefore do ye spend money for that which is not
bread? . . .
Eat that which is good, and let your soul delight itself in
fatness.*

—ISAIAH 55:2

The world is divided into two camps: those who can live happily
on bread alone and those who also need vegetables, meat, and
dairy products. Isaiah and I fall into the first category. Bread is the
only food I know that satisfies completely, all by itself. It comforts
the body, charms the senses, gratifies the soul, and excites the
mind. A little butter also helps.

Isaiah was a first-class prophet but untrained as a dietitian. A
good loaf of bread will not delight your soul in fatness. It contains
almost no fats or sugars and lots of protein and complex carbohydrates because it is made from three elemental ingredients: flour,
water, and salt. If you wonder why I left out the yeast, you have
discovered the point of my story.

Every year I have had an intense bout of baking, but these episodes now seem just a prelude, a beating around the bush, a period of training and practice for this year's assault on the summit: *le pain au levain naturel*, naturally leavened bread. I have slipped into a foreign language here because this is a bread most commonly associated with the Paris baker Lionel Poilâne and his ancient wood-fired oven at 8, rue du Cherche-Midi, the most famous bakery in the world. When the baking is going well, Poilâne's bread defines the good loaf: a thick, crackling crust; a chewy, moist, aerated interior; the ancient, earthy flavors of toasted wheat and tangy fermentation; and a range of more elusive tastes—roasted nuts, butterscotch, dried pears, grassy fields—that emanate from neither flour, water, nor salt, but from some more mysterious source. This is the true bread of the countryside, Poilâne writes, the eternal bread. This is the bread I can eat forever, and often do. This is the bread I am eating right now while trying to type with the other hand.

Pain au levain was the first leavened bread, probably discovered in Egypt six thousand years ago. Professor Raymond Calvel, in his definitive *La boulangerie moderne*, places this breakthrough *"chez les Hébreux au temps de Moïse,"* which is when *les Hébreux* were enslaved by *les Égyptiens*. I would love to believe this account but find it improbable. My own *pain au levain* adventure began much more recently.

Saturday, October 7, 1989. I have collected a three-foot pile of books and articles, popular and scientific, in English, French, and translations from the German, including thirty recipes for creating a starter or, as the French call it, *le chef*. This is a piece of dough in which wild yeast and lactic-acid bacteria live happily in symbiosis, generating the gases, alcohols, and acids that give this bread its complex taste and chewy texture.

Commercial yeast is bred to produce clouds of carbon dioxide for a speedy rise, at the expense of aromatic compounds. Your first loaf of *pain au levain* can take six days to make from start to finish. Then each new batch of bread is leavened with a piece of risen dough saved from the previous baking. Compared with bread using commercial yeast, *pain au levain* is unpredictable, slow, and prey to variations in weather, flour, temperature, and the seasons. "Playing with wild yeast is like playing with dynamite," I was warned by the technical manager of a giant U.S. milling company.

Chez Panisse Cooking (Random House) has a lucid and detailed recipe contributed by Steve Sullivan, owner of the Acme Bread Company in Berkeley and a stupendous baker; he uses organic wine grapes to activate the starter. I am in luck: the New York State grape harvest is under way. I order a variety of excellent flours from Giusto's Specialty Foods in San Francisco, which supplies flour to Acme, and when they arrive I walk around the corner to the Union Square Greenmarket, buy several bunches of unsprayed Concord grapes, tie them in cheesecloth, lower the cheesecloth into a batter of flour and water, squeeze the grapes to break their skins, put the bowl near a pilot light on the stove, and go away for the weekend.

Two days later. What a mess! My mixture of flour and grapes has overflowed, sizzling and seething over the stove and running into those little holes in the gas burners from which flames used to emerge. I start again. There is something terrifying about the violent life hiding in an innocent-looking bowl of flour and grapes, and I lie awake at night wondering where it comes from. Have I mentioned my long-held belief that if the planet Earth is ever invaded by aliens, they will arrive in the form of microscopic beings?

Depending on whom you believe, the wild yeast and bacteria on my stove originated either on the grapes themselves, on the organic wheat flour I put them in, or in the air around me where microbes of every race are ubiquitous. My computer has collected 236 scientific abstracts on naturally leavened bread, but none has a definitive answer—as many as 59 distinct species of wild yeast and 238 strains of bacteria have been spotted in sourdough cultures. The truth is vital to me. Wild yeasts living on the wheat berry would create Montana-Idaho country bread, because that's where Al Giusto says his wheat is grown. If they live on the grapes, it would be upstate New York country bread. But my goal is to bake *Manhattan* country bread with a colony of wild bacteria and yeasts that can grow and flourish only here. I apply to *Vogue* for the funds to run DNA traces and gas chromatographs on all my breads and starters. I have received no reply as of the present writing. Maybe tomorrow.

Saturday, October 14. I have made a few loaves of bread with my grape starter—the early ones were pale purple, and all were dense and sour—but must abandon the project in a few days when I leave New York to eat, professionally, in Paris for three weeks. Besides, I am extremely suspicious of yeasts that live on grapes. They are too fond of wine rather than wheat. I am looking for yeasts that love bread as much as I do.

Monday, April 2, 1990. In the August 1989 issue of his indispensable newsletter, *Simple Cooking,* John Thorne gives instructions for *pain au levain* based on the methods that Poilâne himself employs. But I will wait until I can get hold of Poilâne's paperback handbook, *Faire son pain,* and read it for myself. My friend Miriam promises to find one for me in Paris.

Meanwhile, I turn to *The Laurel's Kitchen Bread Book* (Random House) and its recipe for *desem* (the Flemish word for *levain*), which is fastidiously designed to develop only those yeasts that live on stone-ground whole wheat. Recently milled organic flour must be used so that the microbes will still be alive and well; everything must be kept below 60 degrees Fahrenheit until the final rise to discourage the growth of acid-generating bacteria that thrive at higher temperatures; and everything must be sealed to avoid colonization by airborne yeasts. I telephone Giusto's and ask them to send me a sack of whole wheat flour by overnight

mail the moment it is milled. Then I walk around the house testing the temperature. Bread writers who live in the country typically tell you that the perfect place for this rising or that is on the
creaky wooden stairs going down to your root cellar. Don't they
know that most people live in apartments? At last I create a zone
of 55 degrees by piling a twenty-four-quart stockpot on a cardboard box at the edge of my desk with the air conditioner set to
turbofreeze. Now all I need is the flour.

April 11. My freshly milled whole wheat has carpeted the
floor of the UPS truck; the bag split in half somewhere en route
from California. The UPS man is sliding and slipping from one
side of his truck to the other. I telephone Giusto's for another
sack.

Late April. The flour has arrived. It is a balmy spring, but I
am wearing a winter coat at my desk so that *Laurel's Kitchen desem*
will feel comfortable. My wife has the sniffles.

Early May. Both of us have come down with serious colds,
complete with fever. The *desem* starter smells terrific, a fresh fruity
scent unlike anything I've made before, and the bread is rough
and wheaty, full of complex aromas. But like all whole-grain
breads, the strong taste of unrefined flour obscures the more delicate flavors I am after. Long ago I concluded that the only bread
worth its name is made with good white flour; small amounts of
barley, whole wheat, or rye can be added for their flavor and
color. John Thorne writes that "whole-grain breads . . . whether
made of wheat, rye, oats, or any other grain, retain something of
the seed's stubborn unwillingness to be digested. They remain a
kind of aerated gruel, filling but not ultimately satisfying." If Isaiah were alive today, I'm sure he would agree.

Friday, June 1, late morning. *Faire son pain* has arrived
from Paris. Step One: Create a bowlful of life. Poilâne's instruc-

tions have you make a small piece of dough with one-ninth of the total flour and water you intend to use and leave it covered for two or three days while the wild yeast and bacteria awaken and multiply to form an active culture. This will be the *chef.*

Bakers weigh everything because flour can be packed densely or lightly in a measuring cup and doughs can be tight or aerated; it is their weight that matters. I dust off my electronic kitchen scale and set it to grams. Poilâne says that all ingredients at all stages should be between 22 and 24 degrees centigrade, which equals 72 to 75 degrees on Dr. Fahrenheit's thermometer—a nice, moderate room temperature. Now I can turn off the air conditioner.

I weigh 42 grams of water and 67 grams of unbleached white flour, about a half cup, put them in a large bowl, and squish them together with the fingers of my right hand until the dough comes together into a rough ball. Poilâne has you keep your left hand clean for scraping the dough off your right hand with the blade of a sharp paring knife, which sounds silly until you try it any other way. One writer, who evidently has not read Poilâne, recommends tying plastic bags round the handles of your water faucets to avoid sealing them closed when the dough from your hands dries and hardens on them. Better to keep one hand always clean.

I knead the *chef* with extra flour on my wooden counter for two minutes, put it into a rustic brown ceramic bowl, cover the bowl with a clean, wet kitchen towel, secure the towel with a rubber band, and go about my business. This nonchalance lasts for five minutes, and then I am back in the kitchen, peeking under the towel to see if anything is happening. Twenty peeks and several broken rubber bands later, I scrape the *chef* into a clear glass bowl. It looks less like something from a French farmhouse but does facilitate obsessive observation.

I wash my rustic bowl in hot water and learn a lasting lesson: utensils coated with flour or dough are easily washed in *cold* water; hot water makes the starch and gluten stick to everything, including itself. If the dough has hardened, *soak* the utensils in cold water. If you leave them long enough, your wife may get disgusted and clean them up herself. Do it too often and there will be a price to pay.

Where the side of the glass bowl meets the base, it swells and acts as a magnifying glass. For the rest of the day, at three-minute intervals, I search for the appearance of tiny bubbles in the *chef.*

Two Stars for Bread

It is not possible to understand a meal without bread, wrote a French savant whose name I forget. Any restaurant review that fails to evaluate the quality of the bread is either incomplete or completely invalid; I can't decide which. Fantastic bread can overcome an ugly restaurant with brutish service, recently defrosted desserts, and burned coffee.

Saturday, June 2, immediately after waking. In just twenty-four hours, the kitchen towel has grown dry and stiff, the dough has darkened and crusted over, and two spots of pale blue mold have appeared on it. This is not the life-form I had in mind.

I make the morning coffee and start all over. This time I use bottled springwater. New York City tap water is among the most delicious in the nation, but chlorinated water of any kind can inhibit the growth of yeast. And weeks later, when I grow attuned to small differences in the taste of my breads, I find that you can recognize things like chlorine in the crust, where flavors get concentrated. Distilled water lacks the alkalies and minerals that make water taste good and are said to contribute to a healthy rise and golden crust. Springwater is the answer.

Instead of Poilâne's white flour I weigh out some stone-ground organic whole wheat flour: stone ground because I am under the mistaken impression that the metal rollers in large commercial mills heat the flour to temperatures that can kill wild yeast and bacteria; organic because pesticides and fungicides deal death to microbes; and whole wheat because if yeast do actually live on the wheat berry, it is on the outer bran layer that they will, I figure, be found. Instead of a colorful, charming kitchen towel, I use plastic wrap this time. It may prevent a friendly airborne microbe or two from settling on the *chef,* but it keeps the dough from crusting over.

Sunday, June 3.   Is that a bubble in the *chef* or a flaw in the glass of the bowl? The *chef* still smells like wet whole wheat flour, nothing more.

Monday, June 4.   The *chef* has swelled and smells tangy, somewhere between beer and yogurt! I am proud as a parent.

Tuesday, June 5.   No further change. Maybe I have failed. Maybe my *chef* is dead. But it is time for Poilâne's Step Two, doubling the earlier quantities and building the *chef* into what Poilâne calls the *levain,* which you leave from twenty-four to forty-eight hours to ferment.

Wednesday, June 6, bright and early.   The thing is alive! I think it is trying to talk to me. In only twenty-four hours the *levain* has risen to the top of the bowl and is pressing up against the plastic wrap. Large bubbles proudly show themselves through the glass. There can be no doubt about it: I have created the universe in a grain of wheat!

In Step Three you build the *levain* into two pounds of bread dough, tripling its weight again by mixing it with 252 grams of water and working in 400 grams of flour and 15 grams of salt. The water brings together the two main types of protein in flour, glutenin and gliadin, and the result is gluten—the sticky, elastic substance that makes the mixture stringy and clotted.

With evidence of a happy fermentation, I shift to Giusto's

white organic unbleached bread flour. The kneading begins, twenty long minutes of it, stretching the dough away from my body with the heel of my hand, folding it back toward me, giving the dough a quarter turn, and doing it again and again. Besides aerating the dough, this motion unkinks the protein molecules and lines them up next to each other, where they link into a network of gluten. The dough becomes satiny and elastic; as the yeast produces carbon dioxide the dough stretches and expands around the bubbles of gas rather than falling apart and letting the gases escape.

I find twenty minutes of kneading unendurable. Mine is not the attitude of a true artisan. Hand kneading puts the baker in touch with his living dough, you read, endows him with responsibility for his bread. From now on, I will switch to my KitchenAid K5A heavy-duty home mixer equipped with a dough hook. It pummels and whirls instead of kneading, but it does produce acceptable results, especially when I take over for a few minutes at the end.

Poilâne tells you to let the dough rise for six to twelve hours, not the double or triple rise of yeasted dough, but a more modest 30 percent.

Seven o'clock that evening. Through the glass the dough looks well aerated. Though it may not have risen the requisite amount, I am determined to bake it tonight, after a final rising.

Poilâne is fuzzy on forming a round loaf, so I follow the standard procedure—flattening the dough with the smooth domed surface facedown and rolling and stretching it into a tight spherical package. I have bought a *banneton,* a professional linen-lined rising basket, from French Baking Machines in New Jersey, to replace my makeshift two-quart bowl lined with a kitchen towel. I flour it heavily and lower the loaf into it, smooth side down. Then, to create a moist, draftless environment, I inflate a large Baggie around the whole thing and tie it tightly. My loaf will rise until midnight.

I spend part of the evening in a state of wonder. The first miracle is that a handful of wheat flour contains everything needed to create the most satisfying and fundamental of all foods. Then I marvel for a while about yeast. Why does the yeast that feeds on wheat produce a harmless leavening gas and appealing flavors rather than poisons? And why does wild yeast seem to do best at room temperature? Yeast was created long before rooms were. Is this a coincidence or part of Somebody's master plan?

Last, I wonder at the role of salt. Nearly all recipes call for about 2 percent salt compared to the weight of the flour—much more and you kill the yeast and bacteria, much less and the yeast grow without restraint and exhaust themselves too soon. Salt also strengthens the gluten, keeping it elastic in the corrosive acid environment of *pain au levain* and helping the bread rise. Can it be mere chance that the chemically ideal level of salt is precisely the amount that makes bread taste best?

Midnight.   The loaf has barely budged, and I am getting worried. Better give it another two hours. My wife has already gone to bed. She sees this as a dangerous precedent. But several weeks will pass before my compulsive baking threatens to destroy the marriage.

2:00 a.m.   Through the inflated Baggie I can see that the loaf has swelled by half. I have preheated the oven to 500 degrees with a thick sixteen-inch terra-cotta tile on the oven shelf and a Superstone baking cloche on top of it. This device, manufactured by Sassafras Enterprises, is an unglazed ceramic dish with a domed cover that creates something like the even, penetrating, steamy heat of a brick oven. The tile underneath increases the stored heat in the oven and protects the bottom of the bread from burning. Elizabeth David's *English Bread and Yeast Cookery* (Viking) has a photograph of a nearly identical baking cloche from 500 B.C., excavated from the Agora in Athens.

I invert the *banneton* on the fiery base of the cloche, slash the top of the loaf in a checkerboard pattern with a razor blade to encourage a free rise in the oven—uninhibited by a prematurely hardened crust—pour a quarter cup of warm water over the loaf to create extra steam (a frightening but successful gesture I learned from *The Laurel's Kitchen Bread Book*), sprinkle flour over the top for decoration, and cover with the preheated dome.

2:30 a.m. I lower the heat to 400 and uncover the bread to let it brown. It has not risen as much as I would have liked, and my slashes have become deep valleys.

3:00 a.m. My first *pain au levain* is done! When I tap the bottom of the loaf with my forefinger, it sounds hollow, a sign that the starch has absorbed enough water to turn from hard crystals into a soft gel all the way to the center of the loaf, and that much of the remaining water has evaporated.

As I know unequivocally from both book learning and experience, bread is not at its best straight from the oven. Complex flavors develop as it cools, and if you love your bread warm, you should reheat or toast it later.

3:05 a.m. Just this once, I will break the rule and cut off a slice of hot bread. The crust is crisp and tender; the aroma and taste are complex and nutty if a little bland. But my bread is overly sour, and its crumb is dense and gray. Yet I am not disappointed. Butter improves matters, as it does everything in life but one's health, and I know that the flavor will improve by the morning. Which it does.

3:20 a.m. I am falling toward slumber when my heart starts racing and a wave of dread washes over me. I forgot to hold back part of the dough as the *chef* for my next loaf, the entire point of *pain au levain*. Now I must start all over again tomorrow morning.

3:21 a.m. I can't fall asleep. I drag myself into the kitchen and whip up a new *chef*. This time it takes two minutes, and I am confident it will work perfectly. I eat another piece of bread and sleep contentedly. In the morning, my wife objects to crumbs on the pillow.

Thursday, June 21. I am baking as fast as I can, six successive loaves so far—six generations—with my new *chef.* At each baking the *chef* has grown more vigorous and its flavor more assertive but a bit less acidic. My wife feels that my baking schedule has prevented us from going away on sunny summer weekends. She says it is like having a newborn puppy without the puppy. She has always wanted a puppy.

She is also unhappy that every surface in the apartment has a delicate dusting of Giusto's bread flour. But it is only when I nearly turn down tickets to the Madonna concert for fear that Madonna will interfere with my first rising that she puts her foot down. I refrigerate the dough overnight, as I've done with other breads, and find that the final flavor has, if anything, improved. But my bread is still too dense, and I do not know what to do about it.

Tuesday, July 31. I throw myself upon the mercy of experts. Noel Comess left the post of chef de cuisine at the Quilted Giraffe four years ago, at the age of twenty-eight, to start the Tom Cat Bakery in an abandoned ice-cream factory in Queens, and his sourdough *boule* is the best in the city. He agrees to let me snoop around one evening. His room temperature is 85 degrees, much warmer than Poilâne's, and the proportion of old risen dough to new at each stage is less than I have learned to use. I watch him form several loaves and realize that beating down the dough is the last thing naturally leavened bread needs. The gas bubbles are our friends. We pore over his books. Noel loves baking bread and the continuous, self-renewing process of *pain au levain,* in which nothing is ever wasted.

Back home I round my loaves more gently and find that they bake higher and with a more varied texture. But they still look like my bread, not like Noel's. A warmer rising temperature sometimes helps and sometimes doesn't. And my *chef* is simply not active enough to use the proportions that Noel does.

I turn to Michael London. From 1977 to 1986 Michael and his wife, Wendy, ran a patisserie in Saratoga Springs, New York, called Mrs. London's Bake Shop—Craig Claiborne once compared their creations favorably to Wittamer's in Brussels and Peltier's in Paris—and now from the makeshift kitchen of their Federal-period brick farmhouse in nearby Greenwich they run the Rock Hill Bakehouse, where they bake three times a week. I cannot count the mornings I have rushed down to Balducci's or over to the Greenmarket to buy a giant loaf of Michael's Farm Bread before it all disappears.

An unstable and sweltering little plane carries me to upstate New York. I am bearing my latest loaf of bread and a Baggie filled with four ounces of *chef*. Avis refuses to rent me a car on the flimsy pretext that my driver's license has expired. Who has time to renew one's license, I ask, when the dough may overrise while I am waiting on line at the Motor Vehicle Bureau and later collapse in the oven? I lose the argument, but an hour's taxi ride costs little more than Avis's typically inflated charges. I arrive at the Londons' farm in late afternoon.

Michael and Wendy critique the loaf I have brought. Then we eat it with butter from their cow. Their percipient and blond seven-year-old daughter, Sophie, loves my bread.

I watch Michael make his *levain*, and he shows me how to invigorate my starter. As you build the dough from one stage to the next, the *chef*, the *levain*, and the dough should always be used just at the peak of their activity. We sleep for a few hours, wake at one in the morning, make a ton of dough, sleep until five, when his four helpers arrive, and begin shaping loaves for the final bake.

Michael builds my four ounces of strengthened starter into *levain*—and then into twenty pounds of dough. He bakes several loaves with it, and they look just like Michael's other breads, not like mine at all. The secrets, it seems, lie in the baker's hands, his art and intuition, not just in the bacterial composition of the air, the flour, or the grapes. A fantastically expensive professional French hearth oven does not hurt either.

Thursday, September 6. My baking schedule has become less frenzied, twice a week now, and my wife eagerly awaits the finished product. My *chef* is happy and strong and aromatic, the man from UPS has got used to lugging fifty-pound bags from Giusto's every week or two, and I have vacuumed most of the organic bread flour out of my word processor. Most days the bread is more than good enough to eat, and some days it is so good that we eat nothing else.

November 1990

Staying Alive

Years ago I read somewhere that the absolutely cheapest survival diet consists of peanut butter, whole wheat bread, nonfat dry milk, and a vitamin pill. Eager to try it, I rushed to the supermarket, returned home with provisions for a week's survival, and went to work with my calculator and butter knife. Two generous tablespoons of peanut butter spread on a slice of bread and washed down with half a glass of reconstituted milk added up to 272 calories, including 13.6 grams of protein, 15.3 grams of fat, and a good quantity of fiber and complex carbohydrates. In a day filled with eight glossy open-faced peanut-butter sandwiches and four cool, foamy glasses of milk, I would consume 2,200 calories and many more than the 60 grams of protein an adult needs, and the vitamin pill would take care of the rest.

My new diet was 50 percent fat, but twenty-five years ago nutritionists were worried about problems more urgent than the speculative link between dietary fat and chronic disease. They were concerned with the ravages of malnutrition and poverty, with vitamin and protein deficiencies and the minimum cost of subsistence, of staying alive and healthy. I called the Department of Agriculture the other day. Nobody works on subsistence anymore.

Subsistence, I am happy to report, is not much of a problem for me these days either. I could probably subsist for a decade or more on the food energy I have thriftily wrapped around various parts of my body. And even in the past, when straitened circumstances forced me to live at the subsistence level regarding clothing, home appliances, and sports equipment, I have always been willing to devote more of my resources to food than have any of the people around me. I called the Bureau of Labor Statistics. The average American household spends $30,487 a year on everything, of which it allocates a pitiful 8.9 percent to food eaten at home and 5.4 percent to food eaten in restaurants. In telling contrast, I have spent between 30 and 100 percent of my income on food every year since I became an adult. Except for those few blissful days when I lived on the miraculous peanut-butter diet.

One day I nearly dropped a bowl of oyster stuffing when I read with disbelief and disappointment that the average American family spent only $2.59 a person on Thanksgiving dinner in 1991, down from $2.89 the year before, an undeniable sign of the decay of family and national values under two successive Republican administrations. To be precise, I did not actually read that the average American family spent only $2.59 a person on Thanksgiving dinner. That's what the National Turkey Federation press release wanted me to think I had read. The press release really said that a complete Thanksgiving dinner for ten *need cost* only $2.59 a person, considering how inexpensive turkey is. They're right about turkey. I called the Department of Agriculture. Turkey is the cheapest form of animal protein you can readily buy, or at least it was in June 1991. Three ounces of lean, cooked turkey flesh cost 42 cents; three ounces of cooked T-bone steak were $2.35. The protein in beans is much cheaper, but the USDA's 1991 list of "meat alternatives" left out beans. Incredibly, no one in or out of the government knows how much the average American family *did* spend on its average Thanksgiving dinner. I called everybody.

The government does know that the average American household consists of one and six-tenths adults, seven-tenths of a child, and three-tenths of an elderly person (for a total of two and six-tenths humans), who collectively spend $4,271 a year on food, both in and out of the house. That comes to $4.50 a person a day, or $1.50 a meal. My disbelief at hearing these numbers cannot be entirely blamed on my own gluttonous nature. The French and the Japanese are happy to spend twice as much for their exquisite food. We, the richest country in the world, have simply chosen to scrimp. Among the wealthy countries, only the British spend much less than we do. This says volumes to me.

It seems obvious that the only way to spend as little as $4.50 a day on food is to eat nearly every meal at home. To test this proposition, I took out my 1993 edition of the *Zagat New York City Restaurant Survey*, checked off the ten cheapest restaurants, and began to eat my way through them. If you've never dined at the Wall Street branch of McDonald's at 160 Broadway, just two blocks north of Trinity Church, you have a treat in store. It is a soaring two-story space with marble tables, an electronic stock ticker, a pianist at an ebony baby grand, a doorman, and a hostess in a curvy lavender suit. The back half of the ground floor is a traditional McDonald's counter and kitchen, and the menu and prices are just what you would hope. Nonetheless, my discreetly spiced Mighty Wings, my order of excellent fries, and my Diet Coke totaled $5.34 with tax, effortlessly busting the $4.50 average daily food budget of the average American. I could, I suppose, have ordered much less food and sat there all day like several other patrons who, I surmised from their multiple layers of clothing, were homeless. Our bilingual (English-Spanish) hostess guided them to a warm seat upstairs where the staff would bother them less, and together, underneath the Golden Arches, we enjoyed the pianist's witty rendition of "There Will Never Be Another You."

Three of New York City's cheapest restaurants are called the Original California Taqueria; all are in Brooklyn Heights or Park Slope, and two appear to be owned by the same person. A convenient F train whisked us nearly door-to-door to 341 Seventh Avenue in Park Slope, where a fresh and pungent interpretation of East Los Angeles cuisine, an attractive and friendly ambience, and a boldly painted mural that incongruously included the Golden Gate Bridge awaited us. We exceeded $4.50 apiece by only 12 cents, ignoring the $3.00 for round-trip transportation. If my wife's tostada was not quite enough for a day's ration, my ample *plattio*, which included a beef taco, guacamole, beans, and rice, more than made up for it. Of all the restaurants I visited, only at the Original California Taqueria could I buy something approaching a balanced diet with my limited funds. To celebrate this achievement and our unaccustomed sojourn in Brooklyn, we returned to the F train and rode it to the very last stop, in Coney Island, where close by the desolate ruins of Luna Park and its famous Parachute Jump, and two blocks from the original Nathan's, still stands Totonno Pizzeria Napolitano, historically one of the most important restaurants in America. (Totonno, with its coal oven and thickly painted pressed-tin walls and ceiling, opened in 1924, making it the second-oldest surviving pizzeria in this country.) Though Totonno is unjustly listed by Zagat as only the thirty-sixth-best bang for the buck in New York City, a small pizza with a remarkable crust covered by nothing but handmade mozzarella and a sauce of imported canned tomatoes—all unchanged from the founder's original recipe—cost us only slightly more than the following day's entire $9 food budget for two.

At Gray's Papaya and Papaya King the customer can easily stop short of $4.50 by ordering two first-rate beef frankfurters (70 cents apiece at Gray's, more at Papaya King) or one chicken fajita (only at Papaya King) and one large fresh pineapple juice ($1.75). For a more varied diet I journeyed to Amir's Falafel near the Columbia University campus and to the Cupcake Cafe on Ninth Avenue. Perhaps because I relished the food at both addresses, I failed to keep the tab under $4.50. Next time I will try harder. But dining at New York City's ten cheapest restaurants merely confirmed that eating out is extremely difficult on the average American daily food budget of $4.50. And on a subsistence diet, you simply cannot leave your own kitchen.

M. F. K. Fisher wrote *How to Cook a Wolf* in 1942 to help Americans eat well in a time of scarcity and rationing. A chapter called "How to Keep Alive" was directed to her least affluent readers and gave Fisher's formula for what she called Sludge, a mixture of grain and ground meat and vegetables that she created as "a streamlined answer to the pressing problem of how to exist the best possible way for the least amount of money." I had always wanted to try the recipe.

"The first thing to do, if you have absolutely no money, is to borrow some," she begins. "Fifty cents will be enough, and should last you from three days to a week, depending on how luxurious are your tastes. [Here Fisher veers off into a species of coyness that makes her recipe very difficult to replicate today.] Buy about 15 cents' worth of ground beef from a reputable butcher. . . . Buy about 10 cents' worth of ground whole-grain cereal. Almost any large grocery carries it in bulk. It is brownish in color, coarsely mealy in texture, and has a pleasant smell of nuts and starch. Spend the rest of your money on vegetables. . . . Get one bunch of carrots, two onions, some celery, and . . . a small head of cabbage. Grind [the vegetables] all into the pot. Break up the meat into the pot. Cover the thing with what seems too much water."

You simmer this mixture for an hour, add the grain, cook slowly for another two hours, and let it cool. The most delicious way to eat it, Fisher writes, is by taking some slices of the solidified mass and frying them like scrapple.

"Shame on you, Mary Frances Kennedy Fisher," I muttered under my breath as I scoured the supermarket, trying to shop for her recipe. "Why couldn't you have given the quantities in weight or volume?" I had already called the Commerce Department. From 1942 to 1992, the overall consumer price index increased 8.8 times, while food prices increased 9.5 times. I could have tracked down the price of ground beef in 1942, and celery and onions, but I had no way of identifying what kind of whole grain Fisher had in mind. So I threw up my hands, multiplied all

How We Live Today

Today's mania for take-out food and the disappearance of home cooking have two related causes—smaller households and working women. (No man ever gave up cooking because he went back to work.) Are these trends likely to continue? With the aid of a see-through plastic ruler, I have projected the past twenty-five years of U.S. Census Bureau figures into the future, and the results are chilling.

Item: By the year 2050 the average family size will have decreased to about one person. Everyone in America will be living alone.

Item: All women older than eighteen will be working outside the home.

Item: All women will be older than eighteen.

The inevitable conclusion is that by the year 2050, everybody will order take-out food at every meal.

Eating will become extremely expensive. You will need an annual income of at least $392,114 in current dollars to get by. Grazing my way from one end of Manhattan to the other, I found that a modestly upscale take-out breakfast, lunch, and dinner cost $40 plus $7 for a taxi or $54,896 a year for an average family of 3.2 persons. Department of Agriculture figures show that the average American family spends 14 percent of its income on food. Therefore, it must earn $392,114 a year.

Finding good take-out food is not easy. Searching it out will become your full-time occupation in the year 2050, more than cooking ever was. Ameri-

cans will once again become a lonely race of Meso-
lithic hunter-gatherers prowling the darkened city
streets, wallets honed and sharpened, ready to
pounce on the unsuspecting pint of pasta prima-
vera and snare the slow-footed slice of *pâté de cam-
pagne.* We will scarcely have time to eat.

April 1988

her numbers by 9.5, and filled up my shopping cart with $1.43
worth of ground beef (thirteen ounces on super-special sale), 95
cents of Wheatena (just a half pound), and $2.37 of onions, cel-
ery, carrots, and cabbage, nearly a pound of each. Can you
believe that celery costs nearly as much as beef?

I browned the meat first, ground up the vegetables in my
food processor, added some canned tomato puree, salt, and pepper for additional flavor, grew thoroughly fed up with Fisher's
instruction to "cover the thing with what seems too much water,"
covered the thing with too much water, and then had to let it boil
down for the next five hours. The finished Sludge was an appe-
tizing brown and tasted inoffensive (more onions and tomatoes
would have helped), and I let it cool and solidify in a large baking
pan. The recipe yielded ten very generous half-pound portions (I
was in charge of portion control), one for lunch, one for dinner,
and a half portion for breakfast for the next four days. Total cost
was $5.25, including the tomato puree, salt, and pepper. Cost per
day was $1.31. Add 30 cents for coffee and a little orange juice in
the morning, and subsistence comes to $1.61 a day. Just compare
that with $1.70 a day for eight peanut-butter sandwiches and
four glasses of reconstituted milk—not counting the 20 extra
cents for a deluxe vitamin pill.

Whether Sludge or peanut-butter sandwiches with reconstituted dry milk are nutritionally complete, I cannot prove. I

subsisted on Sludge for nearly a day and then grew bored. But my health never flagged. I should also report that Fisher's Sludge turned to complete mush whenever I tried to fry it up in ample sweet butter, as she recommended, the only way I found it palatable.

I briefly entertained the notion that I could solve my subsistence problems by doing all my shopping at Gourmet Garage, a new outfit at 47 Wooster Street in the SoHo section of New York City. Then I visited Gourmet Garage for the first time. The bargains were terrific. *Pied de mouton* mushrooms and yellow-footed chanterelles were being given away for $8.50 a pound, a 50 percent savings; Eli Zabar's two-pound Manor House Loaf, sold by the baker himself at E.A.T. on Madison Avenue for $5.00, went for only $3.95 here; and free-range chickens cost only $2.85 a pound.

When I came to a shelf holding rows of five-kilogram bags of basmati rice, my mind drifted back to an evening several months ago in a Moorish garden in the south of Spain. I was with the beautiful Indian actress and food writer Madhur Jaffrey. The air was soft with the scent of night-blooming jasmine. I leaned toward Madhur and whispered, "What brand of basmati rice would you recommend?"

"Tilda," she replied. And now, months later, as if by divine intervention, I find Tilda on sale at Gourmet Garage for only two dollars a pound.

But no matter how hard I calculate, I can't fit many *pieds de mouton* and yellow chanterelles into my low-cost cooking. And even at two dollars a pound, basmati rice runs four times as much as the regular long-grain American rice at my local A&P. When I lose interest in subsistence, I plan to shop at Gourmet Garage on an hourly basis.

The United States Department of Agriculture publishes a near-subsistence diet called the Thrifty Food Plan, calculates its cost every month, and uses this number to determine how many food stamps to issue to poor families so that they can cook and eat according to the Thrifty Food Plan. (That's how it is supposed to work; advocates for the poor argue that food-stamp allocations are insufficient for those following the Thrifty Food Plan.) Last October the cost was $49.40 a week for a family of two and $82.50 for a family of four. This comes to $3.53 a person a day for a family of two. The amazing thing to me is that the average American on his or her $4.50-a-day food budget spends only about 25 percent more than the cost of this subsistence diet!

I decided to follow the Thrifty Food Plan for a week and took the USDA's booklet *Thrifty Meals for Two: Making Food Dollars Count* to the supermarket, reading it as I wandered the aisles. I will neither confirm nor deny whether or how often I cheated in the days that followed. Food-stamp recipients do not have a choice.

On Day One, the Thrifty Food Plan required me to eat a breakfast of toast, milk, cereal, and an orange. This fueled a long morning of planning and cooking. Many of the recipes in *Thrifty Meals for Two* are made from other recipes in *Thrifty Meals for Two*, so precise and long-range planning is vital. I began by creating six cups of Biscuit Mix (a homemade form of Bisquick, which would later grow into both Drop Biscuits and Peanut Butter Snack Loaf) and five cups of Pudding Mix (sugar, cornstarch, and nonfat dry milk to which I would later add cocoa and water to produce Chocolate Pudding). Then I began preparations for lunch by braising three turkey drumsticks in water in a covered pan, discarding the bones and skin, turning the flavored water into gravy, setting aside three ounces of the meat for lunch (I fortunately possess an expensive electronic scale), and saving the rest for Days Two and Three. Whereupon I baked a potato, cooked up some collard greens, made Drop Biscuits from my Biscuit Mix and a truly repulsive Chocolate Pudding from my Pudding Mix, and ate all but the Chocolate Pudding. Dinner was a bacon cheeseburger on a roll and a disappointing banana. But only an hour later snack time arrived—peanut butter on toast. I could hardly wait until morning.

Breakfast on Day Two was lavish—a scrambled egg, a few slices of bacon, two slices of toast, and a half glass of grapefruit juice. Lunch was yesterday's turkey in a potato salad on a lettuce leaf with more Drop Biscuits. Dinner brought Bean Tamale Pie, additional lettuce, crackers, and Peanut Butter Snack Loaf. You beat peanut butter, sugar, and an egg into some Biscuit Mix, bake the mixture in a loaf pan for forty minutes, and eat it for the next three days, not without enjoyment. Snack time was cold cereal. I love cornflakes with lots of milk and sugar.

The main feature of Day Three was Turkey Spanish Rice (which happily used up Monday's turkey), more collards (have I discovered a subtle ethnic bias in these menus?), and more of yesterday's Peanut Butter Snack Loaf, which would be finished, toasted, on Day Four. My Biscuit Mix was running low, and I drew up plans to make some more.

And so it went. Or would have went if I had not, several weeks earlier, accepted an invitation to a tasting of black truffles jetted over from the Périgord region of France at dinnertime on Day Four. I spent the rest of Day Four testing several forthcoming recipes in *Thrifty Meals for Two:* Roast Pork with Gravy, Pork and Cabbage Soup (the two sharing the same piece of pork), a Barbecue Beef Sandwich, Stove-Top Beans (I would make these again), and Bread Pudding.

On Day Five I resigned from the Thrifty Food Plan. It had taken most of the fun out of eating. Besides, four days is almost a week. Most of the recipes were not awful, although they stressed the kind of weakly flavored mock-ethnic dishes that American dietitians love and I despise. Green peppers found their insidious way into everything. The recipes expressed a complete catalog of modern nutritional superstitions: salt, cooking oil, and sometimes sugar were reduced to ridiculously small amounts; the turkey was wastefully relieved of its proudest part, its skin; butter was eliminated entirely (even though the transfatty acids in margarine are nearly as dangerous as saturated fat); and milk was always the nonfat dry version, which produced a gray and watery bread pudding. But the planning was clever: buying and cooking in large amounts, using leftovers in other dishes, and eliminating all precooked and convenience foods. If you are poor enough for food stamps, it is assumed, you will have all the time in the world to cook everything from scratch.

But aside from the constant and wrenching hunger that it brought, the Thrifty Food Plan has a deeper problem, which lies in the rules underlying its construction. I called the USDA and learned that the computer program used to design the Thrifty Food Plan aims to satisfy a list of nutritional and economic objectives while *departing as little as possible from the current eating patterns of American families.* The result is an excessive emphasis on meat— even on a budget of $3.53 a day—and an underemphasis on the nutritious but much cheaper grains and legumes. And so the Thrifty Food Plan failed to answer the question that still fascinated me: What is the absolutely cheapest subsistence diet, and can it be turned into something palatable?

The problem looked like child's play. All I needed was a list of all foods, five thousand or ten thousand of them; nutritional information about each food and its cost; a personal computer with a statistics program installed; and somebody to type the first two things into the third. The mathematical problem is generally referred to as linear programming, and the routine commonly used to solve it is the Simplex Method, which somebody once tried to teach me in graduate school long, long ago. You simply ask the computer to choose a group of foods that collectively satisfy your list of nutritional requirements while absolutely minimizing the overall cost. It's like the simultaneous equations we learned to solve in high school, but much more complicated. Yet with a personal computer, the whole problem should take just a few minutes to solve. I planned to patent the answer as the Simplex Subsistence Diet.

I went out and bought a program called *Health and Diet Pro* for $39.95 and installed it on my hard disk. Although the manual is perfunctory and confusing, the apparent purpose of *Health and Diet Pro* is to help you keep track of the various nutrients and poisons you take in, make your recipes healthier, and construct fitness and diet regimens. I am bored by all of this. What interested me was that buried somewhere in the heart of the program is a list of three thousand foods along with nutritional information about each of them. Could I add cost figures to this list and then manipulate the program to solve my subsistence problem?

I think the answer is no. I spent an evening at it without the slightest success. Admittedly, I was on Day Two of the Thrifty Food Plan, and the Bean Tamale Pie had destroyed my concentration and made me grumpy. I might have had better luck after the truffles.

I searched the technical literature. In 1945 the late George J. Stigler, an economist who later won the Nobel Prize, made what he described as the first attempt to design a mathematically precise subsistence diet for an adult male, using food prices from August 1939. It consisted of 370 pounds of wheat flour, 57 cans of evaporated milk, 111 pounds of cabbage, 23 pounds of spinach, and 285 pounds of dried navy beans. The total yearly cost of these ingredients was $39.93. Today they would cost something like $460, or $1.26 a day. By August 1944, relative food prices had shifted and so had Stigler's perfect diet. The evaporated milk and dried navy beans had disappeared, and in their place were 134 pounds of pancake flour and 25 pounds of pork liver.

It took me no time at all to figure out that a year's diet of cabbage bread and pork liver pancakes plus an ounce of spinach now and then was somehow not the answer for which I had been searching. But a similar study done in 1981 came much closer. Jerry Foytik of the University of California at Davis followed Stigler's general method but applied sixty additional rules to ensure variety and palatability. His ideal diet contained sixteen foods that would cost today about $238 a month for a family of four—a mere two-thirds of the price of the Thrifty Food Plan.

Scaled down to one day's ration for a couple like my wife and me, Foytik's ideal subsistence diet consists of three glasses of skim milk, 4 ounces of chicken, 3 ounces of hamburger or other meat, a little more than one egg, ¼ pound of dried beans, a large glass of defrosted orange juice, 1/2 pound of fruit and a bit less than that of vegetables, 1/2 pound each of potatoes and cereals (like rice), 1 pound of bread, 1/4 pound of other baked goods, nearly 6 tablespoons of oil or butter, and 2.31 ounces of sugars and sweets. Cost, at my overpriced Greenwich Village supermarket: a ridiculously economical five dollars a day for two adults.

Now it's your job and mine to make something delicious out of our Simplex Subsistence Diet. Just remember: this is close to the theoretically cheapest diet that will keep you alive and well nourished. Even if we add an extra ounce of sugar, a cup of coffee, and a little olive oil to make our lives more scrumptious, we can still beat the USDA and its Thrifty Food Plan at their own game.

45

The meaty American diet, even when scaled down into the USDA's Thrifty Food Plan, seems ill prepared to cope with subsistence in a delicious way. But Italian and French country cooking are full of recipes that would fit perfectly with the Simplex Subsistence Diet. Even modern French chefs instinctively know how to cook stylishly at just above the subsistence level. I telephoned Daniel Boulud, former chef at Le Cirque in New York City and owner of the brand-new restaurant Daniel, and asked him to dip into the first draft of his forthcoming cookbook for his least expensive recipes. Boulud immediately produced the following soup, which uncannily mirrors our Simplex Subsistence Diet.

Swiss Chard and Bean Soup with Ricotta Toasts

Adapted from *Cooking with Daniel Boulud*
(Random House)

1 tablespoon unsalted butter, 8 cents
2 slices slab bacon, 1/4 inch thick, cut crosswise into 1/4-inch
  lardons, 41 cents

*1 medium onion, peeled and finely chopped to yield ¹/₂ cup,
46 cents*

*¹/₂ pound white mushrooms, caps only, cleaned and cut into
¹/₄-inch dice, about 1 cup, $1.43*

1 garlic clove, peeled and finely chopped, 4 cents

¹/₂ teaspoon nutmeg, plus more for the toasts, 10 cents

*2 quarts chicken stock (made at home by browning 2 pounds of
chicken necks and backs in a 6-quart stockpot with chopped
onion, celery, and carrots; covering with 10 cups of water;
and simmering with parsley, ¹/₂ teaspoon of salt, and a few
peppercorns for 2 to 3 hours), $1.60*

*1 cup dried navy or cannellini beans soaked overnight in cold
water, 34 cents*

*1 pound Swiss chard, leaves only, washed and coarsely
chopped, $1.49*

Salt and freshly ground black pepper, 10 cents

¹/₄ pound ricotta cheese, 50 cents

4 thin slices country bread, 30 cents

1 tablespoon grated Parmesan cheese, 19 cents

Melt the butter in a 4-quart saucepan over medium-high heat and brown the bacon on all sides. Spoon off half the fat and add the onion, mushrooms, garlic, and the ¹/₂ teaspoon of nutmeg, and cook slowly until the vegetables have softened, 5 to 8 minutes. Meanwhile, warm the chicken stock in another pan, and when the vegetables are ready, add the stock and the presoaked beans, bring to a boil, and simmer for 35 to 40 minutes until the beans are just tender. Add the Swiss chard, ¹/₂ teaspoon of salt (or less if the bacon and broth are especially salty), and a pinch of pepper, and simmer for another 15 minutes. Adjust the seasonings. Keep warm.

Spread the ricotta on the bread and sprinkle with the Parmesan and a grating of nutmeg. Toast under the broiler until golden. Ladle the soup into large soup plates and float the ricotta toasts on top. With more toasted country bread, this serves 4 as a complete supper, at $1.76 a person.

Perfumed Rice
with Lamb and Lentils

Lentils and rice eaten together compose a complete and extremely economical source of protein. I have now discovered that lower grades of wonderfully aromatic basmati rice can be had for only $1.20 a pound in many health-food stores (and in the Little India section of Manhattan). The world champions in rice cookery are, I think, the Persians, and so the other evening I took a well-known Persian basmati rice and lentil recipe from the excellent *New Food of Life* by Najmieh Batmanglij (Mage Publishers), cut in half the amount of lamb, dates, and butter and eliminated the saffron (the four most expensive ingredients), and cooked a princely feast for six for $1.49 a person.

3 cups long-grain white basmati rice (slightly more than
*   1 pound), $1.20*
Salt, 3 cents
2 medium onions (1 pound total), peeled and thinly sliced,
*   89 cents*
4 tablespoons cooking oil, 36 cents
1 pound lamb shoulder, bone in, cut into 2- to 3-inch pieces,
* $2.59*
Freshly ground black pepper, 2 cents

¼ *teaspoon turmeric, 3 cents*
½ *teaspoon ground cinnamon, 7 cents*
1½ *teaspoons Persian allspice (approximated by mixing a*
     generous ½ teaspoon each ground cinnamon and ground
     cardamom with a generous ¼ teaspoon ground cumin),
     24 cents
2 cups water
1½ *cups lentils, 58 cents*
1 cup white raisins, 88 cents
4 ounces (about 1 cup) pitted dates, chopped, $1.25
1 stick (¼ pound) butter, 67 cents
2 tablespoons yogurt, 14 cents

Wash the rice vigorously in five changes of warm water and soak it for at least 2 hours in 8 cups of water mixed with 2 tablespoons of salt.

Sauté half the onions in 2 tablespoons of the oil over medium-high heat until soft and golden, about 10 minutes. Add the lamb; season with ¾ teaspoon of salt, a good pinch of pepper, the turmeric, cinnamon, and ½ teaspoon of the Persian allspice mixture; and sauté for another 5 minutes. Add 2 cups of water, cover, and simmer until the meat is very tender, 2½ to 3 hours. Set aside.

In a saucepan, mix the lentils with 3 cups of water and ½ teaspoon of salt, bring to a boil, simmer for 10 minutes, and drain. In a frying pan, sauté the remaining sliced onion in 2 tablespoons of oil over medium-high heat until soft and golden, stir in the raisins and dates, cook for 2 more minutes, and set aside.

Parboil the rice by bringing 2 quarts of water and 2 tablespoons of salt to a boil in a 4-quart pot (nonstick is best), adding the presoaked rice, and boiling for 3 to 5 minutes, stirring every so often, until the grains just lose their brittle core but are still quite firm. Drain the rice and rinse it in several cups of warm water.

In the same pot, melt the butter. Pour half of it into a small bowl and set it aside. Take 2 cups of the cooked rice, mix it in a bowl with the yogurt, and spread it on the bottom of the pot over the butter. Sprinkle a layer of lentils on the rice, then a layer of raisins, dates, and onions, then another layer of rice. Continue until all the ingredients are used up, sprinkling the remaining tea-spoon of Persian allspice mixture between layers. Fluff the rice as you add it. Reduce the diameter of each layer so that the ingredients taper into a pyramid in the pot.

Cover and cook over medium heat for 10 minutes so that a delicious crust will form on the bottom of the rice. Then uncover, pour the reserved melted butter over the rice, put a dish towel over the pot, cover again, and cook over low heat for 50 minutes. Remove from the heat but do not disturb the cover; place the pot on a cold, wet dish towel for 5 minutes (which is meant to help loosen the crust). Then uncover the pot and trans-fer the contents by the cupful to a serving platter, mounding the rice and other ingredients into a fluffy pyramid. When only the crust remains on the bottom of the pot, dislodge it with a knife and spatula, and serve in one or two pieces (if you're lucky) on a separate plate. Surround the rice and lentils with the meat mix-ture and serve.

April 1993

Why Aren't the French Dropping Like Flies?

Last year, while browsing through the latest government report on diet and health, I came across a graph that left me flabbergasted.

In little black bars across the page it traced the incidence of deaths from coronary heart disease in twenty-seven industrialized countries. Japan did the best, which is no surprise because the Japanese eat lots of fish, rice, and little green things. But the identity of the runner-up astonished me. Right behind Japan, with the second-lowest rate on earth—lower than Italy with its olive oil cuisine, half of Scandinavia with its high-fish diet, and a mere fraction of the United States, the most finicky country in the world about what we put in our mouths—was, incredibly, *France!*

Impossible, I gasped. Everybody knows that the French wallow in butter, cream, and egg yolks; gobble pork, cheese, goose fat, and sausages; and guzzle wine like fish. If the French have the second-lowest rate of fatal coronary heart disease in the world—and the lowest in the Western world—then everything the U.S. surgeon general, her predecessor, and their battalions of government doctors want us to believe about saturated fats and cholesterol must be dead wrong. And if this is so, the surgeon general would have resigned in disgrace long ago, which she didn't.

I telephoned a doctor friend of mine, an expert in nutrition who never tires of frightening people about the devastating effects of dietary fats, and asked him the obvious question: "If you're so smart, why aren't the French dropping like flies?"

Maybe the French actually eat more austerely than we think, he suggested. Or maybe it's genetic. Perhaps the French government collects health statistics differently from the way we do. He feverishly proposed every excuse that came to mind, while avoiding what for him would be an awful truth: that we may not need to give up sumptuous food to stay healthy.

The genetic argument is hopelessly feeble because the French are not a homogeneous people like the Japanese. But do the French eat as richly as tourists imagine? After only twenty telephone calls to U.N. agencies here and in Europe, I found a statistician in Rome who was willing to send me the most recent Food Balance Sheets of the Food and Agriculture Organization.

Here are the facts: the French take in about as many calories as we do in the United States, but they consume more cholesterol and saturated fats because they eat four times as much butter as we and more than twice as much cheese and lard. I made a quick calculation that the French consume more saturated fat just from the forty pounds of cheese they eat each year than the surgeon general says we should take in from all sources combined.

If the French have heard of oat bran, it does not show up in the statistics—they eat only one-fifteenth the number of oats we do. They consume less sugar and beef and less whole milk, but the rest of their diet differs from ours in unremarkable ways: slightly less meat of all types and slightly less fresh fruit, a little more seafood, twice the garlic, half the onions, rather more potatoes and bread, and the same number of eggs.

I was about to launch an arduous search for detailed health statistics comparing France and the United States when my doctor friend sent me an excellent article by Edward Dolnick called *"Le paradoxe français."* It had appeared in the May/June issue of *Hippocrates* magazine, and it did all the work for me. Only 143 out of every 100,000 middle-aged French men die each year of coronary heart disease, compared with 315 among middle-aged

American men. French men live about as long as men in the United States, but French women outlive American women by at least a year and have even fewer fatal heart attacks than the Japanese—without jogging or health clubs.

Within France the lowest rate of heart disease is found in the southwest, an earthly paradise of goose and duck fat, sausages and foie gras, and very little olive oil or fish. (So much for the Mediterranean-diet hypothesis.) In Normandy, where the people swim in butter and cream, the heart disease rate is higher than in the rest of France, but it's still lower than in the United States. The French smoke as much as we do, but wherever you go in France, heart disease kills at a lower rate than here and kills later in life. For reasons nobody understands, a Frenchman with the same cholesterol level as an American has only half the chance of suffering a heart attack. Even in France, blood cholesterol levels do count, but something else in the French diet seems to count for much more.

One possibility is that the plentiful calcium in all that cheese binds with the fat and prevents its absorption into the bloodstream, allowing it to be excreted before it kills. Another is wine. The average Frenchman drinks *ten times more wine* than the average American. Dolnick cites one study demonstrating that the more wine a nation drinks, the lower its rate of fatal heart disease. The French may die more often from cirrhosis than we do, but liver disease still accounts for only 3 percent of all deaths in France.

Could Americans cut their heart disease rate in half by switching to a high-cheese, high-wine, high-goose-fat French diet? If I were the surgeon general or head of the National Institutes of Health, I would immediately shift every available resource to answering that question. Last week, I tried unsuccessfully to reach the surgeon general to propose this idea. Then I telephoned the Centers for Disease Control in Atlanta, but nobody cared. Finally I reached Dr. Millicent Higgins, head of epidemiology at the National Heart, Lung, and Blood Institute. She was attending some kind of heart attack conference in Houston, where I tracked her down during breakfast in her room. Intelligent and well informed, Dr. Higgins conceded that the French statistics are extremely puzzling. But she refused to drop everything and find out why. And she grew obstinate when I suggested that she send back her fresh fruit with yogurt and bring on the bacon and eggs.

When I explained the reasoning behind my high-goose-fat diet, she objected that she knew of no epidemiological research that would support the idea. Which is precisely my point.

March 1991

Author's Note:

Edward Dolnick and I are usually given credit for having independently "discovered" the French Paradox. Which of us was first is for historians of Great Ideas of the Twentieth Century to decide. The phrase itself was coined by the eminent French doctors J. L. Richard and Serge Renaud several years earlier in a brief and amusing note in a French medical journal; this was the only other mention in print of the phenomenon.

A considerable time after both Dolnick and I had published our pieces, *le paradoxe français* was "discovered" by both the *New York Times* and *60 Minutes* on CBS—on the same Sunday. The *60 Minutes* piece simplistically insisted on the red wine theory, and over the succeeding month, sales of red wine in America increased by 50 percent—not, I think, because people were trying to cure their heart disease, but because they felt that permission to drink more had been granted by a higher authority.

The French Paradox is not, of course, a true paradox, but the sort of seeming contradiction between scientific theory and real-world facts that is supposed to lead to progress. Most of the American nutrition establishment behaved otherwise, because the new facts threatened to destroy the hypotheses on which many of them had built their careers—principally those regarding the

influence of dietary fat on the health of our arteries and consequently on the rate of premature cardiac deaths; and after a year
or two of engaging in what was meant to pass for scientific dis-
course, they were happy to let the Paradox fade from the fore-
ground.

But they never laid a glove on it. Some nutritionists were
happy to believe that the French do not know how to count heart
attacks. The only basis for this charge was a technical study by a
statistician at the National Cancer Institute showing that in one
regard the French do not "code" their death certificates as World
Health Organization protocols instruct: when the French have
the choice between attributing somebody's death to cancer or to
heart disease, they incorrectly favor the former. But how often do
these errors occur? The answer is critically important to the
WHO's MONICA project (Multi-national Monitoring of Trends
and Determinants in Cardiovascular Disease), whose purpose is
to standardize and compare cardiac risk factors and fatalities
across national boundaries. An emergency meeting was held, a
study was performed, and a resulting MONICA report demonstrated that the French inclination to undercount heart fatalities
is too small to matter. Correcting for it does not budge France
from its standing right behind Japan in the coronary heart disease
sweepstakes.

Just the idea that French cholesterol levels are the same as
ours—while their rate of heart attacks is less than half—is enough
to drive American nutritionists crazy. But not the Europeans,
who, though taking cholesterol and saturated fat very seriously,
assign to them only about one-sixth the influence we do here.
Whether blood lipids end up as arterial plaques depends partly on
whether they are oxidized; a major MONICA study, largely
ignored in this country, showed that circulating levels of vitamin
E, an antioxidant, statistically overwhelmed the influence of circulating levels of cholesterol in our bloodstreams. Besides, serum
cholesterol may contribute to narrowing of the arteries, but for a
heart attack to occur, the blood must clot—thrombosis must

occur. Fat intake seems to have no connection with thrombosis. And other blood factors, such as circulating levels of the amino acid homocysteine, are now believed to be at least as important as cholesterol; consumption of folic acid (which occurs in greatest quantity in the liver of web-footed fowl!) effectively lowers homocysteine, but whether this is an effective therapy or merely suppressing the messenger has yet to be discovered.

A large number of heart attacks appear to result from spasms of the blood vessels, or unexplained ischemia; the causes are unknown, and diet has not been implicated. Finally, a group at Harvard has recently characterized the arterial damage that can lead to a heart attack as an inflammatory disease; again, the marker for this inflammation is as highly correlated with coronary disease as is serum cholesterol. All of this may finally explain why regular intake of aspirin fights heart disease. The suspected inflammation apparently has nothing to do with diet.

The French Paradox cannot be dismissed. It should have been noticed decades ago. And its contribution is to encourage researchers to discover the many other common causes of heart disease besides the saturated fat in our diets. The French Paradox is an embarrassment only to those nutritionists and physicians who had refused to recognize the obvious. We have known for some time that half of all heart attacks occur in people with average or low cholesterol, and that half of all people with high cholesterol never have heart attacks.

Totally Mashed

For some time now, I have been unhappy with my mashed potatoes. This is a pivotal difference between me and Omar Sharif, who is so pleased with his mashed potatoes that, according to the glossy magazine on my desk, he always has a second helping. His mashed potatoes really belong to Joël Robuchon, the brilliant chef-owner of the Paris restaurant Jamin, and for several years they have been the most honored mashed potatoes in the world. They are also an escapade in animal fat. Judging from the recipe in Robuchon's *Ma cuisine pour vous* (Laffont, 1986), he beats a half pound of butter into each pound of boiled potatoes. In the ten minutes it takes Omar Sharif to clean his plate, he will have swallowed ten times the maximum daily dose of animal fat allowed by the U.S. surgeon general, before he gets to his main course. This is precisely why mashed potatoes and the other fashionable comfort foods have become so important to us. They let us feel chic and trendy without having to eat tuna carpaccio and fava beans. Considering the smear campaign against dietary fats being waged by the surgeon general and his ilk, mashed potatoes are a godsend.

But while Omar Sharif swans about Paris, my mashed potatoes still get gummy on me. Sometimes they go cataclysmically wrong, turning sticky and gluey or doughy and pasty, bonding to my teeth and gums and the roof of my mouth, coating my tongue and throat.

As luck would have it, the instant mashed potato industry is even more panicky about sticky potatoes than I am. An average potato, on its long journey from loamy meadow to those packets of dehydrated granules on your supermarket shelves, undergoes such intricate torture that its aptitude for gumminess is amplified many times over. Industry scientists, whose careers depend on preventing potatoes from turning out that way, publish their findings in various technical journals here and abroad, which a teacher in Atlanta named Shirley Corriher, who is writing a book on the science of cooking, showed me how to find with my personal computer. Of the 341 papers written on mashed potatoes in the past twenty years, thirty seemed especially worth reading, as did *Potato Processing*, the bible of the industry. The USDA did much of the early work on instant mashed potatoes, and its expert in California, Merle Weaver, was particularly helpful to me over the telephone.

What follows is a series of small suggestions for making good mashed potatoes and one big suggestion. Whether to label the latter a major breakthrough in home culinary science is for others to judge.

Let's get acquainted with the potato. The potato is the most important vegetable in the world. Ten billion bushels are grown every year, almost half of them in Russia and Poland, where vodka is extremely popular. Mashed potatoes whipped with milk are a nearly perfect food that single-handedly nourished nineteenth-century Ireland until the potato blight struck and things turned rough. Without milk, potatoes will keep you alive for 167 days if you can stomach 3¾ pounds of them a day. The average American consumes one medium potato a day, or 110 pounds a year, as often as not in processed form—chips and other snacks, frozen French fries, and instant granules—and derives more vitamin C from potatoes than from citrus fruits. (Back in the days when citrus was still a tropical rarity, potatoes offered the main protection against scurvy.) Raw potatoes are 70 to 80 percent water (making them almost as wet as milk) and 10 to 20 percent starch, with the remainder in sugars, fiber, minerals, and high-quality protein. A potato contains virtually no fat and about as many calories as an apple or a banana.

The potato plant is a perennial herb of the Solanaceae family with purple or yellow flowers and, occasionally, a fruit that looks like an amiable little green tomato but poisons you like the berry of the nightshade. The edible potato is not a root vegetable at all but a tuber—the swollen tip of the plant's underground stem. The eyes of a potato are not arranged randomly but continue the pattern set on the stem by its branches and leaves: a spiral with thirteen leaves or eyes for every five turns of the helix. Sugar is manufactured in the leaves and transported to the underground tuber, where it is turned into starch.

Why your potato turns gummy.   Like other living things, a potato is composed of millions of cells all cemented together. Lining the walls of each potato cell are hard, closely packed microscopic granules of starch, impervious to the water that fills the rest of the cell. But when you heat a potato to about 140 degrees Fahrenheit, the starch granules begin to absorb the water around them, and by 160 degrees they have swollen to many times their original size. The starch is now a gel, a viscous complex with water, and fills up most of the cell. Separate, swollen, and perfectly intact potato cells make for smooth mashed potatoes. But at 160 degrees the cells are still strongly bound to one another, and if you try to mash the potato now, the cells will split rather than separate, and the starch gel will ooze out of them.

This is called free or extracellular starch, and *it is the enemy.* Free starch turns mashed potatoes gummy.

As the cooking time lengthens and the internal temperature of the potato increases to 180 degrees, the cement between the potato cells—pectic material similar to the pectin that thickens jams and preserves—begins to degrade, and the cells can now separate from one another. This is a good time to mash your potatoes. With further cooking, the cells begin to weaken and rupture, and some of the gelled starch leaks out. That's why over-cooked potatoes become sticky and gluey even though they are easy to mash. If 15 or 20 percent of the cells in your potato are ruptured, you will be very sorry.

Buying your potato. One common way of categorizing potatoes is by their starch content. A mealy or floury potato like the Russet Burbank is dense, high in starch, low in water, and, despite the distasteful sound of the word "mealy," generally preferred in this country for mashing. A waxy potato like the White Rose is low in starch, high in water, and often specified in French recipes. (Joël Robuchon's potato is the BF 15; translated from the French this means a small yellow-skinned potato with dark yellow waxy flesh.) The adjectives "mealy" and "waxy" refer to the texture of the potato after you cook it. Mealy potatoes become fluffy and almost grainy when you mash them; waxy potatoes become creamy and smooth. But waxy potatoes generally require longer cooking and greater mashing force to separate the cells. Some researchers feel that more free starch is thus released, increasing the risk of gumminess.

5 9

Once you have decided which type of potato to cook, just try to ask your greengrocer or the guy stamping prices on laundry soap at your supermarket to point out the waxy potatoes and the mealy ones. Your reward will be an uncomprehending stare. But you can test the potatoes yourself. Buy one of each and, when you get home, mix a bowl of brine with nine and a half cups of water and one cup of salt. If a potato sinks into the brine, it is high in starch and will cook up mealy. If it floats, it belongs in the waxy category—unless it suffers from a potato ailment called hollow heart, in which case it will probably float in anything. All the potatoes at my grocery sank.

I used only large mealy Idaho russets in my mashed potato experiments. Avoid recipes that fail to specify which type of potato to use. Also avoid recipes that call for something like "six medium potatoes" without giving their total weight. Potatoes vary in size even more than human beings. If the cookbook specifies neither potato type nor total weight, discard it immediately.

Peeling and cutting your potato. The potato-peel lobby would have you believe that all the nutrients are in the skin. Nothing could be farther from the truth. The peel does contain a *disproportionate* share of vitamins and minerals compared to its negligible weight, but most of the nutrients are nonetheless found in the flesh of the potato and not in the peel. Cooking a whole potato in its peel does prevent some vitamins and flavor from leaching out into the salted water, but cooking any potato whole, whether you peel it or not, leads to uneven cooking when the rounded ends and outside layers become overcooked before the inside is ready. Overcooked cells will rupture.

If you peel your potatoes and cut them into pieces of the same size, they will cook evenly and quickly. Tiny pieces cook fastest but lose more nutrients and flavor because their total exposed surface area is larger. The best compromise is to cut peeled potatoes into slices between five-eighths and three-quarters of an inch thick. Wash them under cold water to rinse off any free starch released when you cut open the cells in peeling and slicing.

Cooking your potato. This is where we part company from all domestic mashed potatoes that have gone before us.

Years ago the instant mashed potato industry found that if you precook potatoes in 163-degree water for twenty minutes (twice as long for waxy varieties) and cool them, the amount of free starch in the final mash will be reduced by half. Without this discovery the instant mashed potato industry would today be manufacturing laundry starch.

I have experimented with both techniques and am guardedly optimistic that precooking may be the answer to our prayers. It appears to work like this. Cooking a potato is a two-stage process. The starch swells and gelatinizes within the cells when the potato reaches 160 degrees; then, nearer to the boiling point, the pectic cement between the cells degrades, and the potato can be safely mashed. Precooking separates these steps. Cooling the potato slices after the starch has gelled causes a process called retrogradation to take place; the starch molecules bond to one another and lose much of their ability to dissolve again in water or milk, even if you later rupture the cells through ricing or mashing and even if you overdo the final cooling a bit. Retrogradation retards gumminess.

For the first time anywhere industrial precooking and retrogradation can now be brought into the home kitchen. The use of a thermometer is vital. Put the peeled and washed slices into a pan of 175-degree water. Keeping the pan on a low flame and adding a little cold water now and then, you will find it easy to maintain the water within a few degrees of 160 for the next twenty or thirty minutes as you go about your other tasks. The slices will become tough and resilient and lose their translucent appearance. Drain the potatoes and transfer them to a bowl into which you run cold tap water until the slices feel cool to the touch, and leave them there for the next half hour. Then proceed to the final cooking, either simmering or steaming. Some recipes have you put your potatoes into cold salted water before bringing them to the boil. An elaborate Swedish study has shown that potatoes cooked this way produce a stickier final mash and sometimes develop an odd flavor. Other studies demonstrate that more vitamin C is lost if you start with cold water. Better drop your potato slices into actively boiling salted water and lower the heat to just above a simmer.

Last night I tested four versions of mashed potato on my guests. The precooked version came in first. It was smooth, not gummy, and had a robust earthy potato taste. The runner-up had been boiled in salted water in the usual manner. It verged on the pasty but tasted good. The other candidates were hopeless.

Mashing your potato. Mash immediately after you drain the potato slices. The goal here is to separate the cells without rupturing them, and the perfect temperature for achieving this is about 180 degrees Fahrenheit. As the potato cools to room temperature, the pectic cement hardens again, and many more cells break open when you mash them, spilling out their sticky starchy gel. At 50 degrees half the cells will rupture.

Any cookbook that sanctions the use of a blender or food processor for mashing should be carefully shredded. People who like to use a hand masher because the resulting lumps remind them of their mothers' cooking ignore the fact that this technique repeatedly abuses the already mashed portions of the potato while you seek out the solid pieces that remain. A ricer is best because each potato cell passes through it only once, and all the pressure is applied in a vertical direction. In contrast, a food mill shears more cells apart by scraping them across the screen as you turn the handle, but it is possible that our precooking technique will permit the use of a food mill without fear of gumminess and produce a perfectly smooth result at the same time. Further experimentation lies ahead.

Steamy cooked potatoes should be dried either before or after mashing. You can return the slices to the pan, cover them with a folded kitchen towel, and shake the pan every so often for the next five minutes. Or you can rice the potatoes back into their pan and stir over low heat for a minute or two until a film appears on the bottom of the pan. Use a softly rounded wooden spoon. Be gentle.

Enriching your potato. How much butter you add is your business. I find that a stick of butter for every two pounds of potatoes (serves four to six) is a bit austere but that Robuchon overdoes it with three or four. If you beat in the butter first and then *hot* milk or cream (over low heat), you can achieve any consistency you like, from runny to stiff, but if you do it the other way round, it is hard to know how much milk to add. Georges Blanc advises incorporating the butter right away, keeping the potatoes warm, and adding heavy cream at the last minute. If you hold mashed potatoes for a while over warm, not simmering, water, don't cover the pan completely or the flavor will turn on you and gumminess set in.

Should your butter be very hard or very soft when you beat it in? Do you dare to use a whisk? (Michel Guerard says never.) Do waxy potatoes and new potatoes precook successfully? Is steaming better than boiling?

At present I am at a complete loss for answers to these remaining questions, and I will not be altogether happy with my mashed potatoes until the whole truth comes out. My next set of experiments begins tonight.

January 1989

Author's Note:

Joël Robuchon's potato is now the *ratte*—small, waxy, yellow fleshed, and available at some farmers' markets, including mine. Robuchon uses a food mill to mash his potatoes, then arduously rubs the puree through a sieve.

Water

I love the taste of calcium carbonate, or at least I think I do. Zinc leaves me cold, and I am lukewarm about lithium chloride. But silicate can taste just great—up to a point, of course.

Cool, crisp, pure, crystalline water is my favorite nonalcoholic drink, more than the juice of the blood orange and even more than diet Coke. Most Americans would disagree. One day in 1986 we began drinking less water, from both tap and bottle, than we did soft drinks. In future years this will be viewed as an awesome and chilling event, our final break with the natural world, but as far as I can remember, the moment passed unnoticed. I was probably drinking a Tab.

For the past few months I have been racking my brain, which is 75 percent water, to understand what perfect water should taste like. Several experts in the science of flavor have tried to persuade me that we all simply prefer the water we grew up with. I don't believe a word of it. If they were right, the 40 percent of Californians who use bottled or filtered water as their main supply—most of them because of the taste of most California tap water—would be content with what they've been drinking since they were young. We lovers of water are always in pursuit of that pure, clear, ethereal Alpine spring of our imaginations, and we know how it will taste when we find it.

I've been sampling lots of unsparkling bottled waters recently, and several of them approach the ideal. Fiuggi from Italy is one, and the French brand Volvic is another, though Evian is not—it tastes heavy and unctuous to me. In this, I resemble Farrah Fawcett, who is reported to prefer Volvic to all other still waters. She sets her hair with Evian, which is where we part company. Michelangelo was a great fan of Fiuggi, and I couldn't agree more.

The Water Centre in Edison, New Jersey, carries more bottled waters than any other place in the country, and I telephoned it the other day at (800) 345-5959 to find out what's new. The owner, Stanley Siebenberg, was sipping from a bottle of rare Peruvian San Mateo water when I reached him; it comes from a region known as the Land of Longevity. He told me that Lithia Springs is very popular among women who wish to get pregnant; it makes you feel mellow and more receptive to sex. M.G. Voda is rich in free magnesium, which some people say cures headaches and helps them sleep. Stanley himself lost seventeen pounds drinking Hennieze, the best-selling water in Switzerland, which, he said, lifts your energy level. Then, for several weeks, he washed his face in Deliziosa, and the wrinkles on his forehead disappeared. I told Stanley that I had read about a rock formation deep under Louisiana in which water has been trapped, unaltered, for forty million years; so far it is unavailable in bottled form.

The Food and Drug Administration forbids bottled-water companies to make health claims, and unless you drink monumental quantities of the most heavily mineralized waters on the market, you probably eat more of most types of minerals in your food. (A glass of milk has more calcium than a whole liter of the highest-calcium water I could find.) I explained to Stanley that eager as I am to shed both wrinkles and weight, mellow out, and add to my allotted years, I would settle in the meantime for a steady supply of water from an ethereal Alpine spring. He knew just what I meant and the next day delivered thirty-three candidates. Stanley's forehead was admirably smooth—though, meeting him for the first time, I had no basis for comparison.

When I had tasted half the thirty-three waters and become aware of their dramatically different tastes, I began to wonder why so few cookbooks specify the kind of water you should use in their recipes. I have seen recipes for lobster steamed in seawater and recipes for matzo balls formed with seltzer to make them light and fluffy. I've read that very hard water (high in calcium and magnesium) ruins the color and texture of vegetables and the consistency of bread dough, but that bread made with water free of alkaline mineral salts will fail to form a delicious golden crust. The British and the Chinese vary the variety of tea they brew according to the character of the water in their part of the country. I telephoned Paula Wolfert (*Couscous and Other Good Food from Morocco, The Cooking of South-West France, World of Food,* all Harper & Row), who opened up the culinary encyclopedia that inhabits her brain and added to my short list. Carbonated water is used by the Yugoslavs to form *ćevapčići,* sausage-shaped hamburgers grilled on a spit and served with onions; by the Serbs in their *proja,* a corn bread; and by other Mediterranean peoples to lighten their meatballs. The Four Seasons restaurant in New York City insists on San Pellegrino in its chocolate sherbet, and Paula herself includes a recipe for spring vegetables in *World of Food* that works only with Evian or Volvic.

The one world-famous recipe that depends on the water you use is carrots Vichy. Vichy water is salty, sparkling, and brimming with sulfates, bicarbonates, chlorides, and calcium from springs in central France where Julius Caesar once built a spa. Its bitter, salty taste is thought to balance the sweetness of carrots. You barely cover thin rounds of young carrots with Vichy water, add big pinches of sugar and salt, and cook gently until all the Vichy water is absorbed. Then you dot the carrots with butter, sprinkle with parsley, and eat.

Bottled water costs more than gasoline, even at a discount supermarket; despite the frightening facts you read these days, there is still lots of fine, free tap water left in America. If New York City water were not treated with chlorine, it would taste as delicious as anything from a bottle, and even with recent ecological threats to the city's upstate reservoirs, tasters from all over the world seem to concur. Chlorine is a greenish yellow gas with a powerful smell. It violently irritates the nose and throat, but it violently irritates bacteria even more, and so it has become a nearly universal disinfectant in public water supplies in America. Chlorine smells like Clorox bleach, and after you bathe in it, it reacts with your sweat and leaves you smelling like a boiled ear of corn, which some experts describe as the odor of human semen. An article in the *Tea and Coffee Trade Journal* considers chlorine the mortal enemy of coffee taste and aroma. Europeans (and most bottled-water companies) disinfect their water mainly with ozone, which does not dissolve in water the way chlorine does. Europeans apparently care more about the pleasure that delicious water can bring than about its germicidal sterility, and now some American cities are experimenting with ozonation.

My water is piped four miles down Fifth Avenue from Central Park, and after I've drunk my fill, it continues all the way downtown. Chlorine is introduced at Ninetieth Street, and because it dissipates as the water travels, enough chlorine must be added uptown so that some is left to disinfect the people on Wall Street, who are probably drinking Perrier anyway. In order that Wall Street may thrive, I must put up with water that tastes less perfect than it should.

One Star for Water

Sometimes Los Angeles reminds me of Arrakis, the planet known as Dune. One restaurant puts a note at the bottom of the menu announcing that its water is treated by the Aqua West Filtration System. I am not a connoisseur of California filtration systems. But if this becomes a trend, the choice of water-treatment device should definitely be a factor in every restaurant review.

This is just one example of the principle that bad-tasting water is not necessarily hazardous to your health and good-tasting water can possibly harm you. Too much iron or manganese makes water taste unpleasant; iron leaves rusty stains on your clothing; calcium and magnesium, the minerals that make water hard, turn soap into a sludgy mess, leave deposits on glasses and pots, and clog up your automatic coffeemaker. But none of these can hurt you in normal concentrations. On the other hand, many harmful or suspect chemicals can't be tasted or smelled even at dangerous levels.

That's why I sent off my water to be tested. *Consumer Reports* recommends a company in New Hampshire called WaterTest; I telephoned them at (800) 253-3506 and ordered up as many home tests as they have to offer. Within a few days I received a series of kits, snug Styrofoam containers filled with half-frozen plastic cold packs molded around little bottles with color-coded caps, some of them containing chemicals. I filled half the bottles at 7:00 a.m., before anybody else had drawn water, and the other half in the afternoon. The idea was to see whether the "first draw" of water lying in the pipes all night was more contaminated than the "full flush," freely flowing water that has been coursing under the streets and through my building all day. Tap water in older cities on the East Coast and in the Northwest can become polluted with lead as it passes through lead pipes (banned in 1986), joints soldered with lead mixtures, and brass faucets containing as much as 8 percent lead—and the longer water lies in the pipes, the more lead it collects. Even low levels of lead can cause permanent learning disabilities in children and peripheral nerve damage in adults. Some people think that lead-lined aqueducts and pewter goblets caused the fall of the Roman Empire. Some people will believe anything.

When the test results came back, I breathed a sigh of relief and took a cool sip of Quibell, a delicious bottled water from West Virginia, to replenish the water that had left my body in the exhale. (We lose three quarts of water a day from breathing, perspiration, and elimination.) All eleven metals, all coliform bacteria, all twelve pesticides, and all forty-nine organic compounds (solvents, petroleum derivatives, and by-products of chlorination, with names like isopropylbenzene and bromochloromethane) occurred at only small fractions of the EPA's Maximum Contaminant Levels, and most of them were below the lowest levels that WaterTest's sensitive instruments are able to report. The only difference between the water lying around all night and the fresh water in the afternoon sample was that the first contained more iron. Lead was no problem.

If I were more nervous about my health, the reports from WaterTest might not have been so reassuring. Critics blame the federal EPA for leaving hundreds of contaminants unregulated and for not pressing local water systems to comply with the rules. Critics of the critics say that our ability to detect these chemicals in incredibly small amounts has outdistanced our knowledge of what it all means for the public health. Those who drink bottled water to sidestep these controversies will be horrified to read studies by McKone and Andelman showing that the amounts of organic compounds you absorb through your skin in the bath or inhale in the shower can exceed the amount you drink. Think of your shower as a gas chamber.

I am grateful that so many people are worrying about the safety of my water, because they leave me free to worry about its taste.

The first problem to solve was this: How do you describe the flavor of an ideal water? I telephoned Arthur von Wiesenberger, author of two books about bottled water (*H2O*, Woodbridge Press, and *The Pocket Guide to Bottled Water*, Contemporary Books), and he generously faxed me a professional rating sheet. Water should be clean tasting, colorless, odorless, refreshing (not heavy or stale), and thirst quenching (without a residue). Water is downgraded if it is cloudy or smells metallic or musty or like chlorine, plastic, sulfur, or chemicals. Other professional testers add that water should not taste soapy, salty, waxy, muddy, or sour. By these standards, the pristine quality of an Alpine spring is nothing but the absence of flaws.

If this were true, then totally pure distilled water (there is no such thing, but you can come pretty close) would be the ideal. Yet almost everybody agrees that distilled water tastes awful—except for people who sell home water distillers and some friends of mine who are clinically paranoid about chemicals in their environment. I bought a gallon jug at the drugstore, took a few sips, and swallowed them reluctantly. On the theory that the water simply needed to be aerated, I whirled a cup of it in the blender for a few minutes. The taste was still unpleasant in a way that is difficult to describe—certainly not sulfurous or chemical or any of those adjectives, just stale and unrefreshing and slightly bitter. It was obvious that perfectly pure water does not come close to the ethereal Alpine spring.

I telephoned two scientists who have done important research on the taste of water, Linda Bartoshuk at Yale and Michael O'Mahony at the University of California at Davis. They explained that distilled water tastes bad because it doesn't taste anything like saliva. Yes, saliva.

Saliva is salty. But we lose our awareness of its constant presence as our taste buds adapt to the level of salt it contains. As a result, we perceive less salty things as having a subzero kind of taste. Bartoshuk describes this as a kind of bitterness (one of the four basic tastes—bitter, salty, sweet, and sour); if we wash the saliva from our tongue with distilled water for several minutes, we lose our adaptation to saltiness and no longer perceive pure water as bitter. O'Mahony refuses to categorize this taste as bitter; he will not go further than calling it "distilled water taste." Here I discovered a deep fissure in the academic world of taste: the O'Mahony school finds no physical basis for the existence of four basic tastes. After I have found the perfect water, I will return to figure out what this means for the world of string beans and crème brûlée.

I took out a book about saliva from the library and read it with fascination. Did you know that each of us produces three cups of saliva a day? Saliva contains about six hundred parts of sodium chloride—common table salt—for every million parts of liquid. By my calculations, this is about one-eighth as salty as chicken soup. I hurriedly added the right amount of table salt to distilled water and tasted it. After only a month of work I had managed to create . . . mildly salty water. Saliva is not an Alpine spring.

Then what is? Most scientific research about the composition of drinking water looks for the impurities that can make it harmful or unpleasant—not those that make really fine water taste that way—and bottled-water companies are secretive about which of the natural minerals in their products give them a delicious taste. I had heard that Pepsi-Cola is extremely careful about the composition of the water it uses, but the people in its research lab in Valhalla, New York, were completely lacking in the Pepsi Spirit when I asked them to share their findings. Table salt is not found in very many bottled still waters, but other substances are. I've found mineral waters containing gold and silver, platinum and copper, chromium and tin. But I was more interested in the mineral salts that water collects as it trickles and bubbles through the rocks and hollows of the earth. Some of these—calcium, potassium, magnesium, chlorides, and bicarbonates—are also found in saliva. Could it be that saliva minus the table salt equals an Alpine spring?

I turned to the few articles that have been published in scientific journals. A team of Japanese scientists writing in the *Journal of Fermentation Technology* concluded that calcium and small amounts of potassium are indispensable to the good taste of water, but that magnesium tastes rough and bitter. They also found that the silica picked up by water as it runs through *clay* is more important than other researchers had thought. Another study suggested that water with more than five hundred parts per million of minerals tastes salty, alkaline, earthy, bitter, or brackish. (By conventional definition, mineral water has more than five hundred parts per million.) Volvic and New York City tap contain about a third of this, and they, I found after extensive tasting, are the most pleasing to my taste. Evian and saliva are near the upper limit of mineral content and acceptability.

These taste judgments were roughly confirmed by a company in Massachusetts called Ionics, which sells water-purification equipment to Saudi Arabia, Bahrain, and Santa Barbara. Once Ionics has completely purified the best available local water, it adds mineral salts to make the water taste fresh and clean and balanced. After working with taste panels, Ionics has decided on 45 parts per million of calcium, 61 of bicarbonates, 45 of chloride, 2 of sulfates, and 1.8 of sodium. I have doubts about the chloride.

Now I was ready to create my own water. I drew up a shopping list, got out the yellow pages, and found that one of the largest chemical supply houses in Manhattan is located a few blocks from my apartment. At its offices, I presented my list and tried to interest the two employees in my spellbinding project. Chemicals come in all degrees of purity, and I specified the "ingestion grade" whenever possible.

Out of the blue, one of them said that I was crazy. I quoted from *Hamlet* with Mel Gibson and Glenn Close, "Though this be madness, yet there is method in't," but the chemical people were apparently fearful of the lawsuits that would follow upon my death from ingesting their ingestion-grade chemicals. I offered to sign a piece of paper guaranteeing that I would not eat anything they sold me. This trick has worked for me in the past, but not this time.

So I promised to test all concoctions only on my puppy. (I don't have a puppy.) Until then, these two employees had been heavy lidded and lethargic. But the mention of a puppy brought them to life, making them unaccountably but vividly angry. I was about to quote from Horace, *"Ira furor brevis est"* ("Anger is a passing madness"), when they threw me out of their shabby quarters. Threw me out!

From a telephone on the corner I called my wife for moral support, got some, then walked over to my local pharmacist, who was happy to help. We pored over his chemical catalog and ordered sixteen mineral salts. The first step was to dilute each of these to a few parts per million, the equivalent of a minuscule pinch in a bathtub of distilled water. Lacking that much distilled water and that many bathtubs, I dissolved a half teaspoon of each salt in a quart of water, took a half teaspoon of that solution, and mixed it into a fresh quart of water. Voilà, seven parts per million, ready for blending and tasting.

Somewhere among my sixteen bottles, jars, vases, and pitchers of water flows my pristine Alpine spring. When I discover where it is, I will let you know. Until then, some bottled waters come extremely close: Naya, Volvic, Connoisseur, Bourassa, Quibell, Fiuggi, Lora, Poland Spring, St. Michel, St. Jean, and Clairval.

May 1991

Ripeness Is All

Ripe fruit wants to be eaten. It has no other function, makes no other contribution. It does not produce sugar to nourish the rest of the plant, as the leaves do. It does not search for water and collect minerals like the roots or distribute nutrients like the stem. A fruit's only purpose is to seduce animals like you and me into becoming cheerful dupes in its secret reproductive agenda.

The dream of every plant is to propagate its own genes and species. For most, this means spreading their seeds far from the mother tree or bush so that the offspring will not compete with its parents for water, breathing space, and sunlight. Every seed has its own means of transportation, papery wings or balls of fluff that ride the wind, or burs that hook onto your jeans or fur. Fruits have another way. As spring draws into summer, they become plump and juicy and brilliantly colored, sweet and perfumed and irresistible.

At least that is what nature had in mind. Yet last summer I hardly dared to eat a *Prunus persica,* and this year's portents are even worse; I doubt that travelers would have brought today's supermarket peaches from China to Persia to Europe in the first place. Peaches and melons and pineapples—most fruit, in fact— do not get any sweeter or more flavorful after they are picked from the tree, vine, bramble, or bush (though they may improve in texture or color). Yet most of American agriculture, even some farmers at my local green market, seem determined to harvest fruit earlier and greener every year. And there are no laws ensuring that those little "Vine Ripened" stickers on the most expensive produce at your store mean anything at all. The penalty for pasting a sticker on a hard, tasteless piece of fruit should be the same as the penalty for printing counterfeit ten-dollar bills.

Eternal vigilance is the price of ripeness. Make it a habit to return unripe fruit. Throw a scene if need be. Your message may reach the wholesaler or the grower. For the smallest fruit, here's a handy tip: When nobody is looking, remove a berry from its little basket and conceal it in your palm. With your other hand, quickly wheel your shopping cart into a dark corner of, say, the cheese department and pop the berry into your mouth. Chew. Appraise its texture, sweetness, aromatic flavor compounds, and seediness. Then decide whether to invest in an entire basket. But first buy some cheese. You can never have enough good ripe cheese.

This grazing technique is unwieldy with the larger melons. For honeydews and most of your other summer fruit favorites, we must return to basics. Here are answers to the twenty most commonly asked questions about fruit and ripeness:

1. What is the difference between a fruit and a vegetable?

The answer has nothing to do with what kind of plant it came from, and everything to do with what *part* of the plant it was. A vegetable is a plant we raise for food. Anatomically, every vegetable is composed of roots, stems, stalks, branches, leaves, flowers, and fruit. Yes, nearly every vegetable has a fruit. So asking whether the tomato is a fruit or a vegetable is as silly as asking whether that large gray wrinkled tube over there is a trunk or an elephant. A fruit is the ovary of a plant—the seeds and the tissue surrounding them. Not only is a tomato the fruit of the tomato plant, but a green or purple pepper, filled as it is with seeds, is the fruit of the pepper plant. And the same goes for green beans, eggplant, zucchini, avocado, and pea pods—all fruits we eat during the savory part of the meal. When a fruit is juicy and high in sugar, we tend to save it for dessert, and then we call it a fruit, even when it is anatomically a stem, like rhubarb.

Most edible plants have only one part we especially like—and for which the plant has been bred, some for 1,000 or more years. When we eat beets, turnips, carrots, celeriac, and salsify, we concentrate on the roots, underground storage depots for starch and sugar, though we also eat celery branches, and some of us eat beet greens. Zucchini and cucumbers are fruits; we may eat their flowers, stuffed or not, baked or fried, but never their roots or leaves. When we are in the mood for eating leaves, we turn to spinach, cabbage, lettuce, sorrel, and all the herbs. Asparagus is a stalk or shoot. Beans and peas in a pod are seeds; when they are immature and their pods or shells are green and edible, they are fruits. We eat pea shoots but not bean shoots. Most of us ignore the potato flower and the artichoke stem. Potatoes, we need no reminding, are not roots. They are tubers—the swollen, fleshy, starchy subterranean section of the stem between the roots and the outside world.

2. Then what is a fruit?

A fruit is an ovary we eat for dessert. Peaches, apricots, nectarines, plums, and cherries are pretty simple ovaries—one seed surrounded by luscious flesh (the enlarged ovary wall) and wrapped in vividly colored skin. Incidentally, a nectarine is not a cross between a peach and a plum but a fuzzless variety of peach with an ancient pedigree.

3. What about raspberries?

Raspberries are more complicated. They are not true berries like currants and grapes. Each little segment is an entire stone fruit all in itself; a raspberry is made up of many ovaries from the same flower joined together. The strawberry wears its ovaries on the outside.

4. Do you mean that a strawberry is a fig turned inside out?

Just so. And a pineapple is a collection of berries all fused together. Watermelons are placental tissue riddled with seeds, a discovery that has somehow made watermelon less appealing to me.

5. What is the number one poem ever written about plums?

Experts differ, but my favorite is "This Is Just to Say" by William Carlos Williams:

> I have eaten
> the plums
> that were in
> the icebox
> and which
> you were probably
> saving for breakfast
> Forgive me
> they were delicious
> so sweet
> and so cold

6. Isn't ripening a chaotic, degenerative breakdown of the flesh and skin of a fruit as it plunges toward the death and decay that await us all?

Where did you get that idea? Ripening is a tightly structured, programmed series of changes that a fruit undergoes as it prepares to seduce every gastronomically aware animal in the neighborhood. Most fruit tastes best when it is ripest, which is often just when its seeds are ready to germinate.

7. Isn't that a teleological explanation bordering on the religious?

So?

8. When does ripening begin?

Ripening can *begin* only when a fruit has reached its physical maturity—*its full size and intended shape.* Fruit picked earlier will never ripen. And even fruit picked when it has reached physical maturity will undergo only some of the changes that we mean by "ripening."

9. How many changes are there?

Twelve, but I'll mention only a few.

Ethylene, a simple hydrocarbon gas, is a fruit's own internal ripening hormone. In ways yet undiscovered, it triggers and coordinates most of the other changes as the fruit sweetens, brightens, becomes juicy and aromatic, grows less acidic and less astringent, exudes a protective wax to slow the loss of water when it finally plops from the tree and is cut off from fresh supplies.

Most fruits soften when they synthesize an enzyme called polygalacturonase, which attacks the pectin cement holding their own cells rigidly in place. The cells slide around, which makes the fruit soft, and spill out their contents, which makes the fruit juicy. Apples lack polygalacturonase, which is why they remain crisp until they degenerate and decay—the stage beyond ripeness when a fruit becomes subject to microbial attack and rot.

Fruits become much sweeter as they ripen. Some of them have already stored up lots of starch or insipid sugars like glucose either on the tree or off; enzymes convert these into intensely sweet sugars like sucrose and fructose. Other fruits fill up with sweet sap only while attached to the mother plant and can get no sweeter after they are picked. And most fruits become less sour as their acids are used up in other ripening processes.

Fruit begins to separate from its parent when a thin layer of cells (known as the abscission zone) is weakened by a specialized enzyme called cellulase secreted by neighboring parts of the plant. Abscission is the natural separation of a fruit from its tree or vine or bush. Very few fruits these days are allowed to remain attached to their mother plant until abscission occurs.

It takes the average fruit only a week or two to go from full maturity to perfect ripeness.

10. But what about limes?

It is a wonder that the lime, with its abundance of acid and only 1 percent sugar, managed to propagate itself at all before the invention of the cocktail, especially because it stays an invisible camouflage green. Most fruits change to a spectacular, attention-getting hue as their chlorophyll decomposes and fades (in ways that nobody understands) and other pigments are either unmasked or quickly synthesized.

As they say in the fruit business, people buy with their eyes. Humans in the grocery store use color as a test for ripeness, which is good practice with strawberries, raspberries, blueberries, and cherries. But some apples redden before they begin to ripen, and oranges can remain green at the peak of ripeness when grown in tropical or subtropical climates (like Florida) without the chilling temperatures that turn the fruit orange (in California). In response to the irrational demands of consumers (including, until a few months ago, me) perfectly sweet and flavorful green oranges are dyed orange or treated with ethylene to "degreen" them on the way to market.

With mature peaches, nectarines, plums, and apricots, the background color of their skin should show no trace of green (except for green varieties). Pay little attention to the red or rosy blush—new varieties have now been bred to turn red long before they are fully ripe. The purpose is to let growers pick immature fruit and dupe the consumer. Some of the sweetest, juiciest peaches and nectarines never color beyond bright yellow.

11. Then what is a fruit lover to do?

Avoid peaches with a green background, and sniff your way around the supermarket. Aroma may be the best way to tell how ripe a piece of fruit was when it was picked. While attached to its parent, fruit synthesizes a bouquet of volatile compounds, as many as one or two hundred in each ripe fruit. At the same time, bitter and astringent compounds called phenols begin to fade away; their main purpose was to discourage animals and micro-organisms from eating the fruit before its seed was ready. Neither process happens normally after the fruit is harvested.

The aroma of ripe fruit seems to make the deepest impression on us. The fragrance of a melon I ate in Japan, a peach nudged from the tree on a farm in Sonoma, Rainier cherries jetted from Yakima to a fancy greengrocer in Greenwich Village, tomatoes and strawberries eaten in a field near San Diego—these memories nearly obliterate the intervening months of numbing banality. Aromatic compounds are synthesized as a fruit grows riper, a bouquet of esters, alcohols, acids, and things with names like lactones and aldehydes—all of them capable of becoming gaseous or vaporous at room temperature so that they can reach the ten thousand odor receptors in the roof of my nasal passages.

In contrast, most vegetables have weak, uncomplicated aromas until you cook them. As Harold McGee puts it, "All cooked food aspires to the condition of fruit."

12. But doesn't fruit keep on ripening after you pick it?

Up to a point. When fruit is pulled from the tree or drops of its own accord, it remains alive—capable of respiration, complex metabolism, and reproduction. But its life is drastically changed. The flow of minerals and water is instantly cut off. So is the supply of sugars from those little photosynthesis factories we call leaves. (Fruits that stay green as they ripen can continue photosynthesis in a minor sort of way were the sun not eclipsed as the fruit is piled together or packed into a cardboard box.) Many fruits feel physical pressure on their skin for the very first time. The supply of raw ingredients for synthesizing aromatic compounds changes. In a dizzying shift, the pull of gravity is flipped sideways or upside down.

And the only energy a harvested fruit can draw on comes from its dwindling reserve of sugars, acids, and starches.

No matter what the growers and supermarkets would like you to believe, most harvested fruits do not ripen nearly as well as they would on the tree, vine, or bush, and some don't ripen at all.

13. Can you be much, much more specific?

Gladly. Fruits can be divided into two groups, according to their style of ripening. "Climacteric" fruits ripen in a frenzied climax of respiration and activity; peaches, apples, and bananas are climacteric. "Nonclimacteric" fruits ripen gradually and decorously; examples are cherries and oranges. *Only climacteric fruit will ripen off the parent plant.* And of these, it is mainly fruit with stored reserves of starch (like apples and bananas) that can grow much sweeter after harvest, although other types of carbohydrates—protopectins in the cell walls and unsweet sugars like glucose—are also capable of sweeting. So there are really five categories of fruit.

14. Who made up these categories?

I did. But they're quite useful. Category One is fruits that never ripen after they are picked. These include blackberries, cacao, cherries (sweet and sour), dates, grapes, grapefruit, lemons, limes, litchi, mandarins, olives (which don't belong here because they are not eaten for dessert, but I thought you should know), oranges, pineapples, raspberries, strawberries, and watermelons. Except for watermelons, these are all nonclimacteric, calmly ripening fruits that receive all their sugar from the parent plant, though some may seem to get sweeter as their acidity decreases. Most postharvest changes in these fruits do not improve their quality. Like mushy cherries, they may soften after harvest, but more from decay than from ripening. Except for dates and citrus, they have brief storage lives.

All you can do is to buy them ripe and store them carefully. Mature, fresh berries are plump, with none of their little segments pale or green. Wash them (and cherries) only before serving to avoid damaging the skin and inviting decay. Buy cherries only with stems attached; decay begins at the bared opening. With all citrus, buy firm fruits that feel heavy for their size (they will be juicier with more tasty dissolved solids in the juice) and with thin, fine-pored skin (no point in paying for thick skin). With oranges, color is unimportant; early-season oranges that have been degreened with ethylene to make you feel warmer toward them have a shorter storage life. Don't mind surface scars and scratches; but soft spots spell decay. If the tiny flower-shaped button at one end of an orange is green, it was picked recently or handled well or both; a brittle, dark button indicates the opposite.

Mature watermelons are well rounded on both ends with dark, waxy rinds, firm but not hard. In a cut piece of melon, the seeds should be dark against intensely colored flesh without white streaks—which makes it much safer to choose a piece of cut watermelon. White seeds are a sign of immaturity.

Category Two contains the one fruit that stands at the opposite extreme. It ripens *only after you pick it* because a chemical signal sent out by the tree inhibits ripening. It is the avocado. The best way to store an avocado is on the tree. The second-best way is in the refrigerator for up to ten days after you've ripened it at room temperature—but only until the fruit yields to gentle pressure, before the skin loosens.

15. How can you call the avocado a fruit if a fruit is an ovary we eat for dessert, and I eat avocados in guacamole and in California rolls at Americanized sushi bars? Do you eat California rolls for dessert?

I don't eat California rolls under any circumstances. But Brazilians eat avocados for dessert, mashed up with sugar.

16. And the last three categories of fruit do *ripen after harvest?*

Yes. They are all climacteric fruits, and as long as they are picked fully mature in size and shape, they will ripen to some extent and in some ways.

Category Three includes fruits that ripen in color, texture, and juiciness but *do not improve in sweetness or flavor.* These include apricots, blueberries, cantaloupes, casabas, crenshaws, figs, honeydews, nectarines, passion fruit, peaches, Persian melons, persimmons, and plums. They will not grow much sweeter after harvest because they contain no starch to turn into sugar. When you ripen them at home, the most you can expect is an attractive, juicy fruit no more flavorful than the day it was picked. If you're lucky.

But you must buy them physically mature. Mature peaches, nectarines, plums, and apricots have fully developed shoulders (the rounded area around the stem) and sutures (the seam that runs along one side); they have just begun to soften; and the background color of their skin shows no trace of green (except for green varieties). Pay no attention to the rosy blush—it is the background color that matters. You should buy apricots ready to eat, but peaches, nectarines, and plums can be ripened at room temperature in a paper bag.

Category Four is for fruits that *do* get sweeter after harvest—apples, cherimoyas, kiwis, mangoes, papayas, pears, sapotes, and soursops. As they mature, they convert sugars from the plant's leaves into starch; during ripening, they convert these starch reserves back into sugar and will grow sweeter, on the tree or off. They are the darlings of commerce because they can be picked mature but unripe, and the advance of ripening can be arrested by refrigeration, sometimes in a controlled atmosphere low in oxygen. Apples and pears do especially well. Pears, in fact, become mushy and mealy when ripened completely on the tree; a period of cool storage before final ripening improves their texture. We are very lucky that pears can be stored, because a ripe pear stays perfect for less than a day.

Most apples in North America are harvested between July and November; cold storage makes them available year-round, often to the detriment of flavor and crispness. Long cold storage followed by ethylene ripening has been shown to produce kiwifruit with less sugar, bananas with less flavor, and apples and pears with less of both.

Buy mangoes when at least some of the green has turned yellow or red (unless you have run across the evergreen variety); avoid those with black spots, which may later penetrate the flesh.

But don't expect the proper aroma to develop in fruit picked long before it was ripe. Aromatic flavor compounds are not synthesized normally after a fruit is picked; astringent and bitter compounds no longer fade away. That's why aroma may be the best way to tell how ripe a piece of fruit was when it was picked.

Bananas are alone in Category Five because they ripen in nearly every way after harvest. The world champions of starch conversion, they go from 1 percent sugar and 25 percent starch to 15 percent sugar and 1 percent starch during ripening. And the simple banana aroma (also known as isoamyl acetate) does develop off the tree, though it will not quite compare with the more complex perfume of a nearly tree-ripened specimen.

When most commercially grown bananas are picked, they are mature but still completely green. Turn this to your advantage: buy them green, if you have the time to let them ripen. Hard, green bananas are less likely to have been injured in handling than those that have softened and yellowed on the way. Buy them with the stems fully attached and without splits in the skin. Ripen in a paper bag until fully yellow with little brown specks. Then refrigerate what you cannot eat immediately, but expect the skins to turn black.

17. *Why is fruit sometimes gassed with ethylene?*

The industry prefers the word "treated." As we have learned, ethylene is a fruit's own internal ripening hormone. In heavy-breathing climacteric fruit, Categories Three through Five, brief exposure to the gas triggers the fruit's own production of the hormone and with it whatever ripening potential the fruit possesses. When you place these fruits in a loosely closed brown paper bag at room temperature, the natural ethylene concentrates and speeds the process. Putting a ripe apple or banana in the bag can also help because these fruits generate ethylene like mad. The bag must be permeable enough to allow carbon dioxide produced by the ripening fruit to escape and oxygen to enter. Cut off from oxygen, fruit ferments. That's the benign side of ethylene. The fruit industry also uses artificial ethylene treatment to hide incalculable sins.

18. *Didn't you promise to explain the best way of choosing melons?*

I was just coming to that. If only there were one simple rule for all melons, nature's most succulent creation! Remember that melons are climacteric—they can continue to ripen after harvest. But they never get much sweeter than the day they were picked. Buy mature melons—well formed, heavy for their size, without injuries or flat areas. When netted melons like cantaloupes are mature, the netting will be raised instead of flat and the skin between will be tan or yellow, not green. Crenshaws are the king of melons: juicy, perfumed, honeyed, tender. Some mature crenshaws may stay green rather than turn gold, except on the "ground spot," the place where the melon rested on the earth. The background color of a Persian melon can be light green at maturity. In the honeydew, that potentially ambrosial but hard-to-choose treasure, the skin must be cream colored (not stark white), without a trace of green. As with other smooth melons, the skin should feel slightly waxy or tacky.

The round depression at one end of many melons is where the stem was attached; if it is smooth, without ragged edges, the melon was ripe enough to slip easily from the stem. Softening, aroma, and waxiness begin at the opposite or blossom end, which is where sniffing will tell you worlds about how sweet and perfumed the melon is inside. Experts clash on whether the aroma of an uncut honeydew is expressive. Casabas have little aroma and are an inferior species overall. Sorry.

19. Any advice about storage?

At your service. Fruits capable of ripening after they are picked should be encouraged to do so at room temperature, inside a paper bag or out. Then these fruits, and all those incapable of ripening after harvest, should be eaten immediately or refrigerated (to slow respiration) in a plastic bag (to prevent water loss). Dehydration is the greatest enemy of freshness in ripened fruit and other produce. Lettuce leaves wilt when their cells deflate from the loss of water. Try putting wilted lettuce in cold water; you will be amazed.

But don't seal the plastic bag tight, or the fruit will ferment and mold.

Before a fruit is ripe, refrigerator temperature will retard the process, may turn the sweeter sugars into glucose, can permanently deactivate the softening powers of polygalacturonase, and may increase acidity. Given enough time, chilling will injure fruits of tropical and semitropical origin both before and after ripening. Avoid buying very cold fruit in the grocery store. Not only will you be unable to evaluate its aroma, but chilling injuries (such as the mushy, fibrous flesh of a damaged peach) may not become apparent until the fruit returns to room temperature.

20. Is all this supposed to explain why most fruit in American supermarkets, except maybe cherries, is so awful?

Partly. There are other reasons too. Until recently, fruit breeders concentrated only on size, color, firmness, and supernaturally uniform shape, at the expense of flavor, sweetness, and texture. Some growers demand trees on which all the fruit matures at once, making it easier to harvest by machine. Others overfertilize to increase their yield and overirrigate to increase the fruits' weight shortly before harvest. And some years the weather refuses to cooperate. But ripeness is, to paraphrase the poet, the biggest deal of all.

There are four villains in the ripeness story: the greedy grower, the venal wholesaler, the shortsighted retailer, and the ignorant and stingy consumer like you and me.

To save on labor costs, growers use machines to pick, sort, and pack their fruit. Ripe fruit cannot survive a run-in with these machines. And when mechanical harvesters are used, they pick everything in sight—hard green, barely mature, and nearly ripe. Growers know that early fruit commands a higher price; all growers would like to recover their investment as soon in the season as possible; and most would like to sell whatever has not ripened by season's end. Citrus growers pick early when they fear a frost.

Growers complain that fruit brokers and retailers make them compete on the basis of price alone, not with texture or flavor. Brokers contend that retailers refuse to accept delivery of produce too ripe to have a long and happy shelf life. Retailers say that brokers buy only the easiest fruit to handle; they blame consumers for their unwillingness to pay more for more delicious fruit. The magic of the marketplace has somehow failed us when inferior fruit forces out produce of higher quality.

But some rays of hope do flicker through the darkening clouds of American fructiculture. Take Ron Mansfield. He is a grower in El Dorado County, California, in the foothills of the Sierra Nevada, halfway between Sacramento and Lake Tahoe, where he farms several small parcels, leaving his peaches and nectarines on the trees until three or four days before they would drop of their own accord; his tree-ripened peaches have at least twice the sugar of those picked just at physical maturity and ripened off the tree. Mansfield picks and packs them by hand in single-layer wooden boxes, and two days later they are offered at fancy produce stores and restaurants on both coasts (and at his own retail farm stand). Mansfield knows only three or four other California growers who try to ship fruit of equal quality.

Margaret and Bill Skaife of Oceanside, California, near San Diego, have designed hand-harvesting and packing procedures and clever containers (patent pending) for shipping nearly ripe tomatoes, strawberries, and stone fruit to distant markets. (The fruits arc suspended by their stems and cushioned from swinging against their neighbors.) Their first tomato crop, offered to consumers with a gold sticker and a money-back guarantee, was a great success at stores like Balducci's in New York, which sold two thousand pounds of them during peak weeks. But the Skaifes are still dependent on the farming practices and cultivars of growers in California and Mexico with whom they contract.

The methods (and prices) of the LTD company represent a workable compromise for the mass market. Growers who sell to LTD harvest their fruit an average of three days later than other growers; the Stop & Shop supermarket chain in New England, which has developed one of the most active programs in the country to improve the quality of fruit, is one of their big customers. But nothing, I am told, beats a Ron Mansfield peach.

Elsewhere, the future looks grim. Most American stone fruit is grown in California—96 percent of all apricots, 90 percent of nectarines and plums, and 60 percent of freestone peaches and Bartlett pears. The fruit is harvested nearly rock hard, ten or fifteen days before it is ripe, to allow for rough picking, mechanical handling, and prolonged transportation. All but the firmest fruit would be destroyed by this ordeal. Under the California Tree Fruit Agreement—a joint federal-state-industry "marketing order" in effect in one form or other since 1933—growers could not ship their fruit unless it met a minimum standard known as California Well-Matured. This simply guaranteed that most tree fruit would be fully developed and consequently that it would improve at least in color and texture after harvest. Now the California stone-fruit growers want to harvest their produce even earlier.

Last year the plum growers pulled out of the agreement. Early this year a dissident group of peach and nectarine growers persuaded the USDA to add an alternate, lower standard known as U.S. No. 1 or U.S. Mature. This will allow them to harvest even earlier and greener provided they say so on their shipping cartons. One rationale is that Georgia peaches have long been held to the equivalent of the trifling U.S. No. 1 standard and can compete unfairly. And Colorado growers recently abandoned their federal-state inspection program entirely. To fruit fanciers, the old criteria were undemanding enough. The new system promises even less.

In a twist of fate, the predominantly Republican California growers were temporarily foiled by President Bush's election-year moratorium on new federal regulations. For the new two-tier fruit inspection system to circumvent the moratorium and go into effect, the vice president's Council on Competitiveness must certify that the regulations are "pro-growth," a term apparently not intended in its horticultural sense. At this writing, the only person who can save America from a catastrophic plunge in the quality of its peaches and nectarines is Vice President Dan Quayle. Any bets?

July 1992

Hot Dog

Everybody's in a panic these days about the dangers of eating raw shellfish. But I have a plan. I've decided to give up skiing this winter so that I can eat my fill. By my calculations, the chance of suffering a substantial injury in one day of skiing is ten times worse than the chance of getting sick from eating a plate of cold, plump, briny, succulent raw oysters or clams. It follows that if I give up ten days of skiing, I can feast on oysters twice a week for the entire year.

To be perfectly truthful, I've never skied a day in my life or eaten less than my fill of anything. My plan was born at supper with an unfortunate friend, fresh from the slopes and hospitals of Aspen, where he had broken his shoulder by crashing into a shrub on a downhill run. He wore a brace on his upper torso and needed help turning the pages of his menu. I immediately recovered from excessive feelings of sympathy as I watched my friend choose his food with a superstitious adherence to every modern nutritional fad and rumor he had ever heard. For the life of me, I cannot understand why some people are eager to take on all sorts of dangers and then go paranoid over a much less risky endeavor—especially when that endeavor is dinner.

We *do* have ample cause to be worried about seafood safety. An investigation in the February 1992 issue of *Consumer Reports* found that a full 44 percent of the seafood its staff purchased at supermarkets and fish stores contained unacceptable levels of fecal coliform bacteria, which can cause all sorts of gastrointestinal illnesses. The federal government has shirked its duty to ensure the safety of our seafood, and proposals are now before Congress to remedy the situation.

Most bacteria and viruses are destroyed by cooking, which is why the federal Food and Drug Administration recommends that fish be cooked to 145 degrees Fahrenheit or until it flakes easily at the center near the bone; oysters and clams should be boiled for four to six minutes. These are reliable recipes for cataclysmically overcooked seafood.

Raw shellfish is where most of the danger lurks. In 1991 the FDA conducted a risk assessment of fish and shellfish in cooperation with the Centers for Disease Control and discovered that, when raw or partially cooked mollusks (mussels, clams, and oysters) are excluded, only one illness results from every two million servings of seafood. This is an extremely low number compared to the danger of eating chicken, with one illness in every twenty-five thousand servings.

But when raw or partially cooked shellfish is added in, the risk jumps eightfold. Raw clams, oysters, and mussels account for 85 percent of all seafood-borne illnesses. One in every two thousand servings of raw mollusks is likely to make somebody ill.

As high as this number seems, it means that if you eat a plate of raw oysters every week, you will get sick once in forty years or twice in a full and happy lifetime. And you can reduce the risk further by avoiding the main threat—raw mollusks taken from March to October in the Gulf of Mexico, when they are likely to be infected with *Vibrio vulnificus*. The warmer the water and the higher the temperature at which oysters are shipped and stored, the greater the danger. This is the principal rationale for the old rule of thumb that oysters should be eaten only in months whose name contains an *r*, because these are the cold-weather months from September through April. (A second reason is epicurean: oysters spawn in warmer weather, depleting their tasty glycogen and losing their succulence.) These days, Gulf oysters are safe, if at all, only from November through February.

For the very young, the very old, and people with weakened immune systems, including those who are HIV-positive, an infection by *Vibrio vulnificus* from a contaminated oyster can lead to death. But for most diners, the worst outcome is a day or two of unpleasant and unsightly gastrointestinal distress.

If raw shellfish makes you sick once in every two thousand servings, how does this compare to the hazards of going skiing? The statistics are elusive—the skiing industry does not encourage the collection and publication of data. But there seems to be general agreement that a substantial injury occurs once in every 250 days of skiing or, at the least, once in 400. These include leg fractures, spine fractures, contusions, lacerations, and knee injuries. A study in Munich found at least one minor injury in every 59 days of skiing and a really serious disaster in every 500; it defined "serious" as meaning that the skier would be off the slopes for at least 3 days. My last bad oyster kept me from table for only one. And most accident surveys leave out gondola crashes, skiers' smashing into each other in the subarctic cold; the danger of radiation (the yearly risk of cancer from cosmic rays is two-thirds greater at the altitude of Denver than at sea level, where oysters live); and injuries that blossom after the skier returns home, like the newly popular sprain of the ulnar collateral ligament of the metacarpophalangeal joint of the thumb. To say that a day of skiing is ten times more dangerous than a delicious plate of oysters is, I think, an act of generosity to the sport and its hapless participants.

Ski apologists point out that skiers suffer fewer *fatalities* than swimmers, cyclists, or equestrians, and that skiing is, on an hourly basis, no more dangerous than junior-high-school football. This may be a welcome consolation prize to the skiing industry, but it is even better news to me. It means that if I am willing to give up junior-high-school football this fall, I can happily devour all the sushi, sashimi, and ceviche that my heart desires.

October 1992

9 1

Playing Ketchup

In England there are sixty different religions, and only one sauce.
—MARQUIS DOMENICO CARACCIOLO (1715–1789)

When rumor recently reached my ears that U.S. sales of salsa would soon eclipse those of ketchup, catsup, and catchup (these words all mean the same thing), I rushed down to my local supermarket, planted myself in the ketchup department, and stood a lonely, anxious vigil, as though my presence alone could stanch the tide of chunky, piquant salsa that menaced from the opposite end of aisle 5.

I yield to no one in my toleration of multiculturalism in America. I eagerly celebrate Cinco de Mayo, Chinese New Year, the Festa of San Gennaro, and the Decay of the Ottoman Empire with whatever banquet is most fitting. But ketchup's fall to second-class status is another thing entirely, which is what the packaged-food experts predict. According to *Fortune*, sales of "Mexican sauces" will reach $802 million in 1992, leaving ketchup in the dust at $723 million. Even worse, the gap will widen for three more years.

To my mind, ketchup stands in the top tier of the world's cold or tepid nondessert sauces. It is surely our proudest, perhaps our only, homegrown sauce achievement. Marquis Domenico Caracciolo, ambassador from Naples to England, was probably referring to crème anglaise, the greatest dessert sauce ever created, but he might as well have been talking ketchup. Ninety-seven percent of American homes keep ketchup in the kitchen. Each of us blissfully eats three bottles of it a year. A tablespoon of ketchup is packed with flavor but carries only sixteen calories and no fat; it is recommended for dieters and skinny people alike. Four tablespoons of ketchup, the amount you might consume on a hamburger and a large order of fries, is the nutritional equivalent of an entire ripe medium tomato, with none of the fuss and bother.

Ketchup is "one of the great successes the sauce world has ever known," wrote Elisabeth Rozin in the *Journal of Gastronomy* (Summer 1988). In its brilliant red color, its rich flavor, and its marked salinity, Rozin theorizes, ketchup represents the "fulfillment, both real and symbolic, of the ancient and atavistic lust for blood," magically achieved with the use of plant products alone. Rozin also draws an analogy to the Christian Mass and its fruity surrogate for the blood of Christ, but I forget how it goes. All I know is that I discovered a case of Del Monte in one of the celebrated kitchens of Piemonte, in northern Italy, vying with *tartufi* and porcini for the chef's affections. And last year in Paris, in a kitchen soon to receive its second Michelin star, I watched the chef add a dollop of Heinz to his sauce of salmon's blood, red wine, and *verjus*, a postmodernization of Escoffier's *sauce genevoise*. Miguel de Cervantes once wrote, "*La mejor salsa del mundo es la hambre,*" the best sauce in the world is the hunger. Cervantes had obviously never tasted ketchup.

Will 1992 be the year we abandon our own great sauce, our most excellent ketchup?

Not exactly. Briefly leaving my shopping cart on guard, I bought a bag of potato chips (natural flavor, not rancho or nacho) and a plastic squeeze bottle of Heinz ketchup, the standard by which all other ketchups, for better or worse, must be measured. I swirled some Heinz on a potato chip and munched thoughtfully. Before long, my mood had brightened. The article in *Fortune* was surely a false alarm; either the magazine does not know its sauces, or else it has deliberately set out to undermine America's confidence in its own condiments. Comparing the sales of all Mexican sauces to the sales of ketchup, just one sauce, is unjust and misleading. Just think of the multitude of sauces in Mexican cuisine, their *mole de olla* and *mole verde de pepita*, red sesame seed sauce and green tomato sauce, *salsa borracha* and *salsa de los reyes*, *salsa de moscas* and *salsa de tijera*, chili sauces made with *pasillas* and with *cascabels*, with *chiles de árbol* and *chiles de guajillo!* When sales of *mole verde de pepita* exceed those of Heinz, then we will have something to worry about.

94

I edged warily down the aisle to the shelves of salsa. A glance at the unit-pricing stickers under each brand again proved that ketchup still reigns supreme. The average price for a quart of ketchup in my supermarket came to $1.16; the salsas averaged $5.50. Divide the first price into the second, and you'll see that on whatever day in 1992 dollar sales of all the salsas put together exceed those of ketchup, ketchup will still be 4.74 times more popular than salsa because salsa is 4.74 times more expensive. I left the supermarket in a gay and celebratory mood and in possession of every type of ketchup they had on offer, nine in all. Within a few days I had ransacked the other markets in my neighborhood, all the fancy-food stores, and every mail-order company I could think of.

Buying a bottle of ketchup is not a mindless matter of pulling it off the shelf and paying some money. As with wines, there are good years and bad, depending on how sweet and flavorful the tomatoes were. Most brands are made from tomato paste or tomato concentrate, boiled down in late summer when the tomatoes are harvested, and used throughout the year to cook the final product. But ketchup bottled in the summer is often made directly from ripe tomatoes. The ketchup connoisseur will want to know the year and day the sauce was bottled. If Heinz is your favorite, look at the four-digit number on the bottle cap, ignoring the initial two letters. The last digit indicates the year and the first three digits tell you the day when the ketchup was bottled. For example, 0752 means the seventy-fifth day of 1992; 2530, a vintage still on the shelves, means the two-hundred-fifty-third day of 1990. If you prefer another brand, telephone the manufacturer for details.

At last, when thirty-three ketchups stood on my kitchen table, I was ready to begin planning a Festival of Ketchups, a grand competitive tasting. Does Heinz truly deserve 55 percent of the U.S. ketchup market with Hunt's a laggard at 19 percent and Del Monte a wimpy 9 percent, while all generic and private brands add up to 17 percent, and the sum total of gourmet and regional ketchups reaches only 2 percent? I began with the assumption that the answer is yes, because Heinz is the only brand of ketchup I ever buy. Or should I say it *was* the only brand of ketchup I ever *bought?* But that would give away the results of the competition.

The scientific ketchup contests I've read about used either plastic spoons or little dry crackers as a tasting medium, with water or club soda between bites. This seems logical, but so does a hamburger and French fries, with a bubbly gulp of diet Coke in between, which is certainly how ketchup is deployed in the real world. In a preparatory experiment with several of the ketchups in my collection, I discovered that their flavor is transformed by the way you taste them: once the mouth becomes acclimated to the sweetness of Coke, for example, the cloying sugariness of some ketchups disappears, but the decorous sweet-sour balance of others tips toward the acidic. The spicier varieties, usually designer ketchups, are zesty on a plastic spoon but obscure the loveliness of a crisp French fry, which the blander, mainstream brands perfectly complement. The choice of a tasting medium would be absolutely critical.

I worried that eating thirty-three hamburgers in a row would be impractical, as was, I would soon discover, cutting a single hamburger into thirty-three equal wedges. I set out to design a miniature hamburger the diameter of a quarter (four millimeters thick), with a tiny little hamburger bun on top and bottom. Getting the outside of the meat nice and crusty while keeping the inside red and juicy proved impossible on so small a scale, and I forsook this plan even before I had got down to miniaturizing the bun.

A decision was taken: my wife and I would rate our ketchups both on and off French fries from the McDonald's three blocks away, ironically *à côté de* my local farmers' market. McDonald's once fried the most perfect, and certainly the most reliable, potatoes in the nation: then some genius got the idea that deep-frying in pure, golden beef fat is not politically correct. He or she was undoubtedly correct, but now its fries merit a rating no higher than Acceptable Plus.*

My third task was to solve, once and for all, the ketchup pourability problem. During the precompetition experiment, I was largely ignorant of the contribution that the science of rheology can make to our everyday lives. It was only after I had sent a stream of ketchup streaking across my wife's favorite tablecloth, a lovely hand-printed Indian cotton from a shop on the rue Jacob, that I telephoned Professor Malcolm Bourne at Cornell for a lesson in non-Newtonian fluids. Sir Isaac Newton wrote the laws governing liquids that flow like water: the more force you exert on them, the faster they flow. But ketchup is different. Composed of tangled red tomato fibers suspended in a sweet and acidic colorless serum, ketchup behaves like a solid both at rest and under low levels of pressure: but then, at some higher threshold, it suddenly begins flowing like an ordinary fluid. That's why the frustrated ketchup lover who loses patience with gentle taps on the bottle's bottom and prematurely shifts to a powerful wallop ends up with a gush of ketchup over everything. Ketchup and mayonnaise are known as Bingham fluids, named after the scientist who characterized them early in this century.

---

*For a more comprehensive discussion of fries, please refer to the chapter of that name in Part Five.

Professor Bourne has these suggestions: Any ketchup in the neck of the bottle has probably dried out and partially solidified; remove the cap and stir the top half inch of ketchup into the rest with the point of a knife. Then, after replacing the cap, violently agitate the whole bottle vertically, like a cocktail shaker: this should decrease the degree of entanglement among the tomato fibers and line them up in the hoped-for direction of flow. Finally, remove the cap again and invert the bottle over your fries or hamburger. Begin tapping the bottom gently, gradually increasing the force of each tap until the ketchup begins to flow at just the right rate. If this doesn't work, go out and buy a plastic squeeze bottle, introduced by Heinz in 1983 and made recyclable in 1991.

Just before the Festival of Ketchups was to begin, I decided to add two homemade ketchups to my collection of thirty-three store-bought and mail-order specimens. For the first, I was determined to track down and replicate the first ketchup ever eaten. And for the second, I wanted to create a good, honest ketchup from the ground up.

Where did ketchup get its start? The most popular theory is that the word itself derives from *kôe-chiap* or *ké-tsiap* in the Amoy dialect of China, where it meant the brine of pickled fish or shellfish. Some people prefer the Malaysian word *ketchap* (spelled *ketjap* by the Dutch), which may have come from the Chinese in the first place. In either case, sometime in the late seventeenth century, the name (and perhaps some samples and a recipe or two) arrived in England, where it first appeared in print as "catchup" in 1690 and then as "ketchup" in 1711, at least according to the *Oxford English Dictionary.* These exotic Asian names struck an evocative chord among the British, who quickly appropriated the names for their own pickled anchovies or oysters, long in popular use and probably remote descendants of the fishy, fermented Roman sauces *garum* and *liquamen.*

But the history of a word is not the history of a dish. Ketchup is not a Chinese sauce of fermented fish brine, a sickly sweet soy from Java, or British oyster juice. Everybody knows what ketchup is. Ketchup is nothing more or less than a cold, thick, bright crimson, sweet, spicy, acidic, cooked, and strained tomato sauce made with vinegar, sugar, and salt, and flavored with onion or garlic and spices such as cinnamon, cloves, mace, allspice, nutmeg, ginger, and cayenne. The FDA is so sure about this that it requires every one of these elements in anything labeled "Ketchup," "Catsup," or "Catchup." And the tomato seeds and skins must be scrupulously strained out. But more than anything, the FDA's regulations concentrate on *thickness*, giving it as much space as any other ketchup attribute: "The consistency of the finished food is such that its flow is not more than 14 centimeters in 30 seconds at 20°C when tested in a Bostwick Consistometer in the following manner," and so forth. The thickness rules go on for another full column in the Code of Federal Regulations.

Henry J. Heinz began making ketchup in the centennial year of 1876 and sold it at the Philadelphia World's Fair. The Heinz recipe has not changed much since. But H. J. Heinz was neither the inventor of modern-day ketchup nor even the first to bottle it commercially. Its origins are intertwined with the history of tomato cookery in England and America. The tomato is a native of the Andes; but in the early 1500s, while living in Mexico, it discovered an expedition of Spanish conquistadores and followed them back to Europe. There, the tomato found a home in the cookery of Spain, Italy, and Portugal, but northern Europeans dithered for two centuries about whether or not it was poisonous. How the tomato reached North America is a profound mystery. My second-favorite (though nearly unsupported) theory is that the Portuguese brought the plant to Africa and that African slaves later introduced it to the West Indies and Virginia. My most favorite theory is that Sephardic Jews who had fled to Provence from Persia brought the tomato from its new home on the Mediterranean to America, when they immigrated to Charleston, South Carolina. If you are interested in all the details, you'll enjoy reading a recent article in *Petits Propos Culinaires 39*, by Andrew F. Smith, and various admirable works by Karen Hess, as well as exploring the culinary collection of the New York Public Library.

Tomatoes were considered far less exotic and dangerous in the American colonies than popular history suggests. The widespread story that one Robert Gibbon ate a tomato on the courthouse steps in Salem, New Jersey, in 1820, to demonstrate that tomatoes are not poisonous may be true, but his dramatic demonstration was completely unnecessary. Long before then, in 1756, Hannah Glasse had published the first tomato recipe in English in her immensely popular *Art of Cookery*, which was widely circulated in the colonies. Thomas Jefferson recorded his cultivation of "tomatas" (and that of other farmers) in *Notes on the State of Virginia* in 1785. And we know that some version of tomato ketchup was made in the early kitchens of America: in New Jersey in 1782; on the Mississippi River sometime before the end of the century by Francis Vigo, a Sardinian; and in Mobile, Alabama, by James Mease, who wrote in 1804 that " 'Love Apples' make a fine catsup."

At least three or four recipes have some claim to being the original tomato ketchup. Having cooked them all, and several others besides, I can say that the model for the kind of tomato sauce that you, the FDA, and Henry J. Heinz would recognize as the modern ketchup was, in fact, the earliest. The first two tomato sauce recipes published in our language appeared in London in 1804 in Alexander Hunter's *Culina Famulatrix Medicinae: or, Receipts in Cookery*. One of them is, in my opinion, the first modern ketchup ever created! It is often attributed to the better-known *A New System of Domestic Cookery*, by Maria Rundell (1813). But it appears that Mrs. Rundell simply lifted her recipe from Alexander Hunter.

Alexander Hunter's Tomata Sauce (1804)

Take tomatas when ripe, and bake them in an oven, till they become perfectly soft, then scoop them out with a tea-spoon, and rub the pulp through a sieve. To the pulp, put as much Chili vinegar as will bring it to proper thickness, with salt to the taste. Add to each quart, half an ounce of garlic and one ounce of shalot, both sliced very thin. Boil during the space of a quarter of an hour, taking care to skim the mixture very well. Then strain, and take out the garlic and shalot . . . and let it stand for a few days before it is corked up. . . .

This is a charming sauce for all kinds of meat, whether hot or cold. . . . Being a pleasant acid, [the tomata] is much used by the Spaniards and Portuguese in their soups. In botanical language, it is the Lycopersicon Esculentum. Linn.

Confused on some of the details, I turned for advice to Hunter's other tomata sauce recipe. There, the tomatoes are roasted in an "earthen pot . . . after the bread is drawn," which I figured is the equivalent of about 300 degrees Fahrenheit in a brick oven that you fire once in the early morning and use as it slowly cools throughout the day. Instead of the chili vinegar, "some white wine vinegar, with cayenne pepper" may be substituted. Hunter also adds some powdered ginger, which sounded like a good idea to me.

Roasting five large and very ripe tomatoes for an hour and pushing them through a sieve, I followed the recipe, adding a quarter cup of vinegar, a few pinches of cayenne, and a scant quarter teaspoon of ginger. I boiled down the ketchup for longer than Hunter specifies—to something nearer the properly modern thickness. But thick or thin, and despite the lack of added sugar, the taste and texture come closer to true, modern ketchup than any of the competition from the early nineteenth century. Having invented tomato ketchup, the British then avoided it for more than a hundred years. By then, according to a report in the *New York Tribune* in 1896, tomato ketchup had become our national condiment, found on every table in the land. Forty-six brands were sold in Connecticut alone.

Just one thing stood between me and the grand competitive tasting—developing my very own recipe. My objective was to use neither exotic ingredients nor flavorings but to achieve the perfectly smooth, thick texture of Heinz or Hunt's while preserving more of the fresh tomato taste than they do and drawing as much sweetness and acidity as possible from the tomato itself rather than from added sugar and vinegar. But I certainly did not want the final product to taste too fresh or natural to be real ketchup.

The overall outlines of a modern ketchup are simple: a pound of tomatoes ends up as about a quarter pound of thick ketchup containing about 20 percent sugar and 1.5 percent acid; fresh tomatoes contain 3 or 4 percent sugar to begin with, which becomes 12 to 16 percent as the mixture is boiled down; the tomato's natural acids concentrate as well. But the more you cook tomatoes to evaporate their water, the more you damage their fresh flavor and color. My solution is a technique sometimes used in making jam—separately reducing the tomato liquid to a thick syrup before adding it back to the pulp for a brief final simmer. This ketchup is easy to make, and delicious.

Olde-Tyme Homemade Ketchup (1992)

Take 10 pounds of very ripe red tomatoes, remove their stems, chop them roughly, and put them in a heavy, wide, nonreactive pan of at least 8-quart capacity. Cover, place the pan over high heat, and cook for 5 to 10 minutes, stirring every minute or so until the tomato chunks give off their juice and everything comes to a boil. In batches, pour into a large, medium-fine strainer set over a 2-quart saucepan. Gently press and stir the tomatoes with a wooden spoon so that the thin liquid (about 2 quarts), but none of the tomato pulp, goes into the saucepan. Then put the pulp through a food mill fitted with the finest screen (to eliminate the seeds and skin) and back into the first pan. There will be about a quart of pulp.

To the tomato liquid add 4 garlic cloves and a large onion, both chopped medium-fine; ¾ cup of white or cider vinegar; a tablespoon of black peppercorns; a heaping teaspoon of allspice berries; a cinnamon stick; 8 whole cloves; ¼ teaspoon each of cayenne and powdered ginger; and 2½ tablespoons of salt. Cook over moderately high heat for about a half hour, until reduced to 2 thick and syrupy cups. Strain into the pan holding the tomato pulp, pressing to extract all the liquid, stir in 6 tablespoons of sugar, and simmer, stirring often, for 15 minutes, or until the ketchup is reduced by one-third to about a quart. Puree further in a blender or food processor to achieve the authentic texture of commercial ketchup.

At long last, thirty-five ketchups were lined up on our kitchen counter.

"Let the games begin," my wife said as we walked into our neighborhood McDonald's. Next to the deep fryers is a bin where cooked potatoes languish under heat lamps until somebody orders them, by which time they may taste like cardboard. So we stood unobtrusively in the condiment and napkin area and waited and watched. When the holding bin was nearly empty and the assistant manager had dropped some fresh potatoes into the deep fryer, we rushed up to the counter and requested ten large orders of fries. A few minutes later we were walking back home with our crispy treasures.

Ten large orders of French fries may be the precise number you need to sample and evaluate thirty-five ketchups. But what we had failed to anticipate is that eating anywhere near this number of French fries slathered with ketchup is nearly impossible. And as the minutes drew on into hours, we became increasingly confused about which ketchups we preferred and why. I remember reading somewhere that a human being is incapable of comparing more than seven things at one time. Two human beings working as a team are no more capable.

Our solution was to assign each ketchup to one of four general categories: Worse Than Heinz, Heinz, Better Than Heinz, and Not Really Ketchup. Both Alexander Hunter's Tomata Sauce (1804), properly reduced, and our very own Olde-Tyme Homemade Ketchup (1992) usually but not always found themselves in the Better Than Heinz category. If you would like to experience some alternative ketchups yourself, here are our tasting notes (with the New York City sources and prices):

- A&P Tomato Ketchup, 14 ounces for $.77. Good, often seemed Better Than Heinz, with a deeper taste. But overly assertive clove flavor.

- Beyond Catsup, Jasmine & Bread, 9 ounces for $6.00. The V-8 juice of ketchups, with assertive celery notes. But not bad.

- Blanchard & Blanchard New England Chunky Ketchup (Extra Spicy), 12 ounces for $2.49. Very tasty, but more like the dreaded salsa, chunky and thick. Does nothing for French fries.

- Busha Browne's Spicy Tomato Love-Apple Sauce, 6.5 ounces for $4.50 at Balducci's. Tiny little chunks with a fermented, almost fetid, flavor, like the ancestral Asian ketchup: more like a roughly pureed chutney, my least favorite flavor in the whole world.

- Del Monte Ketchup, 17 ounces for $.99 at Sloan's. Sometimes Better Than Heinz, sometimes not; less sticky, less tendency to coat the teeth. But slightly overcooked, caramelized taste.

- Fancy Tomato Catsup, from the Food Emporium, 14 ounces for $.77. Seems identical to A&P's house brand, above.

• Featherweight Catsup Reduced Calorie, from Infiniti Health Food, 13 ounces for $2.35. Anybody who would choose a brand of ketchup to save calories is crazy. But this one has a nice, bright taste, though too much vinegar.

• Foodtown Catsup, 14 ounces for $.73 at D'Agostino's. Tastes like A&P's; see above.

• Hain Natural Catsup, 14 ounces for $2.85 at Infiniti Health Food. Naturally and simply awful. Sweetened with the bitterness of honey, foolishly unsalted.

• Heinz Hot Ketchup, 14 ounces for $1.29 at Gristede's. Slightly tangy. Sometimes seemed Better Than Heinz, though the official contest rules do not allow this.

• Heinz Lite Ketchup, 13.25 ounces for $1.29 at Gristede's. Who needs lite ketchup with half the calories and one-third less salt? Identical to Weight Watchers, below, but priced lite-r, at 25 percent less.

• Heinz Tomato Ketchup, 28 ounces for $2.19 at D'Agostino's. The one and only. Bright color, thick but a bit sticky, quite sweet; less taste than homemade but with a good, fruity acidity, some tomato taste: unassertive and uninteresting spices. With French fries, a marriage made in heaven.

• Hunt's Tomato Ketchup, 32 ounces for $1.69 at Sloan's. Occasionally seemed Better Than Heinz. Thick and spicy, but excessive flavor of onion powder or garlic powder. Too salty.

• Jardine's Jalapeño Texas Ketchup, from Mo Hotta Mo Betta, 11 ounces for $5.25. Not much tomato taste. The powerful flavor of cumin belongs in chili powder or Tex-Mex cuisine but never ever in ketchup.

• Krasdale Fancy Tomato Catsup, from Sloan's, 14 ounces for $.89. Seems identical to A&P's house brand; see above.

• McIlhenny Farms Spicy Ketchup, 14 ounces for $3.95 at Dean & DeLuca. Good, deep taste of the Tabasco sauce for which McIlhenny is famous, but does nothing for French fries and tends to pall in ketchup-sized servings. Slightly runny.

• Napa Valley Mustard Co. Country Catsup, 14 ounces for $4.25 at Dean & DeLuca. Very good, balanced taste, but a little too much like barbecue sauce: more texture than classic, modern ketchup should have.

- Nervous Nellie's Jams & Jellies Hot Tomato Sweet Sauce, 6 ounces for $3.50. Delicious but more like a tomato jam than a ketchup. The only specimen with more sugar than tomatoes on the list of ingredients.

- Tassa Scotch Bonnet Catsup, from Mo Hotta Mo Betta, 5 ounces for $3.75. More a hot sauce than a ketchup. In fact, one of the hottest things I've tasted in months. Slightly musty flavor. My mouth won't stop burning.

- Tree of Life Ketchup, 13.5 ounces for $2.40 at Infiniti Health Food. Brownish color, slightly chunky, too much taste of tomato skins and maybe seeds, doesn't last in the mouth, unaccountably sweetened with brown-rice syrup. Inaccurate drivel on the label regarding the history of ketchup.

- Uncle Dave's Ketchup, 14 ounces for $4.50 at Infiniti Health Food. Tiny chunks with good tomato taste. But why sweeten ketchup with maple syrup and leave out most of the salt?

- Uncle Dave's Kickin' Ketchup, from Mo Hotta Mo Betta, 16 ounces for $6.50. Too much like barbecue or chili sauce, with strong taste of cumin and, I'll bet, celery seed.

- Weight Watchers Tomato Ketchup, from Gristede's, 13.25 ounces for $1.69. Another unnecessary product from an organization that victimizes chubby people like me by charging 33 percent more than the identical Heinz Lite.

- Westbrae Natural Catsup, Fruit-Sweetened, 11.5 ounces for $2.60 from Infiniti Health Food. "Fruit" means grape juice, which does not belong in the same bottle with catsup.

- Westbrae Natural Un-Ketchup, Unsweetened, 11.5 ounces for $2.45. The only brand whose label lists water before tomatoes among the ingredients. Caramelized taste indicates overcooking. And don't they know that "catsup" is synonymous with "ketchup"?

- Westbrae Natural Catsup, Fruit-Sweetened, No Salt Added, 11.5 ounces for $2.60. The most distasteful of the three Westbrae offerings.

• White Rose Tomato Ketchup, 28 ounces for $1.49 at Gristede's. Medium thick, smooth, properly sweet and salty, but not enough piquancy or astringency. Could this be identical to A&P's?

• Wine Country Zinfandel Catsup, from Cuisine Perel, 12 ounces for $6.72. Overwhelming taste of ginger, no apparent taste of Zinfandel. A wine-country rip-off.

August 1992

PART TWO

Help
Yourself

Le Régime Montignac

Day One. Thoroughly disrobed, bone-dry, and advanta- geously evacuated, I step onto my rusty old Detecto Doctor's Scale, the kind with the balance beam and the little weights that you nudge back and forth. The numbers are chest high and easily legible, meaning that you can leave your eyeglasses on the sink and save two ounces. No need to peer five feet down to the floor over a pile of sullied flesh.

Let us say that I weigh 160 pounds. No, let us say I weigh 170; 160 would create a credibility gap. Neither is accurate, of course, but I want to tell you all about my new diet without revealing my precise weight, which is an embarrassment—170 is embarrassing enough.

Let us say that I weigh 170 pounds and need to lose 35 of them. This means that I weigh 25.93 percent more than I should. According to the government, people who weigh at least 20 percent more than they should are legally obese. I prefer to think of myself as corporeally challenged, and so do the thirty-four million Americans with whom I share this condition.

The diet is La Méthode Montignac, and it is all the rage in France. Everybody there is on the Montignac diet. It was named after Michel Montignac, who invented the diet ten years ago, lost twenty-eight pounds, and to this day has gained none of it back. Montignac has written four books about it, all of them best-sellers in France; has opened a restaurant and two boutiques in Paris whose products embody La Méthode Montignac; publishes a bimonthly magazine called *Montignac* with a circulation of fifty thousand; and plans to open a Montignac spa in the Paris suburbs by early 1995.

I will skip breakfast today because I have read only three pages of Montignac's book, and I want to avoid making even the teensiest mistake. The book, translated from the French, is called *Dine Out and Lose Weight: The French Way to Culinary "Savoir Vivre."* Its original title was *Comment maigrir en faisant des repas d'affaires,* or *How to Lose Weight While Making the Business Lunches.*

Calories don't count in the Montignac diet. You can eat as much as you like. This is what attracts me, because I enjoy eating large quantities of delicious food as often as possible. I am also excited by reports that you can drink wine and eat cheese and chocolate and foie gras. Montignac's is a diet for gastronomes.

I spend the morning reading Montignac. It seems that I have already made a ruinous error. "Never skip a meal," writes Montignac. "It is the biggest mistake you could possibly make, and the best way to upset your metabolism." When you miss a meal, your body panics and stores away the energy from your next meal in the form of repulsive fat. This also explains why conventional, low-calorie dieting rarely works for very long. Exercise is irrelevant, he says; "sport has never caused anyone to slim."

"For me, a handshake from a great chef is as sacred as a benediction from the Pope," Montignac writes. "One does not gain weight from eating too much, but from eating badly." Eat all you want but only the right foods and only in the right combinations. No potatoes, no pasta, no white rice, no corn, no sugar, no sweets, no caffeine. Ever. Just proteins and fats and lots of fiber from green vegetables. Fruits may be eaten in complete isolation from other foods, at least a half hour before a meal or three hours after. "The biggest mistake one can make is to eat fruit at the end of a meal," Montignac explains. I could have sworn that skipping a meal was the biggest mistake one can make.

What about the wine, the chocolate, and the foie gras? They're in Phase II, weight maintenance. This is Phase I, weight loss.

At noon I take a taxi to the airport, an airplane to San Francisco, and a late lunch in seat 23-C. Today Delta has achieved a new low in comfort and gastronomy. Are the seats getting smaller and smaller, or am I getting bigger and bigger?

I finish half a bag of peanuts before reading in Montignac that nuts are a carbohydrate-lipid, a very bad thing. I eat an unidentifiable chicken part from which I scrape a thick, sodden layer of breading; some pale green broccoli; and a salad with light ranch dressing. The leatherette dinner roll and the Land O'Lakes Classic Blend, whatever that is, are no temptation, and it takes only the barest restraint to avoid a cold wedge of chocolate cake that has hundreds of tiny marshmallows forced onto its surface. There is no cheese, the only dessert that Montignac allows. "Get into the habit of carrying individually wrapped cheese wherever you go," he advises.

By the time the beverage cart reaches row 23, Delta has run out of red wine, white wine, and beer. They do not even apologize or refund a portion of the ticket price or hand out free headsets. But this does not bother me, because wine is pretty much out of the question in Phase I, beer is the worst thing you can drink at any time, and I have already seen the movie.

My first successful Montignac meal is over.

By the time I reach San Francisco, I have finished *Dine Out and Lose Weight*. (You can order a copy by dialing (800) 932-3229.) This is not an easy book to love, brimming as it is with non sequiturs, pointless anecdotes, feeble humor, self-contradictions, and braggadocio. Considering the very competent prose in another of Montignac's books, published in Britain, I do not know whether to blame Montignac or his American translator.

But the key idea is this: There are bad carbohydrates and good carbohydrates. Bad carbohydrates cause a sharp spike in the level of glucose in the bloodstream. Good carbohydrates cause a much milder and slower rise in blood sugar. The extent to which a carbohydrate raises the level of glucose in the blood is expressed by its glycemic index.

When our blood sugar rises, the pancreas produces insulin, which enables the body's tissues to absorb glucose, removing it from the bloodstream. But many of us have a problem. We have become insulin resistant, and so our pancreas needs to produce more insulin than normal to get the job done. The excess insulin has a disastrous effect on our waistlines: it causes our fat cells to store extra calories, whether from proteins, fats, or carbohydrates, in the form of body fat. Food is not turned into fat in the absence of insulin.

The essential trick is to eat only proteins and fats (these trigger very little insulin production) and good carbohydrates, those with a low glycemic index. Caffeine is forbidden because it stimulates the pancreas to secrete insulin.

The worst carbohydrate is maltose, found in beer; its glycemic index is 110, worse than drinking pure glucose, with a rating of 100. Then come white bread and instant mashed potatoes (95); honey and jam (90); cornflakes and popcorn (85); carrots (85); refined sugar (75); corn, beets, white rice, cookies, and boiled potatoes (70); white-flour pasta (65); and bananas and raisins (60). As you can see, white bread is even worse than sugar. All of these bad carbohydrates should be avoided at all times and under all circumstances.

The best of the good carbohydrates are green vegetables; with a rating below 15, they can be eaten freely with proteins and fats. The other good carbohydrates are not quite as harmless and should generally not be eaten with fats: fructose (20); dark chocolate (22); lentils, chickpeas, dried beans, and dried peas (30); fresh fruits (35); wild rice (35); dairy products and whole-grain cereals (35); whole rye bread, green peas, and fresh white beans (40); whole wheat pasta (45); oatmeal, whole wheat bread, and brown rice (50).

And that's why calories don't count. For Montignac, "the

calorie theory is probably the greatest 'scientific swindle' of the twentieth century." I like the sound of that.

Armed with my newly gained knowledge of good and evil, I cross the Oakland Bay Bridge and approach my motel in Berkeley with a quickening appetite for an ample feast of proteins, fats, and green vegetables. But the hour is late, and I am lucky that room service is still operating. Dinner is chicken wings, chopped steak, cauliflower, green beans, and caffeine-free diet Pepsi. After a trying transcontinental journey, I customarily reward myself with a little treat to help forget the indignities and humiliations I have suffered. Sometimes the reward is a jumbo family pack of bite-sized Snickers bars. This time I refrain.

Days Two to Five. Do I still weigh 170 pounds or has Montignac already started to work? I will not know for nearly a week when I return home to my Detecto Doctor's Scale.

I am in Berkeley to attend three days of baking demonstrations by Professor Raymond Calvel at the Acme Bread Company. Calvel, now eighty-three, is probably still the leading French teacher of bread baking. The Bread Bakers Guild of America has organized the whole thing, and every morning fifty of us meet for breakfast at the motel—coffee and juice and baskets of muffins, Danish pastries, and some of Calvel's breads, baked the day before.

The problem is I am not allowed to eat any of them. And any minute now I expect my skull to implode in a nightmarish spasm of pain from a caffeine-deprivation headache.

But the pain never comes. I have made the transition to a caffeine-free lifestyle without catastrophe, though I miss the happy rush of mental vitality that real coffee has brought to mankind for centuries. My mind feels at half-mast.

Montignac allows you to eat two kinds of breakfast. The first consists mainly of good carbohydrates—dry whole-grain bread (the only kind of bread he ever allows you to eat at the only permissible time of day), whole-grain cereals, skim milk, artificial sweetener, low-fat cottage cheese, and decaffeinated coffee. The other breakfast is full of proteins and fats—eggs, ham, sausage, bacon, cheese, and decaffeinated coffee, with cream if you wish. Cream is dietetic in the Montignac Method.

I am not fond of motel-quality whole wheat bread. So every morning before meeting with the Bread Bakers Guild, as soon as room service opens up, I order the biggest American breakfast it sells, plus various side dishes, throw away the toast and the home fries, and feast upon the rest. (You may eat whole fruit—not juice—twenty minutes before a carbohydrate breakfast or an hour before a protein-fat one. Bananas are banned. There are lots of little rules.) Then, at our communal breakfast, I take a bite of Professor Calvel's bread, chew it awhile, and discreetly spit it out into a paper napkin. Under other circumstances I would kill for a loaf of Professor Calvel's bread.

Keeping to the Montignac diet at lunch at Acme Bakery is easy because a caterer brings in enough cold cuts, cheese, olives, and salad to distract me from the tables piled high with Acme bread, the best in America. I take dinner at Chez Panisse in Berkeley and at Lulu in San Francisco, a dramatic new restaurant where everything is grilled or roasted over a huge open wood fire. At Lulu it is child's play to follow Montignac. I have artichokes with Parmesan cheese, just a little bite of the excellent bread, a few sips of red wine, a plate of eggplant and peppers, and gigantic portions of rib steak, chicken, and lamb. The potatoes look scrumptious, but I follow Montignac's admonition to "look upon the steaming potato in your neighbor's dish with the utmost contempt!" For professional reasons, I eat a quarter of a teaspoon of each of five desserts. My friends can hardly tell that I am on a diet.

One evening I have work to do in my motel room. I have heard about a new Chinese restaurant in Berkeley, so I telephone to ask about its specialities, order twice as much food as I can eat, and spend the next half hour in a taxi searching for the restaurant. Back in my room, I dine alone in front of the television on

Emerald Prawns, Mandarin Pork, Tofu Hunan Style, and Lemon Chicken—nothing battered and deep-fried and no white rice. Montignac's book contains all sorts of lists and charts of bad and good foods. But he lists only foods that French people eat, with scattered concessions to American products, and provides no guidance at all for lovers of Asian food. Most Chinese sauces contain cornstarch, which must surely be an extremely bad carbohydrate, and sugar, which is almost as bad as white bread. I wonder why the Chinese are so skinny.

Japanese food is easier to figure out. Sashimi yes, sushi no.

If Montignac is right, then the distinction universally used by American nutritionists between complex carbohydrates (like pasta, potatoes, and bread) and simple carbohydrates (like sugar and sweets) is not only misleading but possibly harmful, at least to dieters. Traditional nutritionists prescribe a diet low in fat, low in protein, and high in complex carbohydrates. But even complex carbohydrates like bread and potatoes have a high glycemic index and trigger a rush of insulin, while simple carbohydrates like fructose do not. Of course, Michel Montignac is neither a nutritionist nor a doctor. Michel Montignac was director of personnel for Abbots Labs in Europe before he got famous. I will carefully investigate the glycemic index when I get back to New York.

Day Six. Home again. It is late afternoon. If I weigh myself now, the scale will report a number that is two or three pounds higher than it will be tomorrow morning. I will get discouraged and go on a binge. Better wait.

On my kitchen table stands a towering ziggurat of candy boxes and tins and bags, assembled for my Christmas article on mail-order treats. There are four kinds of chocolate-covered toffee, Rainforest Crunch, hazelnuts and almonds covered in Valrhona chocolate, shortbread, chocolate-dipped macadamia nuts from Maui, a ten-pound slab of bittersweet Merckens chocolate, three flavors of brittle, chocolate truffles, bonbons both dipped and filled, and graham crackers covered in thick, delicious dark chocolate from Cafe Beaujolais. I pack nearly everything into two bulging shopping bags and send them off to *Vogue*. Let them gorge on bad carbohydrates.

Day Seven. Down to 167.5! I have lost two and a half pounds in six days—6.66 ounces a day! At this rate it will take me only eighty-four days to lose 560 ounces, precisely the 35 pounds by which the charts tell me I exceed my ideal weight! Eighty-four days is twelve weeks. Eleven to go.

I walk down to Greenwich Village and shop for bran flakes (without forbidden raisins), seven-grain bread, skim milk, diet Sprite, caffeine-free diet Pepsi, French beans and bulbs of fennel, four thick and marbled rib steaks, two ducks, ten pounds of chicken wings (to be roasted, for snacks), a box of NutraSweet, four kinds of French cheeses, low-fat artificially sweetened vanilla yogurt, six varieties of Aidells sausages, a bag of exotic and fabulously expensive salad greens, fresh cured olives from Apulia, and four types of apples. This, with minor variations, will be my diet at home for the next three weeks.

I thumb through a book of Montignac recipes, published in French. I own dozens of French cookbooks filled with dishes that already fit within his rules or can easily be made to do so. But I am not inspired to cook. Slowly, day by day, I am losing interest in cuisine. I wonder if I am suited to any other line of work.

Day Eight. I awaken so hungry that I eat breakfast before I remember to weigh myself. Better not weigh myself now.

My barber of eight years has gone out of business. This is a complete and total disaster. Normally, I would have a candy bar or two to help me solve the problem. Better not go outside. That's where the candy stores are.

Day Nine. 167.5. Not quite as breathtaking as the first time I weighed 167.5, two days ago. My rate of weight loss is down to five ounces a day. Maybe something is wrong with my old Detecto Doctor's Scale.

I dig up the January 1993 issue of *Consumer Reports* and its analysis of bathroom scales. The Health O Meter 840 is the highest rated. The Salter Electronic 971, though rated seventh, is the most accurate and gives the most consistent readings; it must have been downgraded for some other reason. Both use the latest in strain-gauge technology and contain no old-fashioned springs. Both have square white platforms, activate when you step on them, take a tantalizing six seconds to decide what you weigh, and tell you about it in large, red LEDs. The Health O Meter is easier to read, and it measures your weight in half pounds. Neither is as accurate as a full blown balance-beam scale with sliding weights. But those cost two hundred dollars and up.

I go out and buy one Health O Meter and one Salter. Now my bathroom floor is littered with scales. I warn my wife not to trip on the way to the shower.

Day Twelve. Today I weigh 166.5, 166.5, and 167, depending on which scale you believe. I slide the old Detecto into the corner and go totally solid-state.

One bowl of bran flakes takes four little envelopes of Equal to make edible. I have become proficient at emptying all four with one deft twist of my wrist.

I feel wired this morning. The sensation is essentially pleasant, but I am suspicious of the coffee and of the person who brewed it before she left for work. I telephone my wife and launch into an interrogation. She finally breaks down and admits that she substituted full-strength Kona beans for my new Thanksgiving-brand French-roast decaf. She can't stand my coffee any longer. Recently, the *New York Times* ran an article about spouses who sabotage each other's diets. I did not bother to read it. How wrong I was. Now I know the dangers that lurk on the other side of the bed.

The North American Association for the Study of Obesity is holding a meeting in Milwaukee. Reports of breakthroughs are beginning to appear in the newspapers. I obtain copies of all the abstracts:

• A leading and responsible researcher has announced the invention of an ointment that, applied once a day to the upper legs of women, can shrink the circumference of their thighs by as much as 4.25 centimeters! That's 1.66 inches. The ointment somehow alters the receptors in the fat cells of the thigh. But the women do not lose weight. The fat goes somewhere else. Their elbows? Their hearts?

• An experimental combination of two commonly used appetite drugs, fenfluramine and phentermine, was shown to produce very impressive weight loss and to lower the subjects' blood pressure, blood sugar, and cholesterol.

• Drugs are being developed to stimulate beta-3, a receptor in our fatty tissues, in an attempt to burn our body fat more quickly.

• A brain protein called galanin has been identified as the key to our craving for fats. When galanin production is blocked in rats, their weight plummets.

Should I go back to crusty bread and creamy potatoes and wait for the ideal drug? Better stick with Montignac for now.

Day Fourteen. No improvement. This is depressing. But at least my Health O Meter and my Salter are consistent. This means I am a good shopper. Montignac promises that some people lose two to four pounds a week, others a little less. For me, considerably less.

Although I am no fan of nutritional clichés, I am beginning to worry about the amount of animal fat in my new diet. I have experimented with brown basmati rice and other whole grains, good carbohydrates that can be eaten freely on the diet though never with butter, olive oil, or cheese. But without any of these fats, brown rice tastes even worse than it did in the early seventies. And beans without olive oil or butter hardly qualify as food. So I resort to thick and juicy rib steaks and crisply roasted chickens and ducks whenever I do not have much time to think about dinner. I cook them expertly, and they are always delicious, but they ooze saturated fat. When I have time to think about dinner, I prepare fish with beurre blanc.

"Butter, charcuterie, oil, foie gras, fresh cream, cheese, and wine are all part of the French daily diet, and yet the French suffer from neither obesity nor heart disease," Montignac writes. This is true. It is a phenomenon widely known as the French Paradox.* But if the French do not suffer from obesity and heart disease, then why is everybody in France on the Montignac regime?

When Montignac's diet first appeared in France, it was attacked by nutritionists there as a "passport to a heart attack." With each succeeding edition of his books, Montignac put more stress on the difference between bad lipids and good lipids, between saturated, polyunsaturated, and monounsaturated fats, not for losing more weight but for keeping your heart healthy. This makes him sound more and more like your typical nutritionist.

I telephone my doctor and schedule a full set of blood tests on Day Twenty-eight of my diet.

But a ray of hope penetrates my dark forebodings. What the surgeon general does not tell you is that a substantial portion of the population is diet insensitive—their cholesterol and other blood lipids are not much affected by what they eat. Public-health programs and pronouncements are aimed at increasing the greater good, not the good of each one of us. If everybody were diet sensitive, there would be no need for cholesterol-lowering drugs. And if my lipids do not fall on a low-fat diet, they may not soar on a high-fat one.

I sit down at the computer, log on to Medline, and search for "glycemic index." On this subject, Montignac has his facts approximately right. There are surprising and unexpected differences between carbohydrates; some cause sugar spikes in the blood, and others do not. The complexity of a carbohydrate molecule does not determine how quickly and energetically it raises the level of glucose. A food's glycemic index depends not only on

119

*I discuss the French Paradox in "Why Aren't the French Dropping Like Flies?" in Part One.

the raw ingredient itself but also on how it has been processed and the form in which it is eaten. Fiber eaten with other foods reduces their glycemic effect.

Day Eighteen. Both scales agree—166 pounds. Only a half-pound improvement, but better than nothing.

This evening we will attend a cocktail party at restaurant Daniel for Daniel Boulud's terrific new cookbook. Cocktail parties are times of greatest danger for Montignac. "British cocktail parties are some of the most tedious to endure. Do not count on being served dinner before 9:30 or 10 o'clock." But food cooked by Daniel Boulud is always a time of greatest pleasure for me. Tonight will be no problem. I have decided to eat and drink as though I am already in Phase II. How much damage can I do?

In Phase II, although bad carbohydrates are still banned and fruit must still be eaten in isolation, other deviations from the strict rules of Phase I are permitted two or three times a day. Scallops, oysters, foie gras, lentils with pork, for example, are prohibited in Phase I because they combine fat with sugar or starch but are considered only minor deviations in Phase II, as is a half liter of wine a day—three full glasses—always to be drunk with food. So I eat the filet mignon with cranberries, the oysters and caviar with lemongrass and cream, little slivers of *rouget,* and layers of scallops and black truffle, fastidiously leaving behind the little pieces of toast on which most of these are served. Halfway through the party, I begin drinking wine.

Montignac loves wine, though when he repeatedly recommends that we all drink young Bordeaux, it is hard to tell whether the advice is dietary or aesthetic. He goes so far as to include a seven-page chart entitled "How to Cure Yourself with Wine," based on the publications of a Dr. Maury. In the left-hand column is a list of diseases beginning with acidosis and running through neurosis and on to ulcers, and in the right-hand column are lists of wines that will remedy the diseases on the left. For acidosis, drink Pouilly-Fuissé and Sancerre; for allergies, try Corbières,

Médoc, Minervois, and Ventoux; for anemia, turn to Cahors, Côtes-de-Nuit, Côtes-de-Beaune, Côtes-de-Graves, Pomerol, and Madiran; for angina, open a Médoc, a Julienas, or a Moulin-à-Vent. And that covers only half the *A*'s.

Day Nineteen. Disaster has struck. My weight is 168.5, up 2.5 pounds. I am gripped by despair. I guess I am not ready for Phase II.

Maybe there are worse things than obesity. Hunger, for example, or a life without Scotch. Maybe I should quit and return to enthusiastic random eating. But then what would I write about?

I leave the bathroom, wait a few minutes, come back, and weigh myself again. Only a half-pound improvement. And now the two scales differ by two full pounds. The Health O Meter seems particularly fickle.

My wife has finally crumbled. She has joined me on the Montignac diet. Twelve pounds from now, she'll be skinnier than Kate Moss.

Day Twenty. I have returned to my downward path: back to 166 on one scale, 165.5 on the other. This is a new low. Yesterday was a hideous aberration.

A grand lunch in Chinatown with friends: roast suckling pig, roast duck, cuttlefish, clam soup, stir-fried fish cake with pickled mustard greens, squid with Chinese broccoli, grouper with a white pepper coating, and a plate of four types of sausage and cured duck. I avoid the tea and the white rice, and worry a little about the sugars in the marinades and the sauces. Otherwise, Montignac imposes no restrictions on me, even in Phase I.

On television tonight, *PrimeTime Live* has a segment on the Montignac diet. I count at least one error in every sentence. Montignac himself is over six feet tall, slim without being gaunt, and has been on Phase II for nearly ten years. He looks nice. I would look nice, too, with yearly revenues of eighteen million dollars.

Day Twenty-one. No change. What a relief! I had feared the consequences of unbridled Chinatown feasting even though everything I ate was Montignac-approved (or would have been if Montignac were not so French provincial).

I telephone Louis Aronne, M.D., director of the Comprehensive Weight Control Program at New York Hospital–Cornell University Medical Center, to ask about insulin resistance and obesity. He is not a fan of the Montignac Method, which he characterizes as "Atkins revisited," a reference to a once-popular high-fat, high-protein diet considered unhealthy because, unlike the Montignac Method, it eliminated carbohydrates entirely and led to metabolic imbalances. But he concedes that some people do poorly on the high-carbohydrate diet recommended by the American nutrition establishment. A substantial minority of the population does suffer from insulin resistance, he tells me; their excess insulin causes an enzyme called lipoprotein lipase to appear on the surface of their fat cells, and this brings additional fat into the cells. As Montignac says, a low-carbohydrate diet does seem to suppress insulin secretion, making it harder to store fat. But Aronne worries that, even if adherents to the Montignac Method lose weight initially, their bodies may soon find ways around it.

And Aronne tells me something new: he suspects that insulin resistance may be one cause of high total cholesterol and triglycerides and low HDLs (good cholesterol). If I am insulin resistant, then my blood test next week may show an improvement in my cholesterol and triglycerides despite the amount of saturated fat I have been eating.

Aronne believes that drugs are the real future of obesity treatment. "Before now obesity has been seen as either a behavioral problem or a moral failing," he says. "But now, for the first time, we are entering a period of rational medical therapy."

Day Twenty-two. Progress again. One scale says 165 and the other 165.5. I celebrate with a lunch of scrambled eggs, a half pound of bacon, Reblochon cheese made in France from raw milk and smuggled into the United States, and decaffeinated coffee. And more Chinese food for dinner.

People tell me that I look thinner. It's probably my new haircut.

Day Twenty-five. My scales have gone haywire! They are a pound and a half apart! I spend half an hour stepping first on one, then on the other, then on the floor. I move the scales around the bathroom, and they change their minds, slightly. Then I try standing on them in different ways, my heels close together or wide apart. I was penny-wise and pound-foolish to go electronic.

1 2 3

I telephone two leading French nutritionists, Marian Apfelbaum, M.D., and Jacques Fricker, M.D., both of the Hôpital Bichat in Paris. Neither is impressed with the Montignac phenomenon. Fricker concedes that foods rich in fiber and those with a low glycemic index assuage our hunger more effectively than others, but he says that without some high-glycemic starches in our diet, any weight lost is more likely to come from lean muscle mass than fat reserves.

Apfelbaum has been quoted as saying that losing weight permanently is more difficult than being cured of cancer. If people temporarily lose weight with the Montignac method, he tells me, it is not because the diet is particularly clever but because it is a diet. That is, it focuses our attention on what we eat. I ask him whether lowering one's insulin level by eliminating most carbohydrates will automatically prevent weight gain. His answer is no. For centuries before Europeans arrived, Eskimos had subsisted on fish and sea mammals—all fat and protein and virtually no carbohydrates. Yet in their native state, Eskimos were fatty and obese.

But Apfelbaum is pleased that after thirty years in which hundreds of fad diets were imported from the United States to France, at last one has traveled in the other direction.

Day Twenty-eight. My weight is at a new low, 163.5 and 164. But in only ten days my wife has already lost six pounds. I travel uptown to my doctor's office to have my blood taken. Results back in two days.

Day Thirty. No change in weight. Every newspaper you can think of has published an article or two about Michel Montignac in the past year. Everybody stresses the foie gras and wine part. Nobody investigates the science or tries the diet for very long. Today I do a computer search for newspaper articles about Montignac in the eighties, before he discovered the Montignac Method.

I come up with something disturbing. Back in 1987, when Montignac was a personnel consultant, the *Financial Times* reported that "he has resurrected, amended, and renamed the ancient study known as numerology. . . . Numerimetrics, Montignac's name for his version of the arcane system, assigns a number to each letter. Added in various combinations, the numbers give totals that, he says, are clues to a person's personality, strengths, weaknesses, and aptitudes."

Late in the afternoon, my blood test comes back from the lab. The results are terrific! Despite the tons of highly saturated fat I have been consuming, my cholesterol is unchanged, my HDLs are improved by more than 10 percent, and my triglycerides, which had been in the abnormally high 400s, are now in the normal range! This is precisely the result that Aronne suggested might occur with people who are insulin resistant.

I walk down to Dean & DeLuca to buy ten pounds of cheese. As I enter the store, a feeling of deep sadness washes over me. All around me is a celebration of foods from around the world, baskets of bread, trays of tarts and cakes, rows of jams and condiments and olive oils, pasta in every conceivable shape, and the smell of dark coffee beans grown on four continents—a profusion that has never failed to bring me a rush of joy. But now, for the first time in my life, I feel completely apart from it. I buy my cheese and leave the store.

Day Thirty-one.   This is the last mandatory day of my diet. My weight is at a new low: 163 and 163.5. Total weight lost: 6.5 or 7 pounds. Weight lost per day: 3.47 ounces.

My diet is over; my promise to *Vogue* complete. Now I am free to eat my favorite foods—pies, pierogi, pistachios, pizza, popcorn, popovers, potatoes, puff pastry—and that only covers the *P*'s. On the other hand, at 3.47 ounces a day, I can reach my ideal weight in 129 days.

I doubt that I will last that long. But I can surely stick to Montignac for just one more month.

January 1994

The Waiting Game

Two brief months ago, you would not have regarded me as an authority on setting the table. I may have known that the fork goes on the left, but I can't swear that I did. Then I enrolled in the New York Professional Service School, the only exhaustive training course for waiters, captains, and maître d's in this country. And now I know the following things, which you probably don't. I have a diploma to prove it:

• When you order wine and the waiter puts the cork down in front of you on the table, ignore it—you cannot learn anything by smelling or squeezing the cork.

• Serve women first, then the elderly, then children, and finally, if they haven't died of hunger, the men. This applies *even when a woman is the host* and would have been served last if she had been a man.

• When you set a table, the tines of all forks should be level with each other; spoons and knives should be lined up at the base of their handles.

• Soup is a beverage and must be both cleared *and* served from the right like other beverages, an exception to the serve-from-the-left-and-clear-from-the-right rule. Speaking of beverages, coffee and tea cups are placed with their handles at four o'clock. The wineglass goes above the point of the dinner knife.

• One percent of all Americans are waiters.

Dinner parties are so much more diverting when you are a man who knows so much more than your hostess about setting the table. Just the other day in an apartment high above Central Park, at a Yuletide table gleaming with silver pheasants and candied fruits, my hostess's face came alive when I showed her that the tines of her forks resembled a broken comb. It was fun watching the other women form a fearsome phalanx around her. You would be amazed at the number of people who think they can set the table without attending waiter's school.

The course at the New York Professional Service School ran for seven weekly three-hour sessions, each one brimming with information and practical exercises. Some of my twenty-seven fellow students worked at admirable New York City restaurants— Metro, the Post House, Manhattan Ocean Club, Sofi, Smith & Wollensky, Remi—and some were looking for jobs at places like them. Each week we learned about table and plate service, or flatware and its uses, or wine and dessert service, from Karen MacNeil, codirector of the school. Then there was a guest lecture by somebody in the restaurant business—the owner of Union Square Cafe or Lavin's, the general manager of the Four Seasons, or a captain at Aurora. At the end of each lesson we had a wine tasting and sometimes a sampling of fresh herbs, wild mushrooms, or foie gras.

Captains and headwaiters at expensive restaurants in New York earn seventy-five thousand dollars a year from their share of the tips, so the curriculum puts at least as much weight on teaching techniques to increase your tips as on the techniques of service. The moment I opened the school's brochure, I realized that I would soon be initiated into the secret stratagems that waiters use to infuriate us, ruin our dinner, and take us to the cleaners. These are some of the topics that caught my eye:

- How to Increase Tips through Professional Selling Skills
- Handling Difficult Customers
- Controlling the Customer Instead of the Customer Controlling You

- How to Increase Tips through Conversation and Selling Skills
- How to Increase Tips through Wine Sales
- Creating the Right Last Impression—Timing and the Check

The guest lecturer at our first lesson was an expert in all these disciplines. He is a captain at the most illustrious restaurant in New York, and one of the most expensive. We will call it La Clique, and we will call him Philippe. He is dark, handsome, charming, and articulate. As soon as Philippe begins to speak, I know that I am in the hands of a master:

"Don't pour them water, you want to sell them water. If I could sell the bread on the table, I'd sell the bread, but I can't. Maybe someday.

"I want you to underline this," Philippe continues. "I am against pouring water. *Make them ask for water.* There is a water glass on the table, and they wait for the water to come. Eventually nothing comes, and they're getting thirsty. Then five minutes later, you say, 'Would you like some mineral water?' It's a very important sale, especially these days, when people drink fewer martinis and a lot more Evian and Perrier. New York tap water, as far as I'm concerned, is much better than Evian and much less expensive. But do you know how much profit the house does on water? Bottled water is about the price of a cocktail—three dollars and fifty cents for a Perrier. It's no work, no production at the bar, and the customers can pour it themselves. This is fantastic! This is the way you want it to be."

Philippe's goals at La Clique are to help his customers spend as much money as possible and make them come back for more. "I take advantage of my strong French accent," he confides. "If you use the fact that you are very handicapped with the language, they feel they have to give you a break and buy whatever you are selling them. It's almost a handicap not to have an accent."

Two students volunteer to act as customers, a doctor and his wife from the suburbs. Philippe explains that although he knows their table is ready, and although he would like to turn it over as quickly as possible, he wants them to buy a drink first. So, as they enter the room, he greets them and says, "Why don't you have a drink at the bar, and we'll see if your table will be ready in a few minutes." As soon as the bartender pours their drinks—and sometimes before—Philippe fetches the doctor and his wife from the bar, his smile inspired equally by a sense of hospitality and by the knowledge that they have spent ten or twelve dollars before he has shown them to their table.

"This is the big thing," he tells the class. "You want to make money. You're not here just for the glory. You're in business. The more you sell, the better it is—for you, for the house, for every-body. I want to shock you about this: don't forget who goes home at the end of the day. It's your plate and nobody else's. Will it be full or not?"

Philippe never lets a customer choose his own table. "They go to *my* table, the one I give to them. Even if their name is Forbes or Nixon, they go where I put them. But you always make it look like you give them the best. You want to keep them under con-trol, always keep them under control. That's the main thing. You are playing the game, and they are in the game. You reverse that and you'll have problems."

Philippe doesn't waste his charm on regular customers famil-iar with the menu and habituated to the glamour of dining at La Clique. But of couples like the doctor and his wife, who are hon-ored to be here and look around the room at the billionaires and socialites, he says, "You can do whatever you want with them— they are Play-Doh in your hands."

He never lets the customer read the menu for more than four or five minutes. "I have already made up my mind that the doc-tor and his wife are going to have something from me today, not just anything from the menu." Be light and evasive, he advises, and then "at the moment they don't expect, be very precise: 'I recommend something very strongly today. As a main course you *have to try* the bouillabaisse.' You say it as if there is nothing else on the menu, as though everybody eats the bouillabaisse, as

1 2 9

though it will hurt everybody if they don't have it. But say it nice." Then Philippe casually asks the doctor and his wife if they would like some salad, as though it comes free with the meal. "This works many, many times," he tells us.

When Philippe is taking the order, he stands very close to the table. As Karen MacNeil later explains, "When you want something to happen, the closer you stand to the person, the more power you have." When Philippe is clearing the dishes, he stands as far back as the length of his arm allows.

He never asks if his customers have any questions. If he is truly in control of the table and appears to be inviting questions, the customers will comply by dreaming some up. "Then you're stuck at this table and there are seven other tables waiting. I see a lot of waiters do this—it's absolutely crazy."

As an exception to his general approach, Philippe never forces food on a customer simply because it is expensive. "I try to sell them mineral water, try to sell them more drinks, more wine, an expensive dessert. I pay a lot of attention to how much a bottle of wine costs. But with food I never go by the price. That is something you have to sacrifice because it's too obvious. You should sell them food only if you are sure it will please them."

Many restaurateurs instruct their waiters to bring the wine list to the table with or before the menus; this has been shown to increase wine sales, Karen tells us. But Philippe disagrees: "Ninety-nine percent of the time, people know if they are going to have wine or not. The wine list won't change their minds. God knows I want to sell them wine. But the wine list is big and scary, and the customer will get confused."

Philippe is a graceful waiter with impeccable training. This is taken for granted. His movements are balletic and weightless; his manner is airy and nonchalant. He has been drilled in the technical rules of service since his boyhood in France—he insists, for example, on removing the salt and pepper from the table after the main course to set the stage for dessert. But he knows when to vary the rules. Wine should be poured from the right, with the right hand, but Philippe may decide to pour across the table rather than interfere with a conversation. For the same reason he may remove plates from the left. But his arm always stays low to the table so that dirty dishes never pass through the diners' field of vision. If a customer doesn't move when he tries to replace flatware or crumb the tablecloth, Philippe never bulldozes him out of the way. "My goal is to make them almost forget that I am here. I don't want them to move. I want them to keep talking and looking at each other and discussing the business, the love, the weather. You are here to disappear when you do something."

After the main course, many waiters give up on the table. But not Philippe. "It's far from being finished," he says. "Every break is a new beginning. Never treat them like a dead table." A good waiter can double the bill by selling desserts, coffee, and after-dinner drinks. And even after the doctor and his wife pay the bill, Philippe keeps going. "If they stay fifteen, thirty minutes after they pay, sometimes you can open another check. It happens every day." They are not a dead table until they climb into a taxi.

When Philippe's powerful psychological weapons fall into the hands of terrorists, the results can be cataclysmic. A week after Philippe's talk, I had dinner at the Mansion on Turtle Creek in Dallas. Dean Fearing's modern American cooking is wonderful, and I was looking forward to that unique Texas style of hospitality—it blends the graciousness of the Deep South with the openness and informality of the West. Instead, the service was one part somebody's idea of Paris, France, and nine parts Al Capone. The captain bickered with my wife when she ordered an inexpensive pasta for her main course and finally bludgeoned her into submission. Then as the wine was poured I took an elbow to the nose because the waiter was too slothful to shift to my right side or shift the bottle to his left hand. (Never reach across a customer unless you have no choice, and then present the inner crook of your elbow, not the protruding joint.) Late in the meal, when it looked as though the staff had quit en masse and I tried to pour my own wine, the very same sloth galloped in from nowhere and wrenched the bottle from my hand.

The captain's proudest moment came when the main courses

arrived. Although our wineglasses were still more than half full, he hastily poured what was left of the very expensive bottle of red wine we had ordered at the start of the meal, sloshing some on the tablecloth, turned to me with a perfectly straight face, and asked, "Would you like a bottle of wine with your main course?" The Mansion is apparently one of those restaurants where waiters are rebuked if any glass in the room looks less than half full. If the captain had attended the New York Professional Service School, he would know that you never fill a glass more than half full and never refill it until the customer has only about two sips left. Most people who spend money on wine like to see how it develops in the glass; topping off a glass of champagne guarantees that only the first sip will be cold and fizzy.

I left the standard tip when I paid my check at the Mansion at Turtle Creek, though I can't remember why. Maybe because the food was so good.

We learned countless ploys and gambits at waiter's school. Customers love to hear the sound of their own names, we were told. Constantly reinforce the positive and distract from anything negative or embarrassing; when the kitchen runs out of a customer's favorite dish, withhold the bad news until you have some good news to bring. Create an aura of comfort and confidence. People go to restaurants to feed their emotions, not their stomachs. (Some customers want to feel important, others to be entertained; some want the staff to take a personal interest in them, others want to be left alone. Find out precisely what each customer needs.) The previous semester, several students had tried an experiment. Back in their restaurants, they inserted the words "for you" into every sentence, even when it sounded silly, as in "I'd be happy to get a fresh cup of coffee for you," or "Is this steak done all right for you?" Their tips increased by 20 percent.

In this country, waiters no longer carve the roast at your table or fillet the fish or sauté your veal over an alcohol flame. They rarely even toss the salad or cut the cake or tart. Waiters nowadays simply sell you food, rearrange the silverware, deliver the food, and open your wine. Service has become an illusion, we learned in waiter's school, and those who best create that illusion are the most handsomely rewarded.

One day we were all divided into teams, given a cold slice of pizza and a Hostess Twinkie, and asked to come up with an enticing description of each—the way waiters do when they try to sell you the day's specials. My team did particularly well with the Twinkie: "a golden roll of classic lemon genoise, scooped out and filled with a delicate sweet cream." The moral, I suppose, is that a good waiter can transform even a Twinkie into something worth tipping for.

January 1989

Vegging Out

My first love affair with vegetarianism ended on a dark and chilly night in 1975 on the corner of Eighth Street in Greenwich Village with a hot dog from Nathan's Famous. For four years, I had been a lacto-ovo vegetarian, meaning that I allowed myself eggs and dairy products but no fish or shellfish, no chicken or other feathered things, no meat either red or pink. The question of insects never arose because, like most Americans (though unlike members of many other cultures), I have always reacted with revulsion to the idea of eating insects, despite their high nutritive value, crunchy texture, and wide availability. My bible was *Diet for a Small Planet,* by Frances Moore Lappé, published in 1971. The message of this utopian, spiral-bound volume was that consuming meat is tantamount to consuming the environment. My other motivation was the conviction that meat is murder.

Eighteen omnivorous, Lucullan years later, I am a vegetarian again, much stricter this time, a full-fledged vegan, which is pronounced "VEE-g'n" and means that I avoid animal products entirely, including milk and eggs, butter and cheese. My first act as a vegan was to eat a carrot, and my second act was to make a list of sixty vegetarian and natural-food restaurants within a taxi ride from my house. Then I ordered some Archer Daniels Midland Harvest Burgers, the kind you see advertised on television. I've always wondered if they taste as good as they are made to look.

Everybody tells me that vegetarianism is a happening thing. Last year, *Vegetarian Times* magazine, to which I now subscribe, commissioned a study by Yankelovich Clancy Shulman. About 6.7 percent of the adults they telephoned told the pollsters that they are vegetarians, way up from 3.7 percent in 1985. This works out to 12.4 million vegetarians nationwide, an apparent jump of 80 percent. Two-thirds of vegetarians are women. At this rate, I calculate, everybody will be a vegetarian by the year 2024, or at least everybody will say they're a vegetarian by the year 2024. But then how can over half of them possibly be women? Maybe something is wrong with my calculations.

The problem with the Yankelovich survey is that many people who say they're vegetarian have an extremely eccentric idea of what a vegetarian is. Forty percent of them report that they eat fish or poultry or both every week. Maybe I'm using the wrong dictionary, but it seems to me that somebody who eats chicken at least once a week and claims to be a vegetarian is the very definition of an impostor, a charlatan, a pretender, or a mountebank. The survey also discovered a hitherto-unrecognized category— the 10 percent of vegetarians who eat red meat at least once a week. I cannot decide whether to call them bovo-vegetarians or psycho-vegetarians.

The survey's results are broadly consistent with recent trends in food consumption. From 1976 to 1990, the average American's consumption of beef dropped from 94.5 pounds a year to 68, but an increase in poultry and fish more than made up for it. So the real trend is the rise of chicken, turkey, and cod, and of people who would like to think of themselves as vegetarians. Because vegetarianism is a happening thing.

Amazingly, only 4 percent of today's vegetarians avoid animal products entirely, an inconsequential quarter of a percent of the total American adult population, or a mere five hundred thousand people from coast to coast. This is the group I joined a month ago, we few, we happy few, we band of brothers.

Most Americans go vegetarian for their health, giving "not sure" as their runner-up reason, distantly followed by the

135

environment and animal rights. Vegetarians do have fewer heart attacks, lower blood pressure, and trimmer figures than meat eaters. But as vegetarians tend to lead healthier lives in general, and exercise more than average, a vegetarian diet in itself may not have much advantage over an omnivorous diet low in saturated fat, full of fruits and vegetables, and moderate though not phobic when it comes to meat. As a lacto-ovo vegetarian in the 1970s, I more than made up for the presumed health advantages of a vegetarian diet by cooking with generous quantities of butter and cream, consuming cheese to my heart's content, and keeping the ice-cream churn perpetually spinning. That is why I am a vegan this time around.

The day before becoming a vegan, I had my cholesterol tested, and yesterday I had my blood taken again. I expect the results tomorrow. Then I will know whether strict vegetarianism does me any good. People vary widely in how closely their serum cholesterol reacts to changes in their diet. If I am very diet-sensitive, my cholesterol should have dropped by about 15 percent—half the maximum benefit one can hope for after staying on a diet extremely low in saturated fat for several months. But the problem is this: If my cholesterol has fallen by as much as 15 percent, how can I justify eating meat ever again for the rest of my life? I can't decide which way to root.

The food press has recently been full of statements like "Eating low on the food chain has tended to be pretty disastrous from the gastronomic point of view—but not any longer!" The evidence presented is always a photo of an exquisite and sumptuous vegetable feast created by one of the country's top young chefs. I happily sample several of these every year, and the problem with them is usually the same. They may be lovely to look at, artfully cooked, and sometimes delicious, but you would not survive very long on meals like these, because they rarely contain any protein. For that you must consume large platefuls of unglamorous legumes and grains.

Strict vegetarians need to be careful in making their nutritional ends meet. Most would suffer deficiencies of vitamin B_{12},

vitamin D, and iron if they did not take vitamin pills or eat forti-
fied foods such as Total and Special K cereals. These three common deficiencies are the subject of intense controversy, but
pregnant or lactating women, children, and the elderly should be
particularly watchful. Early signs that your body is starved for B_{12}
can be dangerously masked (even until irreversible nerve damage
occurs) by the plentiful folic acid in vegan diets.

An Immutable Law

From too much business they didn't close.

> —A waiter at Ratner's dairy restaurant
> on the Lower East Side, explaining
> why its competitor Rappaport's had
> gone out of business

Back in the palmy days of *Diet for a Small Planet*, protein was
seen as the main thing to worry about. The average American
diet serves up double the amount of protein we actually need
(usually given as 0.36 grams for every pound of your weight, at
least for adults, or about two ounces a day for a 180-pound man),
but getting enough protein as a strict vegetarian does take a bit of
planning. You won't find much protein in a plate of delicate
emerald greens dressed with balsamic vinegar or in a jewel-like
mosaic of asparagus and beets. Lappé's solution was to build complete proteins out of the partial proteins found in plants, either by
supplementing them with dairy products and eggs (not an option
for vegans) or by obsessively pairing plants rich in a few of the
nine essential amino acids (protein building blocks that our bodies cannot produce) with those rich in the others. Nowadays,
matching complementary proteins is easier than in 1971 because,

the experts tell us, essential amino acids can be matched up over the course of an entire day rather than at every meal. A few even claim that we needn't worry about complementarity at all. But the simplest solution is to make dishes, like many of the best recipes in *Diet for a Small Planet,* that draw on the familiar third-world combinations of cornmeal and beans, pasta and beans, rice and soy, rice and lentils, and so forth—all somehow discovered long ago by cultures that depend on plants for much of their protein, and all quite delicious.

Most vegetarian, whole-food, health-food, and organic restaurants pay much greater attention to their ideology than to their cooking. Their dishes are typically artless, often drawing (promiscuously and sloppily) on real or imagined foreign dishes. American vegetarians eat vegetables because they hate meat. Europeans eat vegetables because they love vegetables. Nearly all the voluntary vegetarians in the world (those not vegetarians from poverty or religious belief) live in America and England. Neither group is known for its skills in the kitchen.

The first thing you notice about a restaurant's menu is how high up the food chain the chef has dared to climb and which foods on the lower rungs he or she has chosen to exclude. All pollo-vegetarian restaurants seem to allow fish (though some pesco-vegetarians avoid shellfish on the grounds that these are scavengers and bottom dwellers), but some oddly eliminate the ovos from which the pollos came, not to mention the milk that flows like kindness from the pollos' barnyard neighbors. It is common to find ovos where lactos are excluded and vice versa.

Not even every plant food is welcome. Many restaurants do not offer alcohol, whether fermented from barley or hops or grapes. Some do not even let you bring your own. Others eschew the dark, aromatic liquor of the roasted coffee bean, and most banish the purest, whitest forms of sugar and flour. Restaurants following strict Buddhist rules also eliminate onions, scallions, and garlic, which are thought to inflame the passions, while most macrobiotic restaurants flee from members of the nightshade family, such as eggplants and tomatoes. One man's poison is another man's essential amino acid.

China, Japan, and India—unlike the United States and the countries of northern Europe—have strict native vegetarian cuisines of long standing and great sophistication. The exquisite Japanese *shojin ryori,* or Buddhist temple cooking, does not seem to have immigrated to this country; its principal protein combination is rice paired with the myriad forms of soybean curd. Unlike *shojin ryori,* Chinese Buddhist cooking specializes in what you might call facsimile food, astounding imitations of traditional meat and poultry dishes in which wheat gluten, tofu, textured soybean protein, arrowroot, and chopped yams simulate animal flesh; bean curd and potatoes stand in for fish, fresh walnuts for crab, cabbage for chicken. Versions ranging from crude to creative (with or without onions and garlic) can be found in at least seven New York City restaurants. As 80 percent of the population of India is vegetarian (according to estimates I have read), its cuisine is rich in plant protein combinations, especially if one is willing to supplement the rice-lentils-wheat-chickpea quartet with a teeny bit of *raita,* made with yogurt. I was unable to find a truly admirable vegetarian Indian restaurant in any of the five boroughs.

And so my month of dining at two-thirds of New York City's vegetarian restaurants was, on the whole, excruciating. The intricate vegetarian cuisines of Japan, China, and India should make it obvious that when you eliminate most of the possibilities that nature offers—all animal flesh, plus eggs and milk and nearly everything else that is white, including onions and garlic—you must show greater artistry in the kitchen rather than less. The more foods you avoid, the more imagination and skill you need to keep your life palatable, not to mention scrumptious.

Today's supermarkets and health-food stores are full of imitation meat, usually lower in fat and calories than the real thing (but often higher in salt, to make up for the savory taste of animal protein). In addition to an endless variety of burgers made

139

from grains, nuts, or soybeans, you can find faux hot dogs that at least look right (one cleverly called a Not Dog), simulated breakfast sausage, and phony bacon complete with stripes.

Though the Archer Daniels Midland Harvest Burger is not quite as good as it looks, I managed with a little imagination to extract several satisfying meals from the product. You can apparently buy frozen preformed patties at some health-food stores, but I ordered a variety of its dry mixes direct from the company by dialing (800) 8-FLAVOR—Burger 'n Loaf (original or Italian), Chili Fixin's, Sloppy Joe Fixin's, and Taco Filling 'n Dip. All contain little granules of concentrated soy protein with various flavorings and lots of preservatives.

To make a Harvest Burger you empty a foil bag labeled "Burger 'n Loaf" into a bowl, add a cup and a quarter of water, wait fifteen minutes, and form the thick tan-and-gray mixture into patties (fewer patties than the label calls for if you want a mock hamburger that exceeds 3.2 ounces). I tried panfrying, microwaving, baking, and broiling. All the results resembled overdone hamburgers, edible, even tasty, but not juicy; the broiled version was best because it had a charred flavor reminiscent of grilled beef. In a hamburger bun with lots of ketchup and a pile of natural-flavor Wise potato chips washed down with a tall glass of diet Coke, the broiled Harvest Burger was good enough to eat. Harvest Burgers contain no cholesterol and very little saturated fat, but as with raw soybeans, nearly 30 percent of their calories come from fat.

All the other Archer Daniels Midland imitation-beef creations are fun to mix and eat. You add tomato sauce to the sloppy joe mix and tomato sauce and beans (canned) to the chili package; then you cook them for fifteen minutes. Despite the dried and artificial flavors evident in both products, the results were savory and quick and, because of the heavy spicing, quite like the ground-meat originals.

And then suddenly I thought, in a flash of blinding insight: Wait just one minute! Is this what I have been reduced to? What in the world am I doing, standing in my own kitchen, mixing up packets of microwavable, artificial Tex-Mex convenience food? Is this what being a strict vegetarian boils down to? And in large part, I'm afraid the answer is yes. Only as a vegan would I have been able to stomach more than 30 percent of what I have eaten over the past month. It was then that I decided to let my cholesterol test determine whether I would remain a vegetarian for another month.

I have come to the conclusion that Mother Nature never wanted us to become strict and unyielding vegetarians. There is nothing natural about it at all. Visit any vegan, and you will find his cabinet of vitamin supplements at least as well stocked as his larder. The truth is that humans were designed to be omnivores, complete with all-purpose dentition and digestive systems. Vegetarianism is not our natural diet. Anthropologists know that for most of the past million years of our evolution, humans have

---

Familiarity Breeds . . .

An automatic demerit goes to the waiter or waitress who unfurls your napkin and flattens it onto your lap. This is a pretentious and unsanitary practice. He or she has been handling dirty plates, linens, and money for the past hour; now she touches the snowy cloth that will later brush my lips. I keep a very short list of people who are allowed to touch my lap, and an even shorter list of people who are allowed to touch my wife's. A waiter or even a waitress to whom I have never been introduced is extremely unlikely to have made it onto either.

eaten meat, especially fish and low-fat wild game. The only source of plant protein that does not require cooking to become digestible is, I think, nuts. But cooking was invented only fifty thousand years ago, long after most of our physiology and genetic structure had evolved. I cannot think of a traditional, nonindustrial culture (we used to call them primitive cultures) that practices vegetarianism if it can help it. Vegetarianism is always the product of scarcity, of religion, or of ideology, including nutritional fads and fashions.

The environmental arguments against meat are strong, but they apply mainly to factory farming—vast numbers of animals kept in close confinement, fed with grain and water hauled from long distances and producing more waste than we can possibly use as fertilizer or fuel. I have read that more than half of America's water consumption goes to raising beef and that twenty pure vegetarians like me can be fed on the same amount of land needed to feed one meat eater. Meat has been called a petroleum by-product: you can grow forty pounds of soybeans with the amount of oil consumed in producing a pound of beef.

But unless you insist that we must all eat in the most economical manner possible—though few of us dress in the cheapest way or live in the smallest possible space—these are arguments not for avoiding all meat but for eating less meat and raising it in a sustainable way. Universal vegetarianism would not be an unmixed blessing for the environment. Ecological nutritionist Joan Gussow explained to me that for millennia livestock has been indispensable for its magical ability to convert agricultural waste, failed crops, and the vegetation on unfarmable land into high-quality protein. And without grazing animals, it would be difficult to practice environmentally sound crop rotation. Cutting your meat consumption by 50 or 75 percent makes more environmental sense than becoming a vegan like me.

As you can see, I was furiously preparing myself for the switch back to meat. Everything depended on the cholesterol test. And then my doctor called with the results. I don't know whether to be happy or sad, but my serum cholesterol is, if anything, slightly higher than when I started. Even with a near-zero intake of saturated fat, my cholesterol has not budged. For better or worse, my ultimate fate does not seem to depend on my diet. Tonight I will eat a lobster.

June 1993

High Satiety

Guns will make us powerful; butter will only make us fat.
—FIELD MARSHAL HERMANN GÖRING, 1936

The twentieth-century ideal of the dominant, successful, and emaciated man or woman is nearly irresistible. Even I succumbed to emaciation fifteen years ago. For one entire day in 1976, I weighed 116 pounds. This was the culmination of a yearlong diet composed mainly of low-fat cottage cheese and single-malt Scotch whiskey, plus nine hundred packs of cigarettes and a daily vitamin pill. I hit upon this happy combination all on my own, and it is the only diet that has ever worked for me. Having followed a potentially destructive course of conduct that left me thirty pounds underweight, I was inundated with accolades and marriage proposals.

Since then, the fat man inside me has had no trouble getting out. I've gradually passed from svelte through statistically normal, then on to adorably chubby, and finally well past that point, arriving at thirty pounds on the far side of average. Another ten pounds and I will be legally obese. All it took was a steady gain of four pounds a year, which works out to no more than forty excess calories a day—an extra pat of butter or an Oreo. Yet somehow I doubt that I would still be skinny if I had turned down just one mouthful of food every day for fifteen years. How could I have known when I had eaten precisely enough? Which mouthfuls should I have avoided?

Most animals don't even have to think about it. If they stuff themselves on Monday, they will automatically hold back on Tuesday. Even when some scientist forces them to overdo for several weeks in a row, they will naturally trim their appetites for the next few weeks and slim down to normal. Many humans are like laboratory animals. When they've stored a little excess fat or lost too much of it, a gentle biological buzzer goes off in their brains (probably in the paraventricular nucleus of the hypothalamus), and their appetite adjusts. If you give them a snack before dinner, they will eat less later. For people like me, undereating triggers the urge to make up for what we have missed, but overeating simply whets our appetite for the joys to come.

In our defense, I should mention that modern science has shown chubby people to be more discriminating and discerning than our skinny neighbors, at least at the dinner table. If you take away their food for twenty-four hours, skinny people will breathlessly devour whatever you put in front of them. We, in contrast, will still pick and choose, eating only food we normally enjoy and rejecting what we normally find distasteful. One reason for this is that chubby eaters are rarely truly hungry. We simply have abnormally generous appetites. But let's leave the distinction between hunger and appetite until later.

Obesity is partly—maybe largely—a genetic condition. Australian research has found you can predict whether a male adolescent will become overweight by learning whether his father is. Any diet doctor can tell you about patients who weigh seventy-five pounds too much, eat only a thousand calories a day, and don't lose an ounce. In a study using volunteers from a Vermont prison, men of normal weight consumed twice their regular intake of food, as many as seven thousand calories a day. Some didn't gain a pound; some gained only a few. We all know people like that.

I am cursed with thrifty genes. This sounds like a fine thing, and for about a million years it was. In a triumph of natural selection, my remote ancestors evolved the talent of turning food into energy with extreme efficiency, saving lots of fuel to store as fat for a rainy day, when people with wasteful genes find themselves in a real pickle. The problem is that rainy days are much less common now than they were a million years ago. I, for one, spend only brief periods more than an arm's length from an abundant supply of inviting food.

Always on the lookout for a scapegoat, I have had my metabolism tested as often as possible since boyhood. Every attempt was a total flop. The doctor makes you lie down and breathe through a tube attached to a machine that measures how much oxygen you inhale. People with a low metabolic rate use up less oxygen because they oxidize (or burn) fewer calories every hour. But research in the past two decades has discovered that most chubby people burn just as much energy as they should—given their height, weight, and physical activity. Attempts to tinker with the process are rarely successful. If you take a thyroid hormone to raise your metabolic rate, your appetite is likely to become voracious. The same thing happens when you take drugs that block the burning of sugars and fats from today's lunch or dinner in order to force your body to draw on the fuel it stored long ago in your fat cells. These drugs help you lose weight only if you can ignore your hunger and stick to a strict dietary regime. Appetite is still the enemy.

Hunger and appetite are not the same, at least as scientists use the terms. You probably don't feel hungry while you are making elaborate plans for a week of intensive eating in Paris, but your plans themselves are an expression of boundless appetite. Hunger is an annoying, nagging sensation that triggers constant thoughts of food and reminds you that your body wants to eat. But appetite is a more objective measure. Appetite is simply the tendency to eat. It is difficult to measure somebody else's hunger except by asking him how he feels, but we can gauge the size of his appetite by counting up how much he actually ate. Satiety is the state of being without appetite. It is the tendency not to eat.

The difference is important because hunger and appetite do not always coincide. I don't feel hungry after the main course of my dinner, but I still have an appetite for dessert. Eating lots of fiber may take away my hunger and make me feel full, but as we'll see, it may not do much to appease my appetite—my tendency to eat. There are chemicals that affect one and not the other. The drug naloxone can reduce the amount you eat without alleviating your hunger; dopamine antagonists do the reverse.

Someday medical science may discover a way to transform me into one of those people who can eat as much as they wish and never gain weight. But until it does, I plan to concentrate on trying to calm my appetite. I don't want to eat differently, just to eat less. Not for me a diet of steamed broccoli spears with toasted sesame seeds. And as luck would have it, today's research on appetite is as enterprising and energetic as any specialty in the study of obesity. I've located four hundred papers and abstracts published in the past three years alone.

My current thinking is that if I can only get my hands on 180,000 pounds of raw potatoes, everything will turn out right. As it may take me a while to explain how I arrived at this conclusion, I should first summarize some current findings about appetite that may be helpful in a minor sort of way.

• Protein is more satisfying, calorie for calorie, than carbohydrates. A high-protein diet fed to rhesus monkeys reduced their intake by 25 percent. A high-protein lunch caused human subjects to eat 12 percent less at dinner than a high-carbohydrate lunch. This is bad news for nutritionists, both in government and on best-seller lists, who urge us to emphasize pasta, grains, and beans.

Unfortunately, nature often insists on putting protein and fat in the same package, like cows and chickens. Eating stringy low-fat beef or chicken without its crispy skin holds little gastronomic interest, but high-protein lean fish and tofu, the mainstays of the Japanese diet, are another matter entirely. I lost five pounds on a recent culinary idyll in Japan, and two months later I have not gained them back. Could this be the solution to everything?

• Solid foods are more satisfying than liquid foods with the same caloric content. It's conceivable that the mere activity of chewing helps appease your appetite or that solid food stays in your stomach longer and makes you feel fuller. But both possibilities have been ruled out in the laboratory, leaving us without an explanation for this phenomenon.

• Filling up with fiber does not appear to help much with your appetite. Adding fiber to a very low calorie diet makes you feel less hungry at the end of the meal, but it does not seem to affect how fast your appetite returns afterward. And though a high-fiber breakfast makes you feel fuller than a low-fiber breakfast with the same number of calories, it will have only a slight or short-lived effect on the amount you eat at lunch, depending on which study you read.

This surprised me. I used to think that if I could only work up an interest in those dreary yet bulky high-fiber, low-calorie foods, my appetite problem would be solved. One extreme measure sometimes used to help massively obese people is to place a balloon in their stomachs and fill it up with air or water. The idea is that a gastric balloon—like great quantities of fiber-rich food—will suppress their appetites by triggering "stretch receptors" in the walls of their stomach and intestines, sending signals of fullness to the brain. But gastric balloons are often unsuccessful, and when they work at all, patients feel less hungry and eat less food for only a few weeks and then return to normal. As we'll see later, the messages the brain receives in the course of a meal are so numerous and complex that gastric distension has only a weak effect on lessening your appetite once the body learns that you are not eating your usual number of calories.

- Low-calorie snacks will stave off your appetite for the first few days by fooling your body into thinking that you are feeding it calories along with the bulk. But your appetite quickly wises up and begins to compensate at dinnertime for what it thought you were eating in midafternoon.

- The taste of sweetness in itself, with or without calories, has been widely found to stimulate the appetite; many manufacturers sweeten their packaged foods to make you eat more of them. In one experiment, people were given either a plain yogurt or an artificially sweetened yogurt before lunch; those who ate the sweetened yogurt were hungrier at lunch (and consumed more) than those who ate the plain one.

A cookie or a candy bar between meals—maybe even a piece of fruit—seems a prescription for overeating later. If you offer laboratory animals a sugary snack in addition to their regular diet, they will overeat by 20 percent; when the same sugar is put into their food, their appetite and intake become self-regulating again. This works with nearly every type of sugar, even those that don't taste sweet, like dextrin. Fructose seems to excite your appetite less powerfully than other forms of sugar, but only if you don't eat it with other carbohydrates such as bread or muffins.

Artificial sweeteners have been inconsistently reported to stimulate the appetite for anything that follows, to incite a craving for sugar, to satisfy your need for something sweet, or to have no effect at all. The general feeling is that while sugar stimulates your appetite and then satisfies it with calories, noncaloric sweeteners stimulate your appetite but leave you hungrier for other foods. Still, you will probably take in fewer calories from these other foods than the calories you saved by not eating sugar.

Recently all of this was thrown into question by a study of sweetened and unsweetened cereals. The sweet taste alone was not found to increase food intake for the rest of the day. But subjects who knew that their cereal was sweetened with aspartame (NutraSweet's artificial sweetener) ate more than subjects who didn't know. They were apparently so reassured by having eaten a lower-calorie breakfast that they ended up consuming slightly

more calories overall than those whose cereal had been sweetened with sugar.

Aspartame may have an advantage over other artificial sweeteners. People given doses of aspartame in capsules (so that they
would not taste its sweetness) ate less later, probably because
aspartame changes the profile of amino acids in the blood. Aspartame might act as a mild appetite suppressant if it weren't so
sweet.

• Exercise suppresses your appetite only briefly and only if the
exercise is intense. Astoundingly, there are no conclusive answers
on the question of exercise and appetite. The good news is that
exercise does help you lose weight. Theoretically, you should eat
more after a workout rather than less because your body, trying to
make up for the calories you have burned, will temporarily set
your metabolic rate to a higher level. But at least in the short term,
exercise does not appear to increase your appetite, especially if
you are overweight, and it does burn calories.

• Two kinds of diets are guaranteed to increase your appetite: a
high-fat diet and what is known in the laboratory as a cafeteria
diet. Either of them causes lean animals who ordinarily have no
problem regulating their intake of food and their body weight to
eat more than they should. Most studies agree that dietary fat
appeases your appetite less effectively than either protein or carbohydrates. In one experiment, human subjects who were given
as much low-fat food as they wished consumed 11 percent less
than they usually did; offered a high-fat diet, they ate 15 percent
more than normal. I would love to explain the difference by
pointing out that high-fat food simply tastes better. But experiments in which distasteful fats such as margarine were added to
soups yielded the same result.

A cafeteria diet consists of a wide variety of palatable foods.
Experimental animals fed a bland, balanced diet known as laboratory chow typically maintain their proper weight even when
allowed to eat as much of it as they wish. But when the same animals are offered a range of tasty snacks, they will inevitably eat

more at each meal and increase the number of meals they take. The explanation is an important concept known as sensory-specific satiety. When a human or a rat has filled up on one type of food, and you present him, her, or it with another food that differs in taste, aroma, texture, or even temperature, eating begins all over again. Even though you can't touch another bite of your main course, you may eat as much of your dessert as if you had not already been dining for the past hour. The modern world is one grand multiethnic cafeteria. The modern world is designed to make you overeat and then ostracize you when you do.

Lurking within your overall appetite are lots of little subappetites, and any one of them can make you overeat. Your urge to begin eating (meal initiation, in the technical jargon) is quite different from your need to keep on eating (meal length), how fast you eat (feeding rate, which usually decreases during a meal), how much you eat overall (meal size, which is the previous two subappetites multiplied together), and how much time will pass before you start eating again (satiety). Distinct chemical signals in the body appear to regulate these different appetites; some of the brain's sensors shorten a meal's duration without affecting your feeding rate, and some sensors do just the opposite.

Researchers used to think that chubby people had a special style of eating, taking large mouthfuls in quick succession, each one followed by rapid chewing, but they don't think so anymore. I eat slowly, take small to medium mouthfuls, chew at a slow-average but extremely steady rate. I rarely let my mouth get empty. But worse, I have a meal termination problem. I simply keep on eating long after everybody else is off powdering her nose or longing for his coffee. Something is amiss with my satiety signals. They don't tell me when I have had enough.

The biological systems that control each of these subappetites are so complex and convoluted that researchers are only now discovering how they are regulated. Just the sight and smell of food trigger salivation, secretions from your pancreas, and various events in your stomach and intestines. (An obese person's pancreas turns out four times the insulin when food is sighted or smelled as a skinny person's pancreas; whether this is a cause or effect of obesity and how it affects appetite are unknown.) Then, as you eat, chemical and mechanical sensors in your mouth, throat, stomach, intestines, and liver send signals to your brain, which not only integrates these reports but can also directly sense glucose in the bloodstream. And both your weight and your body fat are constantly monitored in ways that are not fully understood. It is not surprising that when you fill up on a low-calorie snack made with substitutes for sugar and fat, the brain soon figures out what you've done and encourages you to make up for the lost calories somewhere else. Calories, of course, are the most direct and pleasant way to satisfy your appetite, but too many calories are what I am trying to avoid. The only solution is to fool the brain itself.

Several drugs appear to suppress your appetite effectively. These include dexfenfluramine and fluoxetine (the active ingredient in the controversial drug Prozac), both of which increase the availability of serotonin in the brain, which triggers a powerful signal of satiety. In European trials with eight hundred patients taking dexfenfluramine and given psychological counseling, the average subject lost twenty-two pounds in the course of a year; patients who were given counseling alone lost only two-thirds as much. I wish they had tested the drug alone.

Fenfluramine is sold in America under the unappetizing names of Rotondin and Pondimin; the marketing departments must have been on vacation when these drugs were christened. They appear to have more serious side effects, from nausea to impotence, than the European version because they contain a mixture of right- and left-handed molecules. (The latter do none of the work and most of the damage and are left out of the European brands.) I thought I might give Rotondin a try anyway, but calls to my doctor are unavailing. He has not even called me back.

Which is why I am pinning my hopes on 180,000 pounds of raw potatoes. Here's how I figure it.

When food reaches my small intestine, it stimulates cells in the intestinal walls to secrete a class of chemicals known as peptides. Several of these peptides reach the brain, where they turn off appetite and turn on satiety. CCK-8 (short for "cholecystokinin octapeptide") is one of them, perhaps the most important and certainly the most closely studied. Injecting CCK into the bloodstream or directly into the central nervous system reduces food intake in animals and people and may possibly hasten the burning of body fat. CCK works only after you have eaten something, which leads some researchers to think that it amplifies other satiety signals to the brain.

Hooking myself up to an intravenous bottle of CCK would be extremely inconvenient both at home and in the better restaurants. But how can I increase my body's own secretion of CCK? Experiments with animals have shown that various amino acids may do the trick, but there's nothing definite yet. Anyway, I have a more clever method. My own CCK would probably be plentiful enough if it were not foiled by another chemical called trypsin. Like CCK, trypsin is secreted by my small intestine, and for reasons I cannot fathom, it acts as a brake on my production of CCK. If only I could suppress my trypsin.

The cells that produce trypsin do not have a mind of their own. They are slaves to orders sent out from the pancreas. But I am loath to fool with my pancreas, even if I knew how. Besides, merely holding back my secretion of trypsin will not achieve the desired effect. That's because another chemical, known as chymotrypsin, needs to be neutralized at the same time.

Which is where potatoes come into the picture. A potato naturally protects itself against bacteria and mold by producing substances called protease inhibitors, which prevent these microorganisms from being able to digest the potato's protein. At least one of them, protease inhibitor II, carries out this lifesaving work by binding to *both* trypsin and chymotrypsin and neutralizing their effectiveness. If I can only contrive a way to place some protease inhibitor II into my small intestine, my CCK will rise and my appetite will disappear.

I *have* contrived a way: by swallowing it. Incidentally, if I have somehow given the impression that I figured all this out for myself, I should mention that I learned about the effects of protease inhibitor II from a paper in the journal *Physiology & Behavior* by Hill, Peikin, Ryan, and Blundell. They added one and a half grams of it to a bowl of soup and fed the soup to eleven subjects right before lunch. The level of CCK in the subjects' bloodstreams increased by four times only fifteen minutes after they drank the soup and was six times higher another fifteen minutes later. And they ate 17 percent less at lunch than when they drank the same soup without protease inhibitor II. How many days this advantage would last has not been tested.

But my plan to switch to an all-potato diet was foiled by two unhappy facts. Protease inhibitors are destroyed by cooking, and their proportion in the average potato is disappointingly small. To ingest one and a half grams, I would have to eat 500 pounds of raw potatoes before every dinner, the equivalent of 180,000 pounds a year, which would be just as inconvenient as carrying around an intravenous drip of CCK.

It was then that I discovered a company in Des Moines called Kemin Industries, which purchased exactly that number of potatoes a while ago, processed them down to six hundred pounds in an intermediate stage called ammonium sulfate cake, and put them in the freezer. Dr. Christopher Nelson told me that a gram of protease inhibitor II would cost ninety-five dollars and take eight weeks to arrive. But Kemin thinks it has found a way to produce pounds of it at a time and is now raising money to start up the new process. A laboratory at Harvard is also testing protease inhibitor II as an anticancer agent, which would be a nifty bonus.

It seems just a matter of time. With my trypsin and chymotrypsin bound into submission, my CCK will soar like an eagle, my appetite will plummet like a stone, and my weight will return to 116. Luckily I still have some of the clothing I bought on that blissful day in 1976. But I'll probably wait until bellbottoms come back into fashion.

October 1991

Sweet Smell of Sex

Male and female created He them.
—GENESIS 1:27

Whenever a female pig (also known as a sow) is in heat and smells a certain musky chemical, or pheromone, in the breath of a male pig (also known as a boar), she shows an immediate, urgent, and uncontrollable reaction. Her hind legs stiffen, her spine curves downward, her ears cock, and she presents herself for mounting. This physical position is known as lordosis, and it is invariably inspired in a sow, without choice or variation, by the scent of a boar's breath. Since the beginning of time, or at least since I was in high school, man has not flagged in his quest for a substance having the same effect on the female of our species. I cannot count the evenings on which my friends and I cruised around suburban streets in our convertibles, sharing our collection of true stories in which something called Spanish fly played at least a major supporting role. What chemical the girls talked about in their convertibles I cannot say.

These adolescent fantasies are only a dim and distant memory now. But when rumor recently reached me, in the form of an article in the *Wall Street Journal,* that the Erox Corporation, with headquarters in New York and laboratories in Salt Lake City, may have discovered the *human* pheromone and bottled it in a perfume, I hastily packed my bags and jetted out to Salt Lake to see if it all was true.

I regret to report that I found very little lordosis in Salt Lake City. I did meet with a group of interesting scientists, learned of some major discoveries in the science of smell, wore two perfumes that may or may not revolutionize the fragrance business, and ate several bags of gourmet saltwater taffy, made with salt from the Great Salt Lake.

A pheromone is a chemical messenger sent by one member of a species to another that is capable of changing the behavior or internal state of the receiver. The most famous pheromones are sexual, like the signals emitted by female moths and butterflies to attract males from as far away as several miles. This talent of the female silkworm moth was discovered in the nineteenth century and attributed at first to some sort of radiation. Finally, in 1959, her signal was identified as the chemical bombykol, emitted by the female and smelled, or at least sensed, by tiny hairs on the male moth's antennae. This was the first pheromonal puzzle ever solved by human science. In celebration, the word "pheromone" was coined, a compound of the Greek *pherein* (to carry) and the Greco-English *hormone* (to excite). It can hardly have been a coincidence that, in the very same year, these now-classic verses soared to the top of the pop charts:

I told her that I was a flop with chicks.
I've been that way since Nineteen Fifty Six.
She looked at my palm and she made a magic sign.
She said, "What you need is Love Potion No. 9."

I didn't know if it was day or night.
I started kissin' everything in sight.

But when I kissed the cop down at Thirty Fourth and
   Vine
He broke my little bottle of Love Potion No. 9.

Sexual pheromones may get the most attention, but the range of chemical signals in the animal kingdom is astonishing. In various species and under a variety of circumstances, pheromones can say, "Here's the food," "Let's you and me fight," "I'm pregnant," "Let's all infest this tree together," "Let's form a swarm," "Our queen is here, so everything's OK," "Please follow this path," and "Help us carry this terrific chunk of food." Harvard's E. O. Wilson estimates that the smooth running of an ant colony requires ten or more types of chemical messages. Honeybees use thirty pheromonal systems to guide, instruct, encourage, and assign jobs to nurses, soldiers, undertakers, and food gatherers.

The simpler mammals could not get along without pheromones. Most of them are inarticulate and cannot write or speak distinctly. And most of them are nocturnal and need their sense of smell to navigate in the darkness. Humans are the only mammals perpetually ready for sex; the others are willing and fertile so infrequently that they need all the help they can get to be in the right place at the right time. The entire sex life of the male golden hamster is micromanaged by chemical messages; pheromones lead him to the female, announce her reproductive status, reduce his potential for unromantic aggression, rapidly raise the level of his testosterone, and finally bring on his copulatory behavior. Male hamsters who have lost their sense of smell do not even get to first base. There appear to be no pheromones that compel the male hamster to engage in intimate conversation after copulation or send flowers the next day.

But I am not a hamster, nor was meant to be, to paraphrase T. S. Eliot. A human being is articulate; possesses consciousness, free will, lots of brainpower, and a keen pair of eyes and ears; and is nearly always capable of sex. Why do we need the help of chemical messages? Our behavior is rarely governed by the mechanical simplicity of stimulus and response; we interpret and manipulate the messages of our senses.

Or do we? Apart from the current work of the Erox Corporation, the strongest evidence we have for human pheromones comes from women's dormitories. Women living together in close quarters have long noticed that their menstrual periods soon begin to coincide. Dr. Martha K. McClintock, then at Harvard, carefully followed the cycles of 135 female undergraduates living in one large dormitory and found that menstrual synchrony occurred among roommates and close friends, though not among all 135 women. McClintock was able to eliminate most of the possible causes that might occur to you and me—similar patterns of stress, of exposure to light and darkness, of diet—and was left with only one: the more time any two women spent together, the more likely their menstrual cycles were to have harmonized. She also found that the more time a woman spent with men (measured in time, not sexual encounters), the shorter and more regular her cycle was likely to be.

At least in this regard, the human female college student is indistinguishable from the common female house mouse. A female mouse surrounded by other females will have a longer cycle; the presence of a male mouse shortens it. And the timing of a female's puberty depends on whether she spends time with male mice (puberty now) or with females (puberty later). Scientists have discovered that these phenomena are provoked by chemical signals—pheromones—in the little creatures' urine and are sensed by a special receptor, the vomeronasal organ, in their noses.

Are pheromones responsible for menstrual synchrony in humans? The answer is probably yes. And the usual suspect is the chemical androstenol, found both in the underarm sweat of humans and in a boar's saliva, where it triggers the much-sought-after lordosis in the sow. But studies of whether androstenol acts as a pheromone in humans are inconclusive—which is not surprising, because pheromones from one species are not meant to affect another. Nonetheless, androstenol is the key ingredient in two perfumes sold by the Jovan company with the claim that they have been "scientifically created to attract."

Such was the state of my knowledge about pheromones as I flew over the Rockies and descended into Salt Lake City in search of lordosis. To be entirely truthful, I already knew that the Erox Corporation, while it claimed to have discovered a dozen human pheromones, discouraged the belief that it had found an irresistible and urgent sexual attractant. Instead, Erox's pheromones are meant to increase the *wearer's* sense of well-being, to elicit sensuality rather than sexuality.

Erox was founded as a perfume company by physician-entrepreneur David Berliner, and its purpose is to exploit the human pheromones he has discovered and thus claim its share of the ten-billion-dollar world fragrance market. This is an astounding number. Ten billion dollars a year comes to $1.84 a person for everyone on the face of the earth—more, really, because I rarely use perfume. Berliner has also founded Pherin, a sister company working on the basic science of pheromones and their therapeutic potential.

Thirty-five years ago, before the word "pheromone" had been coined, Berliner was doing research on the composition of the human skin, or at least so he tells every reporter who has asked. He obtained skin samples by scraping the inside surface of casts that had been worn by injured skiers, prepared a sludgy extract of this material, and stored the extract in laboratory flasks. He and his coworkers were amazed to notice that their moods became mellow and cooperative whenever the flasks were left open, in sharp contrast to the fractious atmosphere that usually prevailed. Then Berliner moved on to other things and froze his sludge for thirty years. It occurred to him once or twice that he may have discovered a human pheromone, but it was not until 1989 that he turned for advice to a former colleague at the University of Utah School of Medicine—Dr. Larry Stensaas, an anatomist who has worked for the past decade mapping the brain.

I drove to the medical school, where Stensaas was ready for me with a slide lecture. He demonstrated that many reptiles and mammals possess at least two separate sensory systems originating in the nose. One, the olfactory system, has nerve endings high up in the nasal cavity and is responsible for the sense of smell; it sends signals about food and wine and fragrances to the cortex of the brain, where they are examined, interpreted, and consciously considered. A second system senses pheromones through the vomeronasal organ, or VNO (which we have already met in the house mouse). In the lower animals, the VNO sends messages along special nerves not only to the cortex but directly to the hypothalamus, where the emotions and reproduction are regulated. A reptile flicks out her tongue to retrieve chemical information about her environment, then carries it back to her VNO. We can just sniff it in.

Until the team at Erox stirred up interest in the issue, most experts doubted the existence of human pheromones because our nervous systems appeared to lack both a VNO and the requisite wiring back to the brain. But Stensaas and his colleagues discovered that *all of us* possess a VNO, a potential pheromone receptor, and that our VNOs are located just where they should be—inside each nostril, on the septum, which separates the nostrils, about a half inch back from the tip of the nose. According to Stensaas, the human VNO turns out to be one of the largest in the animal kingdom, larger than that of a horse. He showed me one hundred striking electron-microscope slides of the human VNO and the nerves that may possibly carry impulses from it to the brain (this part has yet to be proved). And then, I believe, I saw one with my very own eyes.

We drove to Erox's small laboratory at a nearby research park. There I watched Luis Monti-Bloch, M.D., a neurophysiologist, carry out his most persuasive experiment. A student named Brad lay flat on a cushioned laboratory table; he has served as a subject many times before and possesses a rare degree of discipline that allows him to lie still while people poke instruments into his nose for hours at a time. First, I took a look at Brad's septum through a pair of Zeiss loupelike jeweler's magnifiers—and there it was, a little crimson cavity in Brad's equally crimson septum, with an opening about a millimeter wide, a genuine vomeronasal organ if I've ever seen one. Later Monti-Bloch peered into my nose and reported that my own VNOs were where they should be and in seemingly healthy condition.

Monti-Bloch has invented a device that delivers any chemical you choose to the VNO in a precisely aimed and precisely timed manner. It is a narrow white plastic tube with another tube running down its center and a thin silver wire inside that, all connected to pumps and instruments at one end and open at the other. When Monti-Bloch presses a button, a pump sends the probable pheromone or a placebo down the inner tube; immediately, a reverse vacuum pump whisks it away through the outer tube after it has been in contact with the subject's septum for only a half second—before the whiff can disperse into the nasal cavity and trigger the olfactory system. The silver wire reports back any electrical impulses that have been stimulated in the VNO. Berliner's team has extracted twelve active compounds from his frozen pheromone skin sludge and, by watching the signal picked up by Monti-Bloch's silver wire, has identified two of them as the most potent, ER-670 for women and ER-830 for men. These are the pheromones that will be used in Erox's two perfumes.

I watched Monti-Bloch place the open end of his tube over Brad's VNO and deliver fleeting puffs of either ER-830, a strong-smelling clove oil, or a completely neutral substance. A computer screen showed how Brad's VNO responded. When the clove oil or the neutral substance was sent down the tube, there was no reaction, just a flat black line on the screen. But when ER-830 was pumped through, the flat line jumped to attention, forming the sort of graph—a sharp rise followed by a slower, more angular decay—that is, I was told, the characteristic response of sensory cells in other parts of the body.

Later I telephoned around to several major researchers in

animal pheromones and neuroanatomy. Even the most skeptical are enormously excited by the work done at Erox. But nobody can replicate the Erox experiments, because Berliner and his team will not reveal the chemical structure of their putative pheromones. And the question remains whether Brad's VNO or yours or mine is connected to our brains, especially to the seat of sex and emotion in the hypothalamus. (Monti-Bloch's silver wire had picked up impulses only from the VNO itself.) Berliner responded that to demonstrate conclusively a connection would take years of work. And why bother? he asked. The effect of ER-670 and ER-830 on mood and emotion is obvious to him. But this remains the crucial issue.

When we were finished torturing Brad, I was taken down the hall to Dr. Clive Jennings-White's lab and tantalizingly shown the pure pheromones themselves. He is the chemist on the team and has synthesized the pheromones found in Berliner's natural skin-extract sludge. All of his efforts are contained in two large brown glass jars, one for ER-670 and one for ER-830, each about a foot high and eight inches across and nearly filled with a white crys-

The Ice Between Courses

A few years ago, the *coup de milieu* was introduced to Paris, having been popular for a considerable time in Bordeaux and other maritime towns. . . . A young blond girl, aged between 15 and 19, wearing no ornament on her head and with her arms bare to above the elbow, serves each guest. She . . . should be a virgin if possible (though 19-year-old virgins are extremely rare in Paris).
—Grimod de La Reynière, c. 1804

talline powder. Each contains enough pheromone to stimulate half a quadrillion people.

I asked to smell them, but Jennings-White told me that this would be against all the rules. I formulated a plan to trip the fire alarm and trick him into leaving the room while I pried the jars open, inserted my nose, and breathed deeply—but I decided against it. While nobody on the team would admit to having sniffed the pheromones directly, I cannot imagine that four such curious scientists could possibly have resisted the temptation for more than fifteen seconds. I gathered, though, that the Erox pheromones have absolutely no odor. Their only effect is on the vomeronasal organs in the septum of the nose and, from there, on the hypothalamus of the brain—unconscious, insidious, and subversive—if there is any effect on the brain at all.

I have little doubt that Berliner and Erox were once in search of the overpowering sexual attractant we dreamed of in high school. The vast majority of perfumes for women contain real or synthetic versions of pheromonal secretions from the Himalayan musk deer and the African or Asian civet cat. But in a medical journal published in 1991, Berliner and Jennings-White point out that this is illogical: pheromones operate only among members of the same species. Human pheromones would be "more natural and more effective as true attractants." "The human behavior expected from pheromone stimulation is an enhancement of libido. The effect of pheromones would be . . . profound and irresistible."

But now Erox claims that ER-670 and ER-830 have only a modest sensual effect, making female subjects feel warmer and more open and male subjects feel more confident and self-assured. This is a far cry from the stiffened legs and cocked ears of the sow. Despite the 1991 article, everybody at Erox now says that the discovery of a compelling human attractant would have been a nightmare, at least for the marketing people. The only nightmare I can picture is that they could not have found enough wheelbarrows in all of Salt Lake City to carry their profits to the bank.

Thus far, Erox has no statistically persuasive evidence that its perfumes have even these mild sensual effects. Erox has not scientifically compared its fragrances with and without the pheromones or against some popular but conventional perfumes. It is almost as though Erox were wary of learning the results. Wearing its perfume might turn out to be little different from dabbing yourself with a conventional fragrance while drinking a frosty martini.

Nearly all the major perfumes sold in this country—whether by Calvin Klein, Giorgio, Estée Lauder, or others—are formulated at one of six fragrance companies (also known as essential-oil houses) in or around New York City by a tiny group of extremely talented "noses," or perfumers, and each contains between two hundred and four hundred ingredients. Following the customary practice, Erox's president, Pierre de Champfleury (former head of Yves Saint-Laurent fragrances and cosmetics in Paris), and consultant Ann Gottlieb (to whom many attribute the success of Calvin Klein's Obsession, Eternity, and Escape) wrote a "brief" and submitted it to three of the six major fragrance companies. A brief explains the idea behind a prospective scent, the aura that it is supposed to create, and sometimes even its name, the appearance of the bottle and packaging, its intended position in the market, and how it will be advertised.

The three companies responded with preliminary samples of the desired scents, and Champfleury and Gottlieb chose two: the female perfume from Firmenich and the male fragrance from Givaudan-Roure. (Both companies will supply only the essential oil to Erox; the formulas remain their intellectual property.) The fine-tuning that ensued was more complicated than usual because the pheromones stayed in Salt Lake City; each scent could be tinkered with only after the people in Salt Lake had added the appropriate pheromone and shipped it back to New York. Erox's perfumes contain no musk or civet or castoreum—Berliner's human pheromones replace the usual animal attractants. One dose is meant to emit the same quantity of human pheromone as is given off by a completely naked body.

As we had agreed before I flew out to Salt Lake City, Jennings-White allowed me to try preliminary versions of the Erox pheromone perfumes, to be called Realm for Women and Realm for Men. I chose the back of my left hand for the male scent and the back of my right hand for the female. The male scent was woodsy and spicy though light and simple-hearted; the female scent was warm and cozy with an initial floral impression and an underlying Oriental character. Hundreds of times in the next three days I sniffed at the back of both my hands, much preferring the female scent to the male. Does this mean that I am a lesbian?

Despite all of Erox's disclaimers, I desperately clung to the hope that I was wearing an overpowering sexual attractant. I wondered how I would explain to my wife back in New York that, after supper, in the parking lot next to the restaurant where the Erox scientists and I had dined, I had been overcome by a band of beautiful women, dragged into one of those recreational vehicles so popular in Utah, and mated with repeatedly until I was of no further use. What would this do to our marriage? In truth, I was ten times more anxious about my right hand, with its male attractant, and wore a glove during all waking hours until the scent had finally dissipated.

Dinner and my walk through the parking lot were uneventful. Back at the hotel, I lounged around in various strategic locations and took careful notes on whether I was attracting anybody. In the coffee shop, I had a hard time attracting even a waiter of either sex.

I moved to the bar, where I chose a seat with empty stools on both sides, ordered a Scotch, and waited. A few Scotches later, observing that the stools were still empty, I moved on to the hotel desk, where two young blond women in concierge outfits had just come on duty. I pretended that I needed their help in making elaborate plans for skiing in Park City, and, as we pored over maps and brochures, I made certain that my ungloved left hand was broadcasting its irresistible message. Then I retired to my room and waited for one of the young women to telephone for an assignation. But Erox had been true to its word. Neither pheromone seemed to be a sexual attractant. When I returned to New York with the two scents still active on opposite hands, my wife said that I smelled like a magazine.

A month or so later, when I heard that the Erox perfumes had been further refined, I requested the latest version of the scent for men. This would contain ER-830, the pheromone that, Erox claims, makes the male wearer feel more sensual. I wonder whether ER-830 deserves the name of pheromone, which is, strictly speaking, a chemical that communicates a message between one member of a species and another, not between a man and himself. ER-830 is more like an airborne hormone. Perhaps this scent should be called Onan for Men.

In any event, the odor of the male fragrance had been much improved. Now it was more complex, with an initial impression of bright spiciness over warmer and more sensual notes. I cannot say with certainty whether the Erox male fragrance had any effect on my mood. My wife reported that I seemed consistently more romantic and, on one occasion, that I had not kissed her that way for weeks. But without further investigation, I cannot decide whether my behavior should be attributed to wearing ER-830 or to the fact that I was spending sixteen hours a day reading about the mating habits of pigs and golden hamsters. Do you realize that in the languages of the Maori, Samoans, and Eskimos, the word for kissing means "smelling"? At least that's what I read somewhere.

I don't know about you, but I am beginning to find the idea of human pheromones extremely scary, mainly because they affect us unconsciously, without ever entering our awareness. One speaks loosely about "smelling" pheromones, but many of these messenger chemicals have no odor. We are unaware of them because they are perceived by an organ distinct from the receptors designed to sense a hot apple pie or Chanel No. 5, and their messages are transmitted deep into the brain, before our cortex has had a chance to register and follow or resist them.

How can we struggle against the changes these pheromones may be causing in us? How many of our decisions and actions are influenced by forces of which we are unaware, forces as menacing as the pods in *Invasion of the Body Snatchers*? Or as scary as an adolescent human male with a spray can of Spanish fly in his hand? Or, as Max Lake suggests, as frightening as a thousand Nazis at a rally raising their arms in unison, exchanging pheromones in a ritual of group intoxication?

On the brighter side, pheromones may account for some of the fun of kissing, especially the profound French kind. As a general rule, the human nose is positioned conveniently above the lips and, when pressed closely against one's partner's skin, is in a fine position to draw in whatever pheromones may be produced by the skin and in the saliva. This can also explain much of the joy of human snuggling.

But why would nature have provided us with a chemical like this? The answer is simple. Humans are the only mammals I can think of that are both gregarious and monogamous. For us, socialization is as important as sex. As Michael Stoddart points out in *The Scented Ape*, if a woman's fertility were advertised by an irresistible pheromone that drew males from far and wide every twenty-eight days, monogamy would disappear and our social arrangements would give way to universal warfare. Much more useful is the pheromone that Berliner and his team at Erox claim to have discovered, a family-values pheromone, a chemical signal that makes us feel mellow and assured as we huddle together in small groups and sniff contentedly, without smelling a thing.

June 1993

Going for the Burn

When I arrived at the spanking-new Canyon Ranch in the Berkshire Mountains, I was coming down from an intense eating binge as *Vogue*'s monthly food correspondent. No sooner had I polished off a metric ton of mail-order Christmas treats than I was on a plane to Paris, where I had squeezed twenty-two restaurants into sixteen days. Then it was off to Texas, roaming between Dallas and Fort Worth in an extremely rewarding search for world-class barbecue joints. My weight had climbed into a new zone, and I was getting nervous about it. Five days later, Canyon Ranch had changed my life.

• From now on, I will always use conditioner after shampooing. The shower room had pump bottles of conditioner, which left my hair so much softer and easier to manage. Where have I been all these years?

• I will become a serious weight lifter. See below.

• I will strive to become merely chubby again. That was twenty pounds ago.

• Until then, I will wear sweatpants as often as possible. They bind and chafe less than regular trousers and slip on so much more easily.

• I will become a spa junkie, if I can afford the habit.

Canyon Ranch's publicity material scientifically estimates that more than half of America's population has heard of the original Canyon Ranch in Tucson. I was vaguely aware that it was the first major coed fitness resort, not just another plush pamper palace exclusively for women. And that it was a magnet for socialites, movie stars, and CEOs, a lush oasis where you eat one thousand exquisite gourmet calories a day yet never go hungry. I also knew they were building a Canyon Ranch clone in Lenox, Massachusetts, near Tanglewood and Jacob's Pillow and, for those like me who are old enough to care, Alice's Restaurant. It opened on October 1.

Even if you've been a guest before (three out of four have), the first thing you get is a guided tour with lots of numbers: forty million dollars to build on 120 wooded acres, an inn for two hundred guests with 120 rooms and suites (each with a VCR), a spa with 100,000 gleaming square feet for fitness and health, an 1897 mansion called Bellefontaine for dining and wellness, thirty-two fitness classes daily, sixty massage therapists, three hundred staff members in all. Newcomers may find themselves winded before the end of the guided tour.

Next you fill out some medical forms. The final page strikes you as particularly bellicose and hypocritical. "Do you find yourself obsessing about food?" it asks. "Not at all," you reply, "but I think about almost nothing else." So, you soon realize, does everybody at Canyon Ranch, including the three hundred on staff.

Then you meet with a program adviser who guides you through a bewildering range of possibilities: aquatic fitness, aromatherapy, arthritis consultation, badminton, basketball, behavioral therapy, biking, bingo, biofeedback, body composition, body contouring, breathing, cholesterol evaluation, clay treatment, cranial massage, cross-country skiing, European facial, food habit management, funk aerobics, handwriting analysis, high- and low-impact aerobics, hiking, hydrotherapy, hypnotherapy, inhalation, intensive treatment facial, Jacuzzi, Jin Shin Jyutsu, Lifecycles, Lunch & Learn, makeup, meditation, minitrampoline, nutrition counseling, posture and movement, racquetball, reflexology, rhythms, rowing, running (indoor and out), salt treatment, sauna, shiatsu, snowshoeing, squash, steam room, stop smoking, stretching, Swedish massage, swimming, tennis, treadmills, volleyball, weight lifting, wellness counseling, whirlpool baths, yoga.

I was growing acutely anxious about exercising in public. I flashed back to those agonizing afternoons in summer camp on the dusty baseball diamond—where three of us were always dispatched to far right field and spent two hours in the blinding sun praying that the ball would never come our way. My wife could hardly wait. A dancer and star high-school sprinter in California when she was young, she doesn't get much practice in either of them around me. She immediately signed up for a facial, three types of massage (cranial, sports, and shiatsu), body composition analysis, aromatherapy, and an herbal wrap, and filled in the rest of her schedule with classes in rhythm aerobics, flexibility, and strength training. Then she sprinted across the hall to the Canyon Ranch Showcase shop, unavoidable as you enter the spa building, where they sell athletic clothing, shoes, books, and tapes. She had not gone shopping for thirty-six hours and was beginning to show the strain.

As I had signed up for nothing but a late-afternoon tennis lesson (with an excellent pro), I rented a tape of *Tequila Sunrise* with Michelle Pfeiffer, Kurt Russell, and Mel Gibson, and returned to our comfortable room after lunch. Except during meals, there is no coercion at Canyon Ranch, nobody following you around to make sure you are doing what you should. *Tequila Sunrise*, it turns out, is a much underrated film.

On our second day, my wife's schedule was so crammed with exercise and pampering that we saw each other only at meals. By dinnertime, her skin was pink and smooth as a baby's. The skin-care person urged her to wear plastic bags filled with lotion on her hands all night. The skin-care person is divorced.

I spent my time wandering around, watching but not engaging, until I dropped into Gym 4, where they keep the aerobic and strength-training machines, beautiful glittering things in chrome and brass made by a company called Keiser. The fitness staff were unaccountably squandering their afternoon break lifting weights and futilely trying to climb the StairMaster; when they were done, I asked for a demonstration. Before you knew it, I had completed the full circuit, at modest levels of resistance, of course, and had mounted the treadmill for a snappy walk as I gazed through a huge picture window at the New England countryside. The Appalachian Trail passes just beyond the property.

When I had worked up quite a lather, I signed up for a locker (most guests do this on their first day), tried the men's sauna, steam, and inhalation rooms, took a cool shower (individual curtained stalls), and, against my better judgment, felt almost terrific.

The herbal room was dim and warm. Calming New Age music seeped in through hidden loudspeakers. I lay on a table tightly swaddled in heavy, hot, wet canvas blankets impregnated with five herbs. The herbal therapist could not remember which five herbs they were—I would have preferred a little more tarragon— but promised they would detox me, get all the poisons out of my bloodstream. Like what? Oh, nicotine, coffee, chocolate, like that. With my sanguinary poisons oozing out all over the canvas blankets, I was surprised that she was not wearing a protective suit and helmet. I have always considered people who believe that chocolate is a poison to be twisted beyond redemption.

Then she left me alone. My arms were pinned to my sides by the herbal wrappers, and for five minutes I considered going into a serious panic. At last I settled into a pleasant reverie. I was in Paris again, tucking into a plate of Joël Robuchon's ravioli of *langoustines* and his roasted rabbit under a fricassee of wild mushrooms. Presently the scene shifted to La Cagouille, where tiny mussels are grilled without oil on a bare open skillet. When the herbal therapist returned to unwrap me, I was sipping a dark morning coffee at the Café de Flore, biting into a crusty baguette.

Any of these delights would fit into the Canyon Ranch low-fat, low-calorie regime, yet none of them does. I knew I was in trouble at our very first lunch, the emptiest 285 calories I've ever frittered away. It was a "pizza" with a thin brown leatherette crust covered by a cheese mistranslated as mozzarella and some vegetables that don't even belong in the same room with a pizza. Coffee was a pallid version of brewed decaf. At dinner I would learn how to order a packet of instant Maxwell House to dissolve in my decaf, and the next day I would meet a waiter willing to smuggle out a cup of real coffee from the staff's real coffeepot.

Why all this fuss about caffeine? On my last day at Canyon Ranch, I read a delightful story in the newspaper. Researchers at Stanford have discovered that *decaffeinated coffee increases your bad cholesterol (LDLs) by an average of 7 percent!* Real coffee has no such effect. The decaf crowd has got so powerful of late that you can no longer find a cup of real coffee at the end of a dinner party. Although these people have deprived me of pleasure for all these years, I now feel a profound sense of compassion toward them and am thankful to Whoever has guided me upon the low-cholesterol, caffeinated path.

I was never hungry at Canyon Ranch but never satisfied. Executive Chef Barry Correia has a strong background in modern American cooking, but he faces four insurmountable problems: the Canyon Ranch Nutrition Philosophy, the official recipes he is required to follow, the ingredients he uses, and the organization of the kitchen. The directors of Canyon Ranch should either start over from scratch or erase the words "exquisite gourmet fare" from all brochures, pamphlets, and advertising.

The Canyon Ranch Nutrition Philosophy is strict, though not as draconian as Pritikin: 60 percent carbohydrates, mainly complex, 20 percent fat, 20 percent protein, 1,000 to 1,200 calories a day, high fiber, no caffeine, oils high in polyunsaturates, two grams of sodium, almost no refined flour. Some of these rules are arbitrary, some outmoded. There is no medical reason whatsoever for healthy eaters to limit themselves to two grams of sodium a day. The tasteless gazpacho came alive after I had a little dish of salt brought to the table and added two tiny pinches. Though delicious crusty, yeasty bread is the most wonderful complex carbohydrate in the world, all the breads at Canyon Ranch range from boring to gruesome. All are store-bought but one, and this is made with baking soda instead of yeast. Great breads are not made with whole wheat flour and baking soda. Getting my knife into the whole wheat dessert crepes demanded more fitness training than I had undergone. The Canyon Ranch rule against refined flour (oddly they are happy to buy dried pasta made with refined flour) may raise your fiber intake a gram or two, but popcorn does the job twice as fast.

After straightening out their Nutrition Philosophy, the owners should get rid of half the Canyon Ranch recipes and many of the ingredients they buy. The vanilla extract is half artificial. The melons are unripe, the apples waxed, the bananas green. For at least two years now, polyunsaturated oils like soybean and safflower have been considered dangerous compared with monounsaturated oils like olive and canola. I have been told that Canyon Ranch in Tucson switched to canola last July; I saw no canola oil in my tour of the kitchens.

The ubiquitous rubbery skinless chicken breasts should be replaced with juicy low-fat free-range veal from Summerfield Farm in Virginia; the olive oil I saw in the kitchen was not extra virgin or even slightly virgin; the pasta was precooked and cooled, waiting to be reheated in boiling water; the vegetables were presteamed and reheated in the microwave; the "Maine lobster tails" were tough and dry and came frozen from New Zealand.

Why not steamed mussels, and tuna *tartare*, and cold briny oysters opened on demand, and sashimi sliced at the very last minute, and concentrated, degreased veal or chicken stock for richness and flavor, and naturally low-fat game, and wild mushrooms, and hearty bean stews (a profoundly complex carbohydrate), and vegetables grilled with a little olive oil? What's needed are the freshest ingredients, recipes that go beyond the health-food theology of the sixties, and lots of skilled labor at the last minute. The Canyon Ranch kitchen is run with seven workers in

173

the morning and five at night to feed a hundred guests three times a day. One restaurant kitchen I visited in Paris had a staff of thirteen for forty guests.

I gained at least one piece of nutritional information at Canyon Ranch that was worth taking home, and it may well change my life: *Your metabolic rate is directly related to the amount of lean muscle mass in your body.* Doesn't this mean, I asked young Dr. Robert Heffron, that if I follow a program of weight lifting, I will be able to eat more? Heffron is one of the ranch's great human assets—up-to-date in both traditional and alternative medicine, open-minded and undoctrinaire, skeptical toward the Food Police and their current edicts. He found my theory unusual but grudgingly agreed. Aerobics may be good for your heart, but weight lifters use up more calories all day long, even in their sleep.

I hurried over to Gym 4 for a consultation with a weight lifter named Richard, who burns 2,600 calories before he gets out of bed in the morning. My goal is not to look like Arnold Schwarzenegger, I explained, much to Richard's relief. He taught me a series of home exercises with dumbbells and barbells and a padded bench. Now all I have to do is go out and buy a set of sixteen weights ranging from two to thirty pounds each. I am confident they will change my life once I have figured out how to carry them home.

Pumping up, purifying, and pampering, strengthening and slimming (I lost four pounds), and just plain thinking about your body for sixteen hours a day are inebriating experiences, and Canyon Ranch is a terrific place to do them all. The Berkshires are a land of calm and beauty, and after five more days there, I might even have believed that Yogurt Carob Parfait, the most comical dessert at Canyon Ranch, was really a hot-fudge sundae.

February 1990

PART THREE

Stirring
Things
Up

Salad the Silent Killer

I love salad, eaten in moderation like bacon or chocolate, about twice a week. Adults who require a salad at every meal are like obsessed little children who will eat nothing but frozen pizza or canned ravioli for months on end. They tuck into the dreariest salad simply because it is raw and green. No matter that the arugula is edged with brown, the croutons taste rancid, the vinegar burns like battery acid. No matter that it is the dead of winter when salad chills us to the marrow and we should be eating preserved meats and hearty roots, garbures, and cassoulets. No matter that they are keeping me from my dessert. They think nothing of interrupting a perfectly nice meal with their superstitious salad ritual—heads bowed, snouts brought close to their plastic woodgrained bowls, crunching and shoveling simultaneously—their power of conversation lost.

Salad gluttons, defined as people who eat salad more than twice a week in winter or four times a week in summer, are insidiously programmed with three related beliefs: first, that all foods are either poisons, which make you fat and feeble, or medicines, which make you sleek and lovely; second, that raw vegetables, including salad and crudités, fall into the medicine category; and third, that the plant kingdom has been put there by some benign force for man's pleasure and well-being. All three beliefs are toxic delusions. I have spent weeks combing the scientific journals for data on the poisons that lurk in every bowl of salad and every basket of crudités. My quarry was not the artificial man-made pesticides, fungicides, herbicides, and hormones that hog the headlines of our daily newspapers. I was after the true perils—the fresh and natural poisons that plants manufacture to stay alive and perpetuate their species, just as a cobra uses its venom. Having completed my research, I can confidently predict that by the end of this century the surgeon general of the United States will require the following warning label on every spear of broccoli and every leaf of spinach: "Excess Consumption of Salad Ingredients Can Cause Vitamin Deficiency, Bad Skin, Lathyrism, Anemia, and, Quite Frankly, Death."

Imagine that you are a juicy and attractive vegetable. All around you are predators—germs and fungi, bugs and snails, birds and animals—who see you as nothing more than their next meal. You have no house to hide in, no feet for running away, no money with which to buy a gun. It's a real jungle out there, and even the neighboring vegetables covet your place in the sun. What do you do? You pull yourself together and evolve a complex system of chemical warfare.

Like the walnut and eucalyptus trees, you can secrete a growth inhibitor through your leaves that the rain will wash down into the soil to keep your neighbors at a safe distance, or you can secrete it directly through your roots as apple trees and wheat do. If you lack subtlety, imitate poison ivy and produce an oil so noxious that human predators will teach their children to avoid you like the plague. If you approve of contraception, concoct a brew of juvabiones to delay the reproduction of insects that bite you, or ecdysones to accelerate their growth right past the childbearing years. If you excel in Byzantine plots as the snakeroot does, you might consider tainting the milk of cows that forage on you so that Abraham Lincoln's mother will die when she drinks it. Think of the publicity.

So much for the benignity of the plant kingdom. Generally speaking, there are four categories of chemical weaponry that salad deploys against its human predators: nutrition blockers, toxins, mutagens (which alter genetic material), and carcinogens.

Nutrition blockers are the most delicious of the four, morally delicious, that is, because they rob salad gluttons of the one excuse for their obsessive behavior—the belief that salad is good for you. Nutrition blockers are chemicals that bind with some desirable vitamin or mineral and prevent your intestines from absorbing it. My favorite is the oxalic acid in raw spinach, a vegetable exalted for its high content of calcium and iron. Oxalic acid, it seems, forms an insoluble complex with calcium and iron—not only the calcium and iron in the spinach itself but other sources of them as well—and renders uncooked spinach a nonnutritious green. Lots of oxalates are also found in raw beet greens, Swiss chard, and rhubarb. (But rest assured that the recorded cases of death following the eating of raw rhubarb were probably due to toxic anthraquinone glycosides.)

Raw red cabbage, brussels sprouts, and beets contain an antivitamin that binds with the B vitamin thiamine and stops its absorption. Similar antithiamine substances are also found in mustard seeds, some berries, cottonseed (the oil of which finds its way into the cheaper salad dressings), and some ferns (fiddlehead fans take note). The raw egg in a Caesar salad contains avidin, which binds up the B vitamin called biotin in much the same way. Magnesium, zinc, and copper get the same binding treatment from phytates in uncooked grain protein, which includes the wheat germ that some folks sprinkle on their salads. Raw soybeans contain antagonists to vitamin B_{12} and vitamin D and can cause rickets. And a vitamin E blocker in raw kidney beans, alfalfa, and some peas increases the incidence of liver disease in animals. But at least they won't suffer from an *excess* of vitamin E, which blocks the conversion of beta-carotene into vitamin A.

One of the most offensive phrases used by nutrition buffs is "empty calories," applied to such culinary triumphs as the frozen Milky Way bar. I, for one, would rather eat an empty calorie than a toxic one. And what could be emptier than a bowl of bound and blocked raw spinach, cabbage, or peas?

As you might expect, raw vegetables that would otherwise be alluring as rich sources of protein or starch may be equally rich in

1990:
The Bar-and-Grilling
of Gotham

Wood-oven pizzas and grilled everything are now pandemic. Some call it bistromania, but it has nothing to do with bistros. A bistro is not an expensive hamburger-and-chicken joint with shoestring potatoes, red-pepper puree, and five French words on the menu. A bistro is not a bar and grill. (In New York, a bar and grill is not a bar and grill. The Gotham Bar and Grill, for example, is no more a bar and grill than I am.) If there are fewer than, say, fifty true and honest bistros in Paris, how many would you expect to find in New York? Five? The real mania since 1985 has been trattoriamania, the proliferation of informal Italian-style restaurants specializing in pasta, pizza, salads, and postmodern decor. (Nationally, over the past five years the number of Italian restaurants has grown 50 percent, more than any other category.)

"Bistromania" was always just a muddled slogan. What's really happening now is the Grilling of Gotham. In 1989, according to the National Restaurant Association, *nearly half of all restaurant entrées nationwide were broiled, charbroiled, or grilled.* Frying, the favorite cooking method five years ago, has been demoted to a weak second. Simmering, poaching, baking, braising, boiling, steaming, and roasting—every one of these classical cooking techniques is now history. New York, for over a century the great

center of cosmopolitan cuisine, has finally succumbed to the suburbanization of the kitchen. This
is the food of the fifties, of the Eisenhower years, of
the nuclear family and the single-family house, of
Dads grilling steaks and chickens in backyard
America on Moms' well-deserved day off. It is a
democratic kind of cooking that needs no professional training, teeny amounts of hand-eye coordi-
nation, a few moments of *mise-en-place,* even less
time upon the flames. The little booklet that came
with the grill tells you how to do it. Just don a silly,
floppy grease-stained toque and pour a can of
kerosene over a pile of charcoal briquettes. Everything tastes terrifically the same—the acrid tang of
burning fat and blackened muscle fiber, the haunt-
ing scent of the gas station.

Now fish has been added to the grill and sometimes vegetables; potato chips have grown into pancakes, shoestrings, and hash browns. That's how far
we have come in thirty years.

September 1990

defensive chemicals that render the protein or starch indigestible. Protease inhibitors in raw turnips, rutabagas, chickpeas, bamboo sprouts, cashews, peanuts, and most beans counteract the enzymes in our bodies that digest protein. In a similar fashion, amylase inhibitors in raw red kidney beans and navy beans make their carbohydrate content unusable.

The careful reader will notice that each of these salad ingredients acts as an antinutrient only in its raw state. Like some of the toxins we'll come to later, antinutrients are destroyed by proper cooking. Boiling water dissolves or dilutes chemicals that are soluble in water; high heat denatures many proteins, including most nutrition blockers and some toxins; other toxins quickly oxidize into harmless compounds at high temperatures. It is important to know the right method, temperature, and cooking time for each perilous vegetable. Consult your old wives' tales for further instructions.

This year we celebrate the forty thousandth anniversary of the miracle of cooking. Current anthropological thought suggests that modern *Homo sapiens* rapidly displaced the Neanderthals in Europe because *Homo sapiens* could cook and Neanderthals could not. We have seen that most protein-rich vegetables—grains and beans particularly—require cooking to become nutritious. *Homo sapiens* were able to gain a new and stable supply of protein by disabling the nutrition blockers and toxins in raw vegetables and thus achieved a crucial advantage in the battle for survival. The way I see it, Neanderthals, with their flat receding foreheads and bad posture, continued to eat salad and crudité until they died out, which is why we call them Neanderthals, which means crude and stupid people, and also why we use the term for people who still eat the way Neanderthals did. I cannot say whether they preferred Thousand Island or Green Goddess, but then again, anthropology is not my field.

Vitamin and mineral blockers merely hoodwink people who believe that salad is good for them. Much more sinister are the toxins in raw vegetables, which can make them very ill. Some of these are destroyed by cooking, and some are not. As you would expect, vegetables that have been bruised or attacked by mold or fungus manufacture these poisons many times more enthusiastically than healthy ones.

The earliest published description of poisoning by lima bean is from 1884 in Mauritius. Seven deaths were reported in Puerto Rico between 1919 and 1925 from the ingestion of undercooked beans. Lima and other broad beans contain high concentrations of cyanogens, which poison just like the cyanide in those death-row-on-Alcatraz movies. (Cyanide pellets attached to the underside of the prisoner's chair are released by remote control into a pan of acid below. The lethal gas curls up toward her nose and mouth.) Cyanogens are also found in unripe millet, young bamboo shoots, and cassava (see also manioc, tapioca, and so forth), the starchy root that supplies 10 percent of the world's caloric requirements and still turns up in the Nigerian newspapers as a cause of death. Cassava is unlikely to turn up in your salad, but immature bamboo shoots probably will. Both must be carefully peeled, washed in running (not still) water, and boiled without a lid to prevent the cyanide from condensing back into the pot.

Goitrogens are chemicals that cause extreme enlargement of the thyroid among people with little iodine in their diets by preventing iodine uptake. Goitrogens are found in raw cabbage, broccoli, brussels sprouts, kale, turnips, rutabagas, cauliflower, mustard seeds, and horseradish, and contribute to their characteristic flavors. Some studies blame high cabbage consumption in the Midwest among German and Eastern European immigrants and their families for the high incidence of goiter there. Cows that forage on marrow-stem kale in parts of Tasmania transmit goitrogens through their milk, which accounts for endemic goiter in the population. Goitrogens are largely broken down by cooking.

One reason to travel to France and Italy is that they don't force salad on you with the napkins, the silverware, and the incantation "French, Italian, or oil and vinegar?" When you request a salad, it is not thrown together by the dishwasher between his more demanding tasks. It is treated as food, not fodder. It is thoughtfully composed, animated with duck or smoked fish or foie gras, and often served as a first course. Consequently, it does not delay dessert. On the other hand, France and Italy are the source of the current culinary love affair with foods like fava beans, chickpeas, and plantains—all native to exotic lands where life after forty is not an everyday thing.

Favism is a disease named after the fava bean, or vice versa. This darling of the nouvelle cuisine may well turn up raw in your salad. Mild cases of favism result in fatigue and nausea, acute cases in jaundice. The mathematician and cult figure Pythagoras, who was nobody's fool, forbade his followers to eat fava beans. The Iranians never listened to him, and a recent survey of 579 cases of favism there blamed the broad bean for all but four. The good news is that favism attacks mainly people who have something called G6PD genetic deficiency and eat huge quantities of raw favas. The bad news is that G6PD deficiency shows up in a hundred million people of all races worldwide.

Both the ancient Hindus and the great Hippocrates warned that chickpeas could cause lathyrism—neurological lesions of the spinal cord which result in paralysis of the legs. The sale of chickpeas is illegal in many states in India, where they would otherwise completely dominate the diet of the poor, who make chapati out of chickpea flour, which is ground from raw chickpeas. If you soak chickpeas overnight or cook them in an excess of boiling water, they will not give you lathyrism. But don't try to make chapati this way. As for plantains, eat them in moderation. Africans who ignore this injunction ingest too much serotonin and end up with carcinoid heart disease, apparently whether they cook their plantains or not.

Nor will cooking protect you if you make your potato salad with green immature potatoes, which can contain *lethal* amounts of solanine in their sprouts and skin. Undercooked kidney beans in those popular al dente mixed-bean salads contain hemagglutinins, which make your red blood cells stick together and account for poor growth among children in parts of Africa. Monkeys placed on a diet of alfalfa sprouts develop lupuslike symptoms. Soybean sprouts and yams are high in estrogenic factors, which can wreak havoc with a woman's hormones if she consumes too much of them or if the plants have been attacked by mold. Purple mint, popular as a condiment in Japan and now widely available in the United States, causes acute pulmonary emphysema in cattle foraging on it. Better stick with reliable old garden-variety green mint.

The list is endless. But the government virtually ignores these and other natural poisons in your salad bowl while worrying itself to death about artificial food additives and industrial pollutants. Unmasking this double standard—particularly concerning carcinogens and mutagens—has become something of a mission for Professor Bruce Ames, chairman of the biochemistry department at Berkeley. Ames likes to describe the carcinogenic potential in an average serving of some everyday food by comparing it to the polluted well water in Silicon Valley in California, which has been condemned as carcinogenic by the state Department of Health Services. Aflatoxin, for example, is among the most potent carcinogens known and is present in mold-contaminated grain and nuts, like those peanuts you sprinkle on your salad or enjoy in peanut butter. The FDA permits so much aflatoxin in food that the peanut butter in your sandwich can be seventy-five times more hazardous than a liter of contaminated Silicon Valley water, the amount you would drink in a day if they would only let you.

Almost as hazardous are the hydrazines in one raw mushroom or the basil in a dollop of pesto sauce (which contains lots of estragole). Safrole, a compound related to estragole, is the reason natural root beer is now banned by the FDA. Much worse than Silicon Valley water and almost as bad as basil is the daily spoonful of brown mustard in your piquant salad dressing. The psoralens in celery (which increase a hundredfold if the celery is moldy) regularly cause dermatitis among supermarket checkers.

Healthy celery in your salad does no harm, but can you be absolutely sure your celery is healthy? Some investigators warn that psoralens are so carcinogenic that all "unnecessary exposures should be avoided."

I should mention that Professor Ames himself seems to have nothing personal against salad. (He even speculates about the anticarcinogenic potential of some vegetables.) But great minds sometimes fail to see the full implication of their own work. This task falls upon the shoulders of those who follow. Salad fanatics may notice that I have presented no evidence against raw zucchini or carrots. The reason is that I found none. Mother Nature could never have foreseen that zucchini—which has little taste in its raw state and even less nutritive value—would be used as a food by modern *Homo sapiens*. Then again, should we regard those who eat raw zucchini as modern *Homo sapiens?*

Raw carrots do contain the aptly named carotatoxin; when extracted from this red-orange, spindle-shaped root, carotatoxin does produce a severe neurological disorder in mice. But a human would have to eat 3,500 pounds of carrots at one sitting to consume an equivalent dose.

And what about raw fruit? Unlike the antisocial vegetable, ripe fruit is gregarious and loves to be eaten and have its seeds widely dispersed. That's why all ripe fruits generate chemicals—flavors, sugars, dyes, and softeners—to *entice* animals rather than injure them. Raw ripe sweet tasty juicy fruit was designed to give ceaseless pleasure to man and beast alike, even to Neanderthals and their modern cousins. And you never have to boil it into submission.

June 1988

Just Say Yes

Give or take a few millennia, men and women have brightened their mealtimes with a glass or two of wine, beer, or spirits for the past twenty thousand years. Civilization dawned with the cultivation of grain, the pressing of olives, and the fermentation of grapes. Yet every sixty years or so, a small band of men and women reject their evolutionary heritage and set out to eradicate alcohol in all its forms.

Today the forces of Prohibitionism again stalk the land, those cheerless folks behind the surgeon general's warning label on every bottle of alcohol, behind the call for advertising restrictions and excise taxes to force the 60 percent of us who drink moderately to pay for the sins of the 9 percent who overdo. In schools across the country defenseless little children are even taught that alcohol is one of the three "gateway drugs," as seductive as marijuana and tobacco.

But the fundamental truth is really quite simple, and it has been understood for many years: *People who drink moderate amounts of alcohol on a regular basis have far fewer heart attacks than those who do not drink at all.* And since moderate drinking carries very few risks (except on the highway), *moderate drinkers generally live longer than people who do not drink.*

Heavy drinking is extremely dangerous. The federal Centers for Disease Control (CDC), in Atlanta, lists thirty-six causes of death partly or entirely due to drinking, including automobile accidents, homicide, suicide, liver disease, cardiomyopathy, some cancers, and mental disorders. The CDC estimates that 105,095 Americans died in 1987 from alcohol use and misuse.

But seven times as many people die from heart disease, the most common cause of death in America, with 725,110 fatalities in 1988. Over two-thirds of these were cases of coronary heart disease, the closing of the blood vessels that feed the heart. And coronary heart disease (also known as ischemic heart disease and sometimes abbreviated as CHD) is precisely the ailment that moderate alcohol consumption protects us against.

The three major coronary risk factors that doctors warn about—smoking, high blood pressure, and saturated fats— explain only about half the difference in the rate of heart fatalities among various countries and various individuals. The most striking example is France, where the people eat much more butter, cheese, cream, lard, and goose fat than we do but have only one-third the heart attacks. This has become known as *le paradoxe français* (which I have explored in "Why Aren't the French Dropping Like Flies?" in Part One). But the same violation of modern nutritional rules is also common in northern Spain, northern Italy, Switzerland, and Austria—places where the low incidence of heart attacks is commemorated nightly with dinners full of saturated fat. As the French drink ten times more wine than we do (the people in Spain, Italy, Switzerland, and Austria drink nearly as much as the French), the front-running explanation for solving *le paradoxe français* is that wine (or alcohol in general) protects the heart.

In 1979 a famous study in the *Lancet* by St. Leger, Cochrane, and Moore took the statistics for coronary heart fatalities in eighteen developed countries and looked for correlations with a wide variety of factors, including the number of doctors available in each country, the dietary consumption of various fats, and the amount of wine and other alcohol drunk by the population. The strongest connection they found was with wine—France, Italy, Switzerland, and Austria showed both the highest wine consumption and the lowest rate of cardiac mortality. Total alcohol consumption was nearly as important as wine. The number of doctors in each country did not seem to matter.

But geographic comparisons like these can only suggest a connection, not prove one. The first clinical evidence came early in this century from pathologists who noticed that the arteries of deceased alcoholics were remarkably clean. More recent angiogram examinations of live alcoholics are in close agreement. Alcoholics should take no consolation, of course, because any of the CDC's thirty-six other afflictions, including noncoronary diseases of the heart, is likely to get them early in life.

The most powerful demonstration of alcohol's protective effects comes from what are called prospective studies. Researchers enroll a large group of people; take extensive information about their medical history, smoking habits, diet, alcohol intake, exercise, and every blood component you can think of; and watch them closely for ten or fifteen years.

The first prospective study of alcohol consumption and its effect on heart disease was conducted in Baltimore in the 1920s; the past two decades have seen a blizzard of them. And nearly every study has found that moderate drinkers suffer far fewer heart attacks—between 21 and 60 percent fewer—than people who do not drink at all. In most, moderate drinkers live longer than either nondrinkers or heavy drinkers.

The consistency of these studies is remarkable—with similar outcomes in Chicago and Albany, in Yugoslavia and Puerto Rico, in Finland and New Zealand and Framingham, Massachusetts, among Japanese men living in Hawaii and Japanese physicians living in Japan, among West Australians, Trinidadians, and British civil servants, among 276,802 men followed for twelve years by the American Cancer Society, among 87,526 women nurses and 51,529 male health professionals in separate studies at Harvard, and among 123,840 patients at the Kaiser Permanente medical centers in the Bay Area. Only one study, in Alameda County, California, failed to find that moderate alcohol consumption protects the heart.

Summing up the results, Walter Willett, M.D., chairman of the Department of Nutrition at the Harvard School of Public Health, wrote in the *New England Journal of Medicine* in January 1991: "At present, the only dietary factor consistently associated with the risk of coronary heart disease in epidemiologic studies is alcohol, which apparently exerts [a] powerful protective effect."

Several prospective studies found that the more you drink, even to the point of perpetual drunkenness, the lower your chances of becoming a coronary fatality. But in most, the benefits of alcohol follow what now has become the famous U-shaped curve. The odds of suffering a heart attack drop as you take one to three drinks a day, then begin to increase and come up to the starting point somewhere around four or five—which means that people who never drink have about the same chance of suffering a heart attack as those who take four or five drinks a day. At the bottom of the U-shaped curve, moderate drinkers have a much lower risk than either group.

The protective effects of moderate drinking—on coronary disease, stroke, and overall mortality—are even more impressive for women than for men. But women are also more sensitive to a given dose of alcohol. The reasons are that, on average, women weigh less; their bodies have a higher proportion of fat (also known as curves), and this can increase blood levels of alcohol because fat contains fewer blood vessels and less blood than other tissues; and, most important, women have smaller amounts of a gastric enzyme that breaks down alcohol before it enters the bloodstream. If a moderate dose of alcohol for men is two or three drinks a day, then for women moderate drinking means one or one and a half.

The antialcohol forces found it easy to challenge the earliest prospective studies, which typically failed to disentangle the effects of smoking, preexisting heart disease, diet, exercise habits, age, and gender from the effects of alcohol. What if moderate drinkers in America are also more health conscious than non-drinkers, take more exercise, eat less fat, or do not smoke? Most studies conducted after the mid-1970s made statistical adjustments for these baseline risk factors, and the correlation between moderate drinking and lower levels of coronary disease grew even stronger. This outcome should have been obvious from the start—if alcohol were not protective, drinkers would have *more* heart attacks than nondrinkers because drinkers also tend to smoke and to eat fat. So the neo-Prohibitionists were dealt a double blow: many evils that were once blamed on alcohol are, it was discovered, really connected with cigarette smoking.

In the mid-1980s, the antialcohol forces readied their final (one hopes) onslaught against the overwhelming weight of research. What if, they asked, people who never drink are unusual? What if some of the nondrinkers had quit drinking (or never started) for a good reason, such as a long family history of premature coronary disease or their own ill health? These unhealthy nondrinkers would drag down the odds for the entire population of nondrinkers and misleadingly make moderate drinkers look good.

For two or three years, the pro-alcohol camp was thrown into disarray. Some medical journals and newsletters—most already exceedingly uncomfortable with the notion that alcohol protects the heart—announced that the U-shaped curve was a myth. But soon enough, myth again became reality. The four largest prospective studies, all completed after 1987, were careful to separate unhealthy (or high-risk) former drinkers from the population of teetotalers, leaving healthy lifelong nondrinkers. And again, moderate drinkers had the fewest heart attacks. The U-shaped curve was intact.

The facts now seem airtight. The spiraling costs of American health care could be reduced by at least a few dollars a year if researchers no longer felt the need to investigate the issue. Then we could move on to the more interesting questions. Why does alcohol have this protective effect? Is wine better for you than spirits? And what should you do about it?

Remember a few years ago when we learned that cholesterol comes in two types, one good and one bad? HDLs, or high-density lipoproteins, are the good kind of cholesterol because they lift fatty deposits from the inner walls of your arteries, where they would otherwise cause you untold grief, and carry them to your liver for disposal. (LDLs, or low-density lipoproteins, are the bad kind because they deposit fat there in the first place.) In numerous studies, high levels of HDLs in the bloodstream have been associated with a reduced risk of coronary heart disease. Aerobic exercise increases your HDLs. There is general agreement that alcohol does, too.

But now we learn that HDLs come in at least three (and maybe more) types, or subfractions. The neo-Prohibitionists had been arguing for years that drinking increases only HDL type 3 in our bloodstreams, which performs none of the useful work on the arteries that HDL type 2 does. (The other HDLs are apparently irrelevant to this debate.) Now, to the good fortune of moderate drinkers, several recent studies have shown that alcohol raises the level of both HDL-2 and HDL-3—about 17 percent each. And, in any case, HDL-3 now seems far less lazy than people had once thought.

Just as HDLs were the trendy blood component of the 1980s, something called apolipoproteins will surely become the blood buzzword of the nineties. The latest research tentatively demonstrates that the level of certain apolipoproteins in your bloodstream predicts your chances of having a heart attack even more accurately than the HDLs do. Moderate drinkers can raise their glasses again: alcohol increases the best kind of apolipoprotein, known as apo A-1, just as effectively as it increases the level of HDLs.

The second way that alcohol protects the heart involves the tendency of the platelets in your blood to clump together and form clots, especially around areas on your arteries' inner walls that have already been damaged by fatty plaque deposits. As very small amounts of alcohol do not raise a drinker's HDLs but do affect blood clotting, this seems a likely explanation for the protective effects of very light drinking. Both alcohol and aspirin diminish the tendency of these clots to form, which is why doctors regularly recommend that their older patients take an aspirin every other day. The formation of a blood clot involves a complicated series of steps, and nobody has figured out exactly where aspirin or alcohol intervenes in the process, whether they work in the same way or enhance each other's protective effect. Enough research has been done to suggest that each may reduce clotting in its own way.

Contrary to recent publicity, red wine does not appear to be significantly more or less protective than hard liquor. Few large prospective studies have found a significant difference either way, though wine seems to have a slight edge in some. The effects of wine and hard liquor on HDLs and on blood clotting appear identical; beer usually comes in last in studies that have measured its effects.

Serge Renaud of INSERM (the French equivalent of NIH, our National Institutes of Health), in Lyons, told me that any advantage wine-drinking countries have in the coronary sweepstakes probably comes from the fact that wine is usually drunk slowly with meals and not hastily, with a handful of pretzels, in some dimly lit bar; food slows the absorption of alcohol into the bloodstream, which may, according to a paper Renaud is about to publish, be ideal for decreasing the tendency of the blood to clot. Binge drinking may work just as well as slow drinking on your HDLs, but not on your platelets. Renaud might also have added that wine-drinking countries generally show the highest consumption of alcohol.

Research continues on chemical compounds found in the skins of wine grapes that may find their way into red wine but not into white, which is made without the skins. Resveratrol is produced by grapes and other plants to ward off fungal infections and has been reported in Japanese research to lower cholesterol in rats; a paper on resveratrol by two fruit scientists at Cornell will be published by the time you read this. Another treasure in the skins of vine grapes (and yellow onions) is quercetin, which has powerful antitumor and anticlotting effects in the laboratory. But it will be years before researchers figure out how much of either substance actually enters our bloodstreams after we drink red wine and what effect they may have in our bodies.

Now that you know more about why alcohol protects the heart, how will this change your life? In the course of poring over hundreds of papers and abstracts, I became increasingly convinced that doctors who refuse to recommend a drink or two a day should be liable for medical malpractice and that the surgeon general, with her completely one-sided warning label, should be censured.

Now I'm not so sure, except about the surgeon general. Most health officials feel that publicizing the positive effects of alcohol would do more harm than good because of the dangers of both heavy drinking and alcoholism. As one doctor wrote, "Our inability to recommend [alcohol] is attributable not to the properties of alcohol but to the properties of human nature." But saving a handful of potential alcoholics may be heavily outweighed by the coronary benefits of sanctioned drinking.

Three groups should be careful about even moderate drinking: anybody who is about to drive an automobile, people who have had an alcohol problem (or even a family history of alcoholism), and some women.

Women at high risk for breast cancer should be especially careful; this includes women with a family history of early breast cancer and those who did not have children before the age of thirty. Only 4 percent of women die of breast cancer (compared with 38 percent for heart disease and 10 percent for stroke). And there is no evidence that *occasional* drinking (one to three drinks a week) raises the risk of breast cancer. But breast cancer does strike in the prime of life, while heart disease threatens women mainly after menopause.

Pregnant women should also be cautious, given the effects of alcohol on the fetus. But almost nothing is known about the effects of light alcohol intake during pregnancy. Most research has been done with severely alcoholic women; an occasional drink does not appear to be a problem.

People who have stopped taking one or two drinks a day because they believed that alcohol was hazardous to their health, and particularly bad for their hearts, can certainly resume, especially if it brings them pleasure. Anybody like me who currently averages one or two drinks a day should feel elated and smug. And if you don't drink now but don't know why, you might begin by taking a few sips of good red wine or old malt Scotch. A little alcohol now and then has always made the world a more endurable place.

April 1009

Salt

The Yanomamo Indians of northern Brazil have the most famous blood pressure in the world because it is the lowest. You can hardly read an article about blood pressure these days that doesn't drag in the Yanomamo Indians of northern Brazil. I am amazed that the Yanomami can stay so calm surrounded by giant bugs, snakes, and investigators forever taking their blood pressure, which at last report averaged an amazingly low 95 over 61. The average blood pressure in the United States is 120 over 80—halfway between the Yanomami and hypertension, which is another word for high blood pressure and starts at 140 over 90. A fifth of all Americans are hypertensive, but none of the Yanomami are. This is lucky for the Yanomami because high blood pressure multiplies your chances of having a heart attack, kidney disease, or a stroke.

The Yanomami eat incredibly tiny amounts of salt, and we eat lots of it, which has led some doctors to imagine that eating salt causes hypertension. The Yanomami consume about 87 milligrams of salt a day, which occurs naturally in their food and equals two shakes from a standard saltshaker. This minuscule amount, among the lowest in the world, is explained by the Yanomami's isolation from commerce, the briny sea, and mineral salt deposits. Americans eat 12,000 milligrams of salt a day, about 266 shakes, most of it added in cooking and processing.

(The weight of an average shake has, to my knowledge, never before been investigated. To compute it, I loaded my salt-shaker with 15 grams of salt, counted 330 shakes before it was empty, did it again for accuracy's sake, reached the same result, divided 330 shakes into 15 grams and arrived at 45 milligrams per shake.)

Does eating salt cause high blood pressure? Mankind has a great deal riding on this question, because—no matter what some people may tell you—salt is indispensable to good food and good cooking. It sharpens and defines the inherent flavors of foods and magnifies their natural aromas. Salt unites the diverse tastes in a dish, marries the sauce with the meat, and turns the pallid sweetness of vegetables into something complex and savory. Salt also deepens the color of most fruits and vegetables and keeps cauliflower white. Salt controls the ripening of cheese and improves its texture, strengthens the gluten in bread, and can preserve meat and fish, while transforming its texture. Cooked without salt, most dishes taste dull, lifeless, and lacking in complexity; in some, flavors are unbalanced and sweetness predominates, according to Michael Bauer in a terrific article on salt in the August 30, 1989, *San Francisco Chronicle,* reporting in part on a series of blind taste tests that he and Marion Cunningham had arranged. And in a recent issue of *Cook's* magazine, a vast majority of America's leading chefs lined up behind the culinary value of salt. As Robert Farrar Capon has put it, "To undersalt deliberately in the name of dietary chic is to omit from the music of cookery the indispensable bass line over which all tastes and smells form their harmonies."

There are thirty-five low-salt cookbooks on the market today. Most of them substitute heaps of herbs, spices, garlic, and onions for salt. When you try these recipes, the food tastes mainly of herbs, spices, garlic, and onions instead of what you wanted for dinner in the first place, like a nice plump four-pound chicken rubbed with a tablespoon of poultry fat and then a teaspoon of salt and roasted at 425 degrees for ninety minutes until the skin is golden and crackling and the juices run rich with flavor. Be sure to baste every ten minutes.

We are probably the first generation since the beginning of the world to be paranoid about salt. We would all die without salt. It is the only mineral we eat straight out of the ground. Salt was venerated in primitive cultures and exchanged as money where it was scarce. Our blood and our bodies are as salty as the seas from which life emerged, which may explain cannibalism in places where salt is in short supply. The earliest roads were built to transport salt, the earliest taxes were levied on it, military campaigns were launched to secure it, and African children were sold into slavery for it. Salt gave Venice its start in the sixth century as the commercial capital of Europe, caused the French Revolution, nearly defeated Mao Tse-tung, and helped Gandhi bring India to independence.

Because we need salt to live, we are genetically programmed to crave it starting four months after we are born. Salt phobics argue that since only a fifth of a gram of salt a day—200 milligrams, or a medium-large pinch—is absolutely essential to our survival, anything more than that must surely be excessive. This reasoning is absurd. How much music or poetry a day is essential for our survival? How much sex do we absolutely need to propagate the species? How much salt must we eat to survive, and how much do we need to have a very nice day? Every human society with easy access to salt eats forty times the minimum, and the reason is simple. Salt gives us pleasure by making food taste better. Then, after dinner, our bodies eliminate the salt we don't need. That is why God gave us kidneys.

Even lowering your intake to 500 milligrams of sodium a day, about 10 percent of the American average, would involve exquisite torture. First of all, you would have to eliminate all processed foods—canned, frozen, and packaged—which account for at least a third of the salt in our diet. Canned peas or a frozen side dish of rice can contain a hundred times the salt in raw peas and rice. A cup of fresh corn has only 7 milligrams of sodium, but a cup of canned creamed corn has 671, more than your allowance of sodium for an entire day; a serving of canned soup contains one full gram of sodium, two days' supply. An ounce of cornflakes contains as much salt as the same amount of salted peanuts.

Even after you eliminate processed foods and salt added in cooking or at the table, you will still be eating double or triple your 500-milligram sodium ration. That's because many foods are inherently salty, like dairy products (an ounce of cottage cheese is saltier than a bowl of thirty potato chips), breads, spinach, celery, Swiss chard, seafood, turnips, kale, and artichokes. If you want to eat a wide range of foods, you will have to leach out the salt and most of the taste from these vegetables by boiling them in distilled water. (In some places, tap water is too salty for a 500-milligram diet.) And meat is considerably saltier than vegetables.

If salt caused high blood pressure, the average American would be hypertensive, which is not the case. I eat all the salt I want, much more than the Yanomami do, and my blood pressure is slightly below normal. My wife's is even lower—not much different from the Yanomami—and she eats what I do because I do all the cooking. American vegetarians generally have lower blood pressure than American carnivores, yet both take in about the same amount of salt.

The Yanomami differ from Americans in many ways besides salt. They are very skinny, they drink absolutely no alcohol, they are geographically isolated and therefore genetically distinct, and they get lots of exercise under the lush leafy canopy of their Brazilian rain forest, where automobiles are extremely scarce. The Solomon Islanders used to be almost as popular among salt phobics as the Yanomami—until they were brought into the modern age and their blood pressure rose. But this was not attributable to salt. Obesity and lack of exercise were identified as the causes.

It was while contemplating the vacuous taste of an unsalted potato chip that I decided to read through the medical research about salt and hypertension from the past decade or so and find out why America's public-health establishment gets so steamed up about it. Having done so, I still can't understand what the fuss is all about. The animal studies are completely inconclusive—some animals are sensitive to salt; others are resistant; some get high blood pressure when they are stressed; others do not. One research group managed to raise the blood pressure of healthy laboratory rats only by feeding them an 8-percent-salt diet, the equivalent of two cups a day for you and me. Clinical studies with human beings have never shown that salt can cause hypertension in healthy people. At worst, salt can exacerbate hypertension in some of those already afflicted with it.

200   Nineteen eighty-eight was the year of the great salt showdown, the massive and rigorous Intersalt study. Fifty-two centers were established in thirty-two countries around the world, from Argentina to Zimbabwe (the Yanomami were included, of course, along with three other isolated Stone Age peoples), and 10,079 subjects in all were tested. Each was measured for a small number of variables: blood pressure, sodium and potassium excretion (which in healthy people is an accurate measure of sodium and potassium intake), age, alcohol use, height, and weight. All urine samples were flown to a central lab in Belgium; some samples were split in two and tested separately, and the results were compared to gauge the lab's consistency. All measurements were sent to London, entered twice into a computer, and the double entries compared to ensure accuracy. Never before has such care been taken in a blood pressure study of this size and geographic scope. Funding came from the World Health Organization, heart associations around the world, the U.S. government, and a British foundation.

The results were extremely distressing to those who had hoped to prove a link, once and for all, between salt and blood pressure. The four hunter-gatherer cultures did show extremely low salt excretion and extremely low blood pressure. But the researchers could find no significant link in the rest of the world between salt and hypertension.

The Yanomami eat bananas and starchy roots all day; you need to go to such extremes to lower your blood pressure through diet. Nearly everybody in the modern world eats between 2 and 5 grams of sodium a day (1 to 2½ teaspoons of salt). Tinkering with your salt intake in this range will not affect your blood pressure. As the Harvard Medical School *Health Letter* concluded about the Intersalt study: "It seems unlikely that salt intake is a major influence on the development of hypertension in most of the world's populations."

Obesity and alcohol intake are strongly associated with high blood pressure; you can do yourself a great favor by losing weight and drinking less if blood pressure is a problem. And Intersalt did show that the more salt people eat, on average, the more likely it is that their blood pressure will increase as they grow older. But the numbers are unimpressive. If everybody in America slashed his or her salt consumption from eight grams a day to two, the average blood pressure would go down by only 2 percent.

Some people are extremely sensitive to salt; their blood pressure goes way up when they eat it and down when they don't. Of the 20 percent of Americans who develop hypertension, about one-third of them are salt sensitive—about 8 percent of the population. They should avoid it, as should people with congestive heart failure, liver disease, or kidney disease. If you have high blood pressure, you probably know it already; ask your doctor to help you find out whether you are salt sensitive.

But the other 92 percent of us can handle just about all the salt we feel like eating. Why public-health officials would want the entire population to act as if we were allergic to salt is beyond me, especially since nobody has ever been able to demonstrate that moderate salt restriction makes much of a difference to anyone. It's like making everybody wear eyeglasses just because a few of us need them. Yet that's what most government health authorities urge. They never bother to calculate the profound benefits that scrumptious food can bring to our otherwise desperate lives. In a thousand-plus pages of federal nutrition reports I was unable to locate any instance of the words "delicious," "delectable," "savory," or "yummy." And the committees writing the reports did not include one noted chef, even though they are devoted to telling America, in the most heartbreaking detail, how we should eat.

The Yanomami may win popularity contests in the blood pressure industry, but they really have nothing to tell us about how to live. Their hormone systems are in a constant and unusual state of alertness against the loss of any sodium at all, almost as though their condition were an illness; injury and bleeding can be disastrous for them. And you would be appalled to read anthropologists' accounts of how the Yanomami behave when they're not having their blood pressure taken: almost half of all Yanomamo men have killed somebody, and a third of Yanomamo deaths are the result of violence! Most of these homicides are part of an endless cycle of revenge between warring villages. Killers enjoy high social status and get many more wives than men who have not killed. (I think the Yanomami consider more wives a good thing.) All Yanomami live in constant terror of violent death. They also take psychedelic drugs.

By all accounts, the Yanomami are a bunch of bloodthirsty maniacs who make Abu Nidal look like a scoutmaster. Personally, I wouldn't be at all surprised if their tasteless behavior were due entirely to salt deficiency. I doubt that the blood pressure industry is looking into this.

Growing up in a hysterical antisalt environment, a whole generation of America's future homemakers lack the slightest notion of how to cook with it and how the various types of salt taste and behave. Here are some hints: Water for pasta should be vigorously salted before the pasta goes in (a tablespoon for each quart and four quarts of water for a pound of pasta) or the noodles themselves will taste bland no matter how well you salt the sauce. The same goes for potatoes. But dried peas and legumes should be salted at the end of their cooking; otherwise their skins will harden and split. Usually, salt added at the table becomes the dominant flavor, doesn't bind the other tastes together, and leaves you with a salty aftertaste. But sometimes you love the feeling of salt crystals against your tongue, as on pretzels, crackers, and chips.

Don't salt fried foods before you cook them or they will become soggy in the fryer, but be sure to salt them immediately before eating. Food eaten cold needs more salt in cooking than food served hot. Add salt to your salad at the very last minute or the greens will wilt; tossing coarse salt into a salad immediately before serving it (not into the dressing) will add a sparkle and a crunch.

If you feel a bit less anxious now about salt and are ready to begin exploring the wonderful world of salt, I have a terrific high-salt dish for you to try, which I discovered at a restaurant in New York's Chinatown.

Salt-and-Pepper Shrimp

The Yun Luk Rice Shoppe on Doyers Street in Chinatown was among the best Cantonese restaurants in New York ten years ago when Henry Hugh was chef, and I recently tracked Henry down to see if he would part with the recipe for his delicious shrimp. Salt is the main flavoring, and it seems to bind the sweet juices of the shrimp to the surface of the shells, where they caramelize and take on the smoke-and-iron taste of the wok. The dish uses three teaspoons of salt, about 15,000 milligrams, which is the average salt ration of a Yanomamo family of four, if they have families of four, for six weeks. (But unless you swallow all the shells, you will consume only a fraction of the salt.)

1 pound medium-large shrimp (14 to 16 per pound), shells on
1 tablespoon salt (15,000 mg)
4 cups peanut oil
2 teaspoons cornstarch
1 garlic clove, minced

1 fresh red hot pepper (an inch or two long if very hot, longer if
  mild), chopped fine without removing the seeds or internal
  membranes
1 teaspoon dry sherry
3 scallions, white part only, finely shredded

With a heavy scissors, cut all along the back of each shrimp through the shell and halfway down into the flesh; devein and rinse well under cold water, but do not remove the shell. Soak the shrimp for 10 minutes in 1 teaspoon of the salt dissolved in 1 cup of cold water. Drain and pat dry in paper towels without rinsing.

In a wok slowly bring the oil to about 400° F., just before it begins to smoke. (If you prefer, use 2 cups of oil instead of 4 and fry the shrimp in two batches.) As the oil nears this point, dust the shrimp with cornstarch through a sieve and toss to coat evenly. Fry the shrimp for 1 minute, tumbling them in the oil. Empty the contents of the wok into a large strainer set over a bowl to collect the oil.

Return ½ tablespoon of oil to the wok, heat, add the garlic and chopped pepper, cook for 10 seconds without browning, add the shrimp and the remaining 2 teaspoons of salt, toss a few times, sprinkle with the dry sherry, toss, cover for 10 seconds, uncover, toss a few more times for about 10 seconds, remove to a serving plate, and garnish with the scallions. Eat the shrimp with your fingers or with chopsticks, sucking the burnished salt and juices from the shells before discarding them. Or you can eat the shells too. Serves 2 as a main course or 4 as an appetizer.

August 1990

Pain Without Gain

Last night I played the neatest trick on my wife. I grilled a slice of my best homemade French country bread, spread it thick with Promise Ultra Fat-Free nonfat margarine, set it on the counter, sat back, and waited. Soon the toasty aroma drew my wife into the kitchen. Seeing the bread, she smiled broadly and took a bite. I'll never forget the way her smile froze, as she gagged, stumbled over to the kitchen sink, and gave up her mouthful of bread covered with Promise Ultra Fat-Free nonfat margarine. What fun we have together!

I learned about Promise Ultra Fat-Free nonfat margarine—which is made from water, vegetable mono- and diglycerides, gelatin, salt, rice starch, and lactose, plus a bouquet of chemicals and artificial flavors—from *Butter Busters* (Warner Books), an extremely popular low-fat cookbook. I have been living with low-fat cookbooks for the past month or so—not because it makes any medical sense, as I will explain, but because the low-fat cookbook business has become a bloated and distended juggernaut that threatens to crush everything else on the market. Susan Arnold of Waldenbooks kindly sent me a printout of their best-selling cookbooks, and there, proudly occupying first and second place, were *In the Kitchen with Rosie* (Knopf) and *Butter Busters*. Rosie's book has just gone into its thirty-second printing in eight months, bringing its grand total to 5.8 million copies in print and making it not only the number one best-seller of 1994 in all book categories but also the fastest-selling book since Gutenberg may or may not have invented movable type. *Butter Busters*, with well over a million copies in print, has nothing to be shy about either. And Susan Powter's completely incoherent *Food* (Simon & Schuster) soared onto the best-seller list immediately upon publication.

Most low-fat cookbooks contain long self-congratulatory passages claiming that the author's revolutionary new way of cooking actually tastes better than real food. This is only rarely true. Sure, many traditional dishes should have been lightened years ago. But the vast majority of low-fat and nonfat makeovers sacrifice at least something in texture, taste, and satisfaction. That is indisputable. The key questions are: What do you give up for what advantage? What do you gain for how much pain? *Butter Busters*, America's second most popular cookbook, gives up more than a bit of taste and texture. It gives up food itself.

It could have been called *How to Shop for and Throw Together the Trashiest Food on Your Supermarket Shelves into a Low-Fat, Low-Sodium, and Low-Sugar Imitation of High-Fat Junk Food* (Warner Books). Pam Mycoskie, who wrote and published the book all by herself in 1992 and then sold it to Warner Books in 1994, leaves nothing to chance. Forty pages are taken up by a shopping guide to the many artificial, chemical-laden, low-fat supermarket ingredients demanded by her recipes. (The guide is divided up according to which stores in the vicinity of Arlington, Texas—her hometown—carry which brands. As this information is of passing interest to most Americans, Warner Books must have been in a great hurry to reach a public voracious for junk food, or was loath, for scholarly reasons, to tamper with the original manuscript.) Pam's picks include Butter Buds, Egg Beaters, Egg Mates, Better'N Eggs, Pillsbury Lovin' Lites cake mixes and frostings, Old El Paso fat-free refried beans (doesn't "*refried*" mean anything anymore?), ENER-G egg replacer, Texas B-B-Q Seasoned chicken strips, Peter Eckrich Deli "Lite" roast beef slices, Sea Pak Cooked

Artificial Crab, Auburn Farms fat-free toaster pastries, and nonfat cheeses from Alpine Lace, Borden, Kraft, Polly-O, and Healthy Choice. There must be a law against calling them cheese. Have you ever tasted this stuff?

With these and other ingredients you can make Sloppy Joe Casserole, Mashed Potato Shell Taco Pie, and Pam's Sweet Trash. Her Pineapple Salad Surprise contains ketchup, fat-free Miracle Whip, lobster tails, and Cointreau. I baked Pam's Rich Fudge Brownies because the more opulent Easy Fudge Brownies on the facing page began with a box of Lovin' Lites fudge brownie mix, which I deemed a form of cheating. As it was, the Rich Fudge Brownies included Sweet 'n Low, Sweet 'n Low brown sugar substitute, Egg Beaters, our old friend Promise Ultra Fat-Free nonfat margarine, and Braum's Lite fudge topping. Finding most of these ingredients proved tricky for somebody residing so far from Arlington, Texas, and required a tour of nearly every supermarket in lower Manhattan. In the end, the brownies turned out sticky and rubbery and would have had no chocolate taste without the lite fudge topping. Even mediocre brownies have a brief half-life in my house; five days on, the pan of Pam Mycoskie's Rich Fudge Brownies sits lonely on the kitchen table, nearly intact. These brownies are infinitely shelf-and-table-stable.

I did learn a handy trick from Pam, though it is apparently common in microwave cookbooks: you can cook an entire head of cauliflower in one piece by wrapping it in plastic and microwaving on high power for just six to eight minutes. The results were perfect, ready to sauté in plenty of real olive oil with a little real garlic, not part of Pam's recipe. Her Egg Beaters Benedict was completely inedible, and her Cherry Cheesecake Delight suffered both from a crust made by crushing one and a half boxes of SnackWell's Fat-Free Cinnamon Snacks and from a thick layer of Philadelphia fat-free cream cheese, one of the gummiest affronts to the name of cheese ever concocted. Pam's Potato Pancakes are made from nearly all real food—potatoes, onions, flour, pepper— and were delectable if slightly undersalted when I fried them in olive oil. But sautéed in liquid Butter Buds as the recipe instructs, they are blotchy and grossly undercooked, lacking the fat that would evenly convey the heat to the pancake's surface, crisping them deliciously. Pam Mycoskie cannot resist fake food; her recipe for sourdough bread, which is nearly always made without a trace of fat, bafflingly includes Butter Buds.

Why would anybody in America want to humiliate, degrade, and befoul themselves by eating these dishes or any of the hundreds of fat-free packaged foods that Pam recommends to her million readers? Why did a million of us buy her book?

Because we have become mortally and irrationally afraid that eating fat will make us fat, bring on heart attacks, give us cancer. Fearful of both death and unsightly bulges, we are no longer able to distinguish right from wrong. In the ignorant grip of a national fat phobia, we recoil from the flesh of the velvet green avocado, the benign and perfumed olive, and the golden oil of the crunchy peanut as though these were the moral equivalent of the thick carpet of solid white fat surrounding a slab of beef. "A low-fat lifestyle is as important to you as stopping smoking," Pam opines. This is dangerous nonsense.

What are the facts? The medical literature, available on Medline or in the *Index Medicus* to anybody with a modem or, for that matter, a library card, is quite at odds with the 1988 recommendations of the surgeon general, where most media nutritionists and writers of low-fat cookbooks begin—and then make more extreme. One good place to start is Dr. Walter Willett's thorough review of the literature in the April 22, 1994, issue of the journal *Science;* then track down the research studies on both sides of each issue in his footnotes. But for now, here are a few specifics:

• Heart disease is not linked to the total amount of fat an individual eats. It is associated only with saturated fat, the kind derived from animals and perhaps from some tropical plants, like the coconut and the palm. This has been known for forty years.

• The heart disease rates of various countries are not linked to their total fat intake. In the famous Seven Countries study, the island of Crete showed the lowest rate of heart disease in the world, even though its diet was very high in fat, most of it olive oil. Today the countries with the lowest rates of heart disease are Japan and France. Japan has historically had a very low-fat diet, France a high-fat diet.

• National rates of heart disease are most closely linked to consumption of nonfermented dairy products and red meat. There is no link with cheese, regardless of its fat content.

• Though your blood cholesterol tends to increase as you eat more saturated fat, it actually tends to go down as you eat more unsaturated fat, the kind found in most vegetable oils.

• Not all fats classified as "saturated" will raise your cholesterol. Cocoa butter, the fat in chocolate, hardly increases your bad LDL cholesterol at all. God's in his heaven; all's right with the world.   2 0 9

• A low-fat diet can be dangerous for patients with adult-onset diabetes. A study published last May in the *Journal of the American Medical Association* showed that, contrary to the low-fat, high-carbohydrate diet then recommended by the American Diabetes Association, diabetics can better lower their level of blood sugar, triglycerides, insulin, and LDL cholesterol on a diet very high (45 percent of calories) in monounsaturated fats—olive oil, canola oil, and so on. Why anybody ever thought that non-insulin-dependent diabetics could get control of their blood sugar on a high-carbohydrate diet is a mystery to me.

• As much as 25 percent of the population is "insulin resistant," which means that they may gain weight more readily from eating carbohydrates than from eating fats.

• Consuming lots of omega-3 fatty acids (the oil in marine fish and some plants, like purslane) has been shown in some (not all) studies to reduce your risk of coronary disease. But low-fat diets restrict you to lean fish that lack omega-3.

• Countries with a low fat intake do show lower cancer rates, but the link is with animal fat and meat consumption rather than with total fat or vegetable fat.

• National rates of breast cancer increase with a higher consumption of total calories, not fat intake. (The early studies confounded the two, and then mistakenly blamed the correlation on fat.) In a recent Greek study, women who consumed olive oil more than once a day had a 25 percent lower incidence of breast cancer than women who consumed none.

• Colon cancer rates are associated in some studies with animal fat consumption, in other studies with red meat; there is no link with vegetable fat. Similar results have been found with prostate cancer. Alpha-linoleic acid—found in the fat surrounding red meat—appears to be a major culprit.

• Obesity does not seem to be related to fat intake. In a comparison of sixty-five counties in China, no link was found between the fat intake of each population and its tendency to become overweight—even though the people in some counties consumed less than 5 percent of their calories in fat. Southern European countries have a lower fat consumption than northern European countries but show higher rates of obesity.

• In a recent clinical trial at the University of Minnesota involving moderately obese women, a low-fat diet showed no significant advantage over a low-calorie diet. Though some studies claim an initial advantage to a low-fat diet, the difference typically disappears after a few weeks. Research at Rockefeller University has found no difference in the amount of weight experimental subjects gain or lose on liquid diets that are high or low in fat.

• To summarize: Saturated fat is bad for your health; the fat in red meat and unfermented dairy products is the worst. Unsaturated fats are perfectly OK. Olive oil is probably beneficial. Your body weight is unlikely to be affected by the percentage of total calories you consume in the form of fat.

If all this is true, then how did the mass frenzy of antifat paranoia begin? What keeps it going?

There is enough blame to go around. The National Research Council's compendious and influential 1989 report, *Diet and Health*, correctly targeted saturated fat in some chapters but grossly misread the medical literature in others, warning, without foundation, against total fat consumption above 30 percent of calories. The FDA's new food labels list total fat calories on line 1 and grams of fat on line 2; saturated fat and cholesterol come later. Nutritionists tell me that too much information confuses the public, and that if people lower their total fat consumption, they will automatically lower their saturated-fat intake. This may or may not be true. But asking people to restrict their diet more severely than they need to lowers the chances that they will heed your advice, reinforces the notion that deprivation and anhedonia are critical to the happy life, increases the ambient level of societal paranoia regarding both the natural and the man-made world, and propagates misinformation, which was once thought to be in itself a bad thing.

And then there are cult figures like Dr. Dean Ornish and 211 Susan Powter. Dean Ornish made his mark in the late 1980s by demonstrating, over the skepticism of many in the medical profession, that a program of smoking cessation, moderate exercise, stress reduction (including meditation), social support, and a very low-fat diet could reverse the progress of atherosclerosis and lessen the risk of coronary heart disease—without surgery or drugs. His credentials as a diet doctor are much less impressive. Ornish's very lucrative *Eat More, Weigh Less* (HarperCollins) is a low-fat, vegetarian cookbook preceded by eighty-one pages of half-truths. Since in his earlier research with heart patients he never bothered to isolate the relative benefits of diet, exercise, smoking cessation, and so forth, Ornish's own work is irrelevant to the draconian diet (10 percent fat) he prescribes. His footnotes abound with references to newspaper accounts of other people's research.

Ornish's Life Choice program "takes a new approach, one scientifically based on the type of food rather than the amount of food." This is, of course, the same "new" approach about which every one of the hundreds of low-fat cookbooks that clog the market boasts. The difference is in the fanaticism of the Ornish diet: you must avoid meats of all kinds (including fish), all oils (saturated, monounsaturated, and polyunsaturated—it doesn't matter to Ornish), avocados, olives, nuts and seeds, even low-fat dairy, alcohol, and all other products with more than two grams of fat per serving. "No matter what you may have heard," he writes, "olive oil is not good for you." I remember attending a nutrition conference with Ornish in Boston a few years ago. An expert panel was struggling with the serious and difficult question of whether olive oil really confers benefits that other vegetable oils do not. As though he had been unwilling or unable to absorb the complexities of the argument, Ornish could contribute nothing more than to sputter that olive oil *must* be harmful because it is a fat. He seems to be fixated and obsessed.

Dean Ornish's apparent unfamiliarity with the medical literature has not diminished his influence. One casualty is Sarah Schlesinger and her *500 Fat-Free Recipes* (Villard Books), a solid seller last year. Referring to Ornish and more vaguely to studies from "societies around the world," Schlesinger has become irrationally convinced that cancer and heart disease (plus acne, rashes, vertigo, and "hormonal imbalances") automatically spring from consuming "excess" fat, which she takes to mean any fat at all. She offers us this urgent advice so that we can follow her diet even on trips abroad:

> Learn the necessary phrases to express your needs. For instance, you can say "All my food must be fat-free" around the world in one of the following languages:
> Spanish: *Es necessario que mi comida no tenga grasa.*
> German: *Mein Essen darf kein Fett enthalten.*
> French: *Tout doit être préparé sans gras.*
> Italian: *Niente douvebbe essere fritto.*

Ms. Schlesinger surely deserves a refund for her Italian lessons.

If, contrary to Ornish and his polyglot epigones, there is not much to be gained from cooking the low-fat way, the corresponding pain had better be extremely minor. Absence of pain is the chief criterion I used while cooking for a month from a half-dozen low-fat cookbooks. I chose *Butter Busters* because of its popularity. But the pain one suffers from using—even just reading—this book was so excruciating that no gain, perhaps not even immortality, would make it worth cooking from. Two of the six merited serious analysis and experimentation. Martha Rose Shulman's *Provençal Light* (Bantam) struck me as one of the most attractive and authentic low-fat cookbooks available. And Alice Medrich's *Chocolate and the Art of Low-Fat Desserts* (Warner Books) is the most methodical approach to the subject of low-fat cooking, for reasons I'll explain.

What do these authors mean by low-fat cooking? The American Heart Association and the 1988 surgeon general's report both call for us to take no more than 30 percent of our calories from fat. So this seems a good cutoff. Most low-fat cookbooks aim for it.

As the average American takes in about 37 percent of his or her calories from fat, cutting down to 30 percent does not seem like a drastic step—certainly not enough to have spawned an entire new industry. Seven percent of a 2,500-calorie day works out to 175 fat calories, less than two tablespoons of olive oil or butter. Why does the world need a flood of painfully self-righteous and badly written cookbooks to teach us how to avoid two tablespoons of butter a day? One reason is that nearly all low-fat cookbooks want every dish—every appetizer, every main course, every salad, every dessert, every bite that you put into your mouth—to contain fewer than 30 percent fat calories. This is, of course, unnecessary. The objective of a low-fat diet should be to *average out* your consumption to 30 percent, or whatever your fat goal is, not to force every single dish into the same low-fat straitjacket. But that is what most low-fat cookbooks do, taking a very modest goal and making it extremely difficult and distasteful to attain.

Alice Medrich is in a much more difficult fix. Saturated fat is extremely prominent in chocolate desserts, and so is Medrich. Founder and the owner of the late Cocolat, the dessert and chocolate shop in Berkeley, California, and author of the prize-winning cookbook *Cocolat* (Warner Books), Medrich has taken the job of creating low-fat chocolate desserts extremely seriously, and in *Chocolate and the Art of Low-Fat Desserts* she has succeeded at least half the time by my count, an incredibly good score. Her goal, after all, is to create "truly indulgent," "sensational" desserts, not just desserts that are judged "not bad for low fat." Most of her creations are new, not low-fat versions of her earlier recipes. Medrich cannot help making the kind of apocalyptic and self-congratulatory comments that other low-fat authors do. "These are the new desserts of the future," she writes proudly, and refers to the research for her book as a "journey of discovery." But unlike the author of *Butter Busters,* Medrich uses only high-quality, natural ingredients and no food substitutes. She wants her desserts to taste rich, not light, and she uses fat strategically rather than replacing it.

Grease is good. Grease works. As all low-fat cooks discover, fat serves a remarkable number of purposes: it blends and softens flavors, carries them about the mouth and allows them to linger; in cooking, it conducts heat more effectively than water and allows temperatures high enough for the delicious browning reaction to occur; and it contributes to texture in obvious and less obvious ways. At first Medrich discovered that her mousses did not stiffen, frostings did not hold their peaks, pastry became soggy, and fillings would not retain moisture without "bleeding" or draining. And some flavors became oddly aggressive. Sugar grew sweeter, but eliminating sugar made for drier textures because sugar retains water. Fat holds and stabilizes flavors; low-fat desserts can become tasteless after brief storage, and any inferior ingredients in them will be exposed.

Medrich relies only sometimes on two easy and common but unpalatable solutions: replacing all chocolate (which contains 55 to 75 percent fat calories) with lower-fat cocoa and substituting egg whites for yolks. She also eliminates a good part of the fat in pastry creams and mousses, lightens her sponge cake so that she can use richer toppings, toasts nuts for more flavor and chops them finer so they will go further, and makes an exception to her general principles by including "light" cream cheese in frostings. By the time she is finished, her recipes, through a host of careful and canny compromises, range from acceptable to delicious.

This book is not simply a collection of recipes; it is a manual for the creation of low fat chocolate desserts and devotes several chapters to theory and general principles. The mixture of smooth and crunchy is fundamentally satisfying, Medrich believes. Some flavors, such as caramel, taste inherently rich, though they contain no fat. Medrich uses meringue as a substitute for some of the whipped cream in mousses and to add lightness, volume, and creaminess. But as she considers uncooked egg whites to be dangerous, she has developed a useful but tiresome procedure for pasteurizing them by raising their temperature to 160 degrees over hot water after mixing them with water, cream of tartar, and sugar. (Without these additions, they would scramble.) Occasionally, I wished that Medrich had aimed for a more varied range of sensory qualities than richness alone. Chocolate wears a hundred faces.

The proof is in the pudding, and I cooked eight or nine of them. On the rebound from my repulsive encounter with the *Butter Busters* brownies, I began with Medrich's. They were shiny to gaze upon and moist to consume, with a rich, chocolaty flavor—far superior to any of the commercially available low-fat brownies that I receive almost weekly by UPS. Only by tireless eating was I able to detect in them the flaws that mar Medrich's less perfect recipes (and that destroy the low-fat desserts of less skillful cooks): their texture was slightly rubbery rather than cakelike or gooey, the result of substituting egg whites for eggs; their taste betrayed a hint of the sharp and dusty character of cocoa; and their flavor did not last long enough in the mouth, a common problem with many low-fat foods. These imperfections were all minor in Medrich's brownies, but they suggest the dangers she continually skirts at the stove. Even more successful

2 1 5

were her Bittersweet Chocolate Marquise, a sensational frozen chocolate terrine, and a low-fat version of her well-known Chocolate Decadence (essentially a flourless chocolate cake). Less admirable were the rubbery pastry cream, the dry chocolate soufflés, the uninteresting sugar *tuiles,* and several of the sauces.

Even those of us who understand that low-fat diets are unnecessary should consider Medrich's thoughtful book. The problem is that the fat in chocolate desserts is mostly saturated, the kind found in butter and egg yolks and cream and to a lesser extent in cocoa butter, the kind that wounds, maims, and kills. Cutting back your desserts to 30 percent fat satisfies nobody's criteria if most of that fat is *saturated;* both the American Heart Association and the surgeon general limit saturated fat to 10 percent of total calories. Oddly, the nutritional data accompanying Medrich's recipes leave out numbers for saturated fat. I doubt that this was inadvertent.

Martha Rose Shulman has written several books on low-fat cooking, but *Provençal Light* may well be her best—and, along with Medrich's, the best low-fat cookbook of the past year. It is a warm and knowledgeable appreciation of southeastern France and a fine cookbook in its own right; folklore and food are charmingly intertwined in this well-designed and nicely edited book.

Shulman has lived in Provence and traveled extensively through it, and you will find versions of all your Provençal favorites here—from bouillabaisse (hers is the fabled soup from the restaurant Bacon in Cap d'Antibes) to the wonderful gratins and ragouts of the region. She does not entirely ban eggs, moistens her *brandade* with milk to eliminate some of the oil (a hazardous substitution), cleverly stretches her alternative aioli with mashed potatoes, and bakes her eggplant instead of frying it. But she leaves out bourride (another great fish soup from which she could not artfully remove the fat) and all dishes containing red meat (the region is famous for its fine lamb and often uses a little bacon for flavoring, but Shulman doesn't eat red meat), and quite unsatisfactorily makes all her tarts with phyllo dough, which has little fat in itself.

This is real food made entirely with natural ingredients. But many of Shulman's lightened recipes can be vastly improved by the addition of a little olive oil. And the only reason for leaving it out is a pathological, if remunerative, fear of fat. "Like the other cuisines of the Mediterranean, the cuisines of Provence are inherently healthy," Shulman writes in her introduction. But if this is true, then why monkey with the food?

Take Shulman's Vegetable Soup with Pistou. You boil together a bouquet of vegetables for one and a half hours; add cooked white beans and some fresh vegetables for crunch; cook for another ten minutes, ladle into bowls, and stir in a tablespoon of intensely aromatic pistou, the Provençal paste of basil, oil, garlic, and cheese. The broth itself is hardy, bland, and slightly sweet; the magnificent pistou transforms it into one of the world's great soups. Shulman's recipe is much like those in traditional Provençal cookbooks—three fine versions were published recently, one by Robert Carrier and two by Richard Olney—except that she leaves out most of the olive oil, about a tablespoon in each serving. Without this, her broth lacked flavor, the garlic was caustic, the basil harsh and minty, her beans and pasta bland—until, like the conductor of an orchestra, a good dribble of golden olive oil brought these instruments together into warm and rousing vegetable concerto. By my calculations, her Vegetable Soup with Pistou is only 12 percent fat; adding two teaspoons of olive oil to each serving would still keep her fat calories below 30 percent. Why did she leave them out?

I do have a question about Shulman's title. According to the FDA's regulations regarding packaged foods, "light" may be used on a label only when the food inside the package contains 50 percent less fat than the standard version. I think *Reduced-Fat Provençal* would be more accurate because this means 25 percent less fat than usual, a more fitting characterization of many of Shulman's recipes. Or considering that she avoids the merest trace of red meat, traditionally used as an indispensable condiment in a host of essentially vegetarian Provençal dishes, Shulman should have called it *The Pollo-Ovo-Lacto-Vegetarian Reduced-*

2 1 7

Fat Provençal Cookbook (Bantam Books). Anomalously, her nutritional analysis of each dish leaves out the percentage of calories devoted to fat. Could she have been motivated by the desire to sneak in what looks like a magnificent recipe for Rich Fish Soup, perhaps the crowning glory of the Provençal cooking of the Mediterranean coast, which in Shulman's low-fat version is a whopping 60.4 percent fat, more than you find in French fries? I can't wait to try it.

April 1995

Murder, My Sweet

According to recent surveys, more American consumers are worried about sugar than about anything else in their diets except
cholesterol.

Our national fear of refined white sugar reached a febrile
peak in 1979 and has remained on a plateau ever since. That was
the year that Dan White, on trial for shooting and killing San
Francisco Mayor George Moscone and Supervisor Harvey Milk,
was convicted of manslaughter instead of first-degree murder
after his lawyer raised the Twinkie Defense, the claim that Dan
White's brain had been so deranged by Hostess Twinkies and
other sugary junk foods that he should not be held fully responsible for his actions. Twinkies, the argument went, made him do it.

White sugar has also been blamed for heart disease, obesity,
diabetes, anemia, and hyperactivity in children. These claims
have always made me suspicious. Humans are born with only
one innate taste preference—an attraction to sweetness, to sugar.
The idea that nature designed us to be powerfully drawn to what
harms us most strikes me as perverse and godless and extremely
unlikely. So I recently tracked down the medical facts about sugar
and happily discovered that nearly every accusation is ground-
less.

Simple sugars are the building blocks of all complex carbohydrates, and all complex carbohydrates are broken down into

simple sugars in our digestive tract before being absorbed into our bloodstream. In this sense, one carbohydrate is more or less nutritionally equivalent to any other because they must all be converted to glucose, the simplest sugar of all, before we can use them. Glucose is blood sugar, the principal source of energy in the body; without it our muscles and brain have no use for pasta or candy or fruit or milk, for starch or sucrose or fructose or lactose. If it isn't glucose, it isn't food.

Every authority in nutrition, from the National Research Council to the American Heart Association, recommends that we increase our intake of carbohydrates to 55 percent of total calories—especially complex carbohydrates like starch. These are favored over simple sugars because they are usually found in foods rich in fiber, vitamins, or minerals, such as pasta, potatoes, beans, and bread. White sugar delivers nothing but calories and acute pleasure. But to consider it dangerous is another thing entirely.

The odd thing about the claim that eating sugar makes people hyperactive or even violent is that eating any carbohydrate will reliably do just the opposite. Carbohydrates raise the level of the amino acid tryptophan in the bloodstream, which the brain uses to synthesize serotonin, a neurotransmitter associated with sleep, analgesia, calm, and even the lifting of depression. This is the best-documented (and perhaps the only) example that scientists have discovered of the way a food can change the functioning of our brains. Twinkies make us glad.

Some parents believe that their children become wild and unmanageable after eating sucrose; they have been known to send their offspring to another child's birthday party carrying his or her own little cake made with fructose or aspartame. Yet most studies that have tested such children in the laboratory—away from their parents—have refuted the parents' claims.

The mechanism purportedly at work here is a condition known as reactive hypoglycemia. The theory is that the body may overcompensate for the consumption of large amounts of sugar by releasing too much insulin, which drastically lowers your blood sugar, causing confusion, anxiety, muscular weakness, and personality changes. The idea that unruly children and prisoners are generally afflicted with this condition seems to have arisen in 1977, when an Ohio probation officer, Barbara Reed, told a U.S. Senate Committee that, after reading a pamphlet entitled *Low Blood Sugar,* she had changed the diets of the probationers under her care and accomplished remarkable improvements in their behavior.

But reactive hypoglycemia is a rare condition, and most scientifically controlled research has failed to document its presence in hyperactive or violent people. A 1986 study at the National Institute of Mental Health was unable to find any cognitive or behavioral consequences of eating sugar. A study of hyperactive children at the University of Toronto found that they reacted the same to sucrose, aspartame, and saccharin. And in 1990 a team of researchers at the University of Wisconsin found that a breakfast full of sucrose actually improved the performance of the group of fifty-eight white and fifty-seven black juvenile delinquents they studied.

Does white sugar make you fat? A gram of sugar has the same four calories in each gram as any other carbohydrate or any gram of protein. All carbohydrates have a substantial advantage over dietary fats, which, with nine calories in every gram, are more energy dense and can be effortlessly converted into body fat. The conversion of excess carbohydrate calories—*simple or complex*—into fat is energy intensive, using up as much as 20 percent of the carbohydrate calories in the process. But complex carbohydrates have only a minor caloric advantage over simple sugars; the additional energy you burn away as your body breaks them down is extremely small.

There is an idea floating around that white sugar somehow bypasses the body's regulatory mechanism and tricks us into overeating. This has been repeatedly disproved. In one study, Kool-Aid was prepared in two ways, one sweetened with sugar and the other with aspartame. Both were given to children an hour before lunch. Those who drank the sugary Kool-Aid compensated for the extra calories by eating less at lunch than those whose Kool-Aid contained the noncaloric sweetener. The body sees sugar for what it is.

Do chubby people have a sweet tooth? No. Obese adults actually consume less sugar than skinny adults. And taste tests have shown that neither group craves sugar more strongly than the other.

Does white sugar cause heart disease, diabetes, anemia, and other degenerative diseases? No. *Diet and Health* (1989), the National Research Council's compendious review of everything that was then known about nutrition and disease, summarized hundreds of studies on the subject and concluded that "sugar consumption (by those with an adequate diet) has not been established as a risk factor for any chronic disease other than dental caries in humans." Population studies in Puerto Rico, Hawaii, and Framingham, Massachusetts, found that healthy men consumed more carbohydrates than men who developed coronary heart disease; the type of carbohydrate did not matter. Most authorities recommend that added sugar be limited to 10 or 11 percent of our calories; our average intake today is only slightly higher. But in people with elevated triglycerides, especially diabetics, too much *fructose* eaten alone can aggravate their problem; sucrose consists of one unit of fructose and one of glucose.

Does white sugar give you cavities? Sure it does. But no more than any other fermentable carbohydrate. More important is the form the carbohydrate takes. Sticky carbohydrates like syrups, honeys, and raisins cling to your teeth and have more time to do their damage. Children and adults with a proclivity to cavities should vigorously rinse out their mouths after eating any kind of sticky carbohydrate.

It was the nutritionists of the 1970s who sent America into a panic about white sugar. As a consequence, we consume vast amounts of artificial sweeteners (even though several brands carry warning labels that they cause cancer in laboratory animals). More damaging to American gastronomy, we eat distasteful "sugarless" desserts and jams sweetened with concentrated apple or grape juice or pulverized dried apples, all of which contain just as many sugar molecules as sucrose but taste of boiled fruit juice instead of the pure, crystalline clarity we hunger for. Many nutritionists today are worried that people get so distracted by their irrational fear of sugar that they forget the really serious problems in our diets, especially our prodigal consumption of animal fat. That's what I call sweet revenge.

October 1992

A Fat of No Consequence

2 2 4   High over Cincinnati, heading back to New York, I writhed in my procrustean airline seat and reflected upon the Second Age of Man. For that is precisely what we embarked upon, you and I, on January 24, 1996—the day the FDA approved Olestra.

The First Age of Man, the Material Age, ran from 100,000 B.C. until the evening of January 23, A.D. 1996. It was called the Material Age because, while it lasted, human consciousness was trapped in its primitive physical housing, the body, and pleasure was inevitably followed by painful and expensive consequences. And then, on January 24, everything changed. The Second Age of Man, the Virtual Age, began with the legalization of the first nearly successful virtual pleasure—a virtual food, as it turns out—Olestra. The invention of birth control, coming near the end of the Material Age, was only a halfway step.

Olestra is the fat that passes unchanged, unchallenged, and unabsorbed through the human body. It is the fat without calories, without cholesterol, without heart disease, without cancer. Olestra is the fat without consequence. It is a molecular imitation, almost a parody, of fat.

All the fats and oils we eat are called triglycerides, because they consist of three fatty acid chains, each attached at one end to the same glycerol molecule. Olestra is quite similar, except that it has six or eight fatty acid chains on the outside, with a sucrose molecule, table sugar, in the middle. (That's why the generic name for Olestra is sucrose polyester.) The fat-slicing enzymes in our intestines, accustomed to taking apart triglycerides for easy absorption into the bloodstream, cannot figure out what to do with this Medusa, and so Olestra keeps traveling down the digestive tract and out of the body, fatty acids and all. This smooth and easy transit can also cause problems, but we will get to them later.

Compared with Olestra, fat substitutes like Simplesse are impostors. They are not like fats at all but are carbohydrates or proteins mechanically whirled up to look like fat or feel like fat on the tongue. But eat them or heat them, and the illusion breaks down. Olestra is different. It looks like a fat and it acts like a fat in cooking, and it tastes like a fat—greasy and good. But once it has done its magic in the frying pan and on our palate, it simply disappears down the drain. Have you ever tasted a dish of fake ice cream made with Simplesse? Whoever invented this stuff should be taken out and forced to eat a dish of fake ice cream made with Simplesse.

I had followed the Olestra story practically since I learned to read. The molecule was first dreamed up in 1959; the idea was that all those extra fatty acids and sucrose could supply intense nourishment for premature babies. Somebody must have been extremely disappointed to discover that the new substance supplied no nutrition at all because it could not be broken down and absorbed. And so years passed before Olestra's fabulous potential was understood.

I had read the scientific and medical papers on Olestra and followed the volleys of charges and countercharges about its efficacy and safety. I had spoken with officials who participated in the FDA hearings, and I had obtained all the transcripts, several thousand pages on four floppy disks. I was up to speed. And there *is* a good reason for worrying about Olestra: eating it can bring on side effects, mild to severe gastrointestinal discomfort and problems with absorbing nutrients. But before getting hot and bothered about all this, I desperately needed to cook with Olestra, using meat and seafood and fruit and bread, in sauces and in sweets—sautéed, panfried, deep-fried, roasted, and baked—in all

225

its boundless forms and incarnations. The FDA has approved Olestra only for making savory snack foods, and I yield to no one in my admiration for a fine potato chip. But it is not snack foods that have made me fall in love with the concept of Olestra.

Because here is the Big Point: Olestra is not just some alternate kind of fat, like a bottle of peanut oil or a can of Crisco. Olestra is a *process* for turning any fat—*any fat!!*—into a sucrose polyester that passes right through the body. They can make Olestra butter and bake golden croissants with the fat calories of a piece of dry toast. They can make beef-tallow Olestra (or goose-fat Olestra) for cooking truly perfect French fries, savory and crunchy but with the zero-fat level of a naked baked potato. They can make lard Olestra and roll out piecrust so light and flaky that you will have to nail it to the kitchen table to keep it from floating away. They can make cocoa-butter Olestra and mold bars of smooth, rich, dark chocolate with the three or four fat grams found in a quarter cup of dry cocoa powder. At least I think they can.

I also knew that it was politically incorrect to love Olestra, at least in the world of nutrition. Procter & Gamble had sent hundreds of shiny foil bags of Olestra potato chips to food editors and writers around the country. Some of them—my friends!—had actually refused to open the packages. Me, I tore the samples open before the courier had left my house. I knew that these silver pouches contained crisp little chips of history. And they tasted just fine.

I have to admit it: one of the most delectable reasons for loving Olestra is that it makes most nutritionists squirm. For nearly a decade they have earned a fine living frightening us into believing that consumption of any fat will bring on heart disease, stroke, diabetes, obesity, and various cancers. The scientific truth is that not all fat is bad for us, only saturated fat—mainly animal fat.* But either out of ignorance or from the sheer thrill they get

---

*For more details, please turn back to the chapter "Pain Without Gain," but only after you have finished reading this one.

from controlling the rest of us, the antifat forces have tried to convince us that every fat is a poison. And now they are in a pickle. For if fat is poison, then anything that can keep us from consuming fat, even a diet composed entirely of fat-free junk food made with Olestra, will be a godsend. Olestra calls the nutritionists' bluff!

If Olestra lives up to its potential, the unemployment rate among antifat nutritionists and food writers will soon reach 100 percent.

What were you doing on January 24, 1996? Me, I was thinking about fat. Actually, I was thinking about food, which is the same as thinking about fat, unless you regard thinking about lettuce as thinking about food. Early that morning, as if by psychic awareness, I had placed a call to Procter & Gamble's public relations department to request a bathtubful of Olestra to experiment with. They didn't say no, and they didn't say yes. They forgot to return my call.

For it was that very afternoon that the FDA announced its favorable decision, and all hell broke loose around the Procter & Gamble publicity shop. A few days later, a P & G voice offered to come by my kitchen in New York City and demonstrate Olestra. Two PR people and an excellent culinary consultant named Marilyn Harris were traveling to New York City and making the rounds of the most powerful and influential food writers and magazines. When they had finished with that, they would come and see me. I angrily replied that I would accept nothing less than complete and free access to Olestra, not a rehearsed demonstration available to any Fleet Street hack. When they refused, I grumpily gave in.

The day arrived and so did the three people from P & G. They were in a terrible hurry, late for me and due in only a half hour at *Allure*, some kind of beauty magazine. They set up two tiny deep-fat fryers on my kitchen counter; poured soybean oil into one and Olestra, a very thick and golden liquid, into the other; plugged them in; fried a few corn chips; and unplugged the machines. The results were good to eat, both those done in Olestra and those done in soybean oil. When I asked to keep the Olestra oil, the answer was a peremptory no. I asked if I might fry some potato chips and French fries I had earlier cut up. Again, the answer was no. But when the two P & G public relations staffers went off to the telephone, Marilyn Harris and I surreptitiously plugged in the little fryers and cooked the potatoes. Though the PR people were furious, the resulting French fries and chips were delicious and fat free as a glass of water, and my appetite for Olestra increased a thousandfold. I was frantic to cook with it.

I inundated Procter & Gamble with telephone calls. At first they ignored me, but with the assistance of Marilyn Harris, who had become my ally, I finally received an invitation to Cincinnati to cook for as long as I pleased with any form of Olestra they had on hand. I would soon become the first journalist of the Virtual Age, the only one ever allowed to play with Olestra to his heart's content and tell the world about it, flaws and all. And thus I was to step into the pages of history.

Why choose me over all other writers? I do not know, but I would not discount raw animal magnetism as a major factor.

The days flew by like minutes. I assembled a bundle of fine recipes—no savory snack foods here—and faxed Marilyn Harris a shopping list: apples, lemons, vanilla, flour, sugar, milk, potatoes, garlic, fresh rosemary, thyme, sage, and oregano, a dozen shucked oysters, okra, zucchini, two chickens, a pound of shrimp, and several pints of Graeter's ice cream in assorted flavors. Cincinnatians always tell you that Graeter's ice cream is the best in the world, and I have long wondered if they were correct.

I boarded the plane carrying several frying thermometers, which set off the metal detector, a few extra pairs of tongs, and a bag of chapati flour for making puffy pooris. A few rainy hours later, Marilyn and I pulled into the parking lot of Procter & Gamble's Winton Hill Technical Center on the outskirts of Cincinnati. The P & G Culinary Center consists of four kitchens and several hundred cookbooks on the ground floor of a modest tan brick structure called the Food Building. Three of the kitchens are small home models fitted with standard equipment, and one is a large, professional demonstration kitchen, where we spent most of the day. Ivorydale is a mile or two away, and on rainy days when the wind is right, the air is sickly sweet with a soapy perfume.

First I had to sign a legal release. The FDA's reason for restricting Olestra to the production of salty, savory snack foods is to limit the likely amount of Olestra that people will actually eat, while it studies the long-term effects. The FDA has decidedly not approved Olestra for the kind of home cooking in which I was about to engage. I quickly set up two large, heavy pots on adjoining burners, filled one with peanut oil and the other with the standard FDA-approved form of Olestra made from soybean or cottonseed oil; immersed one of my frying thermometers in each; and fired them up. Soon our memories of Ivory Snow were driven away by the joyous aroma of deep-fried beignets (we cooked these first and dusted them with confectioners' sugar to go with the morning's coffee), zucchini sticks (first dipped into Marcella Hazan's excellent flour-and-water batter), okra fried in cornmeal (Marilyn's crispy recipe), French fries, and my very own excellent potato chips.

Meanwhile, I prepared two versions of the miraculous, to be perfectly frank, piecrust dough from last November's *Vogue* (see page 481), one made with Crisco and the other with a hydrogenated form of Olestra manufactured some time ago in the laboratory and stashed away by Marilyn for a moment just like this. Marilyn peeled ten pounds of apples with only the mildest complaint, and our talented helper Cindy Young rolled out my dough and constructed two handsome pies—which only she could tell apart. And somewhere along the way, Marilyn made her favorite fatless Olestra brownies, southern biscuits, and deep-fried chunks of chicken breast in a Cajun-style recipe.

I was shown many types of Olestra during my visit, including the Crisco-like version and the beef-tallow version for making French fries. This is where mankind truly needs Olestra—as a

229

completely satisfactory replacement for those dietary fats that really do cause us harm, the fully saturated or hydrogenated fats people should avoid but that make many traditional foods so delicious. I was especially keen to lay my hands on some Olestra butter, but I could find none in the entire Cincinnati metropolitan area. I know they've made some. There could be a Nobel Prize in store for someone.

We three cooks were never alone. Every few seconds some P & G executive or scientist or engineer wandered in to have a snack, generously share their cooking advice, answer my probing scientific questions, or talk about New York restaurants. These people have been nibbling on Olestra every day for five years. None, apparently, has suffered any ill effects—or lived to tell about it.

And now for the gastronomic verdict: The Olestra apple pie was universally judged to be superior to the Crisco version—it was considerably flakier and just as tender. Marilyn's Olestra biscuits seemed flakier than her Crisco biscuits, though also greasier. Pooris made from Madhur Jaffrey's recipe puffed just as well in Olestra as in peanut oil, and the taste was similar. Marilyn's fat-free brownies were fine, but I much prefer the chocolate-and-egg taste of real brownies.

There was, in taste and texture, little to distinguish the foods deep-fried in Olestra from the foods fried in peanut oil as long as they were eaten very warm. If anything, the Olestra versions seemed crispier and their flavor more neutral, which allowed the taste of the underlying foods to come through, often in unexpected ways.

But as they cooled down, many Olestra-fried delicacies left the roof of my mouth repulsively greasy, especially when we had failed to blot the food with meticulous care. The reason is that the current version of Olestra has been manufactured to stay quite thick at room temperature—it looks something like Vaseline until it is heated—which is why P & G always demonstrates Olestra melted.

Why did they formulate Olestra this way? Because the early, more liquid versions caused gastrointestinal problems. One of these—"anal seepage," or, in my preference, "passive oil loss"— occurs when fully liquid Olestra separates from the food with which it was cooked and slips along the inner walls of people's intestines, bypassing everything else in its way. Drops of Olestra show up on their underwear or floating in their toilets. (The FDA actually abbreviates this as OIT, "oil in toilet.")

Procter & Gamble discovered that passive oil loss and some— but not all—of the other gastrointestinal effects (cramps and diarrhea, for example) could nearly be eliminated by making Olestra about as thick as mayonnaise at room temperature, which prevents it from separating from food in the intestines. This is the only form of Olestra the FDA has approved. But potato chips with a greasy coating the consistency of mayonnaise are not going to walk out of the supermarkets. So the Olestra potato chips that P & G experimentally produces, in a perfect one-twentieth-scale model of a complete potato chip factory it has constructed in another part of the Food Building, are carefully dried by "steam stripping." That's why in some of the informal taste tests run by several national newspaper food sections Olestra potato chips did not taste greasy enough.

Before Olestra can be used for home cooking, something drastic must be done. Actually, something drastic has been done. I was the first outsider ever shown an experimental form of Olestra that is wonderfully liquid at both room and frying temperatures, but which somehow stiffens within the body. The people at P & G were annoyingly laconic about this apparently perfect, light golden Olestra because they are afraid, they said, of tipping off their competitors. (They obviously wanted me to write about it or they would not have shown it to me—I did not discover it in some broom closet.) But I was allowed to fry with it for hours on end, and the results were excellent—nearly as crisp and much less greasy, with a light, translucent taste. P & G has no immediate plans to petition the FDA because, I suspect, approval will require a massive series of additional animal and human tests. Otherwise, P & G would rush it to market.

Flying back from Cincinnati, still intoxicated by the promise of Olestra, I grew preoccupied with some of the darker questions.

Will Olestra make you too skinny? The FDA did not even consider, officially at least, whether Olestra will make you skinny at all. When somebody applies for permission to introduce a novel substance into the American food supply, the FDA has only one legal responsibility: to find out whether the new food is safe to eat, not whether it is effective or delicious or desirable. (*Drugs* are evaluated also for their effectiveness.) P & G's weight-loss research is promising but very short-term.

232   As for the gastrointestinal effects, I can testify that after a solid day of cooking with Olestra, munching on the results, consuming five times the amount the FDA ever envisioned, and dipping regularly into the bags of Olestra corn and potato chips that now sit next to my computer, I did not have the slightest trouble. My wife, who always claims to have a more delicate stomach than mine, had no problems either, and loved the taste and crunchy texture. There is no doubt that some people, apparently a small number, do suffer from cramps, diarrhea, or passive oil loss. But the FDA assures us that any GI symptoms disappear as soon as you stop eating the stuff—with no lasting discomfort.

There is one very serious potential consequence of eating Olestra, and the FDA sidestepped the issue in a way that may come back to haunt it.

Some of the vitamins in the foods we eat are fat soluble—principally vitamins A, D, E, and K. When they are eaten at about the same time we eat Olestra, some of them dissolve in the Olestra and pass from our bodies unabsorbed. The press has inaccurately described this as "flushing" or "vacuuming" or "sweeping" the vitamins right out of our systems. Olestra carries off only a portion of the fat-soluble vitamins that you consume within two hours on either side of the Olestra. If you eat Olestra potato chips in the afternoon, the vitamins in your dinner will be unaffected.

Procter & Gamble and the FDA have calculated the amount of replacement vitamins that need to be added to Olestra itself or into the foods made with it to set everything right, even for heavy snackers, and this is what P & G has done. The results seem sensible to me. If you are still concerned, read the FDA's research summary in the *Federal Register* (vol. 61, no. 20, January 30, 1996, *Rules and Regulations*). What level of vitamin supplementation will be needed when we consume Olestra all day, every day, in every snack and at every meal, as the main added fat in our diets—as I have hopes we will? The easy answer is to take a vitamin pill every morning, an hour or two before or after slathering your Olestra-lard biscuits with golden Olestra butter.

But there is a much thornier problem: How can we replace all those nutrients we don't yet know enough about? The carotenoids are a group of more than five hundred related compounds found in fruits and vegetables, among which the most famous are beta-carotene and lycopene (in tomatoes). There are fifty respectable epidemiological studies showing that populations consuming large amounts of fruits and vegetables have lower rates of cancer, and that low levels of carotenoids in the bloodstream are associated with heart disease, stroke, and certain eye diseases among the elderly.

Carotenoids are fat soluble, and there is little doubt that eating Olestra sharply decreases the levels of some carotenoids. But are carotenoids the crucial nutrient in fruits and vegetables, or is it something else? (Other possibilities—flavonoids and polyphenols—are not fat soluble.) And is the level of carotenoids in the bloodstream the important thing to measure? Or is it simply a marker for other processes going on in the body? Nobody knows, and so the government has never established a standard—an RDA—for carotenoid consumption. As a result, the FDA did not require Olestra to be enriched with any of the five hundred carotenoids. This is the dilemma: How can we replace nutrients that are beyond our ability to name and to measure?

Is Olestra worth the risk? If fat is poison, sure it is. But if not . . . ?

If Olestra has the epochal effect I am hoping for, if Olestra truly ushers in the Second Age of Man, it could make up 30 percent of our diets. Would it be possible to engineer a form of Olestra that does not allow nutrients to become dissolved in it? This may be our only hope. I trust that the people at Procter & Gamble are working on this problem night and day. For otherwise the Age of Virtual Pleasure will be postponed until further notice. And we will have but a few shiny bags of savory snack foods to play with.

May 1996

PART FOUR

Journey
of a
Thousand
Meals

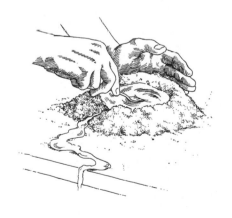

True Choucroute

When I awoke, the morning air was as crisp as bacon and as sweet as liver sausage. I was lashed to the passenger seat of an unfamiliar European automobile, alone and abandoned by the side of a deserted mountain road. The keys were gone from the ignition. Had I been outwitted once again by my very own wife?

I unbuckled and squeezed out of the car. In other circumstances, the scene around me would have seemed altogether sublime. Yellow-green vineyards climbed the steep hillsides, and flashes of autumn color showed through the silvery pines. In the wide valley far below I could make out a tiny farmer on a tiny tractor lugging a tiny wagon bursting with *quintal d'Alsace*, huge white cabbages that would soon be finely shredded, layered with salt and juniper berries, and fermented into choucroute, which is French for "sauerkraut," which is German for "bitter herb." Simmered with wine and spices and everything an Alsatian pig can contribute to man's well-being—its sturdy knuckles and shanks, its dainty feet and meaty jowls, its mirthful belly and brawny shoulders—*quintal* is raised to the dizzying, almost inconceivable gastronomic summit known as *choucroute garnie à l'Alsacienne*. The dream of unearthing a perfect choucroute had plagued me for a decade. But now, alone and deserted in Alsace, my goal seemed as remote as the tiny farmer toiling on the valley floor.

A journey of a thousand meals begins with a single bite. My choucroute obsession had taken hold with the very first version I had tasted, a recipe of Julia Child's. It was sweet with chicken broth, onions, and carrots, aromatic with cloves and juniper berries. The meats were roast pork and sausages, bacon and ham, all luxurious and familiar. I had relished every morsel and imagined that a thoroughly authentic choucroute would be the same, only more so. And thus my quest began.

Years later in Paris on a particularly warm June day, I lunched at one of the Baumann chain of brasseries, thought by some to have the best choucroute in the city. It was the most demoralizing meal of a lifetime, not because the choucroute was poor, which it was, nor because my wife forced me to eat outside in the broiling sun and a pigeon soiled my suit, which they did, but because it dawned on me for the first time that an authentic *choucroute garnie à l'Alsacienne* was not what I was after. The cabbage was tough and acrid and greasy; some of the pork was so amply streaked with soft white fat that it seemed morally wrong to eat more than a bite or two of it; two pieces were so lean and dry that my knife buckled as I tried to cut them. Meals the next day at the Brasserie Flo and at Chez Jenny restored my confidence a bit. I vowed then and there that someday I would voyage to Alsace and uncover the truth.

Whenever I travel to France, I like to hit the ground eating, but my urgency on this trip was even more intense than usual—a brief week in Alsace was barely long enough to sample fourteen authentic choucroutes. I had passed a sleepless night and morning on the trip to Strasbourg—two plane flights and an endless wait for airport connections—while my wife slumbered beside me like a puppy. Anticipating that I would lose consciousness as soon as we rented our car, my instructions to her had been the model of clarity: Drive directly from the airport to Ittenheim on the forlorn outskirts of Strasbourg, avoiding the twofold snare of ineffable scenery and medieval churches. Park at the Hotel-Restaurant au Boeuf and make a reservation for lunch. Enjoy yourself very quietly for the next two hours. Wake me at 1:00 p.m. for our first steaming plate of true choucroute.

Hard as I tried, I could not find a loophole in these instructions. Yet here I was, alone and immobilized, deep in the Vosges
Mountains and their adorable little towns of medieval houses,
lofty church spires, narrow spotless streets, and ferocious dogs on
flimsy tethers.

I fished around in the glove compartment for a dictionary, a
long roll of graph paper, and a stack of postcards. In France as in
no other country they sell postcards with photographs of regional
dishes on one side and recipes on the reverse. I had located five at
the Strasbourg airport while my wife, by division of labor, took
care of the baggage. Three cards featured *choucroute garnie à l'Alsacienne*. I sat down on a tree stump and resumed my master-
work—a chart analyzing every authentic recipe for choucroute I
could get my hands on.

Just then a shadowy figure emerged from the forest into the
bright sunlight. It was my wife, wearing the look she gets when
she believes she has been ennobled by proximity to nature. Too
proud to betray the slightest concern at her absence, guessing
that interrogation would be pointless, and recalling that she still
had the car keys, I smiled carelessly, rolled up my chart, and said,
"To Ittenheim!"

An hour later we pulled into the courtyard of the Hotel-
Restaurant au Boeuf, three stories of white stucco and dark tim
bers, with pink and red geraniums in every window box, like
most of the buildings in the Alsatian countryside. I had chosen
Au Boeuf because its *choucroute garnie à l'Alsacienne* had won the
Concours de la Cuisine Régionale in 1985, a competition run by
an association of modest French country inns. Alsace has more
than its share of superb restaurants displaying international
ambitions. But a good choucroute, I felt, was most likely to be
found in a family establishment serving convivial fare on well-
worn crockery.

After a pleasant interlude with a smooth slab of goose foie
gras—another Alsatian specialty—the choucroute was borne to
our table. Down the center of an oval terra-cotta platter was a

mountain of golden sauerkraut; leaning up against it were nine distinct cuts of pork and charcuterie, and around the outside lay eight yellow potatoes. Four red sausages taller than the others rose to the crest of the mound, where they appeared to support a stout pig's shank, still in its skin. We heaped the choucroute on our plates and chose the meats at random, half a sausage here, a cutlet there, washing everything down with a local Riesling.

We ate until we were satisfied, continued eating until we were full, and kept going until we were bloated and sleepy—not because the dish was flawless but because, among the scores of *choucroutes garnies à l'Alsacienne* I had eaten in restaurants or prepared in my own kitchen, this was the first specimen I knew to be absolutely, certifiably authentic. It was a trophy to carry back home in the form of sensory memories, enhanced body weight, and a recipe that Jean-Jacques Colin, the prizewinning chef, generously shared with me. I might have used more onion than Colin and a less acidic wine to make the sauerkraut sweeter. But who am I to tinker with a genuine regional masterpiece?

After lunch we readjusted our seat belts and drove south to Colmar, which we would use as a choucroute base camp for the next few days. We set out again for two *winstubs*—Alsatian wine bars or taverns—in nearby Niedermorschwihr, one called the Morakopf (Moor's Head) and another whose name a splash of choucroute has obliterated from my notes. I remember that we shared a table at the second with a sullen young couple who lived nearby, and that, as in many *winstubs*, everything in the place had been made from something else. The bar stools had once been wine barrels, a wooden shoe had become a wine cradle, an oval ox yoke was mounted on the wall with eight lightbulbs screwed into its sides, an iron tripod pot had been upended and little shaded bulbs attached to each leg, rough wagon wheels were hung as chandeliers, and so forth. When I first met my wife, she tried to turn every inanimate object she came across into a lamp, and I thought she would be captivated by the interior decoration. But she was too busy figuring out where to hide the day's third slab of poached bacon so that the restaurant would not notice that she hadn't touched it.

The name of the restaurant does not matter much. It could have been the Caveau d'Eguisheim in Eguisheim or the Au Lion d'Or in Kayserberg, the refined Flory in Colmar or half a dozen other places we visited. But it could not have been the Ferme Auberge Deybach.

A *ferme auberge*, in its idealized form, is a working farmhouse deep in the mountains whose hospitable owners welcome guests for lunch or dinner, heaping timeless country food on long communal tables. The owner of our hotel warned us that every *ferme auberge* on the list we showed him harvested its ingredients at the local supermarket and earned its living feeding tourists instead of farm animals. We pressed him for the name of the genuine article, and an hour later, just in time for lunch, he produced the Ferme Auberge Deybach near Schiessrothried.

Our mouths watering, we drove into the cold and misty mountains, asking directions to Schiessrothried every few miles. It was not until our rented car had gotten stuck at a sixty-degree angle on the edge of a ravine in the freezing rain halfway up a hiking trail that we realized that Schiessrothried is not a town but a sylvan lake high in the Vosges. We inched backward several thousand feet to a paved clearing, turned the car around, and followed a series of signs for the Ferme Auberge Himmel-Something, where we would ask for directions. Outside were two scrawny yellow horses, several tons of rusting farm machinery, and four chickens scratching at the earth around the horses' ankles. Inside was a large gloomy room lit by two small candles, a *tarte aux pommes* (yet another Alsatian specialty) baked the previous month, and a dour farm couple who reluctantly redirected us to the Ferme Auberge Deybach.

As it turned out, the Deybach was not far from that paved clearing at the base of our near-fatal hiking trail. We had missed it earlier because we were not on the lookout for a dilapidated wooden shack near a ski lift guarded by two rabid Alsatian dogs.

Inside were seventy-five German students on a walking tour, crammed together at makeshift tables, and an immense proprietress wearing a man's sleeveless undershirt. First she refused to talk to us at all and then spoke only in German, while speaking only French to the German students. Lunch appeared to be a thick potato soup followed by a half-inch-thick slab of raw bacon nailed to a wooden board. We let the students at our table practice their English on us ("A wonderful man is President John Kennedy") while we shared a warm pitcher of local white wine and waited for all seventy-two of their friends to be served. At last the proprietress threw a completely unripe Muenster (Alsace's famed cheese) on the table before us and grunted in German, "Too late for lunch."

We sped back into Colmar, bought five Alsatian cookbooks and more recipe postcards, and snuggled in our hotel room, where I worked on my master chart until dinnertime. Not one of the cookbooks had a recipe for raw bacon slab nailed to wooden board.

My memories of choucroute all run together now, but the crucial variations are preserved on paper. After a while, I could simply take a few bites, ask the chef a question or two, and understand how his version was made. This left us with an acute disposal problem regarding the ten pounds of *choucroute garnie à l'Alsacienne* remaining on the platter each time we dined. A ruthless investigator would have shoved the choucroute aside and eagerly turned to the wealth of other savory Alsatian dishes on the menu. A courteous investigator would bring a plastic garbage bag and scoop up the choucroute when nobody was looking. A guilt-ridden investigator like me, brought up worrying about the starving children of Asia, gets rid of ten pounds of surplus choucroute by eating half and artfully arranging the rest to appear as small as possible.

As the days passed, we discovered an important medical principle that, to my knowledge, has hitherto been undocumented: when you have eaten *choucroute garnie à l'Alsacienne* twice a day for five days, your wife's face turns green, she claims that yours has, too, and you both lie immobile in a netherworld between sleep and wakefulness for the next eighteen hours. Then you can eat again. The French would call this a liver attack, but they call everything a liver attack.

When we recovered, we fled north to the bright lights of Strasbourg and its fabled patisseries, delicatessens, and chocolatiers. We averted our gaze whenever we passed the Maison du Lard restaurant across from the hotel garage and feasted instead on the modern Alsatian cooking of two brilliant chefs highly honored by Michelin and Gault-Millau: Antoine Westermann at the Buerehiesel in Strasbourg's lovely Orangerie and Michel Husser at the Hostellerie du Cerf in Marlenheim. What a relief to eat food that was invented only yesterday!

Westermann does not offer choucroute in his restaurant. There is only one true choucroute, he joked, and gave his family recipe, currently entrusted to his grandmother, Cécile. Husser serves a wonderfully up-to-date choucroute. The sauerkraut is simmered briefly with three traditional meats to give it flavor. These are removed (and served to the staff for lunch), and the sauerkraut is garnished with foie gras that has been smoked over oak for two hours and then sautéed, and with suckling pig, some of its parts roasted in a mustard sauce, others dry-salted a day ahead, poached in broth, and caramelized in honey and vinegar. The dish is a triumph.

It was snowy and cold when we returned to New York, perfect weather for sharing a real *choucroute garnie à l'Alsacienne* with friends. I decided to construct my own recipe, following this convenient working definition of "authenticity": if it *could* have been made in Alsace by a traditional cook, it is authentic. When my chart gave me permission, I chose what most pleased my tastes, which lean toward the spicy, crunchy, sweet, and mellow. But I would not go beyond the flavors, textures, and methods I had found in Alsace. Authenticity seems more a matter of ranges and limitations than of outright prescriptions.

Every traditional recipe includes sauerkraut, water, juniper berries (for their characteristic ginny taste), onions (for their flavor and sweetness), black peppercorns, cloves, garlic, goose fat or lard, and potatoes. Chicken broth is sometimes mixed with the water, sometimes not. Bay leaves and wine are found in most recipes, fresh thyme and coriander seeds less often, butter and cooking oil never. Apples and carrots, which sweeten the choucroute, appear only occasionally, as do cumin and caraway—they are more German than French. Cooking times vary from one to twelve hours; the stove top is heavily favored over the oven.

Cookbooks usually instruct you to soak and arduously squeeze the sauerkraut handful by handful. (I demolished a salad dryer trying to automate the process.) This once made sense in the Alsatian countryside, where preserved cabbage and turnips were the only vegetables available during the long winter months; by April, the sauerkraut had become dark and highly acidic. But when Alsatians use choucroute nouvelle—fermented for only three weeks and used right away like the sauerkraut we get in the United States—the most they do is quickly rinse off the brine.

The meats found in nearly every recipe are smoked bacon, salted bacon, and smoked or salted pig's knuckles or shanks (*jarret, jambonneau*). Nearly as universal are smoked *palette de porc,* Strasbourg sausages, and salted loin of pork, though some cooks prefer the untranslatable *échine,* which Cécile Westermann and others prefer to the shoulder for its flavor. Beef is out of the question. Every recipe includes three or four types of sausages; half of them call for quenelles of pork liver, poached at the last minute. *Les joues* (cheeks) and *épaule* (shoulder) are found now and then, sometimes fresh and sometimes smoked. Surprisingly, most of these terms are too technical for paperback dictionaries like the one I carried in France, and in the end I needed all four volumes of *Harrap's Standard French and English Dictionary* next to my pots and pans. But literal translation is pointless, because French pigs are butchered into different pieces from ours and handled differently later.

I located diagrams of French and American butchering methods, aligned one over the other, and held them up to the light to see where the French cuts fall on an American pig. With my free hand, I telephoned the butcher and asked if he would saw off the part of the shoulder blade near the neck, keeping the backbone and first ribs attached, and could I get it salted. My goal was *échine salée*. I tried again with *jambonneau*, which runs from above the knuckle (also known in pork circles as the hock) to just above the feet. In reply, he pretended to have received a long-distance call on the other line. So I telephoned four ethnic butchers—two Italian, one Polish, and one German. They could provide some of the inexpensive cuts like knuckle and shank, though not the cheeks and neck, and nobody carried unsmoked, salted shoulder, loin, or bacon. Salting was invented as a preservative, but we use it now to deepen and concentrate the flavors of foods.

Before long I was in a taxi bound for Harlem with a picture of a pig in my pocket. From what I knew about the salted meats of the American South, I suspected that the answer might lie there. A friend had put me in touch with Aubrey Foster, general manager of the Pan Pan Coffee House, at 130th Street and Lenox Avenue, where every day in the basement he smokes a great deal of pork over hickory. I met up with Foster at the Pan Pan just in time for an early lunch of juicy barbecued ribs and an excellent chopped barbecued-pork sandwich. We pored over my pig diagrams and drove up Lenox Avenue to Clarence & Sons Prime Meats. I was tempted by the frozen possum and coon but stuck to business and discovered snowy-white salted bacon and smoked jowls (streaked like bacon but with a deeper taste); fresh jowls are available around Christmas, when Clarence's customers order whole pigs' heads. I was told that the *jambonneau* on my diagram is never available, because American hams are cut down to the knuckle, leaving only the lower shank.

While I was in the neighborhood, I bused down to La Marqueta in Spanish Harlem, beneath the elevated railroad tracks on Park Avenue between 112th and 116th Streets, where, if my command of Spanish is accurate, I tracked down some fresh neck meat and what was probably a boned, unsmoked *jambonneau*, though it was much larger than I had expected and was referred to as a "horseshoe." There was no salted loin; that's what they eat in Harlem, I was told. I bought a fresh loin and salted it myself according to a recipe in Jane Grigson's *The Art of Charcuterie* (Knopf). It took several days of work.

Choucroute garnie à l'Alsacienne is so demanding under the best of circumstances that, after two meticulously authentic meals, I lowered my sights a few millimeters and limited myself to meats that can be collected in New York City after no more than two or three hours of shopping. I sometimes splurge by dressing up the choucroute with a roast pheasant or duck legs, grilled quail or confit of goose—all possibilities in Alsace—and enjoy substituting spaetzle or sliced, fried potato dumplings for boiled potatoes.

There is nothing remarkable about the recipe that follows. It is, I think, simply delicious in an everyday, authentic Alsatian sort of way.

Choucroute Garnie à l'Alsacienne

At least 3 hours before the feast, melt a *scant ½ cup of duck or goose fat* in a heavy 9- to 12-quart flameproof casserole or stockpot, add *5 cups of very finely sliced yellow onions*, and cook, stirring, for 10 to 15 minutes until the onions are limp and translucent but not browned. Meanwhile, put *5 pounds of drained fresh young sauerkraut* in a large strainer, pour *2 quarts of cold water* over it, press firmly to expel the water, and leave to drain again. On a 6-inch square of cheesecloth that has been rinsed in warm water, place *25 black peppercorns, 1½ teaspoons of coriander seeds, 5 cloves, and 15 juniper berries;* gather up the corners and tie with kitchen twine. Then make a bundle of *6 branches of parsley, 4 branches of fresh thyme,* and *2 bay leaves;* wrap the *leaf of a leek* or a strip of parchment paper around the middle of the bundle and tie tightly with twine.

When the onions are ready, stir in *1½ cups of dry Alsatian wine* (Riesling or Sylvaner), *2 cups of homemade chicken broth,* and *2 cups of cold water.* Add a well-rinsed *1½-pound slab of unsmoked, dry-salted, or brine-cured bacon* from which you have removed the rind, and which you have cut crosswise into two equal pieces; a *1½-pound slab of smoked bacon,* also divided crosswise; *2 dry-salted or brine-cured pig's knuckles or shanks,* rinsed well; *1 pound of smoked pork butt* from which you have removed the netting, if any; the spice bag, the herb bundle, and *3 carrots,* scraped and washed. Sprinkle *¼ cup of finely minced garlic* and *2 teaspoons of coarse sea salt* over all, and lay on the sauerkraut, fluffing it with your fingers.

Add enough *cold water* to bring the liquid to an inch below the top of the sauerkraut. Cover and, over medium heat, bring to a boil. Immediately reduce the heat and continue cooking at a strong simmer for 1¼ hours, stirring every 20 minutes. The sauerkraut should still be crisp. Remove from the heat and let cool for anywhere between 30 minutes and 1½ hours. Then begin the final preparation, which requires 45 minutes of frantic yet ultimately satisfying work.

Peel *4 medium potatoes,* cut them in half, and cook in 1 cup of the sauerkraut liquid until tender.

Preheat your broiler. Place 4 quarts of water over high heat; when it comes to a boil, it will be used to cook the sausages. Meanwhile, with long tongs, remove everything but the sauerkraut and its liquid from the casserole: Place the two pieces of smoked bacon on a plate. Place the salted bacon, the smoked pork butt, and the pig's knuckles in a large baking dish, moisten with sauerkraut liquid, cover with a wet kitchen towel, and keep them warm in an oven or toaster oven set to low, or over a pot of barely simmering water. Moisten the kitchen towel again from time to time. Discard the carrots, the spice bag, and the herb bundle. Put the sauerkraut casserole over medium heat, stir well, and simmer, uncovered.

When the sausage water has come to a boil, drop in *4 white veal sausages* (**weisswurst or bockwurst**) and *4 smoked country sausages* (**bauernwurst**), and reduce to a simmer. After 5 minutes, remove the white sausages to a skillet greased with *1 tablespoon of goose or duck fat.* After another 5 minutes, add *4 Strasbourg sausages* (**knackwurst**) to the water, remove immediately from the heat, cover, and leave for 15 minutes. Brown the white sausages over medium heat.

Meanwhile slice both the smoked bacon and the salted bacon crosswise into half-inch-thick strips and grill them under the broiler until crisp and deeply colored but still moist within.

Drain the sauerkraut and heap it up on a very large, warmed platter. Slice the smoked pork butt into eighths. Remove the sausages from the water and cut them and the browned white sausages in half crosswise. Arrange the sausages, sliced meats, and potatoes around the sauerkraut and set a knuckle at its crest. Serves 8.

November 1989

Hail Cesare!

I returned home from a week in Cesare's kitchen in Albaretto della Torre, population sixty, with an indomitable urge to cook. I began by heaping two pounds of flour and polenta on my wooden table, molded a deep crater in the center, broke twenty egg yolks into it, and began stirring the eggs with a fork.

Every day all over Italy countless cooks do precisely this when they make pasta, except that using only egg yolks is something I had learned from one of Cesare's neighbors and except that I ran into a problem. As I began to incorporate flour from the crater's inner wall, a wavelet of egg splashed over the top, causing serious erosion, and when I nimbly scooped up a handful of flour from the stable side of the mound and used it to stanch the flow, the crater collapsed. A torrent of egg yolks, now thick with flour and cornmeal, surged across the table, carried off a pile of chopped garlic and, like molten lava rolling over a Hawaiian housing development, leaving death and destruction in its wake, headed toward my handwritten notes. As I snatched away the notebook, the flood plunged on, lifting two rosemary branches as though they were matchsticks and cascading over the edge of the table and into an open silverware drawer.

Cesare never warned me about making pasta near an open drawer. He did suggest that I would do better with an electric mixer to form the dough, kneading it afterward by hand. My wife

contended, among other things, that if I had washed the silverware immediately, it would not have taken on the feel of indus-
trial-grade sandpaper. I replied that if laundry science had been
my goal, I would not have traveled thousands of miles to a
remote hilltop in Piemonte.

"Food eaten in anger turns to poison in the stomach," I
reminded my wife when dinner was ready, quoting a timeless
Sufi saying. But the danger was past, for when the tastes of the
Langhe were spread before her, she grew docile as a lamb and
congenial as a kid turning slowly over an acacia fire.

Cesare is chef and owner of a restaurant called Dei Cacciatori
(the Hunters' Place) or Da Cesare (Cesare's Place) or sometimes
both. Albaretto is a half-hour drive south of the ancient city of
Alba in the part of Piemonte ("Piedmont" in English) called the
Langhe, and to these eyes it is the most magical hill country in all
of Italy. In the autumn, when the grapes and hazelnuts have been
gathered, when truffles ripen under the hillsides and wild mushrooms grow up between willow and oak, the Langhe becomes an
epicurean madhouse. Germans, Swiss, and Italians flock there for
tartufi bianchi d'Alba, the intense white truffles of Alba; for Barolo
and Barbaresco, the noblest red wines of Italy; and for the finest
veal, game, berries, porcini, hazelnuts, and chestnuts you can eat.
Alba is only a two-hour drive from Milan, one hour from Turin,
or a half day north from Nice. Spending a few fall days around
Alba makes for one of the greatest gastronomic vacations you can
take anywhere in the world. Yet travelers from the United States
are rare, perhaps because Alba is not on the way to anywhere
else.

It was a rainy November evening when I had my first meal at
Cesare's. The dining room was rough and warm, dark wood
against stucco walls and tall shelves of wine bottles begging to be
opened. In the stone fireplace at one end of the room, a sizzling
joint of meat turned slowly over a wood fire. The frenzy of the
white truffle season was upon us, and the room was packed
beyond its usual capacity of twenty-five guests.

Cesare's children, Elisa and Filippo, brought us plates of tripe and fresh porcini and a tiny green the size of clover, all hidden under paper-thin slices of white truffle. A wild-duck breast followed, flavored with a sweet sauce of chestnuts and white truffles, and a large onion baked on a bed of salt, scooped out and filled with white truffles, meat broth, pureed onions, and cheese. Each course was Cesare's variation on a Piedmontese theme, robust and refined at the same time, the fantasy food of a country boy. Cesare (pronounced "CHEH-za-ray") is forty-two, with thinning chestnut hair, an ample nose, a full mustache, and sharp gray eyes. He is the son of a farmer who owned the original Dei Cacciatori down the road from Cesare's current place—Cesare has turned it into a guest house—and who cut hair as a sideline. "I would simply like to be thought of as a good cook who continued the traditions of his region with his own imagination," Cesare says. Some consider Cesare the best cook in the Piedmont, one of the best in all of Italy. "Cesare is also a few crazy," I was told by a great wine maker whose vineyards are nearby and who first introduced me to Dei Cacciatori. "But what can you expect of a genius?"

Cesare's wife, Silvana, brought us a baked potato drenched in grappa and a cream of hare with white truffles—somewhere between a mousse and a pâté—and asked us if we would like to start our meal. We were baffled until etymology came to the rescue: "antipasto" literally means "before the meal" or "re*past*" (not "before the pasta"). Piedmont is famous for its antipasti; one local restaurant brings you a procession of seventeen, each served separately or in little groups, never crammed together on a huge platter.

The repast started with a variety of traditional Piedmontese pastas. Some of us had *tajarin,* an incredible type of tagliatelle or tagliarini noodle typically made with only the deep orange yolks of local eggs. Others chose *agnolotti,* tiny ravioli stuffed with meat and cabbage or spinach (or, as tonight, stuffed with pumpkin) and pinched together by hand. Both were moistened with *sugo d'arrosto,* a thin sauce of browned butter, sage, and meat broth, and both were showered with white truffles.

Next we had to choose between oven-roasted wild boar, a guinea hen baked in clay scooped up from Cesare's land, or a spit-roasted leg of kid just taken from the fireplace. The kid was the most perfect piece of meat ever to enter my mouth. The outside was dark and crisp and pungent with herbs and smoke from the acacia-wood fire; the inside was sweet and succulent and practically falling apart, something like the best North Carolina pork barbecue. Now I understand why James Beard once wrote that spit-roasting over wood is the ideal way to cook meat. (Cesare, who typically shows contempt for precise measurement in the kitchen, insists that the bed of the fire must be exactly forty centimeters below the spit. He uses acacia wood because he bought a vast amount of it last year when the government put a road through his friend's property, but says that oak and vine cuttings would be preferable.) I have become obsessed by the concept of spit-roasting, and I am thinking of moving to an apartment where I can set up a motorized spit in a wood-burning fireplace, even if the place lacks windows and running water.

Dessert was a pear poached in Barolo with a sauce of *mirtilli* (whortleberries or tiny blueberries) and a puzzling platter of leafy hazelnut branches. The leaves were pretty enough, though the hour seemed late for a change in the table decoration, and the glossy brown nuts themselves were impenetrable without a nutcracker. At last we discovered that Cesare had replaced one hazelnut in each cluster with a sweet, golden cookie.

When inspiration deserts him, Cesare simply shuts the restaurant for a while. He does not have much patience with restaurant critics. When the Michelin guide to Italy—not the proudest achievement of that company—awarded him his first star several years ago, Cesare posted a sign on the front door of his restaurant: IF YOU'RE HERE JUST BECAUSE YOU READ MY NAME IN MICHELIN OR VERONELLI, PLEASE DO NOT ENTER. More pragmatic than Cesare, Silvana put her foot down, and the sign disappeared.

But the critics have been kind to Cesare. He was discovered in 1972 by Nino Bergese, the most celebrated Italian chef of this century and cook to King Umberto; Bergese told Luigi Veronelli, author of the standard guide to the restaurants of Italy, *I ristoranti di Veronelli,* and soon Cesare became widely known. "Personal, inventive, and refined. . . . A great cook, at once a faithful interpreter of traditional Langhe cuisine and capable of exceptional new dishes" is how I translate Sandro Doglio's appraisal in his *Mangiare & bere in Piemonte e Valle d'Aosta,* the most comprehensive guide to the restaurants of Piedmont. "Inspired . . . moody . . . extravagant . . . at times bizarre" are the adjectives that Faith Willinger applies to Cesare's cuisine in her indispensable *Eating in Italy* (Hearst Books, with a much-updated edition expected in early 1998).

253

We stayed the night in Cesare's snug little guest house. It was snowing lightly the next morning, and we kept inside, gathering strength for our evening adventures. Cesare had persuaded his friend Bernardo, a retired farmer and a *trifulau* (a professional truffle hunter) since age ten, to take us along on this evening's truffle hunt.

By late afternoon, the weather cleared, revealing a vista for miles around—steep green misty hills rising in the middle distance to low mountains and in the far distance, on two sides, the snow-covered Alps, a sparkling pink-lavender in the sunset, a spectacle that makes you gasp. Soon Cesare appeared, bringing us a large, flat package wrapped in butcher's paper and an excellent bottle of Italian champagne. "For the *trifulau,*" he laughed as he unwrapped the paper, disclosing a platter of warm *crostini*—crisp slices of grilled bread brushed with butter and showered with thin slices of white truffle. Their musky pungent perfume filled the room. Then their musky pungent taste filled our mouths. Rossini called them the Mozart of fungi.

Cesare speaks in a mixture of Italian and the Langhe dialect, closer to Provençal than to Italian. There are only twenty-one letters in the Italian alphabet, yet I am proficient in no more than half of them. But as luck would have it, my wife and I had met up with Eugenio Pozzolini, a native Tuscan who manages the importing arm of Dean & DeLuca in New York. Eugenio was traveling through the Piedmont in pursuit of new treats for the people of America to enjoy. He was a fine and selfless translator.

On a dirt road outside town, we found Bernardo and his dog, Lola, and they led us down the slope of a hill and into a hazelnut orchard. From October through January the best white truffles in the world grow under this earth, in the Langhe hills to the south of Alba and the Roero hills just to the north, on the subterranean roots of oak, linden, willow, and hazelnut trees. The pattern and color on the inside of the truffle tell you which kind of tree was its "mother." (Pink streaks, for example, indicate the root of an oak.) On the outside most *tartufi bianchi d'Alba* are smooth and light tan and strongly perfumed. Farther north in the Piedmont, in the area around Asti, truffles grow gnarled and pitted because the earth there is densely packed, and the truffles must struggle for room to grow. "Those truffles grow up angry," Bernardo explained. What did he think about truffles from Tuscany and Umbria? "They are one step up from potatoes."

We walked slowly from tree to tree. The twilight sky was now a luminous blue, and tiny lights appeared in the houses and churches on the hills around us. Bernardo talked softly to Lola, like the gentlest father trying to instill discipline and concentration. She was just eleven months old, playful and impulsive, and lacked the dedication of her mother, whom Bernardo had left behind. This was Lola's first truffle season, but at only three months she could recognize their scent. When Lola is experienced and adept, she will be worth four thousand dollars. But Bernardo would never sell her. Bernardo directed her toward particular trees, urged her to pause before moving on to the next, and called her back when she bounded away from us into the middle of the orchard.

Lola began to dig at the base of a hazelnut tree, and Bernardo hurried over, gently pulling Lola back from the shallow hole she had dug and brushing away some dirt with his hands. He found nothing, and let Lola go at it again for a few seconds. Then he scratched the earth with the small metal *sapin* he carried on his belt and discovered the top of a white truffle. Very carefully he reached around it and pulled it out. My pulse rate soared.

Our first truffle was small, about an inch across, but smooth and well formed, and its perfume filled the air. Bernardo gave Lola a biscuit and replaced the earth, smoothed the surface, and scattered some dry leaves over it. If the tree's roots were protected and the earth was cared for, a truffle would mature in this same spot exactly one year from now by the lunar calendar, Bernardo told us. Besides, an exposed hole would alert other *trifulau* to Bernardo's secret spot.

We passed the truffle from nose to nose. Instantly the truffle feasts of recent days passed before our eyes: white truffles on green noodles moistened with *fonduta;* a mousse of white truffles and guinea hen liver; cold loin of rabbit sprinkled with white truffles; an asparagus flan in a pool of truffled cream; polenta layered with white truffles, raw egg yolk, and the local *rubbiolo di murazzano* cheese; risotto of nettles and strawberries with slivers of white truffle; and hand-rolled, hand-cut tagliarini (*tajarin* in the Langhe dialect) made only of egg yolks and flour, tossed in melted butter, flavored with fresh sage, and covered with paper-thin slices of white truffles. This last is the simplest and incontrovertibly the best way to enjoy white truffles, and it is served in virtually every restaurant in the Piedmont, from the humblest to the most ambitious.

Trifulau work mostly after dark, and it is easier to see a white dog in the late autumn moonlight than a black one. When you harvest truffles in the daytime, other *trifulau* will discover your secret places. "I do my best work between two and six in the morning, several kilometers' walk from here," Bernardo said. "But I would never take anyone with me."

We found two more small truffles in the hazelnut orchard and then descended into a muddy gorge and the woods beyond it. The sky was dark now, and when the autumn mists floated over the moon, the only light came from Bernardo's flashlight. Lola discovered three more truffles in the woods, small and smooth.

As we headed back to Bernardo's house, he reminisced about his largest truffle, eighteen ounces in weight, the size of a grapefruit, and worth over a thousand dollars at today's prices. Ten years ago, Bernardo gave up truffle hunting because he had become possessed by it. He would leave home in the late afternoon, and after a day and a half in the cold damp woods and two packs of cigarettes, he would return home sick and exhausted. Like many others, he had become a truffle junkie—and one day he simply gave it up, except as a moderate and controlled activity to supplement his tiny government pension. "My dream," Bernardo told us, "is to see, together in one place, all the truffles I have found in my lifetime."

Cesare's restaurant was closed that night, and he took us out for an evening of eating and drinking with his friends, including Matteo, a retired *trifulau* who was famous for finding more white truffles than his dog. "You can *see* them," he told us. "In open ground they push up the earth above them, and when the sun is warm, the earth will crack. At night you can feel the bump with the soles of your feet if you wear thin slippers. The grass above a truffle will turn limp and brown when the truffle disturbs its roots. And if you strike the ground with the end of a stick, you can hear the hollow sound of a truffle underneath. But you must be able to distinguish that sound from the sound of a rock or the thick root of a tree."

Matteo's best dog walked into the room and smiled as Matteo continued, "A white truffle takes between forty-four and eighty-eight days to grow, after which it ripens in the space of four hours. If not discovered, it will continue to live for only twelve days when the earth is very wet or up to thirty-five days when the earth is dry. Then it becomes waterlogged and spongy and loses its appeal. If you pick it before it matures, it will never develop its perfume, and you will have destroyed the root, the mother, and no truffle will grow there next year.

"During the four hours of ripening a truffle gives off three distinct aromas—the first is sour and musky like the bottom of a barrel, then a fungus smell like fresh porcini, and finally the stupendous perfume of the white truffle. If you pick a truffle at any time in these four hours, it will continue to ripen because it is a living thing. But if you wait until the third perfume, another *trifulau* may discover it first. Many dogs can detect the last perfume, but only one dog in a thousand can smell the first aroma."

We showed him our six tiny truffles. "My beautiful dog would never have bothered with those." Matteo laughed. The heaviest truffle Matteo ever found weighed twenty-three ounces. "It was so large that it pushed its way up through the earth," Matteo says, "and I tripped over it."

Cesare announced that at five-thirty the next morning he would take us to the truffle market in Ceva, a half hour's drive south. Evening stretched into early morning with the aid of many bottles of Barolo and Barbaresco, glasses of grappa distilled from the pomace of these grapes, and a deep draft from a roadside spring possessing diuretic properties. Cesare's friends sang ballads about the young women of the Langhe and teased us when we grew anxious about getting a few hours' sleep before the truffle market.

A few hours later we had become truffle traders. We arrived at Ceva just past six and parked in a large paved market area, deserted except for fifteen *trifulau*, who stood in groups of two or three in the cold dawn. Somewhere on each of them you could detect the bulge of truffles, in the pockets of their tweed jackets or tucked under their heavy sweaters.

Cesare needed five kilograms of truffles for his restaurant in the coming week, and he brought seven or eight million lire in cash, about five or six thousand dollars. Other towns have more famous markets, like the one in Alba, but they attract tourists who pay too much and unscrupulous sellers who bring in truffles from Umbria and Tuscany or even Bulgaria and Romania and perfume each batch with one genuine *tartufo bianco d'Alba*. The market in Alba is fine for setting the price of local white truffles, but the market in Ceva is Cesare's favorite for stocking up.

As we walked toward one group of *trifulau*, they scattered to the farthest corners of the market, thinking that Cesare had brought revenue agents with him. When Cesare reassured them that we were just Americans, they opened their brown-paper packages and held them up for sniffing. Cesare paid 420,000 lire for a 400-gram batch, or $23 an ounce, a very good price. Restaurants in the Piedmont typically add $16 to your bill for each dish containing truffles. One fine restaurant has a small table by the entrance to the dining room holding a scale, a pile of ten large white truffles under a glass dome—perhaps $2,000 worth—and a carefully lettered sign: TARTUFI BIANCHI. 3200 LIRE PER GRAMMA. Every table chooses its very own truffle, which is weighed before and after the meal, and the bill is adjusted accordingly, at $70 an ounce. The truffle wholesalers in Alba charge between $40 and $50 an ounce for respectable specimens. Beware of stores in the United States that charge less than $60 an ounce for fresh white truffles. If these were genuine *tartufi bianchi d'Alba*, the shop would lose money on every one it sells.

For the next hour Cesare frantically jogged around the parking lot, pulling each *trifulau* off into a corner and collecting as many white truffles as he could before the commercial buyers arrived. His clothes and his van were permeated with the scent of truffles. At seven o'clock the sun was just visible through the mists, and the shops around the market began to open. We stopped in a bar for thirty seconds of coffee and warmth and rushed out again to buy more truffles. The rest of the Ceva market slowly came alive with stalls for game and mushrooms, produce, and dry goods, and Cesare finally turned his attention to huge sacks of walnuts and hazelnuts and flat wooden crates of fresh porcini.

When we returned to Albaretto della Torre for breakfast, Cesare cleaned and weighed his purchases. He had bought 4.6 kilograms of white truffles, about 10 percent of them too small to use in anything but pâtés and sauces. In the past four hours Cesare had worked as feverishly as any commodities trader on the floor of the Chicago exchange. He looked a wreck.

When we left the next morning, our arms filled with Silvana's jam and a gigantic white truffle sealed in a jar of rice, Cesare invited me back to Albaretto to learn the traditional dishes of the Langhe and some of his inventions as well. The secret of his cook ies in the hazelnut branches, though, would remain his alone. "I had a fever for two days after inventing that dish," Cesare told me.

It was springtime when I returned to Cesare's remote hilltop. Rows of hazelnut and fruit trees blossomed along the roads, and a patchwork of ancient vines covered the slopes. But Cesare's life is in the kitchen, and for most of the following week mine was, too, except when I moved to the dining room to eat what we had cooked. Cesare's young cousin, Bianca, who is proficient in English (and whose father was a famous *trifulau*), kept us company, interceding whenever my confusion became evident or when Cesare lapsed into the Langhe dialect. "I am a man of Provence," Cesare inexplicably announces when he has lots to drink. He has successfully refused to learn one word of English.

Cesare began our first morning by collecting the eggs from his hens and a goose, who live behind the restaurant. Back in the kitchen, two of the eggs became my breakfast, along with bread, chestnut-and-thyme honey, and a dark marmalade of sour cherries that Silvana puts up at the beginning of summer. For the next four hours, Cesare was a whirlwind. Fourteen rich Milanese were driving to Albaretto for lunch, and Cesare single-handedly prepared six courses and the broths and sauces that accompanied them, moving urgently between the chopping table, the cold box, and the pots on the crowded stove. Cesare's final chore before his guests arrived was to cook a lavish bowl of spaghetti with tomato sauce for a Saint Bernard called Freida, one of his four dogs. Freida is a vegetarian.

One day when the restaurant was closed, we climbed into Cesare's Lancia for a shopping trip that lasted twelve hours and seven hundred kilometers. We raced over the mountains to Recco, beyond Genoa on the Mediterranean coast, to see the Cafarate brothers and their olive press; Cesare ships them olives from Oneglia, an hour up the coast in the direction of Monte Carlo. "How else can I make sure the olives come from Liguria

When Italy Knew the Noodle

Q Did Marco Polo really introduce pasta to Italy from China?

A. Of course not. In 827, centuries before Marco Polo may or may not have voyaged to China, the Arabs conquered Sicily and brought noodles with them. Some Sicilian pasta dishes still bear Arabic names.

Los Angeles food writer and linguist Charles Perry has found traces of pasta in ancient Greece, in two Latin words borrowed from the Greek, and in the Talmud. (Are noodles leavened or unleavened?) He concludes that Italy knew the noodle long before the Arabs arrived.

Jane Grigson, the late cookery writer at the London *Observer* and author of many terrific cookbooks available in this country, believed that the Marco Polo canard had been hatched in the 1920s or 1930s in an advertisement for a Canadian spaghetti company.

and not from the south or even Spain?" he asks. Cesare dries his own mushrooms, brews his own Barolo vinegar, picks sage and rosemary outside his kitchen door, and manufactures his own salami, *cotechino,* and *coppa.* He often visits the farmers who raise his rabbits and *vitello albese,* a white bovine creature peculiar to Piedmont, halfway between a veal calf and a steer.

We lunched in Portofino, where Cesare spends a few weeks each summer cooking for a Milanese nobleman who winters in Argentina. Then up over the Apennines to Sassuolo, on the outskirts of Modena, where Cesare bargained for Parmesan cheese from a small producer who also sells him *prosciutto di Parma* cured by a good friend. "You can tell the month Parmesan was made and even the field where the cows grazed when you taste it," he explained. Not me. On the exhausting ride home from Modena on the autostrada we stopped at a service area, where I bought Cesare a bag of American tortilla chips. He was extremely gracious.

In my last days with Cesare, I was able to slow him down sufficiently to follow what he was doing in the kitchen. His first task each morning is to prepare the *fondo bruno,* a rich meat broth that underlies so many Piedmontese dishes. It is thin and limpid compared with a French stock: Cesare's version contains wellbrowned pieces of *vitello albese,* to which he adds rosemary and vegetables but no bones, though many Italian broth recipes do. "Bones are for dogs," he says. After the broth has bubbled away for two hours, Cesare ladles it out whenever he needs it, and as lunch approaches, he slides the pan to the back of the stove, where the heat supports only the barest simmer.

Cesare showed me how to cook a *gran bui,* or *bollito misto,* the Piedmontese farmer's feast of ox, rooster, veal, tongue, *cotechino* sausage, and half a calf's head, boiled in three pots and then combined; several risotti (Piedmont grows more rice than Lombardy); a scrumptious apple turnover of *pasta sfoglia,* Italian puff pastry; and his *torte di nocciole.* The Langhe is noted for its hazelnuts, intense in flavor but without bitterness, and also for the *torte di nocciole* made from them—yeasty cakes packed with nuts. Cesare's version is like a huge cookie, crisp and buttery, the size of a dinner plate.

Cesare is also a master of zabaglione, the most famous dessert of Piedmont—a foam of egg yolks, sugar, and wine, which Cesare makes with Moscato d'Asti, a local sweet sparkling wine with the taste of orange, instead of the familiar Marsala. Zabaglione was invented by felicitous mistake in seventeenth-century Turin and was thus named for San Giovanni Baylon, patron saint of pastry. Cesare learned the technique from a destitute priest, Don Camera, who had only the tiniest church to support him but who made a celestial *zabajone*, as they call it in the Langhe. The secret, Cesare told me, is to whisk an *odd* number of egg yolks over a *high* flame (contrary to every cookbook instruction), not in a bain-marie. Only San Giovanni knows why this works, but it does.

We did not have time to do Cesare's famous fritto misto with twenty ingredients, but he did teach me four versions of *bagna caôda*. Three of them contain lots of Barolo (or very old Barbaresco) because they were passed on to Cesare by an eighty-year-old man who was always drunk. *Bagna caôda* is a hot Piedmontese sauce for raw vegetables, typically made with butter, olive oil, garlic, and anchovies—oil and butter flow together in Piedmont like nowhere else in Italy. It is served in a chafing dish or in individual ceramic candle warmers to keep it slowly bubbling, and you dip raw vegetables into it—cardoons, bell peppers, celery, cabbage, and fennel—holding a piece of bread underneath to catch the drippings on the journey to your mouth. Then you eat the bread.

Cesare's favorite recipes for *bagna caôda; fondo bruno,* the wonderful, deeply flavored meat broth he uses in many sauces and soups; and his *sugo d'arrosto,* that brothlike sauce used in Piedmont with many pastas, follow. First I will give you a fine recipe for *tajarin* noodles with white truffles, which I have finally got right. The finest way to enjoy white truffles, and no more difficult to make than any other pasta, *tajarin* are prepared daily in nearly every Piedmontese restaurant I have visited. I have never found them in the United States, even at the most expensive and pretentious Italian restaurants that are proud to serve the first white truffles of the season. The sauce is simple and mild, so that it does not detract from the truffles.

Tajarin al Burro e Salvia con Tartufi Bianchi
All-Egg-Yolk Pasta with Butter, Sage, and White Truffles

White truffles are available between November and late January. Squeeze and smell your truffle before you buy it. Fresh truffles are *very firm* and aromatic. Spongy truffles are old and tired. Many fans believe that large specimens have a more stupendous taste than little ones. Strong aroma is no guarantee of flavor, but if you know of a fancy-food store that lets you taste your *tartufo* before paying for it, please let me know.

Tajarin is Piedmontese dialect for the most rich and delicious tagliarini noodles made with egg yolks instead of the whole eggs used in the rest of Italy (though some Piedmontese cooks mix yolks and whole eggs). They are best consumed after your routine cholesterol test, not before. In Alba they are rolled with a wooden dowel and hand-cut an eighth inch wide. I have found nothing like them, fresh or dried, in any pasta store I know. The Piedmontese refer to the "red" of an egg, not the yellow, because their egg yolks are orange-red and their *tajarin* are a deep golden color. Yours will be paler.

Hand-rolled noodles are generally made with unbleached white flour rather than semolina because its high gluten content makes semolina hard to work by hand. The method given here uses a pasta-rolling

263

machine for thinning the dough and a knife for cutting it into noodles. If you are good at hand-rolling pasta, which I am not, by all means try it; the results will be lighter and more tender. But remember that hand-rolling is not like making pie pastry. The dough must be stretched, not compressed, into a thin sheet. If your hand-rolling technique merely compresses the dough, you may as well use a machine. Those expensive square white electric pasta extruders with the plastic templates are completely out of bounds.

The sauce combines butter browned with sage, uncooked butter used for its fresh taste, and just enough Parmesan and meat broth to add a savory undertone that intensifies the taste of the white truffle. If you can easily identify the Parmesan or the meat broth, you have used too much.

1 pound unbleached white flour
Salt
20 yolks from extra-large eggs
12 tablespoons sweet butter, softened at room temperature
12 large sage leaves, roughly chopped, plus 6 to 8 more for
*   decoration*
Freshly ground white pepper
1 tablespoon well-packed freshly grated Parmesan cheese
2 tablespoons meat broth (Cesare's recipe is given on page 267)
2 ounces white truffles

Put all but 1 cup of the flour on the counter (or, into a wide shallow bowl, if you are wary of repeating my disastrous first try), sprinkle with a half tablespoon of salt, make a depression in the center, and pour in the egg yolks. Stir the yolks with a fork, gradually incorporating all the flour that surrounds them, until you have a sticky mass of dough. With the reserved cup, heavily flour your hands and work surface, and knead the dough, adding flour as necessary, until you have a smooth, soft ball that no longer sticks to your fingers. Cover it with a towel and let it relax for 30 minutes. You can also use a food processor until the dough forms a ball and finish the kneading by hand.

Divide the dough into six roughly equal pieces and roll each one eight or nine times through a pasta machine with the rollers at the widest setting, folding the dough and turning it after each pass. Thin each piece of dough at increasingly narrow settings until you have sheets a bit thicker than ordinary pasta (usually setting 5) and about 20 inches long. Place the sheets flat on a very lightly floured surface, dust with a little flour, and let them dry until their surface begins to resemble leather but before they become brittle. Turn them over to dry the other side. Total drying time will be 15 to 30 minutes.

Working with the sheets of dough one at a time, fold from one short end to the other several times into a compact shape 3 inches long; trim the ragged edges with a flat-bladed knife, then cut into ⅛-inch strips. Unfold the noodles and let them dry as you work on the other sheets. Then let them dry further, for up to a half day.

Just before dinnertime, put 6 quarts of cold water in a large covered pot over a high flame. Melt 8 tablespoons of the butter (one stick) in a small skillet over medium heat and, when it stops sizzling, turn the flame to low and add the chopped sage. Let the butter infuse for 20 minutes as it lightly browns. Strain out the sage. Add 1 teaspoon of salt, two or three grindings of white pepper, the Parmesan, and the meat broth, and keep warm. Warm a large heatproof bowl and your pasta plates in a low oven.

When the water comes to a boil, add 4 tablespoons

of salt, let the water come to the boil again, and add all the noodles at once, stirring until the water boils again. Cook the noodles at a full boil until they lose their rubbery texture but are still resistant to the bite—as long as 5 minutes, depending on how long you have let them dry. After 2 minutes, test them every 30 seconds by fishing out a noodle and eating it.

Drain the pasta very well, and put it into the large warm bowl. Pour the sauce over the pasta and toss. Cut the remaining 4 tablespoons of softened butter into small pieces, add to the pasta, and toss. Divide the pasta among 6 to 8 warm plates, decorate each serving with a sage leaf, and quickly shave the truffles over each serving in paper-thin slices using either a truffle grater or the wide blade on a four-sided vegetable grater. Serves 6 to 8.

Cesare's Favorite *Bagna Caôda*

This famous sauce of the Piedmont is kept bubbling at the table and used for dipping vegetables. Many restaurants in the Piedmont serve *bagna caôda* spooned over wide strips of roasted, peeled red and yellow bell peppers.

Divide a large head of garlic (about 3 ounces) into cloves. Peel and trim the garlic cloves, and cut them crosswise into 1/8-inch slices. In a small saucepan, bring 1 cup of Barolo to the boil, add the garlic, and simmer for 2 minutes. Add 1½ ounces of anchovy fillets (8 to 10 of them) and ½ cup of extra-virgin olive oil, and simmer for a moment or two more. Add 4 tablespoons of butter and simmer very slowly for 45 minutes, until the anchovies dissolve. You can prepare this *bagna caôda* in advance, but do not refrigerate it. Simply reheat it at the table.

Cesare makes a milder version by simmering the garlic slices in 1 cup of milk for 2 minutes and straining out the milk before adding the Barolo, anchovies, oil, and butter. This is the Dei Cacciatori House Special.

Sugo d'Arrosto
Sage and Meat Sauce for *Tagliarini*, *Agnolotti*, and Other Pastas

Melt 1 tablespoon of butter in a skillet, add 6 large fresh sage leaves and a peeled garlic clove, and lightly brown the butter over medium heat. Remove the garlic, add 1½ cups of meat broth, simmer for a moment, and remove from heat. Cook enough pasta for 6 people (¾ to 1 pound as a light appetizer) in ample boiling salted water until it is just al dente—it will cook further in the sauce. Bring the sauce back to simmer, add the pasta and 1 cup of freshly grated Parmesan very loosely packed, and cook for 3 or 4 minutes, tossing until the cheese has disappeared and the pasta is hot. Divide the pasta among 6 warm plates, grate a little Parmesan over each (including the rim, if you wish), and serve. Serves 6.

Fondo Bruno
Piemontese Meat Broth

Cesare uses the rosy meat from the breast of a white bovine creature peculiar to Piemonte, halfway between a veal calf and a steer. This deeply flavored broth can be used as the base for any hearty Italian soup, is indis-

pensable in *sugo d'arrosto,* and adds a savory undertone
to the browned sage and butter sauce for *tajarin* with
white truffles.

Extra-virgin olive oil
2½ pounds vitello albese *or brisket of beef, cut into 3-inch pieces*
3 fresh rosemary branches, each 6 inches long
1 celery stalk
1 garlic clove, peeled
1 onion, 3 to 4 inches in diameter, peeled and cut into eighths
2 tablespoons kosher salt
2 small ripe tomatoes, cored and seeded
3½ quarts cold water

Put a wide 9- to 12-quart pan over high heat, film
the bottom of the pan with olive oil, and brown the
meat very well on all sides, lowering the flame if the
meat juices threaten to burn. After the pieces of meat
have browned on one side, begin adding the rosemary,
celery, garlic, onion, and salt, waiting 30 seconds
between additions as the meat continues to brown.
When the meat juices begin to caramelize on the bottom of the pan, add the tomatoes.

When the meat is well browned, add the water. Let
the water come to the boil, lower the heat, and simmer
for 3 to 4 hours. During the first 30 minutes, skim the
white foam that collects on the surface. Then cover partially and skim occasionally. Strain. Refrigerate any
broth that you do not need for that day's cooking; it
will keep for 3 to 4 days if you boil it for 15 minutes
before using. Makes 3 quarts.

February and September 1989

Where's the Wagyu?

Three hundred dollars' worth of Wagyu quivered and sweated on my countertop. I watched it, paralyzed by indecision and ignorance.

To the unaided eye, it looked like an ordinary, raw, boneless prime rib-eye steak, two pounds in weight and two and a half inches thick. But to my eyes, aided by reams of misinformation, this was Kobe beef, the most famous, expensive, and delicious beef in the world, taken from an ancient strain of Japanese black cattle that are raised on a diet of beer and sake-soaked grain and pampered throughout their lives with massage and acupuncture. *Wa* means "Japanese" in Japanese and *gyu* means "cattle."

Now for the first time ever, Wagyu was being imported into the United States and, to my unbelievable good fortune, was being sold exclusively by my friendly butcher, Charlie Gagliardo at Balducci's in Greenwich Village, for $150 a pound. Minutes after hearing the news, I rushed down to Balducci's, negotiated a ridiculously low wholesale price of $45 a pound, and returned home with a sheaf of press releases and a two-pound hunk of Wagyu. The surface of my Wagyu was intricately laced with delicate veins of off-white fat—by laboratory measurement, *three times* more marbling fat than U.S. prime-grade beef, though with slightly less cholesterol. This is the fat that made Wagyu famous—rich and tender and juicy and sweet, the foie gras of beef.

But with only two hours left until dinner, how would I cook it? I felt like a diamond cutter—one slip and a fortune in Wagyu would be destroyed.

I sat next to my kitchen counter to keep an eye on the Wagyu while I read through my Japanese cookbooks and the articles and publicity I had collected. I discovered how little reliable information is readily available in English about this culinary treasure. The best way to prepare Wagyu, I read, is to grill it or panfry it or cook it in *shabu shabu* or sukiyaki, or not to cook it at all and to serve it raw, like beef sashimi, sliced a generous eighth-inch thick and called *tataki*. When prepared like a steak, it should be left two inches thick or maybe cut down to a half inch, the fire should be very high or very low, the timing will be longer or maybe shorter than for U.S. beef, the external fat should be removed or left on, the ideal state of doneness is rare or maybe medium-well, and the perfect portion is a twelve-ounce slab or a three-ounce sliver.

Now, with only an hour remaining before dinner, I telephoned Mr. Nishi's beeper. A Japanese meat broker working in New York, Mr. Nishi returned my call almost immediately from his car phone as he crossed the Queensboro Bridge into Manhattan. In Japanese steak houses, he told me, Wagyu is either grilled over wood charcoal or panfried, nine ounces of meat for each person, often cooked medium-well, and served with vegetables and rice. It is crucial to achieve a good brown crust on the meat.

My favorite way of grilling a really thick steak—I adapted it years ago from one of Christopher Idone's cookbooks—seemed ideal, so I cut all the external fat from my Wagyu; divided it crosswise into two thick steaks (for purposes of experimentation); salted them a few minutes before cooking so that some juices would come to the surface, where they would caramelize nicely; popped them briefly under a very hot broiler until the outside was crusty but not charred; transferred the Wagyu to a 350-degree oven, where the insides would finish cooking; took their temperature every few minutes with my instant-read meat thermometer; removed one steak when it had reached 120 degrees for rare and the other at 140 degrees for medium-well; lightly peppered them; and let them rest for ten minutes. I called my wife to the table, cut each steak in two, and we began to eat.

The rare steak was tough, and its marbling fat had not melted into the flesh; its taste hinted at a sweet richness but was not strong enough to matter. The medium-well steak was fibrous, mealy, and nearly inedible.

Either I had ruined a king's ransom in Wagyu, or Wagyu is a cruel and evil hoax. I had to know the truth. We took a plane to Hong Kong, boarded a ship for Japan, and two weeks later landed in Osaka. (This is a ludicrous route to Osaka, but my wife had business on the way.) We chose Osaka because its inhabitants are famous for dining to what the Japanese call *kui-daore*, or "surfeited collapse," which coincides with my own aspirations, and also because Kimio Ito, the generous brother of a Japanese friend in New York, was ready to treat us to the best Wagyu feast in town, at a restaurant called Devon Steak.

We entered past a cooler piled high with slabs of beef even more thoroughly marbled than my Wagyu back home, sat in a booth around an immense stainless-steel griddle, and ordered a raw beef appetizer, a beef main course, beer, sake, and melon ice cream. While we ate the velvety rectangles of raw Wagyu (they tasted more like raw tuna than beef), followed by a grainy version of vichyssoise, a salad of iceberg lettuce, and a heavenly little baked Hokkaido potato, the chef stood at the open end of the booth and cooked our steak.

He buttered the griddle, layered cubes of fat and peeled garlic cloves on it, placed a massive rib eye, three inches thick, on top of them, and covered everything with a copper dome for a minute or two, apparently to melt the fat and infuse the beef with the lightest garlic perfume. The cover was lifted, the garlic and fat were scraped to one side, and the beef was doused with cognac and allowed to luxuriate for a minute or two more, again under its copper dome.

Then the cooking began in earnest. With visible concentration, the chef sliced off every bit of surface fat and separated the cap from the body of the rib eye, putting everything but the very heart of the beef to one side. He asked Kimio, who asked us how we liked our beef—we divided between rare and medium-rare—and then he lightly salted the meat, rotated it on the griddle to caramelize every side, and ground a fine sprinkling of pepper over it. Several times the meat was cut in two, the cut sides were browned, and one half was moved to the warm edge of the griddle while the chef attended to the other.

Finally, most of the beef lay resting at the side while he worked on four small pieces of steak, each two inches by one inch by one-half. He frequently tested their internal condition by pressing them with a chopstick, and when he felt they were done, he lifted them onto one of the square mats of aluminum foil that sat on the warm edge of the griddle in front of each of us, scraped the griddle clean of cooked fat, and went on to the next portion. He worked slowly and carefully, with none of the samurai swordsmanship you see at Benihana.

By the end, each of us had received ten strips of steak, deliciously browned and almost crisp on the outside, rosy inside, and brimming with juice. The chef cooked the rib-eye cap last and then the cubes of Wagyu fat, which rendered crisp as goose cracklings. There was a little dish of dipping sauce at each place—soy, garlic, honey, miso, and a secret spice whose identity is known only to Devon Steak.

While my wife was in the ladies' room, I made off with two of her Wagyu morsels for the scientific purpose of comparing her rare with my medium-rare. Mine won. It lacked none of the tenderness and moisture that steak can lose when you grill it medium; like most blood-red meat, hers lacked a rich beefy taste.

Wagyu is not a cruel and evil hoax. It is the best beef I have ever eaten, as tender and closely grained as the finest filet mignon, with the melting juiciness of the richest rib steak and the savor of less expensive cuts like hanger and skirt steak, though with a sweeter, more delicate character. It was also the most expensive meal I've ever had. Kimio would not, of course, let us see the menu, but I noticed a placard on the way out of Devon Steak from which I inferred a price of 40,000 yen plus service and tax, or $340 a person. That makes Paris look like a fantastic bargain.

A few days later I was back in New York, padding down to Balducci's again for more Wagyu. This time, I also bought a U.S. prime rib eye for comparison, identical except for its markedly more modest marbling. I improvised a griddle from a wide stainless-steel sauté pan with a thick copper bottom and clumsily tried to follow the procedure I had observed in Osaka. The Wagyu was wonderful, at least half the equal of its cousin at Devon Steak. Next to it, rare U.S. prime tasted bloody, almost wild, and required lots of savage chomping and tearing; cooked medium, it became stringy and coarse and dry.

I have finally located someone who knows the facts about Wagyu, Dr. David Lunt, superintendent of the McGregor Research Center of Texas A&M University, where they have been raising Wagyu for several years now. Their hope is that U.S. ranchers, with production costs only 30 to 50 percent of those in Japan, will be able to ship Wagyu to the lucrative Japanese market, where it fetches $60 to $150 a pound at retail, depending on the cut and quality.

The Wagyu strain of cattle was probably brought to Japan as a draft animal from Manchuria and down the Korean Peninsula in the second century A.D., at the same time that rice cultivation was introduced. Wagyu worked for at least a thousand years in the rice paddies before they were consumed as food. Most Wagyu are raised as a cottage industry on small family farms throughout Japan, though there are some large operations as well; many farmers haul their cattle to the region around Kobe for finishing and processing, because beef with the Kobe name still commands a higher price. Wagyu are not allowed to graze freely, and massage is used to soothe their stiff muscles, not to disperse their fat; they are occasionally fed beer to maintain a healthy population of microbes in their rumen, or large stomach, not to flavor their flesh or keep them relaxed. The distinctive taste and marbling of Wagyu are partly genetic and partly the result of feeding methods; their fat contains a high ratio of monosaturated oleic acid (also found in olive oil), which accounts for its buttery taste and moderate cholesterol.

The McGregor Research Center has just had its second Wagyu slaughter, and the Japanese flew over to appraise the meat. Just as U.S. government meat graders use a series of color photographs against which to compare the marbling in a slab of beef, Japanese graders use acrylic steaks, like the cute plastic food you see in the windows of Japanese restaurants. The Texas Wagyu was a perfect success—the Japanese experts gave it their highest possible rating.

August 1991

Kyoto Cuisine

Standing on the corner of Takakura-dori and Shijo-dori, waiting for the light to change, I knew that I could eat here forever.

I was in downtown Kyoto, currently my favorite city in the entire world, "home of the Japanese spirit," as someone has described it, capital of Japan for eleven centuries, birthplace of its traditional arts, crafts, and literature, and, more important than any of these, the source of its most refined, restrained, and elegant cuisine. Only my friends in nearby Osaka think that their food is better.

With just a few hours left in Japan, I headed toward the Takashimaya and Daimaru department stores, which I had first visited within minutes of arriving in Kyoto. Throughout Japan, the great department stores devote their entire basements to displays of food that rival the great food halls of Europe. There are exquisitely wrapped Japanese sweets and brand-name European chocolates; Chinese takeout and groceries from Milan; Jamaican Blue Mountain coffee for fifty dollars a pound and melons that fetch seventy-five dollars each; delicacies and delicatessen from Munich. Daimaru's pride is a café and bakery run by Paul Bocuse, complete with plastic models of French breakfasts and a TV screen showing live bread bakers laboring somewhere in the bowels of the store.

But I was tired of grazing, and I had lost interest in most Western food, a potentially perilous condition in my line of work.

I wondered how I would eat when I returned home. Would anything satisfy me but three meals a day of Kyo-ryori, "Kyoto cuisine"? And I blamed it all on Mr. Shizuo Tsuji and Mr. Nagata's bowl of soup.

So I walked two blocks to say goodbye to Nishikikoji. This medieval market street is a quarter mile long, roofed over with red, green, and yellow awnings, and lined with 141 specialized shops selling raw and cooked foods, seaweed and rice and tofu of every description, fresh-roasted tea, sashimi knives, whiskey, pickles, and more fish than in an average-sized ocean—a hundred species in cases and tanks, pickled, dried, and salted fish in barrels and trays, fish being grilled over charcoal, fried as tempura, or cut into sushi. In the early morning, restaurant chefs collect their raw materials at Nishiki; in the afternoon, housewives and grandmothers elbow you aside as they assemble their dinners.

For two weeks before arriving in Kyoto, my wife and I had toured the southern half of Japan on a luxury cruise ship, from Okinawa to the island of Kyushu and then through the Inland Sea from Hiroshima to Osaka. In exchange for our passage, my wife was obliged to deliver six lectures on Japanese art and pretend that the food aboard ship was nearly edible. My job was to play the grumbling spouse, a role so foreign to my nature that an entire hour passed before I got fully into it. My sea change was helped along by the appearance of an unexpected typhoon in the East China Sea, which for several days tossed our ship about as if it were a tiny morsel of tempura in a cauldron of boiling oil. But when the typhoon had moved on, we left the ship whenever its throbbing engines mercifully stopped, and with an adventurous little band of fellow passengers sampled the regional cooking of Japan.

Our constant companion was *Gateway to Japan* by June Kinoshita and Nicholas Palevsky (Kodansha, 1990), an amazingly comprehensive guide to the history, culture, shopping, sights, food, and lodgings of this country. The writing is compact and witty, and the authors have included everything you need to know, from transit diagrams to an annotated list of Tokyo's sex parlors, ranked "in order of difficulty." *Gateway* is not simply the best guidebook to Japan—it is the best single guide to any country I've ever visited. And the restaurant suggestions we followed—mainly in provincial cities where we lacked personal recommendations—were highly rewarding.

I had prepared for Japan by reading *Japanese Etiquette* (Tuttle), compiled by the Tokyo YWCA in 1955. I learned that there are three ways to bow in Japan and one way to drink your soup. First you remove the domed lid from the soup bowl with your right hand, place the lid upside down on the tray or table, lift the bowl with your right hand and place it onto the palm of your left, and drink some liquid. Then you pick up your chopsticks with your right hand, arranging them with your left, and eat some of the contents of the bowl. Next you eat some of your rice. Finally you can eat anything at will. But please don't touch the pickles until you finish your soup.

The first time I tried this, fate quickly carried me beyond the scenario sketched out by the Tokyo YWCA. When I tried to lift the lid from my soup bowl, the entire bowl rose from the table. This is not unheard of: if you waste too much time arranging your chopsticks, your soup cools down and forms a vacuum under the lid. So I grasped the bowl firmly with one hand, I don't remember which, and tried to dislodge the lid with the other. When that failed, I squeezed the bowl with both hands (lacquered wood is flexible), imagining that the lid would pop right off. Then, praying nobody would notice, I lodged the bowl in the crook of my right elbow for extra leverage and tried to wrench off the lid with my left hand. Finally I wedged the bowl between my knees and used both hands to tear it open. This worked like a charm. But the lid slipped from my hands, flipped over, and plopped into the bowl, splashing the thick white soup in a perfect circle over the tatami mat, the gleaming table, the flower arrangement, and me. I shelved my book of Japanese etiquette and thenceforth played the bumbling Westerner with no knowledge of local manners. I simply tried not to offend.

They used to say that it is impossible to get a bad meal in Paris. They were wrong. But try as we might, we could not find a truly bad Japanese meal in Japan. (We did find a wide variety of mediocre Western meals without even trying.) You can eat amply and well for six dollars a person at a noodle shop, for twenty dollars at a place serving everything grilled on skewers, for sixty dollars for a seven-course dinner in a private room at a handsome restaurant in the provinces, and for four hundred dollars a person and up at the most refined *kaiseki* banquet in Kyoto, probably the most expensive restaurant food in the world. The setting, the cost of the ingredients, and the level of artistry may differ, but concern for freshness and the urge to do one's best seem nearly universal.

In Naha, on Okinawa, known as the Hawaii of Japan for its beaches and tropical climate, the cooking shows a Chinese influence in its rich sauces and enthusiastic use of pork and peanuts—a crunchy Japanese version of shredded pig's ears with cucumbers, peanut tofu, and a delicious pig-tripe soup. In Kagoshima, on Kyushu, called the Naples of Japan by someone who has never been to Naples, we were introduced to delectable sardine sashimi with a mustard sauce, and raw chicken breasts and gizzards—thinly sliced, attractively fanned, nearly tasteless, and almost too chewy to swallow. At least there is no sign of salmonella in Japan.

Hiroshima is famous for, among other things, its oysters and its perennially last-place baseball team, named the Carps. At Kakifune Kanawa—a converted barge anchored in the Motoyasu River at the edge of the Peace Memorial Park—oysters are served ten ways. Our oyster banquet included seven: raw, huge, and icy on the half shell; skewered and grilled; crisp juicy tempura; baked in their shells on a bed of salt; raw and marinated in a little cup of vinegar and soy (our favorite); stewed in a miso broth; and pan-fried, chopped, mixed with rice, and arbitrarily called risotto. A half-mile stroll upriver from Kakifune Kanawa through the graceful park is the skeleton of the one prewar structure remaining in a city that has otherwise been completely rebuilt. It stood at ground zero on August 6, 1945.

If the meals we ate before arriving in Kyoto seemed better than most of the Japanese food I've had in the United States, their superiority was more a matter of degree than of kind. The seafood was universally fresh, the flavors were remarkably clear, the spices and herbs were both more delicate and more vivid than in the Japanese food back home. But for our first two weeks in Japan, just as I do when I have a Japanese meal in New York or Los Angeles, I still longed for a hamburger, French fries, and a Milky Way bar after dinner. Kyoto changed all that.

It was May when we arrived in Kyoto. The *tai* were running, the *kinome* was in fine fettle, and *takenoko* were pushing up through the earth in the groves around Kyoto. *Tai* is Japanese sea bream, a firm, lean white-fleshed fish unlike the bream of other waters. Raw and sliced, it makes a fine sashimi (in May, often garnished with a baby cucumber, one inch long and still wearing its yellow flower); when slices of *tai* are wrapped around a long cone of vinegared rice and tied in bamboo leaf, it is called *chimaki*. May is also the month to eat bonito, *karei* flounder, horse mackerel, and sea trout. Westerners know that oysters are delectable only in cold months; Japanese chefs know the ideal time for a hundred kinds of fish.

Kinome is the bright green, newly formed leaf of the *sancho* (prickly ash) tree and the favorite herb of professional Japanese chefs, always used fresh and not, I think, eaten anywhere outside Japan. We found little, fern-shaped sprigs of *kinome* in every meal we had in Kyoto. Commonly described as light and minty, its wonderful astringent taste I find also reminiscent of lemon peel and coriander. A few weeks before our visit, the *kinome* was tiny and tasteless; a few weeks after, gross and bitter. And while in Kyoto, we could feel the *kinome* season slipping away as spring turned into summer and the leaves grew larger day by day.

Takenoko are bamboo shoots. I have spent a lifetime avoiding those stringy, tough, bitter canned bamboo shoots you find in

Asian food in this country and wondering why anyone in the world would bother to cut off the tip of a bamboo plant just before it emerges from the earth, husk the thick woody covering, and eat its pale golden heart. Now, for the first time, I tasted them fresh—sweet and crunchy and tender—in a restaurant on the outskirts of Kyoto called Kinsuitei that serves, in thatched pavilions along a shaded lake, a many-course lunch of fresh bamboo: bamboo grilled on bamboo skewers, bamboo shredded with seaweed, bamboo sliced like sashimi with a soy-based dipping sauce, bamboo floating in soup, bamboo simmered in broth, bamboo deep-fried as tempura, and bamboo chopped in rice. Perhaps that's the problem with impeccably seasonal food—you wait an entire year for the fleeting moment to arrive, and then you overdose.

2 8 0

Kyoto is the home of *kaiseki ryori*, perhaps the most refined and exquisite branch of Japanese cooking. This is formal Japanese haute cuisine, served in nine courses or more on antique ceramics and lacquerware, usually in a small private room. A *kaiseki* meal appeals to all the senses; only seasonal ingredients are used and only at the peak of their freshness.

Our friend Sunja traveled from Kobe to Kyoto and took us to a *kaiseki* lunch at the famous restaurant Hyotei, five teahouses joined by bamboo walkways in a lush garden around a little pond. It was raining when we arrived at the gate, and each of us was given a light, broad bamboo basket to hold over our heads as we walked the twenty feet to a three-hundred-year-old teahouse. I felt as if I had become a figure in a Japanese print.

Inside, a hanging scroll and purple irises in a narrow alcove set the mood of late springtime, as did the patterns and colors on ceramics and lacquerware throughout the meal. We sat on a tatami floor of woven grass, some sections fresh and green, others dry and crackling. The paper window screen was open to the garden, and rain trickled down from the thatched roof.

A little wooden table was placed before each of us, and for the next two hours a set meal was served in groups of dishes on

lacquered trays, seven courses in all, loosely following the traditional order from appetizers to raw fish and soup to grilled foods
to steamed to simmered to fried. We began with a dish of tiny,
sweetly caramelized fish; thin slices of raw *tai* garnished with a
baby cucumber; a white miso soup; and sesame tofu surrounded
by *junsai*, a plant that grows on the bottom of deep, clear, old
ponds such as Midorogaike, north of Kyoto. In late spring, its
immature green buds are surrounded by a gelatinous sheath—
junsai is a texture food.

The next tray held a little rectangular plate with three peeled
fava beans; an egg cut in two (magically, the white was set and
the lightly flavored yolk was liquid); a young ginger shoot that
shaded from lavender to white; a cube of tofu omelet in a round
dish; and two *chimaki*, one with raw *tai* and the other with eel,
tied tightly in bamboo leaves. The tray was decorated with two
tiny green maple leaves, a reminder of spring, in case we had forgotten.

In our clear soup we found a shrimp wrapped in *yuba* (a thick
bean-curd skin), new peas, a tree-ear mushroom, and a lily root.
Suzuki (sea bass) followed, deliciously panfried and brushed with
a glistening, mildly sweet teriyaki sauce and garnished with the
flower of the *sancho* tree, and then rice and pickles and another
soup, this one containing bright green and white vegetables and
abalone wrapped in a rectangle of fish. Bitter green tea was
served with a slice of melon and then a light brown Japanese
sweet that seemed no more explicable than any other Japanese
sweet I've tasted. But the melon was an epiphany of melons: the
skin of a cantaloupe, the green flesh and size of a honeydew, and
the perfume and sweetness of a jungle thick with honeysuckles.

I blush when I consider how much of this food-poem went
by me unnoticed. But ignorance has its own rewards. Japanese
gourmets have always sought the mysterious and exotic in their
ingredients and textures. As Diane Durston tells it in her indispensable *Old Kyoto* (Kodansha, 1986), the warlords and wealthy
merchants of the Edo period played a game of guessing what they

had just been served for dinner. Nothing could be more authentically Japanese than not knowing what you are eating.

A traditional Japanese chef works under a series of demanding constraints. His insistence on cooking foods only at their seasonal peak eliminates three-quarters of the possibilities at any one time. And his concern for freshness rules out most ingredients from other parts of the country. His recipes contain only four or five ingredients; I've made complex French sauces that require twenty. Japanese flavors seem to work as complements or counterpoints to each other; ours are meant to blend and orchestrate. Yet after a week of eating in Kyoto, you are unaware of any limitations. Your palate stops looking for strong, complex Western flavors, just as your eyes adjust to the soft light of a traditional Japanese house.

Japan imported Buddhism in the sixth century from the Asian mainland, where the semitropical profusion of fruits and vegetables made the Buddhist rule against killing easier to live with. But a relatively short growing season and little arable land forced the Japanese to rely on variety and ingenuity instead of abundance in their cooking. Many of the dishes we associate with Japan are relative newcomers. Portuguese missionaries taught the Japanese how to deep-fry in the late sixteenth century (and brought them hot red peppers, too); as with many things, Japanese cooks have become the greatest deep-fry artists in the world, creating the incomparably light, crisp, and translucent tempura. The most familiar form of sushi—slices of raw fish on bite-sized mounds of vinegared rice and properly called *nigirizushi*—was not invented until 1818. For laypeople in Japan, the Buddhist rule against killing applied only to four-legged animals, making fish and fowl available. But cows, sheep, pigs, and goats were taboo until 1873, when the Meiji emperor announced that the Buddhist proscription was "irrational." Sukiyaki appeared only at the turn of this century, and I've read that *shabu shabu* was devised after World War II by a Kyoto chef who had enjoyed a Mongolian hot pot in a Chinese restaurant. Of these, only tempura belongs in a *kaiseki* meal. Three hundred years is long enough, even in Japan, for something to become traditional.

Four fundamental raw ingredients underlie all Japanese cuisine—flavors that until now had struck me as monotonous and bland—rice, soybeans, dashi, and fish. Rice is served boiled or steamed at every meal and never fried; it is also made into sake, *mirin*, and vinegar, and its bran is used for pickling. Soybeans become soy sauce and tofu in all their varieties. And dashi is a simple, delicate broth of giant kelp (an olive-green seaweed) and dried bonito (a member of the mackerel family). Dashi is the base of nearly all soups; chicken stock appears only if one of the main solid ingredients in the soup is chicken. *Every Japanese dish or its dipping sauce is flavored with soy or dashi or both.*

283

Before arriving in Japan, I had arranged an introduction from a mutual friend to Mr. Shizuo Tsuji, the renowned Japanese chef whose cooking school in Osaka—École Technique Hôtelière Tsuji—is the largest and most important in Japan. (There is a branch in Lyons for his advanced students of French cuisine, and Mr. Tsuji has written an astounding illustrated encyclopedia of French cooking, published in a limited Japanese edition.) His *Japanese Cooking: A Simple Art* (Kodansha, 1980) is one of the finest cookbooks published in English about any cuisine, beautifully written without a touch of pretense and crystal clear in its essays, explanations of ingredients and techniques, line drawings, and 220 recipes.

Draconian and petty airline regulations prevented me from meeting Mr. Tsuji, but as soon as we arrived in Kyoto, we felt that we were under his protection and tutelage. He recommended a variety of restaurants, telephoning one of them in advance to order our dinner. And near the end of our stay he dispatched to Kyoto his *directeur de cabinet*, Mr. Kazuo Nakamura, and a professor of Japanese cuisine, Mr. Kazuki Kondo, who took us to dinner at a restaurant named Chihana (A Thousand Flowers).

Chihana is a tiny place with a sandalwood counter and just two tables, all done in a variety of satiny blond woods, and it is presided over by Mr. Nagata, the seventy-five-year-old chef-owner. The food is like a *kaiseki* banquet but served in an alternate manner popular in Kyoto. You sit at the counter, and Mr. Nagata and his oldest son hand you the food the moment it is prepared, discreetly watching your reactions with a sideways glance. First there was a series of tiny appetizers: a little cup of gelatinous *junsai* delicately flavored with dashi, soy, and vinegar (the first time I saw the point of eating *junsai*); plump raw clams with seaweed; the tenderest cold octopus, stewed for three hours in dashi, soy, and sake; sea trout grilled in salt with a sauce of *ume*, soy, and salt (*ume* are called plums but are really apricots); and barely cooked broad beans with a loose white rectangle of something called children-of-the-clouds. This is a welcome euphemism for the sperm of a fish, often cod but in this meal *tai* sperm. Its flavor is bland and difficult to describe, except to say that it does not taste like fish; its texture and appearance resemble tofu or unset custard. I do not expect to find children-of-the-clouds stands popping up in minimalls across America.

Now came the moment for clear soup and sashimi, "the test pieces of Japanese cuisine," as Mr. Tsuji puts it, "the criteria by which a meal stands or falls. . . . The soup and raw fish are so important that the other dishes are merely garnishes." The fish instantly reveals whether the chef sets high standards for freshness and seasonal perfection. That I can readily understand. But a bowl of clear soup as the centerpiece of a complicated feast? This is the course I listlessly sip at Japanese restaurants in New York or Los Angeles, if I touch it at all.

Across the sandalwood counter, Mr. Nagata handed me a covered bowl and said, "It is all right for you to start." Translated from the polite language of the Japanese, this means "You'd better get started instantly or you'll ruin my food." I lifted the lid and was lost in a cloud of aromatic vapor, familiar but intense. I briefly noticed a cube of tofu, a shiitake mushroom, and a sprig of *kinome* in the broth, and I began to drink it. The basic flavors were a summing up of the Japanese concept of *umami*, of savoriness, meatiness, mouthwateringness, the bliss-point of any food. *Umami* is the Japanese fifth taste (our textbooks tell us there are four), and dried bonito, kelp, and shiitake all offer a concentrated dose of *umami.*

On the way to the Osaka airport, I bought another copy of Mr. Tsuji's *Japanese Cooking: A Simple Art* and read it all the way home as though it were a thriller. The mysteries of Mr. Nagata's soup were easy to solve. "If the soup is good," Mr. Tsuji says, "it proves that the chef knows how to blend his bonito stock—the flavor base of all the dishes to come." You begin with a piece of kelp, a dense block of dried bonito fillet, and a quantity of good water. (Giant kelp is harvested from the subarctic waters off Rebun Island, in Hokkaido, and dried in the sun until it becomes amber brown and mottled with a white powder that bears much 285 of its flavor. Bonito is dried in both shade and open air in a complicated process that takes six months.) You place the kelp in cold water over a medium flame and remove it just before the water boils. Then you shave the bonito into thin ribbons, using a special blade mounted on a wooden box, and add them to the broth. Bring it to the boil again, and turn off the heat. A minute later, when the bonito has settled to the bottom, strain the dashi.

To make a clear soup, you add a little salt and light soy sauce to the dashi, heat without boiling, and pour it into bowls with three or four little pieces of solid food. Cover the bowls immediately, or the precious aroma of the dashi will be lost, and serve within thirty seconds.

That's it. The entire process takes twelve minutes. But only the most expensive restaurants in Japan still make dashi this way, and my newly educated taste buds have not detected its presence in New York. Most places use instant dashi powder or at best a plastic bag of commercial bonito shavings. Mr. Nagata's simple, flawless soup sums up a traditional way of life in Japan that grows more remote with every passing day. Many modern Japanese have never tasted this central essence of their own cuisine.

Or even tasted real wasabi. This is the pungent green Japanese "horseradish" you add to dipping sauces, broths, and the rice in hand rolls and sushi. Wasabi is a long root that grows only in the marshy banks of cold, fresh, free-flowing streams (and, it seems, only in Japan). The best wasabi grows on the Izu Peninsula, southwest of Tokyo, is very expensive, and should be grated right before you use it. True wasabi has a mellow, sweeter flavor than the acrid paste we get in this country (and in much of Japan), which is mixed from a powder or squeezed out of a tube like toothpaste and contains very little wasabi.

In M. F. K. Fisher's introduction to Mr. Tsuji's cookbook, she reveals her difficulty returning to Western food after several weeks in Japan. My reaction was similar. The thought of a whole grilled chicken lying on a big round plate to be dismembered by metal weapons seemed repulsive. I tried a few favorite Japanese restaurants in New York but missed the aroma of true dashi and the taste of real wasabi, the sprigs of *kinome* and the silkiness of sea bream. For an entire afternoon, I lost my appetite completely. One day I went out looking for a bonito shaver and came back with a sack of Japanese rice. Mr. Tsuji jokes that it takes twenty years to learn how to boil rice, and I am counting the days until the year 2011. But my first try was not a catastrophe.

Finally realizing that there is no way I can eat as I did in Kyoto, I slowly nursed myself back to health. I began by taking a spoonful of crème brûlée now and then, a bite or two of pastrami on rye. Now, several weeks later, I can eat an entire small Western meal without much difficulty. But after dinner, I still feel a longing for a bowl of rice and two or three slices of fish.

September 1991

Creatures from
the Blue Lagoon

To get the most out of a trip to Venice, the traveler must master several local words and phrases. Two of the most useful are *Senta, portrei avere un'altra porzione colossale di vongole veraci* (Waiter, another gigantic bowl of those tiny little perfect spicy clams, please) and *Ucciderei per un piatto di cannocchie ai ferri* (I would kill for a plate of those charcoal-grilled mantis shrimp, also known as squill, the sweetest crustacean in all creation).

The seafood of Venice and the Adriatic coast to the south is easily the best I have ever tasted, and on a recent trip there I ate nothing but mollusks, crustaceans, and fish for six days and nights. I could have kept it up forever if the lady at Pan Am had not thrown around words like "forfeiture with extreme prejudice" when I tried to extend my stay. It was my contention that the airlines should have warned me, *before* I bought the ticket, that I would completely miss the *seppioline* season. *Seppioline* are baby cuttlefish the size of your thumbnail, quickly deep-fried until they are crunchy and irresistible. As I was explaining this, the lady from Pan Am threw around words like "Ciao!" and the line went dead.

To say that I ate only seafood in Venice is an exaggeration. The Venetians have carelessly left many priceless paintings and mosaics in the churches for which they were created instead of collecting them conveniently in museums, and even a casual survey of the major works requires relentless trudging from church to church. This, in turn, ignites the appetite. Eating seafood in basilicas and museums is considered disrespectful, so you must bring along something else to tide you over. I recommend the roasted corn nuts sold throughout the Rialto market and the pungent, gaily colored licorice pastilles offered in every sweet shop. These put you in the proper mood to understand why the painters Carpaccio and Bellini truly deserve the food and drink that were named after them. Venice also has a wealth of pictures depicting dinner, of which my favorite is Veronese's *Supper in the Pharisee's House*, with its tempting rack of lamb and several round crusty loaves. And don't miss Tintoretto's *Creation of the Animals*, which shows eleven distinct species of fish leaping from the oceans that He had created just two days earlier.

Marcella Hazan tells me that nibbling is not Italian, and she is the reason I traveled to Venice. I had yearned to meet Marcella ever since feasting my way through her *Classic Italian Cookbook* in 1973 and *More Classic Italian Cooking* in 1978. (I am still working on *Marcella's Italian Kitchen*, from 1986.) It was Marcella who gave us the very first detailed instructions in English for making fresh pasta and our first generous helping of northern Italian home cooking. Along with a handful of others, she inspired the flowering of Italian cuisine that has transformed American eating. Do you remember what most Italian restaurants were like in 1973? Do you remember spaghetti and meatballs?

When the opportunity to meet Marcella arose last January, I hurried over to the Hazans' New York City apartment. Our conversation turned to Venice, where Marcella and her husband, Victor, now live most of the year and where Marcella conducts her classes from April through October. They told tales of the remarkable creatures that dwell in the Venetian Lagoon and the Adriatic beyond: of clams the size of quarters and shrimp so small that four could fit inside each clam; of sea dates that burrow into underwater rocks, and fishermen who drag the rocks to shore and crack them open to harvest the little mollusks; of sea truffles eaten cold and raw, and soft-shell crabs two inches across and exquisitely sweet; of eel grilled slowly over charcoal until its fat renders crisp and its skin crackles. Marcella offered to teach me all about Adriatic seafood if I met her in Venice. Her lesson plan would have three parts: buying it, cooking it, and eating it.

Three months later Marcella, Victor, and I strolled across the Rialto Bridge and down into the bustle of the marketplace. The Rialto market is bordered on two sides by water, and in the early morning small boats piled high with seafood and vegetables float down the Grand Canal and converge on the market. The Pescheria itself spills out from under an open, colonnaded Venetian Gothic structure built in 1907 on eighteen thousand larch-wood piles. By nine o'clock, thirty or forty fish sellers have spread their offerings on long tables for both housewives and restaurateurs to inspect. There are few fish stores in Venice, because everyone shops at the Rialto; it is among the best places to buy seafood in all the world. Though some critics consider the market hall entirely without architectural charm, it is for me "the building which occupies the center of the picture Venice leaves in the mind," as Bernard Berenson mistakenly wrote about the church of Santa Maria della Salute.

I scribbled furiously as Marcella and Victor called out the names of every fish in sight, about fifty in all: iridescent sardines and anchovies flashing silver and turquoise, flying fish with pointed beaks and snails creeping nowhere in their glossy spotted shells, tiny gray shrimp jumping like crickets and huge blue shrimp too stately to move, clams with shells bearing Navajo designs and scallops as small as aspirins, delicate flatfish for grilling or frying and bony striped fish for soup or risotto, diamond-shaped turbot and broad fans of skate, ink-stained cuttlefish, octopus, squid. We watched a fishmonger gut and bone a pile of sardines with his hands, while another butchered a monkfish to sell the tail as *coda di rospo,* the cheeks for pasta sauce, and the grotesque head for soup. Nearby a boy played with an eel slithering in its tank while his father watched the fishman flay another as it wriggled. The Italians believe that eels must be kept alive until minutes before cooking, the way we behave toward lobsters.

Leaving the Pescheria, we walked past a long line of vegetable sellers. Marcella admired the baskets of peas, pointing to the stems and leaves still attached to the pods; the leaves wither quickly after the peas are picked and are a sensitive barometer of freshness. For the same reason, artichokes in Italy are sold with their stems and outer leaves, tomatoes are still attached to their vines, and zucchini are displayed with their flowers intact. (These are usually removed before cooking. Large squash blossoms for stuffing and frying are grown separately.) Chickens are hung in shop windows with their feet and heads still on—the feet darken with time, and the head tells you whether it is a rooster or a hen.

For my first eating lesson, we walked to Da Fiore, probably the best seafood restaurant in Venice. The cooking is simple and austere, the ingredients are of incomparable quality, and the fish is not even washed until you order it.

Plates of *gamberetti* appeared almost instantly—crunchy three-quarter-inch shrimp fried whole in the shell with just a dusting of flour—and when I mechanically reached for a wedge of lemon, Marcella proposed that I try it both ways and compare. Her point was that lemon can overwhelm the delicacy of impeccable seafood, and without any doubt she was correct; some restaurants even refuse your request for lemon.

My first taste of *cannocchie* came next—pink-gray crustaceans found only in the Adriatic and Japan, about two inches wide, eight inches long, and flat as a ribbon, with false eyes on their tails and the sweetest flesh you can eat. They are arranged in one layer in a pan with just a little water, covered closely with a wet kitchen towel and a tight lid to trap the vapor, and briefly steamed. Half the shell is snipped off in the kitchen, and you pry up the white meat from the other half as you eat it.

"*Poppa*," I said proudly when the warm young octopi were brought out, demonstrating that I had learned some Italian in the market that morning. "*Poppa* is the breast of a woman," Marcella corrected, and looked around to make sure that nobody had heard me. "*Polpo* is octopus. Young ones are *folpeti*." When the Hazans were courting, octopus was sold on the street and eaten right out of the pot, doused with oil and a little vinegar.

Bowls of little clams were placed before us, *vongole veraci*—oblong and slightly pink, only an inch across, sweet and peppery and impossibly tender. Like everything else, they were cooked very simply: garlic is lightly colored in a little oil, chopped parsley is added, and then the clams; the pan is covered, the heat is turned high, and within a minute or two the *vongole veraci* have opened, surrendering their juice to the oil and garlic, composing a sauce. No salt or pepper is added, no wine or broth, no herbs. "We have a saying in Italy," Marcella told me, "that what you leave out is as important as what you put in."

Our lesson continued with cuttlefish risotto bright with peas and dark with ink, plates of shredded *granzeola* (the local spider crab), and grilled eel. From these I learned that cuttlefish ink is milder and sweeter than squid ink, that lemon is also too assertive for perfectly fresh crab, but that a little olive oil is ideal, and that everybody in the United States should grill eels on their barbecues this summer.

Mere hours after it had begun, the eating lesson at Da Fiore was over, and we made plans for my cooking lesson at ten the next morning.

The Hazans' apartment occupies the top floor of a small palazzo built in 1520 by a branch of the Contarini family, whose Ca' d'Oro on the Grand Canal, begun in 1424, was the finest house in Venice. Marcella's kitchen is white, with sloping dark wood beams and polished gray granite countertops, just the right size for her classes of six students but, as Marcella pointed out when I made a far-reaching mess later that morning, slightly too small for one of me.

Venetian Seafood Glossary

Photocopy this glossary and head for the Adriatic as soon as convenient. If it does not include everything edible in the waters and restaurants of Venice, it comes pretty close. The Italian names are given first and the Venetian in parentheses. I use the plural for creatures you eat lots of, like *cozze,* and the singular for creatures you eat one at a time. The Venetian names will make you sound like a native within twenty-five kilometers of San Marco, and like a Martian beyond that. If you think that I lifted this information from some book, just try to find one. After I had exhausted my notes from the Rialto market, *La pesca nella Laguna di Venezia* (Amministrazione della Provincia di Venezia, 1981), Alan Davidson's *Mediterranean Seafood* (Penguin, 1981), and a gigantic Italian dictionary, Victor Hazan graciously returned to the fishmongers on the Rialto to help fill the gaping holes.

Acciughe (sardoni): anchovies, called *alici* around Rome

Aguglia: garfish, sometimes found in the better sushi bars

Anguilla (bisato): eel

Aragosta: rock lobster, called *langouste* in France

Astaco (astise): like Maine lobster; imported from Yugoslavia or France; *astice* in vernacular Italian

Bianchetti: whitebait; also known as *gianchetti*

Branzino (bransin): bar or *loup de mer* in France; Marcella compares it to striped bass; others say it's a sea bass of a different species (*Labrax lupus*) from ours; *spigola* or *spinola* in Rome; delectable in and on any tongue

(Cagnoleto): very small shark, often stewed with tomato sauce

Calamaretti: baby squid, one and a half inches long, fried whole, incredible

Calamaro: squid

Calamarone: large squid

Canestrelli (canestreli): minute scallops, tinier than bay scallops and spicy in taste; nearest U.S. cousins are Peconic and Digby Bay scallops; here, as elsewhere (for example, *schile*), Venetians don't pronounce the final *i*

Cannocchia (canocia): squill, or mantis shrimp, found only in the Adriatic and Japan, pinkish gray and flat, two inches wide, eight inches long; grilled or steamed, the sweetest crustacean you can eat; also *pannoccia*

Cannolicchi (capelonghe): razor clams

Capitone: a long, fat type of eel

Cappe sante (capesante): large scallops, sweet and tender

Carpa: carp

Cefalo (lotregan, verzelata, bosega, caustelo, volpina): varieties of gray mullet, of which the *cefalo durato (lotregan)* is the most esteemed

Coda di rospo: monkfish tail; literally tail of the toad, though most of this fish is an extremely ugly head; formally, *rana pescatrice*

Cozze (peoci): mussels; also called *mitili*

Datteri di mare: sea dates, related to mussels; eaten in soup or spaghetti sauce; embed themselves in rocks, which must be

hauled from the sea and
smashed to harvest them

Dentice: sea bream

Folipetti (folpeti): baby octopi,
boiled and served warm
with a drop of vinegar

Gamberetti: small gray shrimp,
which jump like crickets
on trays in the market

Gamberi (gambari): shrimp;
gamberi di fiume are crayfish

(Go): yellow and black, used
for soup and as a base for
risotto

Grancevola (granzeola): spider
crab, delicate and sweet;
the crabs are boiled, and
the meat is meticulously
picked from the shell

(Granzoporo): increasingly rare
shore crab; small, slightly
furry, with powerful pin-
cers; much sought after in
the south of France

Latterini (anguela): sand
smelts, like long, silvery
sardines

Lumachine (bovoleti): tiny sea
snails, similar to periwin-
kles

Mazanette (masanete): tiny
crabs, a little larger than
your thumbnail; boiled,
chopped into two or three
pieces, and served with

chopped garlic; you chew
on the shells to extract the
flesh and juice

Mazzancolle: large, blue-gray
shrimp

Mazzola: sea robin, pinkish
gray and used in soup;
Marcella says that the
broth is as esteemed as
capon broth; discarded in
the United States; called
gurnard in England and
pesce capone in Liguria

Merluzzo (merluso): hake, small
and gray; cooked as in
recipes for whiting

(Moleche): soft-shell crabs, two
and a half inches across,
like the smallest and most
prized specimens in the
United States; found
nowhere in Italy but Venice

Mormora: small striped bream,
silver and black, excellent
grilled

Moscardino: tiny curled octopus, often brought to
Venice from Liguria, won-
derful deep-fried

Murici (garusoli): snails that
live in a murex shell,
unlike French snails or the
Italian *lumache*

Orata (orada): gilthead bream,
called *daurade* in France;

the highest attainment of the bream family; like the apotheosis of a U.S. porgy

Ostriche (ostreghe): oysters, now rarely harvested in Venice

Paganello (paganelo): small and creamy gray, used like the larger *go* for soup and broth

Pagello: reddish sea bream

Papalina: sprat, halfway between an anchovy and a sardine

Pesce spada: swordfish

Polpo (folpo): octopus

Razza (raza): skate, ray

Rombo chiodato: turbot, diamond shaped, with nail head–like protuberances, prized for its delicate flesh

Rombo liscio (soaso): brill, like *rombo chiodato* but less esteemed

San Pietro (sampiero): John Dory; called Saint-Pierre in France; a dark mark remains on its side where Saint Peter touched it; also called *sampietro*

Sardina (sardela, sarda): sardine, sleek and silvery with turquoise reflections

Scampo: langoustine in France, Dublin Bay prawn in England, unavailable here;

rose-gray or pink, with claws and feelers like a small lobster; among the most delectable of all crustaceans; scampi are not large shrimp, as Italian menus in the United States pretend

(Schile): the tiniest of shrimp, they remain gray when cooked; increasingly rare; sometimes known as *gamberetti grigi* in Italian

Scorfano: scorpion fish, bony, reddish, used for soup; *racasse rouge* in France and indispensable to bouillabaisse; *scorfano* is slang for "ugly person"

Seppie (sepe): cuttlefish; eight tentacles but more tender than octopi; their ink is sweeter and milkier than the squid's in risotto and gnocchi; their broad, flat bones hang in birdcages the world over

Seppioline: baby cuttlefish, as small as your thumbnail, irresistible when deep-fried whole; season begins in August

Sgombero: mackerel

Sogliola (sfogia, porato): sole, the world's finest flatfish, says

Marcella, and unavailable in United States

Tartufi di mare: sea truffles, a kind of clam, usually eaten raw

Tinca: tench, a type of carp

Tonno: bluefin tuna

Triglia di scoglio (tria): red mullet, called *rouget de roche* in France; larger and more deeply colored than the *triaglia di fango (rouget barbet),* sometimes called *barbon* in Venetian

Uove di seppie (latticini): egg sacs of female cuttlefish

Vongole (bibarase): small clams, one and a half inches across, round, with a zigzag shell pattern reminiscent of Native American pottery; wonderfully tender and sweet; sometimes called *vongole gialla*

Vongole veraci (caparozzoli): clams, a bit larger and more oblong than *vongole,* with fine lines in both directions on the shell; the muscle has two little horns like the U.S. steamer clam; more highly prized than *vongole,* but this is a competition among minuscule culinary Olympians; known as *palourde* in France

•   •   •

Our menu was fried sardines and anchovies, grilled *cannocchie,* spaghettini with *vongole,* monkfish with red wine and vegetables, green tomato salad, and lemon gelato. My first duty was to zest two firm lemons with a vegetable peeler. Before long I had zested my thumb and gouged out deep chunks of lemon peel with the bitter white pith attached, about my average performance at this task. Marcella showed me how the zest comes right off if you move the peeler back and forth in a sawing motion. (One of Marcella's students told her this trick alone was worth the trip to Venice; I would agree if you throw in a *fritto misto di pesce* or two.)

Marcella's teaching is not about kitchen tricks, but you pick up lots of them working alongside her. When sautéing onions or garlic, Marcella does not wait for the butter and oil to stop foaming before adding the vegetables, as we are usually taught to do, and she can think of no reason why anyone would; once the butter stops sizzling, it is so hot that the garlic instantly burns. After steaming mussels or clams, Marcella does not discard the ones that refuse to open. If this were an infallible test, how could anyone eat raw clams pried open with a knife? she asks. When she parboils zucchini, Marcella cuts off only the rounded end; if you remove the stem end too, the vegetable will take on too much water. When cooking a pasta sauce containing olive oil, Marcella adds a little uncooked oil at the end to freshen the taste of the dish; for sauces cooked with butter, she adds a little butter.

Marcella showed me how to butterfly fresh sardines with my thumb, as the fishmonger in the market did. (Here are the delectable details: You hold the sardine parallel to the table and snap off the head behind the gills with your other hand, pulling horizontally to extract the intestines. Then you slide your thumb between the backbone and one side of the flesh, scraping the end of your thumbnail against the bone all the way to the tail. You break off the bone at the tail and lift it carefully from the other side of the flesh. Finally, you open up the sardine and with a scissors snip off the fins and sharp edges all around and wash the fish under cold running water.) Then Marcella prepared the *cannocchie* for grilling by snipping away the meatless parts of the shell with kitchen shears and cutting the shell lengthwise along the top to aid in marinating and cooking. She turned the *cannocchie* in olive oil, bread crumbs, salt, and lots of pepper, and left them for an hour.

We gutted the anchovies together, and Marcella cooked the little clams for the spaghettini and the vegetables for the monkfish, a savory recipe from her third book. Our preparation took the better part of two hours.

Marcella began to fry the sardines, holding each one by the tail, dipping it in flour, and immediately frying four or five in a quarter inch of hot vegetable oil in a skillet. They curled instantly because of their freshness. Soon a rhythm was established: when one sardine was done and lifted out to be drained, salted, and eaten with our hands, another was floured and laid in, perfectly maintaining the temperature of the oil. Marcella is a most distinguished fryer.

Victor joined us to help eat the sardines. Then he went to work on the *cannocchie*, arranging them in a flat, hinged rack that would go over the glowing charcoal. We moved to the south terrace adjoining the kitchen, where the Hazans have a wonderful grill made by a company in Rimini called Bartolini that supplies many of the best fish restaurants on the Adriatic. As Victor labored, we sat in the sun drinking wine and gazing over the rooftops of Venice, and when the *cannocchie* were done, we took them inside to the dining table and ate them with our hands, marveling at their sweetness, the pungency of the pepper marinade, and the charred bitterness of the shell.

My next eating lesson was convoked the following day at the restaurant Barbicani, where the syllabus included small whole squid, crispy from the grill, black gnocchi under a profoundly pink sauce made from four fish and four herbs, and grilled sole with a sauce the waiter made at the table by mashing the head and skin of the fish with olive oil and a touch of garlic and then pressing everything in a strainer to extract the juices. Marcella points out that unlike the French, Italian cooks rarely make a separate sauce for anything but pasta. Instead, they allow the main ingredient to create its own. Marcella considers Adriatic sole the world's finest flatfish, far superior to what passes for sole in the United States, which is really flounder. Her favorite Atlantic fish is striped bass because of its compact texture and delicate taste.

After leaving the Hazans, I practiced my eating lessons as often as possible, and I will mention two other fish restaurants of high quality: the famous Corte Sconta, where I ate, on newsprint mats, *uova di seppie* and a perfect mixed grill of fish, and Osteria al Ponte del Diavolo on the island of Torcello, fifty minutes by water bus from Venice and open only for lunch except on Saturday. When you have eaten like this for several days and then stumble into a place that boils its crab and *cannocchie* several hours ahead of time, the contrast is excruciating.

Speaking of excruciating contrasts: high over the Atlantic on the trip back to New York, I began to suffer from Adriatic-seafood-deprivation syndrome, the symptoms of which are too hideous to relate.

Minutes after depositing my bags at home, I hailed a cab and toured the major fish stores of Manhattan, widely known as a great place to buy seafood. Twenty dollars in taxi fares later, I headed back home, dejected and empty-handed—the selection was narrow, the shrimp were frozen, the sole was flounder, the clams were huge, the scallops were larger, and the eels were dead.

When my depression lifted a few days later, I reviewed the sections of Marcella's books that show you how to cook Atlantic seafood the Adriatic way, remembered what I had learned in Venice, and went on to concoct a reasonably authentic

Grigliata Mista di Mare
Mixed Grill of Shrimp, Eel, and Sardines

Each fish is handled differently and each is delicious. The sardines and shrimp are adapted from *More Classic Italian Cooking* and Marcella and Victor's terrace. Marcella was not in a flaying mood when we cooked together and declined to skin an eel for me, but I watched two restaurant chefs grilling eel slowly over charcoal and tried it successfully at home.

You can use a little hibachi or a fancy barbecue, but the fuel should be hardwood charcoal, not briquettes, which are made from small particles of carbon glued together with distasteful chemicals and may contain resinous softwoods that make your food taste as though it were basted with turpentine. In each recipe, you arrange the fish in a flat, hinged rack; this prevents them from curling, allows you to turn them all at once, and leaves the skin undisturbed, at least until the last minute. Even if you use an oven broiler, the hinged rack is quite a help.

Throw a few bay leaves on the coals just before you grill the fish. Buy the best Italian extra-virgin olive oil you can find. Serves 6 as a main course.

Shrimp Grilled Like
Cannocchie

Buy 1½ pounds of medium shrimp (about 24 to the pound), still in the shell but with the head removed and fresh, if possible. Rinse them in cold water and dry with paper towels. Insert a sturdy toothpick into each shrimp along its back, between the shell and the meat, to keep it straight. Put the shrimp in a large bowl, add ⅓ cup of extra-virgin olive oil, and turn to coat them well. Add 1 teaspoon each of salt and freshly ground pepper and 1¾ cups of fine, homemade toasted bread crumbs. (These hold the other ingredients on the shells during marinating and cooking.) Turn them again and allow to marinate for 1 to 2 hours. Put the shrimp in a hinged rack, gently shaking off any excess bread crumbs, and cook close to the hot coals for 2 minutes on one side and 1½ minutes on the other, until the shells are partly charred. Eat them immediately with your hands, peeling the shell and sucking out the meat as you go.

Grilled Eel

Have your fishman bone a long center piece of eel, or do it yourself by cutting around the backbone through the flesh side and removing it. You should wind up with a reasonably flat rectangular piece of eel with skin on one side and flesh on the other. Cut this crosswise into 4-ounce servings and place them in a hinged rack, latched tightly. Slowly grill the skin side at a good distance from the coals (I measured the temperature at 300°) until it is very crisp and bubbling and the fat under the skin has rendered and drained, about 20 to 30 minutes. Lightly salt and pepper the skin side, and cook the flesh side for 5 minutes, this time nearer the coals, until it is golden. Salt and pepper this side and serve. Lemon is optional.

Grilled Sardines

"There are some smells that have the power to summon intact a whole period of one's life," Marcella writes. "For me it is the odor of sardines roasting over a slow charcoal fire . . . and an image of my father's mother in never-changing long black dress and black kerchief, bending over a wobbly grill set on bricks in our yard, waving at the embers with a fan of rooster-tail feathers."

Marcella says that the silvery fish sold in the United States as sardines are probably small, strong-tasting herrings or large Atlantic anchovies, but they work well in some recipes all the same. Or you can use small smelt. In any event, scrape and gut 2 pounds of

> fresh "sardines," each about 6 inches long, or have your
> fishman do it. Wash out the belly cavities, draining the
> sardines well. Dry with paper towels, and lay them on
> a platter. Sprinkle with ½ teaspoon of salt, ¼ teaspoon
> of freshly ground pepper, and ¼ cup of olive oil, and
> allow them to marinate for 20 minutes, turning once or
> twice. Put the sardines in a hinged rack and cook them
> close to the glowing coals, 2 to 3 minutes on each side.
> To eat, hold the head and pull the meat from the back-
> bone with your lips and teeth.

August 1989

Author's Note:

Da Fiore is still the best fish restaurant in Venice, especially
good at lunchtime. Barbacani has changed hands and is, according to Victor and Marcella, no longer worth trying. Marcella's
fourth book, *The Essentials of Italian Cooking*, was published by
Knopf in 1993. Indispensable and fundamental, it combines her
first two books, adding fifty new recipes and improving several of
the old ones.

Rosemary and
Moon Beans

It was one of the last sessions of the 1988 installment of the Oxford Food Symposium, and Lourdes March was conducting a seminar on paella, which means both the wide shallow pan and also the food you cook in it. (Lourdes wrote *El libro de la paella y de los arroces,* published in Madrid in 1985, and has been collaborating on a book about olives and olive oil with Alicia Ríos.) She began with the history and etymology of paella and its symbolism as "an ancestral rite of the cyclical fecundation of the earth performed away from the kitchen and thus away from the feminine hand." Then she attacked false paellas and their jumble of ingredients that "have nothing to do with the well-balanced and true formula," which she proceeded to reveal.

The real Valencian paella is a traditional lunch for workers in the vineyards. There are four rules for making one. It must be cooked outdoors, by a man or men, over a fire of vine cuttings and citrus wood. It must contain chicken and rabbit (no lobsters crawling all about). The grains of rice must be three millimeters long, like the arborio rice you use in risotto. And you must add either twelve snails or two sprigs of rosemary, but not both.

The rest of us were skeptical on several points. Few of us had ever met a paella we'd liked. And how can two sprigs of rosemary substitute for twelve snails? we asked, thinking that Lourdes, who is just now learning English, must have confused "or" with "and," or "snails" with "rosemary," or something like that. As would often be the case over the next few hours, Lourdes humbled the skeptics among us. In Valencia, when you catch snails for your paella, you feed them rosemary for a few days, both to purge them and to give them flavor. Herbs from the sunburned gardens of Spain are so intense that twelve snails contribute all the rosemary flavor you need.

Why bother with vine cuttings and citrus wood? Lourdes explained that as the cooking liquid evaporates from the wide surface of the pan, it mixes with the smoke and then condenses back, bestowing an indispensable flavor to the dish. Vine cuttings and orangewood have a high acid content, which creates a hotter fire. Their smoke contributes an aroma absolutely required in all the true Valencian paella.

Paul Levy, a transplanted American who is food and wine editor of the London *Observer*, author of the very funny *Out to Lunch* (Harper & Row), and one of the pillars of the British food world, lives in a seventeenth-century farmhouse ten miles northwest of Oxford, with his wife, Penny, who edits art books, and their two daughters. When the symposium was over, Paul and Penny invited ten of us back to their farm to join Lourdes and Alicia in adapting their ancestral rite of cyclical fecundation to the Oxfordshire terrain. Paul had a good supply of plump corn-fed chickens, but the only rabbit in sight was Leonard Woolf, a family pet. When Penny defended Leonard Woolf against our offers to dress him for the pot, Lourdes settled for Paul's frozen pigeons. Paul had neither collected snails from his garden nor gorged them on herbs, so Lourdes sent one of us off to pluck some branches from Paul's pungent rosemary patch.

We gathered round as Lourdes and Alicia meticulously leveled Paul's U.S.-made barbecue grill so that the oil and broth would lie perfectly even in the pan and lit the fire of vines and apricot branches and, finally, in a desperate act, an old crate. For the next two hours they composed the paella, continually dispatching the rest of us on vital errands to other parts of the garden and the farmhouse. First the fowl were browned on all sides in olive oil. Green beans and chopped tomatoes were added and sautéed for a few minutes, then the heat was reduced. To say that the heat was reduced is to summarize a complex process in which Lourdes made the rest of us reach into the dense billows of smoke engulfing the paella, the grill, and most of Lourdes to pull out and somehow dispose of huge bundles of flaming wood. Tedious micromanagement of the fire continued throughout the endless hours of cooking. My slacks and jacket lost their perfume of Valencia-on-Thames only after two dry cleanings back home in New York, where you regulate your cooking fire by turning a knob.

Paprika, some broad white beans in their cooking liquid, and additional water now went into the pan. Lourdes had brought the dried beans from Spain, and Alicia had boiled them indoors before the fire was started. Lourdes and Alicia called them limas, but nobody else agreed. We argued aimlessly about whether they were really dried favas, butter beans, or broad beans, until Lourdes silenced us all with their Latin classification, *Phaseolus lunatus,* which Paul nicely translated as "moon beans." When I returned to the hotel that night and opened the *Oxford Book of Food Plants,* I realized that Lourdes had tricked us, because *Phaseolus lunatus* covers all the eligible candidates.

After an hour, when the chicken and pigeon were tender, Lourdes and Alicia added the two sprigs of rosemary, some powdered saffron, and a little salt, mixed them around, and removed about two cups of the dark broth, so that the remaining liquid came just to the handle rivets on the inside walls of the paella. All paellas are manufactured so that the rivets tell you how much broth to use for cooking the rice, which will soon resemble nothing more than a crusty, russet risotto. Vine cuttings were added to enrage the fire, and a kilogram of rice sprinkled evenly over the surface of the broth. After ten minutes of vigorous cooking the fire was damped, and the simmering continued for another ten minutes until the rice was just al dente. All the while, reserved broth was added in small doses as the rice swelled.

All of us were ravenous, but Lourdes let the deep reddish-brown paella stand for five minutes as the grains of rice absorbed more flavor and loosened from one another. Our conversation, which had degenerated into a cross-cultural comparison of methods for cooking udders among the English, Romans, Mexicans, and Yemenite Jews (who on top of everything else need to make them kosher), ceased as soon as we began to share the true Valencian paella. The rice lining the bottom of the pan was browned and crusty; the meat was tender and deeply flavored. Everything was imbued with the smoke of vines and fruitwood and the aroma of rosemary, and the *Phaseoli lunati* were, well, incomparable.

Max Lake, an Australian doctor turned wine maker, broke out a case of his best Australian red, and when no more than half of it had been drunk, one of the British writers among us revealed that, at the age of sixteen on a vacation in the south of Spain, she had been courted by El Cordobés, the greatest bullfighter who ever lived.

November 1988

Going Whole Hog

Raymond's taxi clattered through the humid night, carrying me
from the Memphis International Airport to the East Memphis
Hilton.

"I am a firm believer that the sauce and the slaw have a great
bearing on the matter," Raymond was saying.

"Granted," I replied, "but a mere sauce or garnish can never
alter the greatness, or lack thereof, of a slab of ribs." I had discovered in only a few deft questions that Raymond was a Memphis
native and an expert in eating barbecue; the topic for our half-
hour ride was set. Raymond nodded. Momentarily we were in
complete agreement about barbecue.

Whenever I travel to the South, the first thing I do is visit the
best barbecue place between the airport and my hotel. An hour
or two later I visit the best barbecue place between my hotel and
dinner. In Memphis, making these choices is not easy. The metropolitan Memphis yellow pages list sixty-one barbecue restaurants; in truth, there are probably more than two hundred.

The clock struck nine-thirty as Raymond exited from the
expressway and headed down Poplar. Time was running out. If I
acted fast, I could cover two restaurants before closing time. But
which to choose?

I had not come to Memphis merely to engage in some shabby
and dissolute eating binge. This year, no doubt in recompense for

a noble deed I had committed in a former life, I was invited to be a judge at the Memphis in May World Championship Barbecue Cooking Contest! When the call from Memphis came, I thought I had died and gone to heaven. But even before my plane landed, the awful responsibility began to press painfully upon my brain. Memphis is the pork-barbecue capital of the world, and the Memphis barbecue cooking contest is the preeminent barbecue event in the known universe. The 1990 *Guinness Book of World Records* deems it the largest. But when lovers of barbecue call the Memphis contest simply the Big One, they are referring to its moral and aesthetic authority as much as to its size. Would I be up to the job?

I decided to stifle these solemn thoughts until the next morning, or at least until after I had eaten a couple of dinners. Raymond's thoughts were as follows: The best barbecue he had ever eaten was in Terre Haute, Indiana, eight hours and a stiff cab fare away, both of which I considered for fifteen seconds longer than I should have. His Memphis favorite is Jim Neely's Interstate on South Third, at the opposite edge of town from my hotel, closely followed by the world-famous trio of Leonard's, Corky's, and Charlie Vergos's Rendezvous. In the black neighborhoods of south Memphis, Raymond directed me to the tender and juicy ribs at Hawkins Grill, in the 1200 block of McLemore, and Al's Tasty Burger Inn, at McLemore and College. Raymond recommended that if I managed to eat my way through all of these, I try the Raines Haven Rib House on East Range Road, the Commissary in Germantown, and Brown's Barbecue, just down from Neely's Interstate on South Third.

Raymond's palate turned out to be as discriminating as any, at least judging from the two handfuls of barbecue restaurants I was able to try. In both sandwich and rib, Neely's Interstate Bar-B-Que Restaurant serves the best commercial product I had ever tasted. (Notice that real barbecue lovers often refer to their favorite food as "product.") And by the time I had left Memphis four days and four hundred ribs later, I had added several of his other picks to my permanent list of barbecue shrines. In the meantime, I collected another ten places to visit when the opportunity arises—among them Cozy Corner, Payne's, Gridley's, and the Bar-B-Q Shop Restaurant, all in Memphis—plus others from human settlements too distant for this visit: Bozo's in Mason and Bar-ba-rosa's in Millington (both Tennessee), L. C. Murry's BBQ in De Valls Bluff and Freddie's B-B-Q in Stuttgart (both Arkansas), the universally revered Dreamland Bar-B-Q Drive Inn of Jerusalem Heights, just outside Tuscaloosa in Alabama, and Freddie's, a little beer joint sixty-five miles from Little Rock. This last suggestion emerged from an exhaustive conversation with Jerry (J-R) Roach, who runs the School of Southern Barbecue and whose J-R Enterprises makes championship barbecue cookers. "The best sandwich I've ever put in my mouth," he had confided. Now that I have returned from Memphis, I leave a light suitcase packed and ready, just in case the chance to fly to Stuttgart or Jerusalem Heights unexpectedly presents itself.

My official duties commenced early on Thursday morning, when I and twenty-five others reported to the crumbling old New Daisy Theater on Beale Street for a grueling day of instruction in judging barbecue according to Memphis rules. The Memphis in May World Championship Barbecue Cooking Contest has three main divisions—Ribs, Shoulder, and Whole Hog. When I was asked to serve as a judge, I had signed up for Ribs, because I felt thoroughly unqualified to judge the other two. Ribs, I figured, was easy. Volunteering for Whole Hog would have been the height of irresponsibility.

Before flying down to Memphis, I knew four things about real southern barbecue: (1) the origin of the word, (2) the dramatic difference between grilling meat and cooking barbecue, (3) the happy chaos of barbecue styles around the South, and (4) how much I love to eat any style of real barbecue.

1. If you think the word "barbecue" comes from the French *barbe à queue*, "from beard to tail," then you are one of those silly people whom *The Oxford English Dictionary* accuses of an "absurd

conjecture." Coming from the *OED*, these are fighting words. "Barbecue" derives from the Spanish *barbacoa* or the French *babracot,* both adaptations from the Taino and Arawak languages of Haiti and Guiana. The Indian words referred to a framework of sticks set upon posts either for sleeping or for supporting meat above a fire. But though the word may have been invented by the Indians of the Caribbean, the technique was probably not: Waverly Root considers it "a method of cooking so natural under primitive circumstances that it would practically invent itself everywhere, especially in societies accustomed to living outdoors most of the time."

    2. Real barbecue has absolutely nothing to do with grilling. Did the Taino Indians grill or did they barbecue? Was the technique of real barbecue known to the North American Indians, or was it developed by Mississippi slaves? The answers are lost in the mists and drizzles of time itself. Backyard grilling (which nearly everybody outside the South calls barbecuing) is quick cooking over intense dry heat (often 500 degrees or higher) on an open brazier. Real barbecue is slow, enclosed cooking at gentle temperatures in moist hardwood smoke. A whole hog typically takes twenty-four hours in a barbecue pit or cooker, a shoulder takes twelve to fourteen hours, and ribs average five or six. Most people grill their meat to rare and juicy. Real barbecue is always well done. Any sign of blood, any trace of unrendered fat, is a serious flaw. All the tough connective tissue must be dissolved. The meat must pull cleanly from the bone and separate in long, moist shreds. Real barbecue never sizzles; it just lies there quietly, slowly and imperceptibly reaching what Boyd Atkinson described to me as a higher plane of existence. Boyd himself cooks an extremely good rib.

    The cooker (also known as the pit, the smoker, the rig, or even the grill) must be covered, and the atmosphere inside must be moist. The temperature should range between 170 and 250 degrees. (Some experts advocate even lower temperatures. "But if flies begin to land on your meat," they warn, "you know it's not hot enough.") Sometimes wood is the only fuel; sometimes chunks of hardwood are burned with charcoal or even (but never in Memphis) gas. Especially when large cuts of meat are cooked, the heat is usually indirect, generated by coals and hardwood chunks burned in a separate chamber called a firebox; the heat and the smoke are then piped into the main compartment. A water pan can be used to humidify the air inside the cooker and catch the drippings, but the meat inside a well-sealed cooker will generate its own moisture.

No reputable barbecue cook parboils or presteams his meat, which reliably turns the meat gray and leaches out its sweet pork taste. Sauces can be used for marinating the raw meat, for inject- 311 ing flavor deep into a hundred-pound hog, for basting, as a fin- ishing sauce when the product is nearly done, and as a table or serving sauce. Some championship barbecue cooks use several sauces, some none at all, instead sprinkling on a layer of dry rub only at the very beginning. The miracle of barbecue is that this ancient process flavors and tenderizes the meat all by itself. The greatest barbecue cooks use sauce in ascetic moderation.

3 and 4. Real barbecue is one of the most delicious foods ever devised by humankind. It takes on various forms and shapes. In Memphis, a pork-barbecue sandwich consists of pulled shoulder (or pulled and then chopped) on a hamburger bun (or a length of what in this country is called Italian bread, a squat baguette with tapered ends, all flecked with sesame seeds), doused with a tomato-based sauce that is tangy, mildly sweet, and barely piquant—and topped with a scoop of coleslaw and the upper half of the bun. In Memphis, coleslaw is raised to a level that, while never scaling the heights to which pork soars in this city, is in my experience without peer or equal. I cannot say the same for bar- becued spaghetti, another Memphian speciality.

In St. Louis, potato salad replaces coleslaw and is served on the side. In Kentucky, pork becomes mutton. In some parts of the South, fluffy commercial white bread, often toasted, stands in for the bun or Italian bread. In North Carolina, the mild tanginess of

Tennessee spice rub becomes the corrosive power of vinegar, and in South Carolina the tomato-sauce base is replaced by unadulterated mustard. Drive one hundred miles into Missouri, and whole pork shoulder yields to the smaller butt portion. In some places along the Southeast coast, fresh ham replaces shoulder, and if you travel farther west than central Arkansas, pork gives way to beef and poultry. But in Memphis and its culinary sphere of influence in northern Mississippi, western Tennessee, and eastern Arkansas, pork is king.

This much I knew. The daylong seminar in the dark theater on Beale Street concentrated more on the practicalities of judging and the fine points of pork. Our excellent teachers were Mike Cannon (judging chairman of the Memphis in May World Championship) and Steve Gray (chairman of the Memphis in May Sanctioned Contest Network, a circuit of pork-barbecue cooking contests run according to Memphis rules). We started by taking a test of fifty multiple-choice questions. May whole hog be cooked in two or more pieces? What is the red layer below the surface of a piece of barbecue? What cut of meat makes an acceptable shoulder? What is the most difficult aspect of cooking a whole hog? Can natural gas or propane be used as fuel in the Memphis World Championship?

After we had all failed the test, which was our teachers' intention, we sat in the old New Daisy for the rest of the day, listening to their lectures, watching a film from a meatpacking plant, running through the simulated judging of a real live pork shoulder. Only a small percentage of Memphis judges subject themselves to this seminar, but I don't see how anybody can hope to be a fair, consistent judge without it. Finally we took the test again—exactly the same questions but in a different order. All but two of us passed. I got a 96.

By Friday morning my wife had arrived, which meant an obligatory visit to Graceland for the complete Platinum Tour. This included the mansion, the Elvis Presley Automobile Museum, the Sincerely Elvis Museum, and Elvis's two airplanes. We had arrived early to leave time for a late-morning barbecue brunch at Cozy Corner in preparation for a full barbecue lunch at Payne's. But the Platinum Tour was so excruciatingly comprehensive that we missed brunch and were forced to postpone lunch until three in the afternoon. Two days of anger and depression lifted when I read in the Memphis papers that at the very moment my wife was dragging me around Graceland, the Shelby County Commission had filed suit to reopen the investigation into Elvis's death. The guides at Graceland never mentioned the King's fondness for controlled substances. Or that his favorite snack was fried peanut-butter-and-banana sandwiches. They did not mention barbecue even once.

Late Friday afternoon my wife and I drove over to Tom Lee Park in downtown Memphis, where all 241 barbecue teams had already set up for the World Championship Barbecue Cooking Contest. The contestants stretched a half mile along the east bank of the Mississippi, and the air was thick with perfumed smoke, pork and hickory and applewood. On its assigned plot of ground, each team had erected its temporary quarters, a tent or a bungalow, a cabin or a cottage, a shed or a shack, a shanty or lean-to, a trailer or a pavilion, a kiosk or an entire prefabricated suburban house. Some structures hugged the earth; others soared three stories toward the skies. Some were rough and homely, others magnificent, with decks and balconies overlooking the great river.

Each team had brought at least one barbecue cooker. Most were painted black, but some came in red, and one in pink; most teams had two or three cookers, some converted from five-hundred-gallon propane tanks, others in the shape of outsized coffins, still others bulbous affairs with tall smokestacks. One cooker was a converted 1975 Datsun with a firebox in the engine compartment and racks of meat in the driver's seat. The U.S. Porkmasters, sponsored by the Postal Service, had made its smoker from a small mail-delivery van. The Paddlewheel Porkers had the largest display of all, a forty-three-foot replica of a riverboat steamer complete with decks and galleys and a revolving paddlewheel. Each team had a name—the Adribbers and the Big Dawg Hawg, the Crispy Critters and the Great Boars of Fire, the Not Ready for Swine Time and the Party Pigs, the Super Swine Sizzlers and Hazardous Waist. (Swine Lake Ballet was not in attendance this year.) Of the 241 teams, I was told by an insider, 100 are serious and expert competitors who enter ten to twenty contests a year, traveling around the South with their five-thousand-dollar cookers and their twenty-thousand-dollar eight-wheel trailers. "This is our country club," one team captain explained to me, "this is our bass boat." (A bass boat is apparently an extremely fancy and expensive speedboat that rides high on the water, carries sonar and other costly toys, and is used in fishing contests in the Mississippi Delta.) Barbecue competitions are largely a white man's game; no more than twenty of the Memphis teams were dominated by blacks or women. Still, the very first Memphis world championship sixteen years ago was won by a black woman named Bessie Louise Cathey.

Each of the serious teams had a long table that sagged under the weight of its twenty or thirty proudest trophies. The most breathtaking example had three tall and lustrous blue metal columns supporting a black triangular platform, on which were three pink metal pigs each standing on a golden rectangle. In the center, between the three pigs, stood a loving cup surmounted by a tall golden figure in the form of the *Victory of Samothrace,* this one not headless and chipped like the version at the Louvre, but fully formed and with a slimmer, more modern body, her wings shimmering with speckles of blue and pink, her saucy breasts straining through gauzy drapery, one arm raised to hold a torch aloft, its flame a rosy radiance.

Saturday was judgment day. The sky was blue, the air was filled with smoke and tension, and the ground was getting dusty. When it rains on a Memphis in May World Championship Barbecue Cooking Contest, Tom Lee Park turns into a hog wallow. But today the event went off with benign military precision. Many among both the public and the contestants wore pink rubber snouts; your present correspondent did not. There was also a sprinkling of Elvis impersonators. Admission for the public was four dollars; the crowd was later estimated at eighty thousand.

Teams had driven in from seventeen states to vie for twenty-five thousand dollars in prize money, most of it divided among the winners and runners up in the three categories of pork barbecue—Ribs, Shoulder, and Whole Hog. Some judges visit each team's site, and some participate in a blind judging, in which each team's product is carried in a numbered Styrofoam box to the judges' tent, where four judges evaluate (in order of importance) the entry's flavor, tenderness, and appearance or doneness—on a scale from 5 to 10. In the on-site judging, three judges make independent trips to each team's location and assign points for the quality of the food, the cleanliness of the team's area, and what is called the team's presentation, a lengthy speech explaining the history of the team; its theories of barbecue cookery; the source of its meat, fuel, and machinery; the secrets of its sauce. Truth is not an indispensable element. As long as a speech is consistent and intelligent, a team is allowed to say, southern style, anything that may impress you. "It's like sitting around an old pit late at night, swapping stories," one of our teachers had explained. I have never sat around an old pit late at night, but I can imagine what he had in mind. Appearance and presentation are given minor weight. The meat comes first, and flavor is its most important attribute. Garnishes do not count, not even Memphis slaw.

The on-site judges are repeatedly warned not to get drunk before visiting all three assigned teams, but I saw no judge who was anything less than stone-cold sober. Each on-site judge is given an apron (a different color for each category of pork) and an assistant to guide him or her around the crowded park to three teams within a precise sixty minutes. Then the scoring cards are tallied by Price Waterhouse and its computers. The three highest scorers in each of the three categories become finalists. All nine finalists are visited late in the day by a group of four special judges who decide the winner in each category and the grand champion of the entire contest.

Every cut of pork presents its own particular challenge to the barbecue chef. The rib section is the most delicate of a pig's assets, we had been told in the judging seminar at the New Daisy Theater. It is the hardest part to cook, both because of its delicacy and because "anybody that's ever owned a Weber thinks he can cook a real dynamic rib." Only two rib cuts are eligible, the fatty, dense spareribs from the hog's belly and the lighter loin ribs from the hog's back, called baby back ribs when they come from a young hog. Ineligible are country-style ribs, which have a piece of the tenderloin still attached, almost like a pork chop. A slab of loin or baby back ribs, which have narrow bones separated by ethereal flesh, weighs less than two pounds; taken from high on the hog, they are favored in barbecue competitions. When a four- or five-pound slab of spareribs is entered, it is usually first trimmed down to a St. Louis cut—all visible fat removed along with the gristly "brisket flap" that runs obliquely across the back of the slab.

Some teams skin their ribs, and some do not; all of them argue about which is the best policy. The tough membrane lining the underside of the bones may hold in moisture, but it prevents the penetration of smoke and spice. When any cut of pork is exposed at length to hardwood smoke, its outer layer takes on a rich pinkish tint, sometimes as much as an inch into the meat. In Texas, entries are judged on the depth and color of this "smoke ring." In Memphis it is simply a harbinger of deeply flavored meat. For some odd and unaccountable reason, the tasty, crunchy part of a barbecued rib does not matter. "It may taste great," the head judge explained to me, "but it's not Memphis barbecue."

As pork is barbecued, it goes from tough to tender to mushy, and it can dry out if it is not cooked in moist surroundings. Competition cooks often use a thick glaze to mask a mushy or dry entry. On the barbecue pit, ribs pass through the perfect state of doneness for only fifteen minutes. If the bones slip right out of the slab, the ribs are mushy; if the meat refuses to separate from the bones, it is tough. As with all pork barbecue, the meat must have body but separate easily from itself with a gentle pull. Most teams throw on a fresh slab of ribs every twenty minutes for two hours early in the morning so that one slab will be perfectly done six hours later for each of the three judges. An hour or two afterward, perhaps on an auxiliary grill, they begin again—just in case the team reaches the finals and needs some fresh slabs for the second round.

A whole hog must weigh at least eighty-five pounds (suckling pigs do not count in Memphis) and is cooked either whole or halved down the spine, on its back or on its belly, for twenty to twenty-six hours, with or without its head and feet, skinned or unskinned. (The skin of a mature pig is too thick and tough to eat.) Whole Hog teams stay up all night before judgment day, basting and fussing and adjusting the heat. The challenge of barbecuing a whole hog is to get the huge, thick shoulder (the mass of muscle above the front leg) and the ham (above the hind leg) done at the same time as the delicate central portions of loin and rib—while making sure that the flavor of spices and smoke penetrates deep inside the hog. Accordingly, a Whole Hog judge must sample, at the very least, pieces of the shoulder, the ham, and the loin. He or she is also allowed to taste the delightful bacon and the amusing rib section, but these cuts do not count.

A pork shoulder can weigh fourteen to twenty pounds and in its raw state is riddled with fat. The trick is to cook it long and slow, without drying out the meat, until every bit of fat disappears and the cooking flavors permeate every morsel. This is even more difficult under Memphis rules than elsewhere, because an official shoulder must include both the picnic shoulder and the Boston butt, which together make up a vast quantity of meat and bones. An on-site judge should ignore how easily the leg bone slips from the meat; the team may have cut it out earlier and replaced it. Instead, he or she should sample one piece of meat from the very center and another from the crispy, flavorful

317

coating known as bark. Blind judges cannot determine whether a shoulder was properly cooked, because a team with an underdone shoulder can pack into their Styrofoam box only the tenderest pieces.

Just after noon, judging in the Ribs division began. The first team to which I was assigned was the Sporty Porkers from Vienna, Georgia (pronounced "Vy-anna" and home of the Big Pig Jig, Georgia's official championship event), sponsored by the Pitts Gin Company. Its area in the park was carpeted with Astroturf and surrounded by a wooden rail fence. Captain Danny Cape greeted me at the gate, introducing himself and the other members of the team, all trim and immaculate in their snappy Day-Glo yellow T-shirts with black inscriptions. "Deep in my heart," Cape told me as he led me to their huge black cooker, "we feel that the rib we'll serve you today is a top-notch rib. It's got an excellent chance to win the world championship." Sporty Porkers won third place in Ribs in 1991, nothing last year.

Cape explained that their loin back ribs had been bought from a local farmer in Georgia. The underside ribs had been skinned with a wide and toothy catfish skinner; rubbed with secret spices (a combination of Cajun seasonings, lemon pepper, and a pinch of garlic salt); then put on the grill. The Sporty Porkers' fuel is Natural Glow hickory charcoal and blocks of hickory wood, their temperature is 200 to 225 degrees, their fire is started at four in the morning, and their total cooking time is nine or ten hours. For the first eight hours, the ribs are placed on their long edge in an angled rack thirty-three inches from the coals. As the cooker has no exhaust, the steam created when the juices drip from the meat down onto the coals keeps the atmosphere moist. For the last hour of cooking, a light coat of finishing sauce is brushed on.

"We feel really good about these ribs," Cape told me as he opened the cooker to reveal a perfect slab of ribs. (Under Memphis rules, a judge's first view of a sample of rib, shoulder, or hog must be right there on the grill.) Then Cape led me to a striped tent decorated with hanging ferns and two pots of yellow daisies. In the center was a small table set just for one. He placed a single rib on my plate next to a little bowl of sauce—the result, he explained, of six years' experimentation with Hunt's ketchup, red and black pepper, chili powder, and French's mustard, plus cayenne, brown sugar, and apple-cider vinegar. "We feel they're the best ribs we ever cooked," Cape continued. He offered me juice, tea, beer, wine, or cold water. Soberly, I chose water.

I took a bite out of the rib meat. It had been carved in "competition cut," one bone flanked by wide strips of meat. If a team is especially confident about the tenderness of its product, it will serve you what is called "two bones with big meat on either side" and invite you to separate the bones yourself. With perfectly cooked ribs, the meat between the bones should separate down the center and not from the bones. Competition cut denies you that opportunity; it is the conservative choice, but it is less revealing.

I had rarely tasted ribs as good as Sporty Porkers'—sweet and succulent, juicy and tender; the meat was still well attached to the bone but pulled off easily. If they had any flaws at all, the ribs may have been just slightly too white and fatty, a sign of under doneness; a perfectly cooked rib would have been drier and more thoroughly penetrated by smoke. Surrounded by all six members of the team, I tried to convey my admiration without violating judicial decorum. They remained anxious. But I was not to decide precisely how many points to award to the Sporty Porkers on each of the six criteria until I had visited the two other teams to which I had been assigned. I remembered a warning from one of the contest officials. "Northerners are too easily impressed by so-so barbecue when they come down here," she told me, "because they can't get any decent stuff up there where they live."

I sat under the Sporty Porkers' tent, eating ribs and drinking water in a stuporous reverie until my assistant stepped in to tell me that a full fifteen minutes had passed. I had five minutes to walk to the next team, Ol' Hawg's Breath of Memphis, sponsored by Schering-Plough. And then on to M & M Cooker of Francisco, Indiana.

"Great barbecue makes you want to slap your granny up the side of her head," the southern saying goes. Only Sporty Porkers made me feel quite that way. M & M cooked up a very fine rib, but not quite equal to the artistry of Sporty Porkers. Walking back to the judges' tent with my assistant, I filled out the three score-cards, awarding mostly 10s to the Sporty Porkers, 9s and 10s to M & M, and 8s to Ol' Hawg's Breath.

At the end of the day, after the final round of judging, as the sun swooped low over the mighty river and burnished the teeming masses like so many tiny bronzed trophies, the winners were announced. A team called Apple City BBQ from Murphysboro, Illinois, placed first in Ribs; Delta Smokers from Cleveland, Mississippi, came in second; and Backwoods Boys BBQ of Trenton, Tennessee, was third. The grand champion of the entire event and winner in the Shoulder category was the Other Side, from Poplar Bluff, Missouri; the team was named after Captain Mike Clark's business, the Other Side Dental and Medical Supply. The Whole Hog prize was won by the very visible and dedicated Paddlewheel Porkers.

My first reaction was to feel depressed for the Sporty Porkers, who had placed only eighth in Ribs. They had spent seven thousand dollars to participate in the Big One.

My second reaction was to swoon at the thought that within walking distance there existed multiple slabs of barbecued ribs superior to any I had ever tasted.

My third reaction was to grab a map of Tom Lee Park and hurry over to Apple City BBQ to get me a taste of a world championship rib. Apple City's red-and-white-striped tent was surrounded by a white picket fence and carpeted with Astroturf, an immaculate oasis among the dust and smoke that stretched for hundreds of yards around it. In contrast, the Apple City cooker looked like a charred hydrogen bomb—a huge, bulging black cylinder resting on its side with great spherical ends and two stubby smokestacks rising from the top. In the chaos and press of the congratulatory crowds, I did not even get near an Apple City rib. My wife tried to interest me in a display of country line dancing. But all I could think about was what the future would bring.

Three days later I was back in New York and on the telephone to Mike Mills, Apple City's congenial captain, who was back in Murphysboro. I was in luck. While most competition barbecue teams cook only ten to twenty times a year in contests across the Deep and mid-South, Mills cooks barbecue nearly every day at his own 17th Street Bar and Grill. Soon three slabs of ribs were heading my way by Federal Express overnight delivery.

Apple City BBQ cooks its loin and baby back ribs skinned and bone down for six to six and a half hours on a Ferris wheel that revolves in its menacing cooker amidst indirect heat from the sides and direct heat from underneath, both generated by Holland-brand pure hickory briquettes made in Crossville, Tennessee, site of the largest hickory grove in the nation. Southern Illinois is apple-orchard country, and right before every contest, Apple City cuts green applewood prunings that will produce an aromatic smoke in its cooker. The team believes that taking dry applewood and soaking it in water would remove its aroma; fully grown applewood logs contain too many harsh tars and resins.

Before they go into the cooker, the ribs are rubbed with a secret mixture of eighteen spices. Sometimes Mills claims that each of the six team members knows only three ingredients; no two team members are allowed in the kitchen at the same time. Other times Mills says he'd be happy to tell me all the ingredients, but then he'd have to shoot me.

"We go on the theory of low, slow, and long," Mills explained. For the first couple of hours, the temperature in the cooker is kept down near 100 degrees so that the pores of the meat open up and take in the smoke and spices "like Mother Nature would take in a seed in the springtime." Then fuel is added and the heat rises to 180 or 200 degrees, where it is maintained until the last hour and then boosted again, this time to 250 degrees, hot enough to form a crispy bark on the outside of the slab and render out that last bit of fat. A rib will go through at least two sweats, as the surface opens up and the natural juices break through, and that's when the Apple City team sprinkles on its spices. After two or three hours have passed, the ribs are basted with freshly pressed apple juice whenever they look dry, usually about every half hour. And in the final thirty minutes, Mills and his teammates apply two light coats of finishing sauce, which they dry up with more of the spice rub and a little salt. The result is known as a wet dry rib.

Apple City won first prize in Ribs and the overall grand championship in both 1990 and 1992. "Nineteen ninety-one just wasn't our day," Mills says. Last year Apple City won thirteen of the seventeen contests it entered.

Early the next morning, before I had dressed, a crisply uniformed man from Federal Express arrived with a cardboard box enclosing a Styrofoam cooler in which lay three slabs of Apple City world championship ribs. Mills's instructions were to microwave each slab on low, just until the ribs were hot, but not to cook them further. This went without incident. Then, still in my bathrobe, I sat down at the kitchen table, a roll of paper towels on the left and a tall glass of water on the right. In front of me sat the highest expression of America's proudest vernacular cooking tradition. I recalled the late Jane Grigson's claim that all of civilization was founded on the pig. Giving muted thanks to the entire species, I took a bite.

Apple City's were unlike anything I have ever tasted. I grasped two bones and pulled them apart. The firm flesh instantly separated, sending up a puff of steam with the aroma of a clean-burning wood fire and the ineffable, God-given sweetness of pork. The meat was nearly red throughout, moist and entirely free of fat, and deeply flavored with spices and smoke. (Its color and texture resembled pastrami or long-smoked fish as much as it did pork.) And it was profoundly delicious, satisfying every need that the human body and soul have for food, unless you consider cold and slimy greens to be food.

In the blink of an eye, a completely bare bone lay on my plate, then three completely bare bones, and soon a dozen. I considered microwaving another slab or maybe both, but then remembered my wife, who had already left for work. For a girl, she has a remarkably healthy appetite for real pork barbecue, fixed according to Memphis rules.

September 1993

Ingredients in Search
of a Cuisine

The pilot guided our little seaplane slowly across Lake Union in Seattle, aimed us at Vancouver Island eighty miles away, revved the engines, and off we went. Soon we were floating over the city and Puget Sound beyond. It was that rare event in the Pacific Northwest—a brilliantly sunny day. The pilot handed me a pair of bright green earplugs to block the roar of the engines as I tried to figure out why the heater was melting my sneakers.

I peered down at the rocky coastal beaches and at the islands dotting the Sound. A friend back in New York once told me that the most wonderful oysters he had ever tasted were gathered at low tide on one of these beaches. His guide foraged for wild onions in the nearby forest, built a driftwood fire, roasted the oysters, and, when their shells opened, tossed in the onions.

This is why I had traveled to Seattle. All the way from New York I could taste the chubby oysters poached in their own sea-salt liquor, rich with woody smoke and the grassy sweetness of wild onions.

I searched the islands below for any trace of a roasting oyster, but there was none. Wild Pacific oysters are nearly extinct now, and most of the prized bivalves of the region are cultivated; the productive beaches in Washington State are leased to commercial oyster farms. And except for today's sunny interlude, it rained or snowed incessantly during my trip to the Northwest, a discouraging ambience for a beach adventure. I would return to New York no closer to my goal than when I had left. But in the meantime I feasted for ten days on what is without doubt the finest fish and seafood in North America.

In half an hour our seaplane was over open water, the Strait of Juan de Fuca, which, my historical research discloses, was named for Juan de Fuca. Juan was a Greek seaman, sailing under both the Spanish flag and a Spanish pseudonym, who in 1592 may or may not have discovered the strait separating Vancouver Island in Canada from Washington's Olympic Peninsula. We dipped low and glided toward the seaplane terminal in the city of Victoria.

It was no coincidence that at precisely the same moment, thirty miles along the Vancouver Island coast, a Canadian diver named Francis hastily pulled on a wet suit and mask and jumped into the choppy gray waters of Sooke Bay off the Strait of Juan de Fuca. Recent storms had stirred up the bottom, and Francis could see only three feet around him instead of the usual fifty as he searched for long-spined sea urchins, purple-hinged rock scallops, acorn and gooseneck barnacles, sea cucumbers, and orange crab. He bagged some urchins and sea cucumbers, but the crabs were elusive, and when he swam along the edge of the bay with his knife unsheathed to pry off the purple scallops, fierce currents threatened to drag him against the rocks. Not realizing the importance I place upon lunch, Francis thought of his own personal safety and pulled himself from the water.

When I reached Sooke Harbour House later that morning, Francis apologized that my table would not swarm with as much local seafood as he had hoped. To Sinclair and Fredrica Philip, who own the inn, "local" means seafood taken from the waters outside their dining room window an hour or two before lunch or dinner. Divers using scuba gear and air tanks go deeper than Francis; they bring up giant sea urchins, pink singing scallops, sea whelks, octopi, clams, and geoducks (which look like a cross between a giant clam and an elephant), abalone, cockles, and ten kinds of sea snails. Fifty-pound salmon are caught from boats in the same waters; only prawns, oysters, and ocean fish like black cod are bought from commercial fishermen who dock at the government wharf next door.

Sinclair and Fredrica are economists (they married while in graduate school at the University of Grenoble) turned naturalists-innkeepers-restaurateurs, and their dedication to the freshness and seasonality of local ingredients is monomaniacal. The neat white clapboard buildings of Sooke Harbour House are surrounded by astonishing terraced gardens where, with the help of Byron Cook, they grow four hundred varieties of edible plants, including flowers and weeds—sea rockets and nodding onions; wild sorrel, cress, and chrysanthemums; garlic chives in white, mauve, and yellow; all the cabbages and six varieties of leeks; five kinds of rosemary, six types of lavender, fifteen of mint, thirty lettuces, and forty other salad greens. Kid, rabbit, goose, and lamb are raised organically by farmers a few miles away. Local foragers gather wild berries, fifty types of mushrooms, ten varieties of seaweed.

In the kitchen I met my lunch, a tub of dreadful giant red-and-purple sea urchins, each a foot across, and a nightmarish landscape of sea cucumbers, writhing and slithering over each other like tumescent, warty maroon worms, a foot long and three inches in diameter, glistening and slimy. I also met the young bearded chef, Ron Cherry, a shy and unassuming man who was classically trained in some of Canada's best restaurants. Ron's talents are tested at every meal—the day's catch remains a mystery until a few hours beforehand, and it can include twenty species.

Lunch was served in the warm, windowed dining room before a huge stone fireplace, and it was delicious—a soup of oysters, pale orange sea urchin roe, and tiny clams; a sauté of abalone and sea cucumber (just the thin strips of muscle that line the tubular body cavity) with Hubbard squash puree and celery leaves; rich slices of pink-roasted goose breast with one sauce of Oregon grape and another of rosemary-garlic cream; a salad of chickweed, lamb's-quarters, and Siberian lettuce; and salmon mousse wrapped in walking-stick cabbage (the woody stalk is used to make furniture on the Isle of Skye) and garnished with steelhead trout caviar, tuberous begonia, and horseradish butter.

I barely noticed the absence of purple-hinged rock scallops; besides, the best and freshest way to eat them is underwater, according to Sinclair, snipped from their shell before they have had time to clamp shut, and slipped between your lips. I did notice that lemon, lime, olive oil, and other culinary common-places were missing from Ron's cooking. The Philips' interest in local products rules out most plants and animals that don't grow in the Northwest. To replace lemons and limes, Ron has developed other sources of acidity, such as rhubarb juice and apple cider, and the Phillips have found a mill that cold-presses cooking oil from locally grown seeds and nuts. Common Asian spices like black peppercorns are suspect; I wondered about vanilla. At its best, the result is a rejection of all culinary clichés, a rediscovery of the natural world at every meal.

I am still wondering about vanilla because the seaplane schedule back to Seattle deprived me of dessert. I wish I had stayed overnight in every one of the inn's thirteen lovely rooms, all with fireplaces and all facing the strait and the snowy Olympic Range on the U.S. side. But I had a dinner engagement to keep, and a week of lunches and dinners after that. The Pacific North-west overflows with such good food that one grows frenzied trying to nibble and gnaw on it all.

My trip was planned for late winter because that's when oysters are best. In the springtime, as the water grows warm, oysters prepare to spawn, and their flesh becomes milky and soft. After spawning, oysters, like men, are good for nothing until they rebuild their reserves of glycogen. But in winter (when, coincidentally, the names of the months contain an *r*) they are crisp and glistening and incomparable.

My culinary base camp was Seattle's Pike Place Market and the Inn at the Market hotel, which overlooks it. Visiting at the

327

ideal time for oysters meant that I would forgo the wild blackberries and tree-ripened cherries of June, river crayfish trapped
between April and October, the peaches and apricots of late summer, and the May debut of white and golden beets, sweet onions,
red and white chard, white carrots, and twenty kinds of salad
greens. But the local pears (unlike most fruit, pears improve after
they are picked) were the best I've tasted. The Manila clams and
the mussels from Race Lagoon and Penn Cove were a delight—
sweet and creamy and mild—as were the fresh sturgeon and
black cod. And the oysters! Every day I held a little contest among
the Shoalwaters, Quilcenes, Hamma Hammas, Kumamotos, and
Olympias. In the end, the tiny oceanic Olympias won, and I celebrated by eating seventy of them one evening just before dinner.

It seems incredible that Seattle was a culinary wasteland *fifteen years ago,* but that's what everybody says. Supermarkets sold
frozen fish, and restaurants served it deep-fried. The oyster industry produced only shucked meat in gallon containers, and my
exquisite little Olympias were just being nursed back from extinc-
tion. Pink singing scallops were an uneaten oddity, mussel cultivation was unknown, geoducks were spurned by everyone but a
few fishermen, and the salmon caviar was shipped abroad. Fancy
restaurants imported oysters, mussels, and lobsters from the East
Coast.

But Seattleites loved to go fishing and clamming, foraging for
berries and wild mushrooms. They knew what was fresh and seasonal even if their supermarkets and restaurants were slow to
understand. In 1980, Jon Rowley—an Alaska fisherman for ten
years after quitting Reed College—began working with fishermen, supermarkets, and restaurants to revolutionize the way
Pacific fish were caught, handled, and delivered to the city. (Julia
Child has named Jon the Fish Missionary, and his company—Fish
Works!—is now active in ten other cities.)

Stylish American cooking arrived, by some accounts, when
Karl Beckley opened his Green Lake Grill in 1979. The young
chefs who followed him demanded fresher and more varied

ingredients. Small farmers, cheese makers, and fish smokers responded. By the mid-eighties, the culinary excitement here was reminiscent of the Bay Area ten years before. Inventive restaurants sprang up like wild mushrooms, with young chef-owners composing fanciful platters of the most impeccable and expensive regional products: restaurant goers breathlessly followed. Now nearly every restaurant menu lists the pedigree of its ingredients, even when there is none. At one place, I was served a tall parfait glass of good Dungeness crab under cups of red cocktail sauce, which the menu described as "a homemade sauce of Heinz ketchup, extra hot horseradish, and fresh lemon." But where else can you find a waitress, like the one who took my order at Ray's Boathouse, who can explain why she prefers Race Lagoon mussels to those from Penn Cove and why one method of catching salmon is superior to another?

The local food press is as active and alert as any in the nation and a pleasure to read. John Doerper, food editor of *Pacific Northwest* magazine and an encyclopedic guide to me during my stay in Seattle, tirelessly explores the coast from Oregon to British Columbia (he has been known to drive two hundred miles for lunch); his *Eating Well* (Pacific Search) is an essential appetizer for the foods of the Northwest. Schuyler Ingle is now at *Washington* magazine; his graceful essays in *Northwest Bounty* (Simon and Schuster) are models for us all. The *Seattle Weekly* offers the most ardent and informed food coverage of any city weekly I know, as well as a column by Tom Douglas, owner of Dahlia Lounge and one of the chefs who started it all eight years ago at Cafe Sport. And Alf Collins, restaurant reviewer for the *Seattle Times* until recently, now has his own business newsletter, with the most knowledgeable food news around.

The Pacific Northwest has everything a food lover could possibly desire—with two exceptions. The first is bread, and the second is cuisine.

Everybody in the Northwest serves home-baked bread, and everywhere it made me yearn for the factory-made version. The bread is of two types: home-baked health-food-style bread (poorly leavened, crumbly, weak crusted, slightly sweet, speckled with carrots, herbs, olives, or nuts) and home-baked Parker House roll–style bread (traditional American, sweet, white, fluffy, fun on occasion but not three times a day and not with food).

Bad bread wrecks my outlook on life. The pathetic loaves at Seattle's proudest French restaurant immediately made me paranoid about everything on the menu, everybody who had recommended the place in print or in person, and all the other customers. How could they sit there and smile and eat that bread-shaped impostor on the table?

But relief is on the way. Eight months ago the old Grand Central Bakery in Seattle—after a transfusion of talent and an oven from Italy—began turning out chewy, crusty, yeasty loaves of real bread, and within a few months it was operating at its full capacity of one thousand loaves a day. Others are sure to follow.

I had collected a year of restaurant reviews before coming to Seattle, and I visited plenty of restaurants after I arrived. I won't tell you where to eat because I tried no restaurant more than once, I missed several leading contenders, and besides, I did not come to evaluate restaurants. I wanted to understand how Northwest chefs transform the incredible bounty of sea and sod into cuisine. I will reveal that my mouth still waters as it relives the smoked, steamed black cod at Ray's Boathouse, the sweet Dungeness crab and Olympia oysters at Elliott's, the Quilcene oysters at Emmett Watson's, and much of Barbara Figueroa's cooking at the Hunt Club. But only the last can be considered cuisine.

Does the Pacific Northwest have a distinctive style of cooking? The best culinary minds in the region worry about this question every day, write articles, and meet with each other every few months to disagree about it. But the answer is simple. Either there are a dozen distinctive Northwest cuisines, or there is a single Northwest cuisine, but nobody can tell which one it is.

You can't name a cooking style that is not represented here. There are classical French and Italian restaurants, though most

Seattle chefs seem to have come no nearer to Europe than a year or two in Santa Monica. Some menus speak in the dominant idiom of today's regional American cooking—New Southwest with a few Cajun phrases mixed in. California cuisine has oozed up the coast, which usually means underflavored, undersalted modern French cooking hidden under edible flowers and Mexican fruits. Eclectic is in. An odd combination known variously as Pacific Rim, Pan-Pacific, or Pan-Asian is spreading fast; it typically combines every known Oriental cooking method and ingredient, minus India and Japan. One restaurant dishes up, simultaneously, the food of Mexico, the Caribbean, Brazil, Santa Fe, and someone's fantasy of Native America. The *Weekly* characterizes this as "post-ethnic mélange," "post-pre-Columbian," and "neo-Mayan Span Tex." One local food writer recently put her foot down: "I insist on one nationality, indivisible, per plate at a time."

The profusion of tastes and techniques from every corner of the globe gives Northwest chefs no incentive to explore their own natural niche as intensely as the Philips do at Sooke Harbour House. The desperate pace of culinary borrowing and experimentation often overwhelms the exquisite quality of the region's produce and seafood. Many of the ethnic culinary models here were developed in places without impeccable raw ingredients and employ methods of cooking and spicing that do nothing to enhance fresh, natural tastes. In reaction, some Northwest chefs follow principles like these guidelines from the Herbfarm (whose acclaimed restaurant was closed during my visit):

• To be true to our local roots, stay away from food that could only be grown or raised in another climate—oranges, tropical fruits, coconut, etc. . . .

• Here are a few examples of items that should not be used: swordfish, mangoes, tiger prawns, blue crabs, grapefruit, and lobster. . . .

• These items could be grown in Washington but should be avoided as inappropriate and trendy: blue corn, sweet red pepper sauce (maybe), black beans, chilies, avocado, polenta, and the other overt manifestations of California, Cajun, and Southwest cuisines.

When I first read them, these admonitions sounded austere, xenophobic, almost Stalinist. But I became a convert one evening when I spent ten minutes extracting the carambola and sapote from a perfectly nice piece of fish to a waiting ashtray, and then tried to taste the chunks of fresh crab in my wife's Thai-Cajun chowder.

As I drove from Canada to Oregon, the restaurants that interested me most were those that follow, more or less, and often inadvertently, the Herbfarm principles. The Raintree in Vancouver is one, though my afternoon snack there was only a glimpse of how Rebecca Dawson uses what her corner of the region offers. Salishan Lodge in Gleneden Beach, Oregon, is on everyone's list, but my drive down the coast from Seattle was cut short by a savage storm that everybody told me was unprecedented but that, I suspect, occurs on a weekly basis.

I did get as far as the Long Beach Peninsula at the extreme southwest corner of Washington for dinner at Ann and Tony Kischner's Shoalwater Restaurant at the Shelburne Inn. Chef Walker's restrictions are not as severe as at Sooke or Raintree or the Herbfarm. But products from twenty miles around rule the menu. Local gardeners bring Ann their seed catalogs every February to find out what she would like them to plant in the spring. A fisherman who lives a half hour away supplies salmon and sturgeon caviar, which he prepares by a method taught to his father by a Russian émigré. In summer, an elderly neighbor lady collects blackberries from a vine that bore fruit for her mother.

I ate scrumptious Willapa Bay oysters poached in whiskey and served with Columbia River sturgeon caviar in a beurre blanc; an Italian vegetable-lentil soup (Washington lentils, of course); sturgeon baked with a creamy sauce of sake and wild mushrooms; and a deeply flavored pear sorbet made with a Washington Riesling. The next morning, the owners of the Shelburne Inn, Laurie Anderson and David Campiche (who has lived here all his life), fixed one of their famous breakfasts: David's handmade caviar, smoked salmon, and potato-clam cakes; Laurie's pastries and sourdough rolls—the starter may be a hundred years old—and gallons of hot coffee from Seattle's Torrefazione.

Then we walked to the lighthouse at the mouth of the Columbia River. The storm had lifted for the first time in a week, and the morning sun on the Pacific was dazzling. But there was a culinary tragedy in the making.

The salmon fishing season on the Columbia had opened at midnight, fully ten hours earlier. As salmon do not feed as they swim upstream to their spawning grounds, they are at their fattest and most luscious at the mouth of the river, just as they begin to run. This is the only perfect place to catch them and the only perfect time to eat them. Grown men swoon as they describe the taste of spring-run Chinook. And I had come here, at no small risk to my safety and that of my rent-a-car, to taste of this perfection.

But there was not a boat in sight. Either fearful that the storm would resume or wary of the crosscurrents it had left behind, every fisherman for a hundred miles around had simply decided to stay at home. A day later I would leave the Pacific Northwest without even a bite of fresh salmon. If the Columbia River were in New York City, I thought bitterly as I boarded the plane for home, it would have been choked with boats by 12:01 a.m., all vying with each other to catch the first and fattest salmon of the season and rush it to my table. Pacific fishermen are fair-weather sailors, I decided. It is no accident that Captain Ahab set sail from Nantucket, not Santa Barbara, in his quest for Moby-Dick.

June 1990

333

Out of North Africa

334   *Malsouka, masfouf, makfoul. Malsouka, masfouf, makfoul.*
Malsouka is a thin leaf of pastry. *Masfouf* is fine-grained couscous. *Makfoul* is the bottom of a couscous steamer. I can't imagine
why people say that Arabic is impossible to learn. *Zgougou* is a
kind of pine nut. *Zgougou* is my favorite word so far.

But sometimes I think that if I had learned the Arabic
words for "Where on earth is my tour bus?" I would have been
far better off. I was in the medina, the old walled town, of
Sousse, Tunisia's third-largest city. In the heart of the medina
are the souks, the medieval maze of market stalls and shops.
And I had gotten lost in the souks of Sousse. I was innocently in
search of a certain type of flat bread—thin, round, unleavened,
stretchy, dense, wheaty, tender, and dotted with dark bumps
and blisters from contact with the hot earthenware griddle on
which it is baked. I wandered the souks in vain, encountering
only a poor version of French bread and airy, biscuitlike flat
breads.

And then I came upon the real thing. Unfortunately, someone was already eating it, sitting in front of his hardware stall. I
inquired in French; most Tunisians are at least bilingual. He
swallowed, gestured up the narrow, crooked street, and told me
to walk fifty meters and then turn right. My head down, I paced
off fifty meters and turned right, nearly slamming into a huge,

furry cow's head that hung before a butcher's stall, an advertisement for the freshness of the meat on offer. After refusing to
sell me his gigantic triangular cleaver—I have never seen one
like it—the butcher also directed me to walk fifty meters up the
street and turn to the right. But this brought me to a shop selling boom boxes; unlike those in this country, Tunisian boom
boxes have a circle of flashing colored lights surrounding each
loudspeaker. Again I was directed fifty meters up and then to
the right. On the way, to tide me over, I bought a freshly grid-
dled leavened bread stuffed with *merguez*, the local hot sausage,
and green *harissa*, the famous North African paste of hot chili
peppers and spices that usually comes in red. Now I was hopelessly lost. Time was running out, and I was prepared to give up
on my flat bread.

"Take me to the Casbah," I implored a passerby. I have always
wanted to say that. But this time I was in earnest. If I could find
the Casbah, which simply means the fortress or keep of the old
city, then I would find the port, where our tour buses were
parked. If I didn't find the Casbah soon, I would become a permanent and involuntary resident of Sousse.

Luck was with me, for the Casbah was right under my nose,
and this gave me time to brunch on a prodigious beignet (crisply
deep-fried and dipped into sugar syrup) before our bus left for the
Islamic holy city of Kairouan and the Roman coliseum in El Jem,
and then on to Tunis.

I was four days into a two-week trip to Tunisia. I have always
been suspicious of countries (or subcultures) in which a majority
of the men wear mustaches, but Tunisia is a delight. It is the most
tolerant and progressive country in North Africa and also the
smallest.

Here are the vital statistics:

National dish: Couscous.

Population: 8,531,000, predominantly Muslim. (But women
are encouraged to take up professions, and Muslim religious dress
is discouraged.)

Area: 63,378 square miles—as though you had pasted England and Wales together and sandwiched them uncomfortably between a massive Algeria on the west and an enormous Libya on the southeast.

Capital city: Tunis.

Climate: Mediterranean in the north and east along the 805-mile coastline; semiarid in the interior; pure desert in the Saharan south.

Economic growth rate: 8.1 percent.

Average annual personal income: $1,750, the highest in the region but low by Western standards.

Food: Self-sufficient in fruit, fish, and olive oil. (The fish are red mullet, bonito, bluefish, sea bass, and shrimp. The fruits are citrus, dates, melons, apricots, figs, almonds, and cactus fruit.) Fourth most prolific producer of olive oil in the world, possessing fifty-five million trees.

Favorite spices: Hot pepper, coriander, and caraway in nearly every dish, plus cumin, anise, and cinnamon.

Favorite vegetables: Eggplant, onions, garlic, tomatoes, and peppers.

Favorite color: Blue.

The first week of the trip was organized by the Oldways Preservation & Exchange Trust, an extraordinary foundation that brings together—often in romantic foreign climes—nutritionists, environmentalists, historians, anthropologists, chefs, and food writers from the United States, England, Australia, and Japan, to enjoy and argue about traditional ways of eating that seem much healthier than the way we eat in most of the industrialized world. Then, after the first week, when most of the group had returned to their home countries, I planned to stay behind with my good friend Paula Wolfert. My wife would join us from New York, and we would set off to roam around Tunis and the Tunisian countryside in search of the best traditional home cooking we could find.

This is the sort of work that Paula Wolfert is famous for, and I had wanted to watch her in action ever since reading *The Cook-*

ing of South-West France in 1983, her third cookbook and still my favorite (she has written six in all). There was Paula, tromping through Périgord and the Gers, through the Landes and the Béarn, working with a chef in his restaurant kitchen, knocking on a housewife's door, searching indefatigably for the epiphanous cassoulet, discovering dishes that had never appeared in print. Paula is part anthropologist, part amateur scholar (she rarely attacks a subject before learning the rudiments of the language and collecting and digesting a dozen or two cookbooks written by natives), and part culinary interpreter, often improving on a dish she has eaten—but always telling us exactly how she has changed it. And Paula is a very good cook. If her food were not delicious, I would be much less interested in the rest.

The amazing thing about Paula's explorations is that she cannot drive a car. She failed her driver's test twice in the United States and four times in Paris. Only in Morocco were they willing to give her a license, which made me very nervous about the drivers of North Africa.

We had planned our tour of Tunisia in as much detail as we could, considering that Tunisia is half a world away. Paula had just returned from Turkey, where she spent two weeks in and around Gaziantep, a remote provincial city near the Euphrates River and the Syrian border. Paula brought me back a *saç*, which is pronounced "saj" and looks like a very large wok without handles. You invert it over a gas burner and, when it is hot, bake Turkish flat breads on its convex surface. Whenever I telephoned Paula at her house in Connecticut for a planning session (she lives there with her husband, William Bayer, a well-known crime-fiction writer), she was practicing one dish or other that she had discovered in some tiny Turkish town with a name like Nizip. Paula is the only food writer I know who spends much of her time in towns with names like Nizip.

Never having been to Africa, I had made an appointment with an infectious-disease specialist before leaving New York. Thanks to a nurse who thought I had said "Tanzania" over the

337

telephone, the doctor was about to administer a series of agonizing inoculations against meningitis and yellow fever and force me to swallow a bottle of malaria pills. When I told him that it was only Tunisia, he backed off. As long as I did not eat the food or drink the water, he said, I had nothing to fear.

Our trip began on the island of Jerba, off the southeast coast of Tunisia, the island of Homer's lotus-eaters and the home of one of the oldest extant Jewish communities anywhere, probably dating from the years after King Nebuchadnezzar of Babylon captured Jerusalem and sacked the temple of Solomon in 586 B.C. Oldways had arranged a lavish banquet for our arrival, and despite Paula's initial belief that the best Tunisian food is to be found in private homes, this was one of the best meals of our two-week trip.

Spread before us were specialities from the southern regions of the country, from the Mediterranean coast to the edges of the Sahara: a variety of salads and Tunisian breads; stuffed calamari; red pumpkin stewed with chickpeas and onions; a steamed square pasta from the town of Gafsa; a gelatinous meat stew with dried mallow leaves from the city of Gabès; a flat, stuffed semolina pie from the oasis of Tozeur; a vegetable soup from ancient Tataouine; a dish of tomatoes, eggs, and local sausage from somewhere else; and the ubiquitous seafood *brik,* wonderfully thin *malsouka* pastry folded into a triangle around a piece of cooked tuna and a raw egg and deep-fried until it is perfectly crisp. Dessert was fresh dates, still attatched to their branches; pomegranates; a variety of citrus; and *thé à la menthe,* a strong, sweet mint tea with pine nuts floating on its surface. Tunisia grows the best and most varied citrus fruits I have tasted—clementines and mandarins, sweet lemons, also called bergamots, and a succession through the seasons of twelve varieties of oranges.

The following days were filled with sight-seeing, sumptuous dinners, and seminars (all with simultaneous translation into Arabic, English, French, and Japanese). On Jerba, Paula and I searched the souks for an unusual triple-decker couscoussier, a steamer made specially for the famous fish couscous of Jerba; the steamer holds a spicy fish broth on the bottom, fish in the middle, and the grains of couscous on top. Paula thrives on the profusion of the marketplace, but she was afraid we had arrived too late in the morning. Throughout the Mediterranean, the first customer

The Last Undiscovered Cuisine

Q What will next year's food of the moment be?

A My candidate, admittedly a long shot, is Visigoth cuisine. The Visigoths ruled Europe from Gibraltar to the Rhône for 250 years after the Fall of Rome, until the Arabs forced them out of Spain in 711. History has dealt the Visigoths an unfair hand, picturing them as rude barbarians vaguely connected with the destruction of European civilization. Sure they were, but consider their accomplishments. Their laws, written in Latin, strongly influenced South American jurisprudence. They became Christians as early as the sixth century, setting a fine example for the much later Spanish Inquisition by forcing the Jews to accept baptism in the year 600. And most important, their sweet-and-sour cooking left its mark throughout southwest France and Iberia, especially in Catalonia. Yet you will search in vain for a Visigoth cookbook, restaurant, or food shop. It is the last undiscovered cuisine of Europe, and its day may now have come.

339

of the day gets the best bargains; shopkeepers believe that if they lose their first sale, the entire day will go badly. Jessica Harris, one of our fellow travelers and an expert in sub-Saharan Africa, told us that the same holds true in Senegal.

Paula seems to breathe in recipes the way I breathe in air. By the time we had left Jerba for the mainland, her notebook was bursting. On her previous trip to Tunisia, in the city of Sfax, Paula had heard about a meatless couscous dish flavored with fennel greens, onions, and spices. Fennel was out of season then and in season now, and when we arrived in Tunisia, Paula immediately began asking people about it.

Behind my back—I believe that I was engaged in a restorative nap—Paula had somehow managed to interview Aziza Ben Tanfous, curator at the Sidi Zitouni museum on Jerba, and snagged a terrific recipe for the dish. Tanfous had given us a lecture about the food and agriculture of the Berbers. These were the aboriginal inhabitants who dominated North Africa long before successive migrations and invasions of the Phoenicians (with whom the Jews arrived), Romans and Vandals, Arabs, Turks, and French. The Berbers are said to have invented couscous, originally made from barley instead of the hard wheat that was discovered in Abyssinia or Eritrea many centuries later. How Paula knew that Tanfous had a grandmother who made the perfect version of couscous with fennel greens, I will never understand. But a grandmother she certainly had.

Couscous is, for want of a better description, a form of tiny pasta. When couscous is formed by hand, the artisan places coarse semolina flour on a broad, round tray, adding small amounts of water and fine semolina flour as she slowly rubs the surface of the mixture with her palms in a repeated circular motion. Soon the fine semolina and water begin to collect around the grains of coarse semolina, and little balls of couscous begin to appear. Twenty minutes later, when the process has been completed and nearly all the flour has been formed into couscous, the pellets are sieved to ensure that they are all about the same size, then steamed and dried in the sun and packed away for future use.

To prepare couscous for eating, whether it is hand- or commercially made, you bring water or a spiced broth to a boil in the bottom of a steamer; then you soak the grains of couscous in water and place them into the top of the steamer (which is perforated like a colander and always kept uncovered in Moroccan kitchens and mostly covered in Tunisia). The steam and wetness of the couscous prevent it from falling through the holes in the steamer, and soon the grains swell and become light and digestible. Never cook it in boiling water unless you are following one of those rare recipes (usually requiring a very fine couscous unavailable in the United States) that traditionally call for an alternative to steaming.

Paula insists that to prepare the best and lightest couscous, you must steam it twice. (Her first book, the product of seven years spent in Morocco, is called *Couscous and Other Good Food from Morocco;* published in 1973, it is still one of the standard cookbooks on the subject.) After the first steaming, the grains are tipped out onto a platter or into a wide bowl, the lumps are broken up, and cold salted water and sometimes butter or oil are rubbed into the grains as they are raked with the fingers, separated from one another, and fluffed up. Then a second short steaming takes place.

But couscous with fennel greens breaks several of these rules: the grains are steamed only once, and the couscoussier or steamer is covered throughout. The result is delicious and handsome as well, one of the best dishes Paula brought back from our trip to Tunisia.

As we learned in the central market in Tunis, untrimmed fennel has a small bulb attatched to a huge mane of greens; in the United States, you will quickly run out of fennel tops and find dill a handy substitute. And another thing: Tunisians use tomato paste in half their dishes. By sautéing it briefly in oil, they manage to remove its metallic, preserved taste. This is one of Paula's favorite Tunisian kitchen tricks.

Couscous with Fennel Greens
Aziza Ben Tanfous and Paula Wolfert

½ pound fennel greens and dill
½ pound parsley
Handful of carrot tops
½ pound mixed scallions and leeks
½ cup olive oil
1 cup chopped onions
3 tablespoons tomato paste
2 tablespoons crushed garlic
2 teaspoons sweet paprika
2 teaspoons salt, or more to taste
2 teaspoons ground coriander seeds
1 teaspoon caraway seeds, finely ground in a spice mill or
    with a mortar and pestle
2 teaspoons red-pepper flakes
2 cups water
2½ cups couscous
1 fresh hot green chili, stemmed, seeded, and minced
1 red bell pepper, stemmed, seeded, and cut into 6 sections
6 garlic cloves, peeled

Wash the greens, dill, parsley, carrot tops, scallions, and leeks under running water and chop roughly. Fill the bottom of a couscous steamer with water, bring to a boil, attach the perforated top, add the chopped greens and vegetables, and steam, covered, for 30 minutes. Remove from the heat and allow to cool, uncovered. Squeeze out the excess moisture from the greens and vegetables and set aside.

Over a medium flame, heat the olive oil in a 10- or 12-inch skillet. Sauté the onions in the oil for 2 or 3 minutes to soften, then add the tomato paste and cook, stirring, until the paste glistens. Add the crushed garlic, paprika, salt, ground coriander, ground caraway, and red-pepper flakes. Lower the heat and sauté slowly until the mixture is well blended. Add 1 cup of the water, cover, and cook for 15 minutes.

Remove the skillet from the heat, and stir in the couscous. Add the steamed greens and vegetables, and mix well. Fold in the green chili, red bell pepper, and whole, peeled garlic cloves. Bring the water in the bottom of the couscous steamer to a boil, attach the perforated top, add the contents of the skillet, and steam, covered, for 30 minutes.

Turn out the couscous onto a large, warm serving dish. Fish out the whole garlic cloves and red bell pepper slices and reserve. Use a long fork to break up lumps in the couscous. Stir in the remaining cup of cool water, taste for salt and pepper, cover with foil, and set in a warm place for 10 minutes before serving.

Decorate the couscous with the red-pepper slices in a star pattern, alternating with the whole garlic cloves. Some Tunisians eat this dish with glasses of buttermilk. Serves 6.

343

The city of Tunis was an hourly surprise, with its sprawling souks, Ottoman Casbah, public baths, modern hotels, and, on its outskirts, the ancient city of Carthage, founded by Queen Dido in 814 B.C., and the Bardo National Museum, with its fine antiquities, including the largest collection of Roman mosaics under one roof. (The art of mosaic may have been invented in Carthage, centuries before the Romans arrived.) Tunisia is the northernmost country of Africa—the city of Tunis is only eighty-five miles from Sicily across a narrow stretch of the Mediterranean, and so it is nearer to Europe than to Algiers, Tripoli, or Cairo. The

Phoenicians brought spices from Asia and the olive tree itself; the Romans brought vineyards and fruit trees; the Andalusians came with refined cooking techniques; and the Turks brought sweet nut desserts and the delicious *brik*. For centuries, Tunisia was the breadbasket of Rome, supplying wheat to feed the two hundred thousand Roman citizens receiving public assistance. Tunisians have been cosmopolites for more than three thousand years.

One day in Tunis, an acquaintance arranged for Paula to meet with a group of women in a modest private house. Paula began the session with a question: Which of you makes the most delicious couscous? All eyes turned to one of the women, famous for her couscous with raisins. As she explained how she went about preparing the dish, the other women would either nod or shake their heads in disagreement. Every so often, Paula asked them how their versions differed. A friendly argument ensued, and then the first woman continued. Paula came away with the rough outlines for three new dishes and many alternative ways of cooking them. The session ended when the man of the house came home. He was wearing his best traditional Friday Sabbath dress, a low fez, and shoes that curled to a point.

When the Oldways group left us in Tunis, we were taken under the wing of Lynn and Salah Hannachi, a generous couple whom Paula had met a few years before on her first trip to Tunisia. Lynn is from a small town in Kansas, and Salah grew up in Jendouba, in Tunisia's northwest. They met in graduate school in the United States, where both of them earned their doctorates. Lynn teaches American studies, and Salah is a government official; his card reads, "Secrétaire d'État, auprès du Ministre de la Coopération Internationale et de l'Investissement Extérieur." I think this means that he is a deputy minister.

Lynn and Salah had made detailed plans for nearly all of our waking hours, starting with a long drive across northern Tunisia through undulating farmland, vineyards, and olive groves to the resort town of Tabarka and then on to Jendouba, the Hannachi family seat, where Salah's mother, Jamila Hannachi, and several of his brothers still live. At brother Rashid's house, before we sat down to a lavish midday dinner, Mrs. Hannachi made a scrumptious flat bread filled with green onions and green peppers, garlic, sausage, spices, and sheep's tail fat (a delicacy in many Arab countries), cooked on a ceramic griddle. I would give you the recipe, but I have not yet come close to duplicating the dough in my own kitchen. If I ever succeed, I will rename the dish. *Khobs bisshham* in Arabic, it means "bread with grease."

The Hannachi clan let us disrupt their lives for several days. Cousin Faisal showed us around the beautiful Roman houses in the ruins at nearby Bulla Regia, and his wife, Mona, and her mother spent a day preparing the lamb couscous of Béja, full of nuts and dates and very sweet. The food of Béja is famous for its Berber and Moroccan influences.

Salah's mother gave us her recipe for what she considers her finest dish; she is afraid that her version will be lost after she goes. It is called Chakhchoukha, and it consists of a thin, handmade flat bread baked on a ceramic griddle, three or four layers at a time, then torn into bite-sized pieces and eaten like pasta, surrounded by a sauce of chicken and tomatoes. The dish takes three women at least three hours to prepare.

One day Lynn took us to Les Moulins Mahjoub, an idyllic estate in the countryside an hour or so from Tunis, where olives are grown, harvested, and pressed into oil using the same traditional methods I have seen in Tuscany and in the south of France. It was December, and the picking had begun two days before; the first olives had been brought to the mill and were stored outdoors in two whitewashed cribs. In a few minutes, the year's pressing would begin.

We stood outside the mill building and chatted in the warm morning sun with Salah Mahjoub, one of three brothers whose family has been producing olive oil since 1492, and on this property since 1899. We watched a farmer leading a sheep to an inner courtyard beyond the mill, and we sipped coffee and snacked on date pastries that had been baked on a griddle that left a circular ribbed pattern. Mahjoub, who wore a gray business suit, excused himself for a few minutes, and when he returned, we entered the mill building and watched the first olives, green mixed with black, as they were pushed under the huge millstone. A little girl rushed in excitedly, waving what appeared to be a small, white translucent balloon with a pool of dark liquid inside.

Mahjoub explained that they had just sacrificed a sheep in the courtyard to ensure that the harvest and the pressing would be a success. The sacrifice is made to God, he told us, but the meat goes to everyone. In the girl's hand was the gallbladder or bile duct of the sheep; the more bile it contains, the more money your future holds. I rushed into the courtyard, but all that remained of the sheep was its skin, which looked like a bloodstained shearling jacket on the concrete.

Everybody seemed happy with the message of the entrails. As I watched the old engine turning a long pulley attached to the millstone, I noticed that a lucky horseshoe had been tied to the engine, just in case. The new extra-virgin olive oil was raw and bitter, as it would remain for some days after the pressing, but a sample of last year's oil was excellent.

Years ago Paula had read about *bkaila,* a Tunisian specialty in which huge volumes of Swiss chard are cooked in oil until they are reduced to nearly nothing and become amazingly concentrated in flavor. So early one morning Lynn's driver took Paula and me to Carthage to meet Lola and Georges Cohen, retired teachers who live in a white corner house across from the ruins of the Roman baths. Georges's forebears arrived in Tunisia in the late fifteenth century, when the Jews and Arabs were expelled from Spain; Lola believes that her family has lived here many centuries longer, perhaps since before the Arabs conquered North Africa in the late seventh century. The Cohens are disappointed that their three children have left Tunisia for France. They told us that in 1956, when Tunisia won its independence, the Jewish community numbered sixty thousand. Now there are fewer than two thousand.

Bkaila takes nearly all day to make, which is why, Lola said, it is normally reserved for *les grandes fêtes juives* and for weddings. We watched her stuff two kinds of sausages, both called *osban*, with ground beef, beef liver, beef tripe, parsley, coriander, mint, dill, garlic, red onions, *harissa*, and rice. The sausages were parboiled, then combined with the reduced Swiss chard, white beans, pieces of beef, and a thick and gelatinous piece of cow's skin; covered with water; and cooked over a low fire for four hours until everything was tender and took on the black-green color of the greens.

That evening, which was the last night of Hanukkah, we 3 4 7 returned to Carthage with Lynn and Salah and shared the *bkaila* and many other courses with five of the Cohens' friends. We used paper napkins, because the reduced Swiss chard stains cloth indelibly, and drank *boukha*, a white eau-de-vie made from figs.

I will probably not prepare *bkaila* on a weekly basis. But I will surely make endless bowls of *mechouia*, one of the simplest Tunisian dishes and also one of the best. *Mechouia* (mesh-WEE-uh) is a diced salad of grilled tomatoes, grilled sweet and hot peppers, grilled onions, and grilled garlic. Sometimes it is garnished with tuna and eggs. Sometimes it is pounded into a mush and used as a dip for bread, which is how Paula likes it. There are as many formulas for *mechouia* as there are people (8.5 million) in Tunisia.

Considering the current fashion in America both for grilled vegetables and for hot peppers, it is a wonder that *mechouia* is nearly unknown on these shores. But it can safely be predicted that with the publication of this recipe, *mechouia* will soon find its place on every street corner in America. I have relied on the formula in the French edition of Mohamed Kouki's well-known cookbook, *La cuisine tunisienne*. Kouki, you might say, is the James Beard of Tunisia.

Mechouia,
or Salade Tunisienne Grillée

4 large plum tomatoes (about ½ pound)
2 green bell peppers (about 6 ounces)
1 or 2 fresh poblano chili peppers (about ¼ pound)
1 yellow or red onion, about 2½ inches in diameter (¼ pound),
     peeled
1 large garlic clove, unpeeled
¼ teaspoon ground caraway seeds (you may need to grind
     them up yourself with a mortar and pestle or spice grinder)
¼ teaspoon ground coriander seeds
1 teaspoon coarse salt
Juice of ½ lemon
3 tablespoons extra-virgin olive oil
12 small green and black olives, cured in oil
½ tablespoon capers

   Grill the tomatoes, the bell and poblano peppers,
the onion, and the garlic clove on a charcoal grill (or
under the broiler or over a gas flame), keeping the vegetables close to the source of heat and turning them
often until they are well charred. Remove them as they
are done. Put the peppers into a paper bag, close the
bag, and let them steam for 10 minutes. (The paper-bag
method loosens the peppers' skins. A common alternative, peeling under running water, dilutes their flavor.)
   Meanwhile, peel the grilled tomatoes, chop them
into ½-inch pieces, and put them into a 2-quart bowl.
Remove the charred outer layer of the onion, chop the
rest into ¼-inch pieces, and add them to the bowl.
Then peel the peppers, stem them, and seed them. Cut
the bell peppers into ½-inch pieces and the poblanos
into ¼-inch pieces, and add them all to the tomatoes.

Peel the garlic clove, and crush it with the back of a wooden spoon in a small bowl along with the ground caraway, coriander, and salt. Mix well with the vegetables. Stir in the lemon juice and the olive oil.

Turn out into a shallow bowl for serving. Garnish with the olives and capers. Makes 4 modest servings as a side dish, but the quantities can easily be doubled.

My photos have just come back from the lab. There is a picture of a blinkered camel turning a mill wheel in a cave dwelling high in the Berber town of Chenini. And there is my favorite, a snapshot of my wife, having her hands painted with henna in the manner of a Tunisian bride. Paula is still systematically plowing her way through forty or fifty dishes we brought home from Tunisia. Yesterday she made *kadid*, preserved mutton thigh, and, for dessert, sweet balls of coarse semolina bread stuffed with nuts and dates. Tonight her family will feast on a lamb's head with barley grits. I think I'll make do with *mechouia*.

March 1994

Variations on a Theme

Trader Vic's was the first theme restaurant I ever visited, thirty years ago, and it would probably have been the last if I had not recently dedicated myself to deciphering the theme-restaurant tidal wave now on the verge of submerging my home city. Why would tourists come to New York to eat meals they can find in suburban malls? Why would anybody buy a T-shirt, baseball cap, denim jacket, or boxer shorts with somebody else's name on them? Why visit a Planet Hollywood or a Hard Rock Cafe in New York when you can find its identical twin in Atlanta, Aspen, Phoenix, or Tahoe? New York City is hotter and more humid in summer than Aspen, colder in winter than Atlanta, and dirtier than either. The subways are confusing; the taxis require a working knowledge of Urdu and, in summer, a snorkel for drawing some of the air-conditioning through those three little holes in the thick, bulletproof Plexiglas shield meant to protect the driver from you or vice versa. You can't beat Aspen for sensible roads, clean streets, pleasant people, and mountain air. You'd have to be crazy to come to New York for a visit to the Hard Rock Cafe.

It is easy to understand the attraction of owning a theme restaurant: earn a small profit on the hamburgers and make a fortune on the T-shirts and other souvenirs. The profit margin on a Buffalo chicken wing or a beef fajita is 10 percent, on a baseball cap with a logo more like 50. Here are the typical numbers for a successful theme restaurant in the heart of a major city: The place costs $5 million to build and open (though some are now creeping toward $10 million). Gross revenues can be $10 million a year, of which about a quarter is profit, $1.75 million from merchandise and $650,000 from food. Your capital is returned in two or three years. Why invest in anything else? Why not turn every last square inch of real estate into theme restaurants? Why not convert entire neighborhoods, entire cities? That's what happened to Orlando.

If theme knickknacks alone were enough to attract customers, these places would probably drop the food. Even the famously bumbling Los Angeles County Coroner's Office has opened a gift shop to cash in on the celebrity-trinket craze. Along with the usual T-shirts and boxer shorts, the coroner sells authentic toe-tag key chains, ready to be personalized, and beach towels decorated with a facsimile of the chalk outline that police draw around a corpse on the sidewalk. "Reserve your place on the beach," the brochure says. At press time, the L.A. coroner had no plans to expand to New York.

But Warner Brothers has evidently decided that food and souvenirs are inseparable. Its three-story store at Fifty-seventh Street and Fifth Avenue—which, by offering clothing and novelties decorated with images of Daffy Duck, Tweety, and Bugs Bunny, has become one of the most successful shops in the world—reportedly grosses $100 million a year. Warner Brothers' rumored expansion of forty thousand square feet will include *three restaurants*.

Fifty-seventh Street is the new epicenter of New York's theme world. For generations it had been the royal road to Carnegie Hall, once home base of Bergdorf's, Bendel's, and Bonwit's, Rizzoli and Steinway, the Osborne apartments and Hammacher-Schlemmer, the Fuller Building. Then, in 1984, the Hard Rock Cafe arrived, and by 1995 the boulevard had acquired the nickname Theme Street, in honor of the arrival of Planet Hollywood, Le Bar Bat, Brooklyn Diner, U.S.A., and the fabulously successful Warner Brothers store, all of them right on Fifty-seventh; the Jekyll & Hyde Club and Harley Davidson Cafe a block away; and Fashion Cafe in the general vicinity.

And more are yet to come. Opening soon will be the Motown Cafe (beating out Steven Spielberg's Dive! to take over the site of the New York Deli, which had supplanted the great Art Deco Horn & Hardart Automat); Dive! (the decor is bathysphere, the cuisine "reinvented" submarine sandwiches); and Nike (a four-story sneaker theme park behind a copy of the Ebbets Field facade, near Fifth Avenue). Dolly Parton is whispered to be ransacking Fifty-seventh Street for an addition to her country-and-western restaurant chain. And the vultures are waiting for Wolf's Delicatessen on the corner of Sixth Avenue to stumble. Suddenly this once-obscure patch of earth makes downtown Tokyo look like small change. Soon you will stand on this corner and not know what city or even what country you have landed in.

Nearby, Television City will open its theme restaurant and shop at Rockefeller Center; (Ed) Sullivan's Restaurant and Broadcast Lounge has parallel plans for a site on Broadway. One subway stop south, in Times Square, look forward to a huge Disney complex (to complement its studio store down Fifth Avenue from Warner Brothers, right next to the Coca-Cola gift shop), entries from MTV and HBO, and from Robert Earl (towering genius of the theme movement, high Hard Rock executive in the eighties, a founder of Planet Hollywood in the nineties), Marvel Mania and the Official All-Star Cafe, which expects backing from Shaquille O'Neil, Andre Agassi, and Wayne Gretzky, all reported to be internationally famous athletes. And I can't wait for Tito Puente's 275-seat Puerto Rican theme restaurant on City Island in the Bronx, somehow combining Latin jazz and family fare. Puente (the salsa giant) has chosen the estimable Yvonne Ortiz (author of *A Taste of Puerto Rico*) to direct the kitchen. They expect their Frozen Mango Mambo to be the next piña colada. Las Vegas interests are rumored to be shopping for a property in which to establish their *Saturday Night Live* theme chain. And in a late-breaking development, Madonna is said to be looking for her very own site.

But why would a tourist come to New York to eat mall food in this city of fifteen thousand restaurants? Manhattan does have one mall, at South Street Seaport on the East River, and I visited the food court there for the first time to deepen my understanding. It was a brilliantly sunny day, and the river view from the third floor at the end of Pier 17 took my breath away, south to the Statue of Liberty and north to the Brooklyn Bridge, both of them erected in an age of stupendous engineering triumphs, when the city was eager for immigrant workers from everywhere in the world and rich beyond counting.

Just behind me was the food court. I eagerly tasted something at every counter. The Chinese food, from a regional chain, was distasteful and gummy—just footsteps from New York's Chinatown, the largest aggregation of Chinese outside of Asia. The mealy, spongy bread was a disgrace, in this city with the finest bread east of San Francisco. The pizza was mediocre, a mile from Ellis Island, where this country welcomed the first Neapolitan immigrants, and two miles from the first pizzeria in the United States, on Spring Street, opened ninety years ago. Most painful was a delicatessen counter that could have prospered in St. Paul or Tucson (it's one in a chain of 450), serving dank, reconstituted turkey loaves and albino, boneless boiled hams, in this city that was once a megalopolis of real delicatessens, and where the torch of true pastrami is still, today, held aloft.

A native New Yorker leaves the city he loves when he enters South Street Seaport. Nearly all the customers are tourists, and they could be anywhere in the country, spending and eating at Body Shop and Brookstones, and a dozen fast-food chains. I was once proud that establishments like these had never penetrated into my prismatic and unique city. Now, standing at the end of Pier 17 and ruminatively chewing on a thick and floppy pizza, I felt that I was nibbling on the corpse of a great metropolis.

I rushed down the stairs and into a taxi, hoping that the

meals on Theme Street would be better than this. Both menus and food were, for the most part, indistinguishable at Fashion Cafe, Planet Hollywood, Hard Rock Cafe, the Jekyll & Hyde Club, and the Harley Davidson Cafe. If Planet Hollywood were serious about its theme, it would serve famous meals from the movies, like the lusty eating scene in *Tom Jones* and the dinner in the *Godfather* when Al Pacino assassinates the corrupt Irish police official played by Sterling Hayden, and a thousand more. Elvis's favorite foods have been well documented, yet Hard Rock seems oblivious. And Harley Davidson Cafe could serve its theme drinks in miniature hubcaps or motorcycle gas tanks.

But interesting food is not the point. Above all, the menu must be familiar, inoffensive, and inexpensive. A family or a group of friends with diverse tastes should be able to dine together comfortably, order lots of alcohol, then concentrate on the merchandise. What better choice than fast food and theme drinks, which for five or six dollars extra come in twenty-three-ounce logo glasses you can take home with you?

Some of the foods deserve special mention. The ribs at Hard Rock were remarkably good (most other fast-food kitchens parboil theirs first, turning both the meat and bones gray and diluting their sweet pork flavor), and most of the food at Harley Davidson was inedible. Le Bar Bat has real food and slightly higher prices than the others (tender lettuces, good bread and pecan pie, deliciously charred lamb, but an impenetrable ice-cream sandwich). Come to think of it, Hard Rock was also the most fun, with sixties mantras on the wall that brought a nostalgic mist to my eyes. ALL IS ONE. LOVE ALL, SERVE ALL. Most theme restaurants take no reservations and make you wait, even when there is no need to. Nowhere did the espresso have a layer of *crema* on top. Espresso without *crema* is not espresso.

Why are these places so successful? People in the business tell me that most tourists need to feel safe and comfortable. Brand names do that for them. The streets of New York do not. In a city where the nightlife is stratified according to so many baroque and

Why Eating Out in New York Costs Seventy-five Dollars a Person Except When It Costs Even More

A celebrated chef explained it to me this way: Take an entrée of Skate with Brown Butter. Fourteen ounces of skate costs $1.31 wholesale. The ingredients for the quart of *nage* in which it is poached cost $1.92. The sauce requires four ounces of butter ($.44), an ounce of capers ($.26), two ounces of fish stock ($.22), salt and pepper ($.04), and a half ounce of vinegar ($.01). Total cost of these ingredients is $4.20, plus a 5 percent allowance for waste and spoilage, or $4.41.

The restaurant lists every dish at five times the cost of its ingredients to cover rent, labor, and interest on bank loans and yield a profit. *This is the key.* This is why what sells for $25.00 in a New York restaurant sells for $8.00 in the suburban Midwest, if you can find it. The customer is renting an extravagantly decorated twenty square feet of Manhattan for two or three hours.

So the Skate with Brown Butter will be priced at $22.00. The cost of an appetizer, dessert, and coffee approximately equals that of the entrée, say another $22.00. Half a modest $30.00 bottle of wine is $15.00; half a bottle of sparkling water is $2.50.

The total so far is $61.50. Tax adds $5.07, a 15 percent tip another $9.99. Grand total: $76.56.

And it all started with $1.31 worth of skate.

September 1990

unknowable rules of inclusion and exclusion, the theme restaurant is the ultimate in democracy: stand on a line and you are sure to get in, and once you are inside, your table will probably be assigned by a computer. In a nation growing less literate by the day, where the dominant culture has become Hollywood and Disney, anything connected with the movies—in fact, anything remotely *famous*, even Kato Kaelin—draws vast and milling crowds. So tourists travel from city to city and country to country, collecting Planet Hollywood T-shirts, identical except for the name of the city of origin printed below the logo. That's why Planet Hollywood and Hard Rock refuse to sell their goods by mail.

These national chains with their shoddy, overpriced mementos are neither the first nor the only theme restaurants in Manhattan. When you're on the prowl, it is amazing how a new specimen turns up every place you look. Near my house on Twelfth Street is the oldest theme restaurant of them all, the seventy-year-old Asti, where the theme is waiters who sing opera. And scattered around the city are Mickey Mantle's and Rusty Staub's and scores of lesser sports pubs.

Neither Fifty-seventh Street nor Times Square is a patch on the real boom area for the hottest trend in theme cafés and restaurants. The neighborhood around St. Mark's Place on the Lower East Side has become home to the cybercafé movement, including Internet Cafe on Third Street; Cyber Cafe at 273A Lafayette Street, which offers full T1 access, eight multimedia computers, and a sparse collection of muffins and soft drinks; Heroic Sandwich on Fourth Street; and the most elaborate of them all, @Cafe at 12 St. Mark's Place, which opened nine weeks before I arrived there.

@Cafe (http://www.fly.net) is a wonderful place whose only problem is that it opened nine weeks too early. Despite the full T1 access, ten Power Macs, three Windows, two Unix, two huge projection screens, Japanimation, a lovely blonde technical-support cyberfairy named Jessica, and an ambitious menu of Asian appetizers and Cal-Ital main courses, nothing worked right during our visit. At least the farfalle with spinach and the grilled chicken sandwich tasted fine, though the bread was inexplicably closer to Wonder bread than to the real thing. I still have high hopes for @Cafe and will return when it has had a chance to work things out.

I will probably never return to Medieval Times. We boarded a $7 bus to Lyndhurst, New Jersey, and twenty minutes later pulled up at The Castle, where we joined many large families of fun-loving suburbanites (including Cub Scout troop 266) climbing out of their station wagons. The Castle is covered in beige simulated-stone-textured siding. Once inside, we were handed paper crowns (nearly everybody wore one for the next few hours) and were then continually battered by attempts to lighten our wallets before the dinner and jousting began. These included three extensive gift counters, two long cash bars, an extra-charge dungeon displaying a dozen gruesome medieval tools of torture I had never even read about ($1.50), computers that investigate and print out your personal heraldic devices ($19.99 and up), the opportunity ($7) to have your picture taken with the Count or Countess (she's a native of Lyndhurst and has been the Countess for six months), and the rare chance to participate in a single ($10) or double ($20) knighting ceremony, complete with clumsily calligraphed scrolls.

After an hour and a half of this, in large and gloomy rooms that reminded me of American Legion halls, we were finally herded into the Grand Hall of Dinner & Tournament. In the center was an oval arena 50 by 100 feet in size and paved with sand; surrounding the arena were five stepped tiers of tables, at which hundreds of us sat and ate and watched the show. Hanging from the ceiling among the air-conditioning ducts, loudspeakers, and electrical conduits were bright red and yellow squares of cloth meant to set a medieval tone. The only medieval thing about the food was the total absence of utensils with which to handle the vegetable soup, bagel pizza, whole roast chicken, ribs, and cherry pastry. The horse show (mainly Iberian dressage) and the extremely violent jousting and combat (with lances, swords, whips, and maces) lasted two excruciating hours but were not without interest, though everything was choreographed like professional wrestling conducted in *Ivanhoe* costumes. The horses were amazingly fast. The people around me had a much more positive attitude than I— one woman cheered and stamped so deafeningly that I considered asking the management to calm her down, until I looked over and saw that it was my wife. Near the blessed end, our serving wench reminded us that gratuities were not included in the prepaid charges ($35.95) and then went from person to person shaking hands. Several large and festive frozen theme drinks in novelty glassware would have relieved some of my pain, but there was nothing to drink besides tiny glasses of feeble sangria.

Which brings me to my own theory about why the major theme places along Fifty-seventh Street and across the nation thrive. I remember my very first theme-restaurant experience, a million years ago when I was twelve, at the Trader Vic's in the palmy Beverly Hilton Hotel. Trader Vic's was the ultimate goal, at least for my sister and me, of our family's automobile trip from New York City to California and back, in our turquoise-and-white Oldsmobile 98. And what an exotic theme it was. Polynesia! How many people, except the natives themselves, had ever visited the real island of Samoa or the actual country of Tahiti? So Trader Vic's could take liberties with its grass and bamboo huts, its Pu Pu platters laden with deep-fried delights and fueled by reeking purple Sterno, and its widemouthed frozen drinks. The mai tai was the most justly celebrated—decorated with mint and lime and orange paper umbrellas. The Trader created it himself in 1944.

It is in these distant memories of Santa Monica Boulevard where it crosses Wilshire that I have discovered the fundamental reason why somebody would be attracted to the national theme restaurants. The secret lies in their long lists of frozen specialty theme drinks. Sipping from these frosty beverages surely made for my happiest moments at the dinners I endured along Fifty-seventh Street. Fresh fruit and rum, novelty glassware, straws a foot long—where else can such pleasure be found? If the real restaurants of New York City—the ancient pizzerias and hand-sliced-pastrami places, and the palaces of haute cuisine—would simply add frozen theme drinks to their standard menus, Fifty-seventh Street would, I feel sure, soon return to its historic and stately character. For starters, they might try these recipes for the original Trader Vic's Mai Tai, Tito Puente's Frozen Mango Mambo, and Jekyll & Hyde's Dracurita.

Trader Vic's Mai Tai

Adapted from *Frankly Speaking:*
Trader Vic's Own Story

2 ounces 17-year-old Wray & Nephew Jamaican rum
(Appleton Estate Dark rum makes a good substitute)
1/2 ounce curaçao
1/2 ounce orgeat or other almond syrup
1/2 cup rock-candy syrup (made by dissolving rock-candy sugar
in an equal volume of water)
16 ounces shaved ice
Juice and rind of 1 fresh lime
Sprig of mint

Pour the spirits and syrups over the shaved ice in a double (16-ounce) old-fashioned glass (or something more festive and evocative). Add half the squeezed lime and the rind, and garnish with mint. (If you lack shaved ice, put 16 ounces of small ice cubes in a blender, add the other ingredients, and blend until smooth.) A "fruit stick" is completely optional; this is a short wooden skewer spearing a maraschino cherry and a cube of pineapple.

Tito Puente's Frozen Mango Mambo

*3 ounces frozen mango puree (two good brands are Perfect
Puree and Goya)*
1½ ounces Bacardi black rum
½ tablespoon fresh lemon juice
½ tablespoon fresh lime juice
*1½ ounces sugar syrup (made by mixing 2½ tablespoons hot
water with 1½ tablespoons granulated sugar)*
10 ounces crushed ice or ice cubes
Garnish: 1 slice of fresh mango

Put the ingredients in a blender and blend until
smooth. This will fill a 22-ounce glass. Garnish with
the fresh mango.

Jekyll & Hyde Club's Dracurita

1 ounce white tequila
½ ounce Chambord
½ ounce Triple Sec
Splash of fresh lime juice
Splash of "sour" mix
16 ounces crushed ice or ice cubes

Combine everything in a blender and blend until
smooth. Serve in a 16-ounce hurricane glass.

Note: One ounce of liquid equals 2 tablespoons; 8
ounces equals 1 cup. Small ice cubes work much better
in a blender than large ones.

September 1995

The Mother of All
Ice Cream

As our plane circled Palermo, a snowcapped Mount Etna unexpectedly swam into view. "Etna of the snow and secret changing
winds," I said to my wife, pointing toward the eastern end of the
island. "Not many men can really stand her without losing their
souls."

Actually, I was reading from D. H. Lawrence. I can never
understand why Lawrence got so hysterical about Mount Etna.
Sure, she is the largest volcano in Europe, brooding, dark, and
gloomy. Sure, her eruptions have destroyed countless human
beings and entire Sicilian cities. But to me, Etna was something
more. To me, she was the Mother of All Ice Cream.

Or so I thought when we landed in Palermo. Sicily's coloniz-
ers—Greeks, Romans, Saracens, and Spanish—used to harvest
Etna's snow, pack it into grottoes along her slopes, and, in summer, retrieve their chilly treasure to concoct refreshing iced
drinks and snow cones drenched with wine and sweetened fruit
essences. "In these climates the lack of snow is feared as much as
the lack of grain, wine, or oil," reported a traveling Frenchman in
the eighteenth century. Today Sicilians are still crazy for frozen
things, which they eat four or five times a day, starting at breakfast. They are most famous for their granita.

It was granita that had lured me to Sicily—pure and penetrating half-frozen crystalline concoctions of water and sugar, flavored with rose petals or jasmine, coffee or cocoa, fresh fruit

juices and syrups. Our plan was to make a counterclockwise circuit of the island, learning the secrets of granita, and then, climbing up to Etna's snowy peak, taste the primeval origins of every ice and ice cream that came after.

Palermo's heyday, at least one heyday, was around A.D. 965, when, under Arab rule, it was the second-largest city in the world—crowded with palaces, markets, and three hundred mosques—vying with Baghdad and Córdoba as the greatest Arab seat of learning, culture, and cuisine. The Arabs brought sugarcane, mulberries, and citrus fruits (along with many things that have nothing to do with granita), and innumerable recipes for *sharbat*, their sweetened, aromatic drinks flavored with fruits, blossoms, and spices, and often chilled with mountain snow. Many writers casually declare that the Arabs in Sicily made the momentous jump from snow cones to granitas and water ices by freezing their *sharbats*. This means that the Arabs either invented artificial freezing in Sicily (or in Andalusia or Baghdad) or brought the method from China long before Marco Polo claimed the discovery. But I was becoming skeptical, particularly after dipping into two books I had brought with me—Weir and Liddell's excellent *Ices* (Hodder & Stoughton and Grub Street, London) and Elizabeth David's *Harvest of the Cold Months* (Michael Joseph).

Our first morning in Palermo dawned at a little *gelateria* named Cofea, among the oldest and perhaps the best in town. A crowd of Palermitans stood at the counter and spilled onto the street, taking their breakfast, which in spring and summer consists of a sweet, flat brioche sliced almost in half, filled with a wide paddleful of coffee ice cream, and trimmed with whipped cream, or a tall glass of coffee granita—in fact, any granita—with pieces of brioche to dunk into it; and, of course, an espresso or a cappuccino. Your first brioche dunked into a slushy granita is an unforgettable treat. So is every one that follows.

(The Sicilian brioche, which Mary Simeti—who writes so memorably about Sicilian food and history—believes was introduced in the nineteenth century by Swiss pastry chefs who had come to Catania, is a flat, round, sweet, yeasted roll with a little ball of dough on top, resembling a French brioche flattened to a third of its height, or a gigantic hamburger roll. The recipe varies from city to city around the island, from the recognizable golden combination of sugar, flour, eggs, and butter or lard to an uninteresting, white, and doughy specimen made with margarine and without eggs.)

The granitas at Cofea were wonderful and the ingredients utterly simple, or so it seemed. Piero Marzo, the ice-cream maker, demonstrated his recipe for lemon granita in a neat little white building behind the shop, squeezing lemons and adding their juice to a solution of sugar and water. Back in the bustling shop, he poured the mixture into one of two dozen cylindrical metal tubs set into the long, refrigerated stainless-steel ice-cream counter; as the liquid begins to freeze, he will stir it every so often, and then, after it has solidified overnight, he will defrost it slightly for ten minutes and scrape the surface with a wide, flat, triangular ice-cream paddle and scoop the crystals into a footed glass. All this seemed simple enough.

But as I would soon discover, Sicilian lemons taste different from ours—sweeter, more complex, less acidic, more perfumed. One Sicilian pastry chef told us that the second time he came to New York to give some classes, he brought a suitcase full of lemons picked in the groves near his hometown. The lesson Sicilian granitas teach you is simplicity. Their aim is to celebrate the essential flavor, at the perfect time of year, of *one* fruit or flower—not to prove the cleverness of the cook and his ability to combine and transform flavors. How would I be able to duplicate even this simplest of granitas back home? Using lemons with less perfume, I would increase the proportion of lemon juice. But then the acidity would climb so high that I would need more sugar. And the higher the sugar content, the less icily the mixture will freeze—more than about 22 percent sugar by weight and granita will stay mushy no matter how long you freeze it. (Fruits with lots of

363

pectin, such as strawberries, make things even worse.) Zesting the lemon for more flavor can add bitterness. And after all these adjustments, the pure, transparent, ethereal flavor will be lost.

Worried about what the future would bring, we left Palermo and headed westward along the northern coast of the island. It was midspring, and we saw nothing of the dusty roads and parched fields of popular imagery. Now Sicily was a cool and abundant garden, and we drove through fields of wildflowers and almond groves. Erice was our first granita destination, a perfectly preserved medieval stone village on the peak of a solitary mountain at the western end of Sicily. On a clear day you can see Tunisia, in North Africa, eighty miles away. The Greek goddess Aphrodite, whom the Romans called Venus, rose from the sea foam down below. And near the central square, on the Via Vittorio Emanuele, is the shop of Maria Grammatico, one of the best-loved pastry chefs in Sicily.

When Maria was eleven, she was put into an orphanage in Erice, the Istituto San Carlo, which housed seventeen girls and fifteen nuns and supported itself by baking pastries, some from recipes dating to the fifteenth century. It was run like a convent, and neither the nuns nor the girls were allowed much contact with the outside world. Customers would appear at an iron grate and pass their requests and money to the dim, cloistered figure within. Ices were made for visiting priests and other celebrities. The orphans were rarely allowed to taste them. For Maria's full story and her pastry recipes, you should read Mary Taylor Simeti's *Bitter Almonds* (Morrow, 1994).

Late one evening we met Maria for a glass of sweet wine made in the nearby town of Marsala and a granita lesson in her beautiful old kitchen of limestone, tile, and wood. Maria showed us how to make the famous Sicilian almond granita from almond paste, sugar, and water. Every artisanal pastry shop makes its own version of almond paste (known as *pasta reale*, "royal dough") by grinding approximately equal amounts of sugar and skinned almonds (those from Avola on the eastern end of the island are the best) between chubby green marble rollers. Then the paste is diluted with about five times its weight in water and sometimes flavored with a pinch of cinnamon; this is almond milk, a popular Sicilian drink often favored over Coca-Cola. (A more refined version is made by placing a muslin bag filled with almond paste in water and squeezing it tirelessly until the water is milky white.) Maria's almond granita is made by adding sugar to almond milk, freezing it with a technique like Piero Marzo's, and scraping crystals from the surface the following day. The result is a refreshing mountain of tiny, discrete, icy crystals that collapse and implode on your tongue like caviar pressed and popped against the roof of your mouth. It is delicate and very delicious.

The almonds of Avola—and those from North Africa, Sardinia, and southern France—contain a small percentage of bitter almonds, which give marzipan and almond milk their characteristic bitter fragrance and taste. Bitter almonds cannot be imported into the United States because they contain the chemical amygdalin, which, when moistened, breaks down into benzaldehyde (the chief flavor in marzipan and almond extract) and prussic acid, which releases a toxin similar to cyanide. Even batches of foreign almonds that inevitably contain a few bitter almonds cannot be brought here. Europeans seem unconcerned with the problem. But without a source of bitter almond flavor, how would I replicate Maria's almond granita back home?

From Erice we drove for two days across the island, through Segesta and Agrigento, known less for their granita than for their stupendous Greek temples. My pulse quickened as we approached the baroque city of Modica, famed for its proud tradition of *toasted*-almond granita. There we discovered pastry shops that still bake the exotic Modican turnover called *mpanatigghi* (filled with cocoa, spices, sugar, and ground meat—probably devised by the chocolate-crazed Spanish during their rule of Sicily in the later Middle Ages), and pastry shops selling the impenetrable sesame brittle known as Cobaita, from the Arabic word for sesame seed. But toasted-almond granita was nowhere in sight. We left Modica well fed but dejected.

That evening we reached the city of Siracusa on the east coast of Sicily, the gastronomic capital of the Western world and the greatest city in Europe, rivaling Athens in power and prestige—in the fifth century B.C. The great mathematician Archimedes was born in Siracusa and worked there all his life, Aeschylus held the world premiere of *The Persians* (he also played the lead) and *The Women of Etna* in the great amphitheater, and Sappho and Pindar visited the city. Most important, the first cookbook written in the Western world (the lost *Art of Cooking* by Mithaecus) was composed here, and the first professional cooking school established.

The following century, Plato came to Siracusa to teach the ruler, the tyrant Dionysius, how to be a philosopher-king. Plato was disgusted by the gastronomic excesses he found there. "One's existence is spent in gorging food twice a day and never sleeping alone at night and all the practices which accompany this mode of living," he wrote. Dionysius soon sold the grumpy Plato into slavery; friends back home in Greece chipped in and bought him back.

Using Siracusa as our base, we drove a half hour south through flowering orchards of lemon and orange trees to the crumbling jewel that is Noto, destroyed in 1693 by an earthquake and completely rebuilt in the Sicilian-Spanish baroque style from lovely, soft golden and pinkish stone. Near the central square stands Corrado Costanzo's pastry shop, probably the most famous in Sicily. We tasted Costanzo's ice creams, flavored with rose petals, jasmine blossoms, and Avola almonds, and his cheerful marzipan stars covered in dark chocolate. My mission was to learn Costanzo's mandarin-orange granita, which has earned world renown, and for that Costanzo made us return the next morning.

First he gave us breakfast, an espresso and a bowl of *fragoline*—the sweet and aromatic wild strawberries for which Noto is also famous—sprinkled with sugar and the juice of a half lemon and a half blood orange. I tried to remember if I had ever tasted anything more ambrosial. Then we watched Costanzo prepare his mandarin-orange granita, juicing and zesting the mandarin oranges by hand and freezing the mixture to a smooth texture in an electric ice-cream machine. Costanzo would not let me measure any of his ingredients, but when he left to take a phone call, I cheated just a little. The ingredients are elemental (the fruit is a relative of the clementine and tangerine), but the granita's flavor was ethereal, with transparent layers of sweet and subtle perfumes. Would I have anything more than tangerines to play with back in the United States?

A rising contender for Noto's granita crown is the century-old Caffè Sicilia nearby and the young Assenza brothers who own it. They specialize in exceptional, briefly cooked marmalades and creams—barely sweetened and very modern—made from Sicily's finest produce: citrons, bergamots, lemons, mandarin oranges, almonds, chestnut honey, and pink grapefruit. After tasting them all, we noticed that the blackboard over the gelati counter prematurely advertised *gelso nero*, "black mulberry," one of Sicily's favorite ices. As *gelsi* would not come into season until midsummer, we practiced with *fragoline*. It was here, too, that I discovered the secret of the elusive toasted-almond granita of Modica. The Assenzas' father was born and raised in Modica and often returned there for the one taste that revived his fondest memories of childhood. Toasted-almond granita is no longer made in Sicily, it seems, but now it can be re-created in my kitchen and yours. Corrado Assenza's secret is to roast shelled almonds for *five hours*.

A few days later we headed north from Siracusa, past Catania (the second-largest city in Sicily, totally destroyed by an eruption of Etna in 1669, and the only place in Sicily with a tradition of chocolate granita), past the Isole dei Ciclopi—rocky outcroppings in the Ionian Sea just off the coast that were long ago thrown at the fleeing Odysseus by an enraged, blinded Cyclops—past Mount Etna, and up to Messina, where Shakespeare set *Much Ado about Nothing*. We briefly peered out into the water to spot Scylla and Charybdis, the female sea monster who, Homer tells us, devoured ancient Greek sailors and the powerful whirlpool that wrecked

367

their ships; turned left onto Sicily's north coast; and stayed the night in Milazzo. The next morning we would take a hydrofoil to the Aeolians and the island of Salina, noted for the alluring Sirens of mythology, for its Malvasia wine, and for the tiny town of Lingua where, I had been told, a *caffè* owner named Alfredo makes the best coffee granita anywhere.

The hydrofoil took eighty-five minutes, even in the rain and even with a stop at the island of Vulcano, in whose hideously scary-looking volcano the god Vulcan had his forge. On Salina, we stopped at the Portobello restaurant to make reservations for a late lunch and took one of the island's two active taxis to run us up to Lingua, ten minutes away. Walking a narrow path between houses and shops and threading our way through a vineyard, we came again to the sea and a line of beachfront shops, all shuttered except for Alfredo Oliveri's Bar-Café. We tasted his excellent lemon and strawberry granitas, discussed his white-fig, melon, and kiwi versions, and finally tasted the coffee. It was perfect, not because of the perfection of his ingredients—these are easy to duplicate here—but because of his fifty-year-old broken-down Carpigiani gelato machine, which with its battered blade and erratic temperature produces the perfect granita texture: tiny, regular, moist, and highly flavored crystals of ice. Even without Alfredo's Carpigiani, his recipe—quite a standard one—produces a delicious, crystalline coffee granita. On Salina, whipped cream is served with all granitas except lemon.

The next day we awoke at dawn for the four-hour sprint to Mount Etna and the airport near Catania. A heavy, dark rain began to fall. Our plan had been to ascend Mount Etna's ancient peak and retrieve enough snow to make, with the wine and mandarin oranges we had brought, a Certifiably Primeval Snow Cone. But as Etna's huge black bulk loomed through the clouds and rain, our need to accomplish this feat suddenly evaporated. It was not due to the awful weather or the prospect of finding many chocolate granitas in Catania with the time we could save or the fact that the mandarin orange was brought as late as 1805 from

Canton in China to England, from where it spread through Italy and the Mediterranean—a date so recent that it would render our snow cone anything but primeval.

No, the true reason was that my investigations and reading had yielded a major revelation: *Etna is not the Mother of All Ice Cream!* The Romans may have drunk iced wines and the Arabs may have iced their *sharbats* with mounds of her snow, but neither was able to make true granitas and sherbets, because neither knew the scientific secret of artificial freezing.

Decades ago, when the nuns in Erice taught Maria Grammatico to make almond-milk granita, they cracked a block of ice in a wide stone basin, sprinkled it with coarse salt or saltpeter, placed a terra-cotta container of almond milk in the center, and scraped and stirred it as it hardened. Salt lowers the melting point of ice; a mixture of salt and ice melts into a very cold slush—colder than the freezing point of water—and can solidify another liquid through conduction. This was the earliest technique of artificial freezing, and it is called the *endothermic* effect. If you flavor the second liquid and stir it every so often, you will soon have a granita. If you stir it constantly, you will have discovered the water ice and the sherbet.

The earliest mention of the endothermic effect was in a fourth-century Indian poem, "Pancatantra," in a verse that said that water can become really cold only if it contains salt. And the first known technical description of making ice comes from the great Arab historian of medicine, Ibn Abu Usaybi'a (1230–1270), who attributes the process to an older author, Ibn Bakhtawayhi, of whom nothing is known. The first European mention comes in 1530, when the Italian physician Zimara wrote his *Problemata*.

But for centuries artificial freezing seems to have remained little more than a party trick—nobody thought to make granita, sherbet, or ice cream this way until water ices began appearing in Naples, Sicily, Paris, Florence, and Spain in the early 1660s. There are no earlier mentions in letters, books, recipes, or menus anywhere in the world. Italian visitors to Muslim Turkey reported a rich variety of cooled, liquid *sharbats,* but no ices. The earliest recipe appeared in Paris in 1674, the first Neapolitan recipe twenty years later. And the first book on ices, Baldini's *De' sorbetti,* came ninety years after that.

And so the nineteenth-century legends that Catherine de Médicis brought ices to France when she married the Duc d'Orléans in 1533—and the notion that Marco Polo brought ice cream back from China—cannot possibly be true. Not only does Polo fail to mention the Chinese fascination with harvesting, storing, and using snow and ice for cooling food, but some historians suspect that he never got closer to China than a Persian jail.

The endothermic effect is the Mother of All Ice Cream. And Mount Etna is just another gigantic old brooding volcano.

The sky over Catania and the Ionian Sea beyond had turned a dazzling blue, and we drove through the city, nearly empty on a Sunday morning, and sought out several pastry shops, some renowned, some at random, to sample their chocolate granitas and talk recipes. Then we drove west for a while for a last glimpse of Etna and a brief reading from D. H. Lawrence, and nearly missed our plane.

In some ways, it might have been better if we had, because back in New York, trying to duplicate Sicily's granitas was nearly as difficult and time-consuming as I had feared. But the recipes that follow will make the job a snap. Serve your granita in a goblet, a footed ice-cream glass, or a martini glass. Serve it alone, with other granitas, with whipped cream and a brioche, or layered in a parfait glass or goblet with an ice cream of the same flavor.

Making Granitas

Each recipe ends with the sentence "Cover, chill, and freeze." There are numerous ways to turn a flavored, sweetened, chilled liquid into a fine granita; I give three below. As we discovered in

Sicily, there is no one official way of freezing granita. The desired texture seems to vary from city to city. In Palermo and on the west coast, granita is chunky and grainy; in the east, it is nearly as smooth as *sorbetto;* and in the northwest and the Aeolean Islands, it falls somewhere in between. It can be scraped from the inside of the container, chipped or scraped from a block of flavored ice, made in a crusher, or produced in an ice-cream machine.

My favorite way of making a granita is to pour the mixture into a strong, shallow plastic container with a lid; one measuring ten by ten by two inches works fine. Place it in the freezer. After an hour and every half hour thereafter, scrape the iced rim around the inside of the container with a fork; beat, mash, and fluff the ice to achieve a uniform texture. After three to five hours of this, the ice crystals will become separate and somewhat dry in appearance.

Preparing the granita liquids will take about a half hour. Elapsed time for freezing the granitas is about four hours; the actual work occupies five minutes or less every half hour. Yield is about one quart.

Now the granita can be eaten immediately or stored in the freezer for up to three days. To revive the granita, place the container in the refrigerator section for a half hour to defrost slightly, then beat and fluff with a fork, and finally refreeze it for another half hour.

This method was adapted from Liddell and Weir's *Ices.* Here are three alternatives you might try. Methods using a food processor work poorly.

1. Pour the mixture into one or more shallow metal trays and place them in the freezer. After a half hour to an hour, when ice crystals begin to form, stir them into the liquid. Repeat a half hour later. Freeze overnight. Remove, leave at room temperature for five minutes or so, and scrape the surface with the tines of a fork. Spoon the crystals into chilled serving dishes.

2. Bicycle around Manhattan's Lower East Side, as my assistant Tara did, looking for a Hispanic seller of snow cones. Ask him

where he bought his ice shaver, which looks like a wood plane made of dull aluminum with a compartment on top to trap the shavings. Buy one. Freeze a granita mixture solid, defrost briefly, and scrape shavings of snow from the top of the frozen block.

3. Buy the amazingly effective though overpriced Hawaiice Ice Scraper (model S-200) from the Back to Basics catalog, (800) 688-1989.

Lemon Granita
Corrado Costanzo in Noto

As I had feared, when you use regular supermarket lemons and add sugar to compensate for the acidity, a proper balance is hard to attain.

Then I discovered that Meyer lemons from California make a fine substitute for the green summer lemons of Sicily. (Meyer lemons were named for agricultural adventurer Frank N. Meyer, who discovered them in 1908 growing near Peking in an ornamental pot. They may be a cross between a lemon and a mandarin orange, but nobody knows for sure.) And even when Meyer lemons are unavailable, ordinary lemons can be used to make a satisfying granita by diluting their juice with water and using the zest with great discretion. When Corrado Costanzo zests a lemon, he passes it over a hand grater with such delicacy that he removes only the very outer layer of the fruit's yellow peel and never even approaches the bitter white pith.

1¼ cups superfine sugar
3 cups spring water
4 Meyer lemons (see Note), either organically grown or
    carefully washed

Dissolve the sugar in the water in a 2-quart bowl. Very gently grate the lemons with a hand grater held over the bowl. Swish the grater around in the liquid to recover the zest that sticks to it.

Juice the lemons. Pour 1 cup of lemon juice into the bowl and mix well. Pass the mixture through a strainer coarse enough to let through a little of the lemon zest and pulp.

Cover, chill, and freeze.

Note: If you cannot find Meyer lemons, use 3 normal yellow lemons (to yield ¾ cup of juice), 3½ cups of water, and 1½ cups minus 2 tablespoons of sugar. The granita will freeze slowly, but the taste will be excellent.

Maria Grammatico's Almond Granita

The search for an authentic bitter almond taste took me to various almond extracts (both natural and artificial), commercial almond pastes (European brands once contained real bitter almonds, which can be imported only when they are a minor ingredient in almond paste, not by themselves), and apricot or peach kernels, which also contain amygdalin. This breaks down into benzaldehyde—the essential bitter almond flavor—and prussic acid, a poison. I spoke with several scientists in the flavor industry and learned a lot about the differences between "natural," "pure," and artificial benzaldehyde.

I prepared eleven versions of almond milk and

arranged a blind tasting. There were three clear winners: (1) the version made by diluting an almond paste we had brought back from the Caffè Finocchiaro in Avola, near Noto in Sicily, full of bitter almonds; (2) my own homemade almond paste containing peach and apricot kernels, blanched and toasted for safety's sake; and (3) the same homemade paste flavored instead with McCormick "pure almond extract." Imitation or artificial almond extracts, even McCormick's, are sorry substitutes, containing synthetic benzaldehyde alone, with none of the numerous other aroma compounds found in true bitter almond oil.

According to the FDA's labeling standards, "natural" bitter almond oil and almond extract can be made from caccia bark, with a result somewhere between artificial benzaldehyde and the real thing. "Pure" oil and extract must be made from bitter almonds, or from peach, plum, or cherry kernels, which, though they may be chemically distinguishable from bitter almonds, come extremely close. Most commercially available almond pastes on the market today—even those made in Europe—substitute an inferior artificial bitter almond oil for true bitter almonds.

Now it is child's play to prepare an authentic almond granita—look for the word "pure" on the almond extract label, not the word "natural." Or start from scratch with peach pits.

1/2 teaspoon pure almond extract, or 30 peach or
  apricot pits
2/3 cup raw shelled almonds, without their skins
1/2 cup granulated sugar
1 cup plus 4 tablespoons hot water
3 cups spring water

If you are using peach or apricot pits, put five at a time into a plastic bag, crack them open with a hammer, and remove the kernels. You should have about ⅛ cup (2 tablespoons) of kernels. Blanch the kernels in boiling water, uncovered, for 1 minute and slip off their skins. Drain, and toast in a preheated 300° F. oven for 10 or 15 minutes until they turn light brown. Reserve. This procedure will eliminate the prussic acid while leaving much of the bitter almond taste.

Put the skinned almonds, sugar, and pure almond extract—or the blanched, roasted peach or apricot kernels instead of the extract—in a food processor and grind to a fine powder, alternating 30 seconds of pulsing with 30 seconds of steady power, for a total of 6 minutes or more, scraping the sides and bottom of the bowl halfway through and at the end. Then, with the processor running, add the 4 tablespoons of hot water, a tablespoon at a time, letting the machine run steadily for a minute after each addition. The result will be an incredibly delicious almond cream.

Gradually add the cup of hot water to dissolve the almond cream. Pour and scrape into a 2-quart bowl and add the 3 cups of spring water. Cover, chill, and freeze.

Roasted-Almond Granita from Modica

Follow the previous recipe for Maria Grammatico's Almond Granita, but substitute shelled, unskinned raw almonds for the skinned raw almonds, and dark-roast them as follows: spread the unskinned almonds in a heavy baking pan (or several thin pans stacked together), and roast in a preheated 300° F. oven for 5 hours, stirring every hour or so to keep the almonds on the bottom from burning. Let cool before proceeding.

Mandarin Orange Granita
Corrado Costanzo in Noto

5 mandarin oranges, clementines, tangerines, or satsumas (or more if they are small)
3 cups spring water
1 cup superfine granulated sugar
Juice of 1½ lemons (about 6 tablespoons, or ⅜ cup)

Vigorously grate the skin of the fruit (unlike lemons, there is no bitter pith) into a 2-quart bowl containing the water and the sugar. Swish around the grater in the liquid to recover all the zest. Juice the fruit into a measuring cup and pour 1¼ cups of it into the water-sugar mixture. Add half the lemon juice, mix well, and taste. Remember that the granita will taste much less sweet when it freezes; the lemon flavor should not be assertive in itself, but should add enough acidity to balance the sugar. Add more lemon juice until you can nearly—but not quite—taste the lemon flavor.

Strain the liquid through a medium or coarse strainer so that only a little of the zest and fruit pulp passes through. Cover, chill, and freeze.

Black Mulberry or
Wild Strawberry Granita
Caffè Sicilia in Noto

Gelsi neri—"black mulberries"—grow on great trees, not on bushes, as the nursery rhyme would have it; are rarely the object of commerce because they are fragile and easy to squash; and are not in season in most parts of this country until summer. This did not trouble me at first, because I needed to find only *one* part of the country where they are in season. The day I returned from Sicily, in mid-spring, I telephoned the most reliable hunters of produce and other delicacies, without success. Then I telephoned a friend in Tucson, renowned for its mulberry trees and early growing season. After what I learned, it should be renowned for its cruelty to mulberries: within the Tucson city limits, mulberries are an endangered fruit, threatened by the vanity of man. Planting new male mulberry trees is prohibited by law because their pollen is a powerful allergen, and Tucson gains profit and riches as a refuge for allergy sufferers and hypochondriacs. Female mulberry trees must be maimed and crippled each year by chemical spraying to prevent them from fruiting (if they somehow get pregnant without the male pollen) because the people of Tucson become very cross when ripe mulberries fall on their parked cars, splattering them with crimson. I am making plans to sue the Tucson allergy and parking lobbies for keeping me from my *gelsi neri*. But for now, I turned to wild strawberries and quickly found an importer of costly but excellent *fraises des bois* flown in from Périgord. I can still taste and smell the results.

½ pound of black mulberries or fragoline *(wild strawberries,*
  known in France as fraises des bois; *see Note)*
2 cups spring water (see Note)
½ cup superfine granulated sugar
Juice of ½ lemon

Puree the black mulberries or *fragoline* in a food
processor. You will need ⅔ cup of puree. Scrape into a
bowl and mix well with the other ingredients. Pass the
mixture through a strainer coarse enough to let through
just a few seeds and a little fruit pulp. Cover, chill, and
freeze.

Note: Black mulberries are available from Oregon in
the summer. A small quantity of *fraises des bois* is grown
in the United States; excellent imports from France can
be purchased from the Mushroom Man in Los Angeles,
(800) 945-3404, and are available from May to October.
Do not use either unless they are completely red, juicy,
and full of aroma.

I have tried a similar recipe calling for 3 cups of
water instead of 2. Though less intense in flavor than
Caffè Sicilia's version, it was more transparent and
refreshing. Though once I pursued intensity as the ultimate goal of granitas, I have found that added water
increases the crunchiness of the ice crystals and gives
you another, more panoramic, vantage point on the flavor—like stepping back from a painting.

Espresso Granita from the Isle of Salina

24 fluid ounces espresso lungo
1 scant cup granulated sugar

A "long" espresso contains more water than usual. In an espresso machine, you will need to make 7 or 8 cups of espresso. Each time, use one dose of coffee (7 grams, or 1½ tablespoons), but a larger cup, and let the hot water run through the espresso until you have 3 to 3½ fluid ounces (6 or 7 tablespoons, or a scant half cup). Pour into a 1-quart measuring cup and repeat until you have 24 fluid ounces, or 3 full cups. With a drip machine, substitute dark-roasted espresso coffee for your usual brand and triple the amount of coffee you would ordinarily use to obtain 3 full cups.

Let the espresso or drip coffee cool for 15 minutes in a 2-quart bowl. Stir in the sugar. Cover, chill, and freeze.

Chocolate Granita from Catania

None of the chocolate granitas we sampled on the way to the Catania airport was perfect, but back home in New York a few days later, with guidance from Luca Caviezel's *Scienza e tecnologia del gelato artigianale* (Caviezel was a Catanian pastry chef renowned for his ice creams), I was able to turn the recipes I had collected into a good granita that includes a little milk.

1½ ounces "Dutch-process" cocoa (⅓ cup very densely packed
or ¾ cup very lightly spooned)
2¾ cups water
¾ cup superfine granulated sugar
½ cup whole milk
Pinch of ground cinnamon (optional)

Sift the cocoa into the water in a pan, bring to a boil over medium heat, stirring frequently, lower the heat, and simmer for about 5 minutes, stirring constantly and scraping the bottom of the pan to prevent burning. Pour and scrape into a 2-quart bowl and let cool for 30 minutes. Add the sugar and stir until it dissolves. Add the milk and stir well. Add the cinnamon if that taste pleases you. Chill in the refrigerator for several hours or overnight. Then proceed to turn the liquid into a granita by following one of the methods explained on pages 370–372.

And if you would like to convert your granita into a famed eighteenth-century treat known as chocolate *in garapegra,* a "holy and noble elixir of fresh life," add vanilla, orange zest, and a few drops of distilled jasmine.

June 1996

Hauts Bistros

With a napkin of creamy starched linen, my wife wiped some wild mushrooms and a crepinette of lamb from her chiseled chin, gulped down a half glass of fourteen-dollar Bordeaux, and, referring I think to the six-course meal we had just shared, said, "Poetry is tradition compressed."

I could not have agreed more, though my way of putting it would have been slightly different. But one thing I have learned after thirty visits to Paris is never to trust your reaction to the first night's dinner, befuddled as you are by jet lag, the romance of Paris, and your half of the wine bottle. These distortions disappear nearly overnight. After drinking two bottles of wine a day, you quickly come down with, I find, a case of temporary alcoholism. You know that this has happened when you wake in the morning and reflexively feel around the night table for a glass of wine. From then on, your judgment is faulty only between meals.

And it *was* amazing food.

I do not remember which restaurant we were at on the night of my wife's revelation. I have been eating these days on the edges of Paris, because that is where my favorite food is, *la cuisine moderne* at *les bistrots modernes*. It could have been La Verrière or La Régalade, L'Épi Dupin or even Chez Michel. But I suspect it was L'Os à Moëlle because dinner there is always six courses, and the wine list offers mainly 70-franc bottles, $13.60 at July's exchange rate of 5.15 francs to the dollar, which, I predict, will only improve until the November election. On the other hand, if I could foresee exchange rates, I would be rich enough to buy this publishing house. And then you would see some changes! But even rich as Croesus, I would still eat at these five *bistrots modernes* and others like them.

Dinner averages 170 francs ($33) plus wine—lunch is less— the food is delicious, and it maps out a new path for the future of French cuisine. In case you have not been paying attention, haute cuisine in France is skirting the edge of calamity.

The origin of these things is always obscure, but we can start in 1992 with Yves Camdeborde, then twenty-six, one of four young sous-chefs at Les Ambassadeurs, the formal, sometimes transcendent, two-Michelin-star restaurant at the Hôtel Crillon. As a teenager, Yves had come to Paris from Béarn in southwest France to apprentice in the great kitchens of the Ritz Hotel, the Relais Louis XIII, and Tour d'Argent before he was hired as a sous-chef by Christian Constant, the esteemed chef at the Crillon. Constant is a fine teacher, but after six years Yves was ready to move on. In earlier years he might have stayed in haute cuisine as the second in command at one of the grand French gastro-nomic shrines or as chef at a dressy hotel dining room. Instead, he decided to open his own bistro in the Fourteenth Arrondisse-ment, or, as he now considers it, a small restaurant as might exist in the provinces, attracting customers from both the neighbor-hood and around town. He would offer a limited choice, draw on the recipes of southwest France, charge just 165 francs ($32) for every meal, and call the place La Régalade, which refers to the practice you once saw in Spain and southwest France, where drinkers would squirt wine from a leather bag into their mouths. I suppose it was their way of having fun, like getting a bull to step on your foot in Pamplona.

Yves was taking a great gamble. His fellow sous-chefs at the Crillon helped out now and then, and watched to see if he would succeed. And he did, completely and famously, both in the quality of his food and in his clientele. Soon it was impossible to get a dinner reservation at La Régalade unless you telephoned three weeks ahead. Yves's business has never slackened.

I have visited La Régalade on nearly every trip to Paris since it opened, with its bright, creamy walls and six-by-ten-foot kitchen. The menu changes a little every week, so by the end of a month nothing is the same but for some specialties whose disappearance might cause a riot among the regulars, like the *cochonnaille*—a wooden board of salamis, sausages, pâté, and cornichons, some made by Yves's father. And the perfect little Grand Marnier soufflés Yves learned to make at the Tour d'Argent.

I have eaten his crispy lamb sweetbreads with a hearty pan sauce sharp with peppers; the spicy chopped blood sausage nestled under a circle of mashed potatoes and then gratinéed; crunchy *langoustines* wrapped in Vietnamese spring-roll skins and served with garlic chips on the cutest, tiniest salad called *mouron des oiseaux;* potatoes filled with braised cow's cheeks and marrow; and his positively epitomic cassoulet. Most of it is robust regional food, perhaps updated in appearance or garnish, but always true to the original, and cooked with the skills Yves learned in four of the great kitchens of France. And some of it is spring-roll skins. I love spring-roll skins.

By 1995, Yves's fellow sous-chefs at the Crillon had decided to follow him into the *bistrot moderne* business, as had other young cooks around town, many of them also trained at the fanciest restaurants. An endless economic recession in France had both lessened their chances for advancement in the haute cuisine and lowered the price of leasing a vacant restaurant. And Yves had shown his friends what they could accomplish on their own. For a while, Yves's 160-franc menu set a maximum for the chefs who followed him; now some have crept toward 180. When you order the budget menu in an expensive restaurant, you feel like a second-class citizen; at a famous old bistro I was once told that I would be served supermarket ice cream while my wife and

383

everybody else in the room would be treated to the handmade version. At La Régalade, there is no way for a tycoon to spend more than the student at the next table.

Meanwhile the grand cuisine of France was descending into a state of near collapse. Where two decades ago fifty or a hundred great establishments were thriving, it was now hard to list more than a dozen. The culinary world bubbled with rumors that several great chefs recently awarded their third Michelin stars—the highest accolade in France—were in a financial pickle. Each order of Bernard Loiseau's $60.00 frogs' legs with garlic puree and parsley juice earns him only $1.20—after he has covered the salaries of fifty employees and paid off his investment in silverware impressive enough for the Michelin inspectors. Loiseau's profit comes from his boutique and the adjoining inn. The economics differ only slightly from those of haute couture, a dazzling show of artistry meant to lure the public to a designer's more modest and lucrative productions.

Three years ago, I flew from Orly to Lyons in a driving rain, waited two hours for the airline to find my luggage, rented a car, returned fifteen minutes later to get windshield wipers that worked, and drove an hour and a half to Saint-Étienne, a tedious and dying provincial city where Pierre Gagnaire had his restaurant. Gagnaire had just received his third Michelin star, once a guarantee of fame and at least a little fortune. My memory of every morsel is indelible—I thought at the time that Gagnaire had lifted mankind to a new level of eating.

Then last summer a friend visiting Saint-Étienne reported that on a Saturday night at the end of July, a moment when the demand for tables should have been overwhelming, Gagnaire was only two-thirds full. That very night you could not have forced yourself into La Régalade with an assault-type weapon. I knew something was hideously wrong—wrong with Saint-Étienne, with France, and with the cosmos. I learned that Gagnaire's revenues had dropped by more than half since my first visit and that he had let half his employees go. And by spring, after a strike of government workers paralyzed the nation's transportation system and made travel to Saint-Étienne even more difficult, Pierre Gagnaire's restaurant closed.

This was an inconceivable disaster, no less grotesque than if the Louvre itself had crumbled into the Seine. The French newspapers could write about nothing else. Gagnaire blamed Michelin, whose standards had forced him to borrow millions to buy and restore a spectacular Art Deco house in Saint-Étienne. Gagnaire's wife, Chantal, blamed nearly everybody else, including the French people. If I can travel from Manhattan to taste her husband's food, why can't the French drag themselves one-tenth as far? Pierre Gagnaire is a goddamn genius in an art form that the French nation worships, one of the greatest cooks in the entire world, the ultimate product of an ancient system of ruthless apprenticeships meant to identify, like incarnate lamas, the three or four godlike cooks born in every generation.

Most of the problem is probably price. Meals at places like Gagnaire's run two hundred dollars a person, much more if you buy a very good wine. Though the French economy has been in the doldrums for most of the nineties, prices at Michelin-rated restaurants have climbed by 900 percent since 1974, more than double the rise in consumer prices. In 1994, the madness stopped. For the first time in more than twenty-five years, tabs at the better restaurants rose by less than the cost of inflation.

Gastronomic pundits list other causes of the collapse of traditional French eating habits: longer workdays, *le stress*, shorter lunch hours and vacations, diets, *le cocooning*. And there is a more ominous and foreboding possibility. With fewer women free to cook at home and restaurant prices out of reach, the French are forgetting how to eat.

But not if Yves Camdeborde and the other young chef-owners of *les bistrots modernes* continue to have their way. They aim at nothing less than the revalidation of French culture. At least that is what Camdeborde told me over a plate of sautéed sweetbreads.

These young chefs begin with classic regional fare full of the deep, strong flavors of provincial France. Then they apply their training in modern French cooking—really the discoveries of the nouvelle cuisine in the 1970s before it took a disastrous turn into preciousness, luxury, decoration for its own sake, and intellectual pretense. Pan juices replace meat glazes and cream sauces. For the most part, cream and butter are used as flavorings, not as major ingredients. Vinegar supplants sugar in savory dishes, and desserts become less sweet. Much of the cooking is done at the last minute. And the plate has been simplified down to three elements: the main ingredient, a sauce, and a vegetable or two as a garnish. Giving pleasure has returned as the aim of cooking.

By charging thirty dollars for a meal, the young chefs attract a mixture of workers, artists, businesswomen, pensioners who watch their pennies, and gourmands who would squander any amount for food like this. To keep costs down, they have had to reinvent the methods of *la cuisine moderne.* It is easier to please with a pot of caviar, several of these chefs told me, than with a plate of potatoes. At the central market every morning, they insist on the finest fresh products—nothing frozen, precooked, or packaged. But instead of searching for the best ceps and truffles, our chefs look for the finest carrots and potatoes. They use the top butchers but buy only the cheaper cuts—oxtails, ham hocks, and beef cheeks. They purchase excellent bread, but usually in large loaves instead of rolls, which turn stale in half a day and go to waste. They use the stems of herbs for broths and pan juices, saving the tender leaves for soups, sauces, and garnishes. By offering only one cheese—a perfect Camembert or Brie or sheep's cheese that can be easily divided without any waste—they avoid charging extra for the cheese course. They shop at the central market, not because they have keener eyes than the leading suppliers, but because they can afford the more costly ingredients, such as *langoustines,* asparagus, and cheese, only by waiting for bargains. And they work all the time, keeping employees in the kitchen to a minimum. This means that they must know precisely what cooking can be done in the morning and what must be done at the very last minute.

I have eaten at twenty-five *bistrots modernes* in Paris over the past two years. The five best, in addition to La Régalade, are La Verrière, L'Os à Moëlle, L'Épi Dupin, Chez Michel, and Le Bamboche, which all opened this year or last. Three of them are owned by young chefs who had worked with Camdeborde under Christian Constant at the Crillon.

Eric Fréchon was the last to leave Constant. He had earned the title of Meilleur Ouvrier de France—the highest accomplishment of a French artisan—and had risen to become Constant's second in command. But in November 1995, at the age of thirty-two, he opened La Verrière in ample, cheerful quarters in the 387 Nineteenth Arrondissement in northwest Paris. Every dish I have eaten at La Verrière has been something of a revelation. Warm oysters roasted in their shells or cold oysters with little slivers of foie gras; salted breast of pork, lacquered with spices, and served on a mound of "sauerkraut" made from shredded turnips; a circle of gratinéed buttery mashed potatoes over a rich oxtail stew; roasted cod in an herbed crust—all of Fréchon's dishes are deeply satisfying and true to both French regional traditions and Fréchon's own imagination. The desserts are old-fashioned and modern at the same time, like the roasted mango on puff pastry with almond cream and a sorbet of lemon with basil—this is French technique on a frolic in the tropics, all for 180 francs.

L'Os à Moëlle means "marrow bone," Thierry Faucher's symbol for the robust and essential tastes that he transforms with his nearly haute-cuisine magic. The third of our sous-chefs from the Crillon, Faucher brings something like the *menu dégustation* of a grand gastronomic palace to a residential neighborhood in the Fifteenth. And he succeeds with nearly every dish I have tried. When you enter his place, an old restaurant built on a triangular plot with windows on two sides, you remember that this is why you, or at least why I, born with an immunity to shoe stores, come to Paris: a happy room, groups of all ages in animated conversation, people eating very, very well.

Lunch is three courses for 145 francs ($28), with a number of choices for each course, and dinner is six courses for 190 francs ($37) but with no choice at all. Faucher's food is amazingly, continually changing, with new ideas on every menu. Soup might be Jerusalem artichokes or asparagus with morels, or in the summer cold melon with ginger and ham; the second course a rabbit salad hiding under a rosette of crispy potatoes, or a fricassee of wild mushrooms—*pleurotes* and *girolles*—with chicken pan juices and somehow a quail's egg. Then comes the fish, a generous piece of skate in browned butter and vinegar; or roasted rascasse scented with branches of dried fennel and surrounded by a pool of peppery, sweet crustacean broth, not easy to forget. Meat comes next, and then a salad with a wedge of cheese. For dessert, you may be offered the silkiest dark-chocolate quenelle with a stylish Asian sauce of saffron, star anise, and cinnamon, or hazelnut cake topped with crème brûlée. Can you imagine a restaurant in the United States with a fixed menu, a place that ignores the phobias and hypochondria of its customers, where everybody gladly eats the same dishes? Don't they have lactose intolerance in France, or allergies to peas?

François Pasteau, thirty-four, did not work at the Crillon before opening L'Épi Dupin, on the rue Dupin in the Sixth, just beyond Poilâne's revered bakery. But he did apprentice at Faugeron, Duc d'Enghien, and La Vieille Fontaine in the Paris suburbs (all holders of two Michelin stars). A cold terrine layered with every little treasure from a pot-au-feu and served with a surprising compote of pears and tomatoes; small chunks of spiced lamb long stewed with eggplant and called *capitolade;* a guinea hen flavored with fennel and anise; a crispy square of phyllo and apple concealing dark, spicy sausage meat; a generous puffy flaming crepe soufflé of chestnuts; a deep, dark molten chocolate *dariole* streaming into a brilliant green pool of pistachio; a perfect Brie—these are what Pasteau exchanges for your 153 francs

($30), nearly everything delicious, intelligently made, and exceedingly generous.

Do you crave some *kig ha farz* or *kouingaman?* This is Breton dialect for stewed pig's cheeks with stuffing and an unusual, caramelized flaky pastry. And one of the few chefs who dare bring to the capital the real food of Brittany is, fittingly, Thierry Breton, which takes us back to the Crillon Four (or Five if you count chef Christian Constant, who himself has opened Le Camelot on the rue Amelot and charges an impossible 120 francs for dinner). Breton's Chez Michel, near the Gare du Nord, has nothing to do with Michel, if it ever did, but with a young chef who once was named Apprentice of the Year; worked at the Ritz, at the Tour d'Argent, on Joël Normand's team for President Mitterrand, and at the Crillon; and now runs a place so retro-provincial it almost looks intentional. This is country food from the Nord—lots of fish, to be sure, plus *la cuisine d'armorique,* dishes like ceps stuffed with oxtail and *terrine d'andouille* (smoked tripe) served with little pancakes fried in salted butter—plus occasional trips into fantasy—with all the twists in technique and *méthode* we have come to expect from this crowd.

One of the best of the small new restaurants is Le Bamboche, in the Seventh, owned by the fine young chef David Van Laer, who first became well known at the cutting-edge haute-cuisine restaurant Apicius. Though its style of cooking is similar to (if slightly more tailored than) that of the others, Le Bamboche could not be mistaken for a bistro. It is beautifully decorated and probably 50 percent more expensive and 30 percent more dressy. The special 180-franc budget menu is excellent and honest, but this is not the same as at the *bistrots modernes,* where everyone eats the same food for the same price. Whenever I stick to Van Laer's 180-franc menu, I always wonder what I am missing.

This is a wonderful time to eat in Paris, to which I sneak away as often as I can. But ruminatively chewing on my savory *jarret de porc* and *joues de veau* over the past two years, I have wondered whether the trend Yves Camdeborde started may be self-limiting.

His talent, and that of the Crillon Four and the other young chefs, were recognized, polished, and disciplined in the vast, well-staffed kitchens of the haute cuisine. Where will the next generation of cooks get their advanced culinary education if the haute cuisine becomes just a sad thing of memory?

I've spent many happy afternoons in the tiny kitchens of my favorite *bistrots modernes,* learning tricks, techniques, and recipes. Here is one of my favorite dishes, from Eric Fréchon.

Roast Squab with Green Lentils
La Verrière

4 squabs, about 1 pound each
6 tablespoons cooking oil
2 tablespoons coarsely chopped garlic
¼ cup sliced shallots
3 sprigs of fresh flat-leaf parsley
3 sprigs of fresh thyme
1 bay leaf
8 cups homemade or canned chicken broth
Salt and freshly ground pepper
1 cup (about ½ pound) lentils, preferably the small, green
    lentilles du Puy *from France*
1 medium-large onion, peeled and halved, each half stuck with
    a clove
2 carrots, peeled and halved crosswise
3 slices (about 2½ ounces) smoked bacon
2 tablespoons softened butter
4 branches of fresh thyme, as a garnish

Wash the squabs under cold running water, reserving the neck, gizzard, and heart. Butterfly each squab as follows (or ask the butcher to do it for you): With poultry shears or a sharp knife, remove (and reserve) the backbone by cutting on both sides of it. Cut off and reserve the first two joints of each wing. Skin side up, press down on the squab to flatten it. Turning the squab skin side down, remove the ribs and breastbones by inserting a sharp, thin knife between the bones and breast meat. Using your fingers, twist off any bones that were attached to the backbone. Wash and dry the squabs, wrap them in plastic, and refrigerate.

At least 4 hours before dinner, make the squab *jus:* Chop the reserved backbone, neck, tail, wing joints, ribs, bones, and innards into ½-inch pieces. In a 3-quart saucepan over high heat, darkly brown the squab pieces in 2 tablespoons of the oil for 10 or 15 minutes. Pour out the oil (without discarding any of the little browned bits in the pan, which are the point of this entire procedure), add the garlic, shallots, parsley, thyme, bay leaf, and 4 cups of the chicken broth, bring to a boil, and simmer, partly covered, for 2 hours, skimming any foam and adding boiling water to prevent the liquid from reducing by more than half. Pass through a fine strainer into a 1-quart saucepan and reduce over medium-high heat to a cup. Season well with salt and freshly ground pepper. The squab *jus* should now be incredibly delicious.

An hour and a quarter before dinner, preheat the oven to 500° F. Remove the squabs from the refrigerator and season them well on both sides with salt and pepper. Cover and let them warm to room temperature.

Meanwhile, prepare the lentils: Wash them under cold water, pick out any visible stones, and place them in a 3-quart pan with the onion, carrots, and bacon. Add the remaining 4 cups of chicken broth, bring to a boil over high heat, reduce to a simmer, partially cover, and cook for 40 minutes to an hour, stirring every 10 minutes. The lentils are done when they have absorbed all the liquid and are soft to the bite; they should not be al dente. Remove and discard the onion halves, the carrots, and the bacon. Stir in the butter and half (½ cup) of the squab *jus.* Season with salt and freshly ground pepper. Simmer over low heat for 5 minutes more; then keep warm, covered, over the lowest flame. The lentils should be unbelievably savory.

Fifteen minutes before dinner, cook the squabs: Place a small heavy metal roasting pan (or two large ovenproof skillets), just large enough to hold the squabs in one layer, over high heat on your stove top. Add the remaining 4 tablespoons of oil and begin browning the squabs, skin side down, flattening them with a spatula. After half a minute, transfer the pan to the preheated oven and roast for 8 minutes (rare) or 10 minutes (medium), with the squabs still skin side down. Check after 5 minutes: if the skin is a perfect, deep shade of brown, turn the squabs; otherwise, leave them as they are. The French and I prefer squab breast meat just this side of very rare, like red meat. It is most delicious this way, and its texture is wonderful. Cut into the breast meat if you need to check—the juices should run a deep pink.

To serve, warm four plates. Warm the squab *jus.* Stir the lentils and divide them among the plates, in a 5-inch or 6-inch circle in the center of each. Place the squabs on the lentils. Season them with salt and freshly ground pepper. Dribble the remaining squab *jus* in a concentric circle around the lentils and decorate with a sprig of thyme. Serves 4.

September 1996

PART FIVE

Proof
of the
Pudding

The Smith Family
Fruitcake

I was eighteen when I tasted my first fruitcake, which may explain why I liked it so much. My family never celebrated Christmas, except by watching the first fifteen minutes of *Amahl and the Night Visitors* on television every year, and nothing in my grandmothers' repertory had prepared me for that first wondrous mouthful of fruitcake at the house of a friend from college. It was a moist, alcoholic plum pudding, full of dark, saturated medieval tastes and colors—currants, dates, and black raisins, aromatic orange peel, mace and allspice and nutmeg, brandy and molasses—aged for a year and then set aflame at the very last minute, carefully spooned out like the treasure it was, and topped with an astonishing ivory sauce made only of butter, sugar, brandy, and nutmeg. They called it, simply, hard sauce. No more belittling name has ever been conferred upon so massive a culinary triumph.

Nowadays mail-order companies advertise fruitcakes for people who can't stand fruitcake, which makes no more sense to me than concocting an inferior version of foie gras for people who can't stand foie gras. I've ordered several of them over the years; most are loosely cemented blocks of nuts and hard, dried fruits (no sugar added) with barely any cake in between; one is baked in the shape of the state of Texas. Cookbooks inexplicably offer creative alternatives to hard sauce, and a few years back, Hallmark issued a series of antifruitcake greeting cards. I'll bet the most widely published food joke in history is Calvin Trillin's libel that there is just one fruitcake in the world, never eaten but simply passed on from year to year.

Many Christmas customs still puzzle me. Why, for example, would you want to celebrate a joyous event by going out and killing an innocent pine tree, draping it with shredded aluminum foil and dyed popcorn, and throwing it in the garbage a week later? But fruitcake is another thing entirely. By now I have eaten as many fruitcakes as any God-fearing Christian, and I can't imagine what everybody is complaining about.

Fruitcake entered my life on a permanent basis twenty years ago, when the woman who was to become my wife moved in, bringing with her all the edible mores of a Mormon upbringing. (Her family abounds with members of the Daughters of the Utah Pioneers, though an errant granduncle once joined the Butch Cassidy gang in Baggs, Wyoming.) Every year, right after Thanksgiving, her mother, Marjorie Smith, mailed us several small white fruitcakes neatly wrapped in waxed paper and meant to be aged and ripened in the refrigerator until Christmas. We would observe this rule with only one of them and polish off the others, paper-thin slice by paper-thin slice, long before December arrived. Two weeks later Aunt Vivian from Salt Lake City would send a large, dark, spicy fruitcake suspended in a shoebox with her patented protective caramel-popcorn insulation. Sometimes the shoebox was large enough to hold another little package containing delicate sugar cookies decorated with red and green sprinkles. In keeping with Mormon religious rules, none of the family's fruitcakes included any alcohol.

Marjorie's white fruitcake quickly became my favorite. The recipe was created by Aunt Esther in Twin Falls, but Esther never sent us fruitcake and Marjorie never failed to, which is why I always think of it as Marjorie's. It is, at bottom, a rich yellow lemon pound cake, unleavened, slightly underbaked, and filled with a volume of fruit and nuts equal to that of the cake batter— green and red candied cherries and pineapple, walnuts, and yellow raisins. When you have kept it in the refrigerator for a week or two, it becomes dense and less cakelike, and when you slice it thin, the result is a translucent, frolicsome mosaic of yellows, reds, and greens, two of which, I believe, are the official colors of Christmas. Marjorie collected her candied fruit and her packing boxes by Labor Day to avoid the year-end rush.

The other day, as I was thumbing through women's magazines from Christmases past—searching for good advice on making and mailing edible gifts and finding nothing better than a recipe for chocolate-chip pretzel bread—I came across several warnings not to use popcorn or breakfast cereals as the filler in your Christmas packages. They are thought to entice insects and absorb noxious fumes. But let me assure you that the candied popcorn protecting Aunt Vivian's fruitcake never attracted the tiniest insect or the merest wisp of a noxious fume. The magazines suggest using crumpled newspaper instead. That works fine if you mail your gift from Salt Lake City and crumple up a copy of the *Deseret News,* but if you live in New York or Los Angeles, your hapless recipient is likely to read "Store Santa Slashes Tots, Self, on Sleigh" before he or she reaches the delicacies within.

When my wife moved in, she had twenty-two living aunts and uncles, and you never knew whether Aunt Melva would send a box of her taffy or Aunt Frances a jar of her jam cooked from berries she had picked the summer before near her house in Olympic National Forest. Some years Aunt Evelyn in Salt Lake City would send us a tin of her famous butter mints, a delicate, creamy candy arduously made from hand-pulled sugar. At the age of eighty, Evelyn recently supplied butter mints to the four hundred guests at her granddaughter's wedding (two per customer), and once a year she makes them for the twenty-eight widows living in her ward and put under her charge, but she never sends enough to us. Evelyn also does cookies, including Date Swirl; fruitcake, light and dark; and Million-Dollar Fudge. Evelyn is one reason why Utah is called the Beehive State.

If I detect a competitive or compulsive edge to the food giving of the Salt Lake City area—I once observed two women frantically trying to force platters of fudge on each other as though they contained toxic waste—it is a contest from which the observer can only benefit. But as the years pass and Christmases come and go like clockwork, fewer of my wife's relations are able to bake as much as they would like, and most of the younger generation seems more skilled with the can opener than the canning jar. Marjorie and Aunt Vivian kept the fruitcakes coming until the end. Five years ago, after an illness, Aunt Vivian substituted what people in Salt Lake call TV Mix or TV Crunch, which is a mélange of Wheat Chex, Corn Chex, Rice Chex, peanuts, and pretzel sticks tossed with onion salt and soy sauce and intended, presumably, to be enjoyed while watching television. Trying not to sound ungrateful, we phoned Vivian to let her know how much we missed her fruitcake. The following Christmas she came out of retirement at the age of eighty-eight.

398

Now Vivian and Marjorie are gone. Last year, as Christmas approached, I finally acknowledged that no matter how many times I ran down to the mailbox, the fruitcakes would never arrive. The idea of baking them myself did not instantly occur to me. Real men do not bake fruitcake.

One night I could stand it no longer. My kitchen was well stocked with flour, butter, eggs, raisins, and walnuts but sadly lacking in the lemon extract and candied fruit departments. Unlike Salt Lake City, New York is a twenty-four-hour town, so I hopped in a cab and traveled from one all-night bodega and Korean grocer to another in search of red and green candied cherries and pineapple. By midnight I was desperate. I toyed with the idea of buying thirty boxes of Jujyfruits and removing the licorice ones. But at last some candied fruit miraculously appeared, plastic tubs of bright candied cherries, sufficient even without the pineapple for my immediate needs, and by two in the morning the fruitcakes were done. I aged one of them for nearly five minutes and cut it open, and it came close enough to Marjorie's white fruitcake to pacify us until the stores opened in the morning. Since then I have baked the cake many times, using Aunt Esther's advice to clear up various ambiguities in the recipe and add some new ones. My wife can't tell it from her mother's.

Smith Family White Fruitcake
Marjorie Smith, Aunt Esther, and Aunt Vivian

¾ pound candied red cherries (Aunt Vivian increased both the
  cherries and the pineapple, below, by ¼ pound each)
1 pound mixed green and red candied pineapple
1 pound yellow raisins
1 pound walnut halves
1 pound unsalted butter, at room temperature
1 pound (2¼ cups) granulated sugar
6 large eggs
4 cups (1 pound) sifted all-purpose flour
1½ ounces (3 tablespoons) lemon extract (Aunt Esther uses
  twice this amount)

Halve the candied cherries and cut the pineapple into ½-inch pieces. Put all the candied fruits in a strainer and wash them under cold water. Mix them thoroughly with the raisins and walnuts in a bowl with at least a 6-quart capacity.

Beat the butter in a standing mixer or with a hand beater until it is light, add the sugar, and beat until fluffy. Beat in 3 of the eggs, half the flour, the other 3 eggs, and finally the remaining flour. Beat in the lemon extract. Pour the cake batter over the fruit and nuts and thoroughly fold everything together with a large spatula.

Butter two large loaf pans and line them with parchment paper or brown paper. (The Smith family uses brown paper, which they feel prevents the cakes from becoming dark and crusty on the outside, a fatal flaw.) Butter the paper. Pour and scrape the batter into the pans, leaving at least ¼ inch for the cakes to expand.

Bake the fruitcakes in a preheated 300° F. oven for

45 minutes, cover tightly with aluminum foil (leaving space above the top of the cake), and bake for another 45 minutes. Do not overbake. These fruitcakes should be slightly underdone and very moist; remove them from the oven as soon as they resist the pressure of your fingertips or show the barest sign of pulling away from the sides of the pan. Let the fruitcakes cool in their pans on a rack, unmold them and remove the paper, wrap tightly in plastic, and refrigerate for at least a few days and as long as 3 weeks before cutting them into thin slices while they are still cold. This recipe makes 16 cups of cake batter, enough for two 8-cup loaf pans. Or you can make a dozen small fruitcakes in miniature nonstick loaf pans; decrease the baking time accordingly.

December 1991

Fries

For weeks I had been preoccupied with horses. Every time I saw a horse dragging tourists across the snow in Central Park, or standing under a policeman on the cobblestones of SoHo, I began to salivate. In truth, it was the fat of the horses, the fat around their kidneys, that excited me.

It had all started several months before, when a friend in Paris telephoned to announce that Alain Passard, chef of the famed Michelin two-star restaurant L'Arpège in the Seventh Arrondissement, cooks his French fries only in horse fat. "They have a not-disagreeable horsey flavor," he told my friend Frédérick Grasser, a prodigious cook and food writer, "a lightness and a true crispness you cannot obtain with other fats and oils."

Lightness, crispness, savory flavor—the words instantly put my appetite on alert. Isn't it a miracle, I reflected, that French fry lovers the world over—which includes nearly everybody the world over—share the same standards for greatness in fries? I noticed this again when reading a manual for French-fry professionals. Crispness, a golden-brown color, tenderness (instead of toughness), a fine fried flavor, lightness (instead of a soggy interior), and absence of greasiness—these seem to be cultural universals, like the fear of snakes.

Only texture gives rise to argument. Americans look for a dry, granular, "mealy" interior, and so they usually choose high-starch, dense Idaho russets. Europeans prefer a moister, smoother texture, which comes from a "waxier" tuber of lower density and starch content—but not as waxy as the small, yellow-fleshed *rattes*, fingerlings, and new potato varieties they generally use for mashed potatoes. In America, this would describe the BelRus, Centennial Russet, Chieftain, Katahdin, La Rouge, Sangre, Sebago. All but the Katahdin are difficult to find in American supermarkets, where six starchy varieties command 80 percent of the business. Unless your nearest farmer's market sells yellow fingerlings or other boutique potatoes, you will have to settle for a round, white boiling potato from the supermarket if you are not particular about flavor and want to go in the waxy direction.

Frédérick went on to explain that Alain Passard's preferred potato is the Charlotte de Bretagne (whose mealiness or waxiness I have not yet ascertained). He cuts it into the *pommes Pont-Neuf* shape—classic French fries about one centimeter square and eight centimeters long, or three-eighths inch by three inches. He uses a kitchen knife, not a French-fry cutter or food processor, because this produces a slight irregularity in the fries. Passard poaches the potato strips in rendered horse fat, a clear and golden liquid, kept at a relatively cool 265 degrees Fahrenheit, for ten to twelve minutes; drains the potatoes; waits six minutes; and immerses them again in the horse fat, this time raised to 365 degrees Fahrenheit for the two or three minutes needed to make them crisp, golden brown, and a little puffy.

Frédérick had barely hung up when a fresh sense of purpose and drive animated my spirit. Someday soon, I was sure, I would cook my own French fries in the fat of a horse. When and how this would be accomplished were questions that made the future seem alive with prospects and possibilities.

And then I was having a drink with Nora Pouillon, whose two restaurants in Washington, D.C. (Nora and Asia Nora), and fine new cookbook (*Cooking with Nora*, Park Lane Press) are nationally admired for both their food and their dedication to organic farming. Nora wanted to talk about sustainable agriculture, but her charming Austrian accent made it impossible for me to focus on anything but Lipizzaners, those fine, white Austrian Imperial equines. Nora was soon to leave for Vienna for a Christmas visit. Keenly aware that Austrians, while worshiping horses, also like to eat them, I tried to interest her in my French-fry mission.

When Nora began to reminisce guiltily about the fine Hungarian salami stuffed with donkey meat she had enjoyed as a girl, I knew I had her. I administered the coup de grâce by telling her, in complete truthfulness, that an anthropologist has demonstrated that in those countries where horses are used for food, the animals are treated much more humanely after they are no longer fit for work. Within a few minutes she had agreed to bring back six pounds of horse fat—as long as it was legal. President Clinton is fond of her restaurant, and Nora would not risk embarrassing her commander in chief with the scandal of smuggled fat.

I had two weeks to prove that my plan complied with the law of the land. But the problem was this: ruthless radical Republican right-wing religious maniacs had shut down the U.S. government! At the best of times, it is exquisite torture to get a straight answer about food from the Customs Service. Now there was no one even to ask.

And then, as if by divine intervention, the federal government went back to work for a few days. Still, nobody in Washington had the courage to give me the go-ahead. The FDA would take charge only if the horses were wild, and sent me to the USDA, which thought the FDA was wrong. Then I reached one Richard Scott, who supervises the agricultural import inspectors and needs to make these decisions every day. He checked a manual of horse diseases, made sure that Nora's fat was not from Argentina or Paraguay, performed further occult acts, and announced that if my horse fat had already been rendered and properly packed, she could carry it in without going directly to jail.

Now it was just a matter of time before fries cooked in horse fat would be mine.

My dedication to French fries is so profound that it undoubtedly has intrauterine origins, and for as long as I can remember, friends have telephoned me from the farthest reaches of civilization whenever they stumble across a particularly lofty French-fry achievement. Have I tried the fries at the little restaurant on the northwest corner of the Place des Vosges in Paris or at the new McDonald's in Pushkin Square in Moscow? The Cafe de Bruxelles in Greenwich Village or Benita's Frites in Santa Monica? Or the rotisserie near the Antibes market on the French Riviera, where crisp, golden chickens drip and dribble their juices upon the excellent fries piled in the bottom of the rotisserie for the few minutes that pass after they are fried and before they are sold?

Sometimes Fate puts the finest fries right under my nose. One summer we drove an hour into the hills overlooking the medieval walled city of Lucca, in Tuscany, to a tiny village called Pieve Santo Stefano and the restaurant called Vipore, the "Viper," named two centuries ago for its fearsome owner, who successfully kept local bandits from preying on customers as they stopped at his inn to break the day's long ride from Florence to Forte di Marmi on the Tyrrhenian Sea. We sat at wooden tables in a garden planted with flowers and herbs and black cabbages, watching the lights come on in Lucca and the stars come out overhead, and enjoyed the wonderful cooking of Cesare Casella, son of the owners, whose inventions include potatoes deep-fried with garlic and branches of fresh rosemary, thyme, oregano, sage, and *nepitella*, and served on paper made from straw. The herbs become crisp and perfume the oil, the garlic grows soft and mellow, the crunchy potatoes take on all their flavors, and they are wonderful. Tuscans are known for frying their potatoes with a little rosemary (I have read a scientific paper showing that rosemary is an antioxidant that retards rancidity in frying oil), but nobody uses herbs as expansively and skillfully as Cesare.

Somehow I left Pieve Santo Stefano without the recipe. Years later Cesare arrived in New York. Late one Sunday afternoon we shopped for ingredients, returned to my house, and within minutes the smells and perfumes of Tuscany filled the kitchen. Only the *nepitella* was lacking, an herb indispensable in Tuscany, where it grows like a weed, but virtually unknown in this country, despite the plague of eating places calling themselves Tuscan. At Vipore, Cesare's family makes a lunch of fried potatoes with a salad of green radicchio and sometimes a dish of eggs cooked with chopped fresh tomatoes. In Lucca, Cesare's potatoes are called simply *patate frite*, but in America they become

Herbed Tuscan Fries
Cesare Casella

8 cups (approximately) peanut oil
1½ pounds medium-large all-purpose or boiling potatoes
4 garlic cloves, unpeeled and lightly crushed
4 sprigs of fresh rosemary (each 6 to 8 inches long), cut in half
10 sprigs of fresh thyme
4 branches of fresh sage
2 sprigs of fresh oregano
2 teaspoons sea salt
Black pepper in a pepper mill

Special equipment:
9- to 10-inch pan for frying, with sides at least 4 inches high
Frying thermometer (one that covers the range between 200° F. and 400° F.)
Long cooking fork
Round skimmer about 5 inches in diameter

Fill the pan with 1¾ inches of peanut oil and place over the highest heat on your most powerful burner. (Owners of commercial stoves should reduce the heat by nearly half after the potatoes go in.) Immerse the thermometer in the oil. Wash and peel the potatoes and, with a French-fry cutter or a kitchen knife, cut them into long strips with a square cross section about ⅜ inch on a side. Do not wash the pieces but dry them carefully with a cloth and keep them tightly wrapped. Get the garlic and herbs ready.

When the oil reaches 360° F. to 370° F., add all the potatoes. Do not use a frying basket. Be careful not to splash the oil. The oil will bubble furiously and drop to between 240° F. and 270° F. before the temperature rises again. Stir continually with the long fork until the potatoes are done, in 10 to 12 minutes, adding the herbs and garlic as follows:

About 2½ minutes into the frying, stir in the garlic cloves.

Six minutes into the frying, the potatoes should begin to take on a golden color, and the temperature should reach 280° F. to 300° F. Stir in the rosemary sprigs.

A minute or so later, stir in the thyme, sage, and oregano.

Nine minutes into the frying, sprinkle with the salt. (Yes, right into the potatoes and oil.) The potatoes should now be a deep golden color, and the oil temperature should have climbed to about 320° F.

A minute later, fish out a piece of potato with tongs or chopsticks, blot it on a paper towel, wait a few seconds, and take a bite. It should be crisp, and instead of bending, it should be stiff. The insides should be creamy, with no hint of a raw taste. You are not likely to need more than another minute or two of frying before the potatoes attain this state. If the temperature reaches 360° F., lower the heat.

When the Tuscan fries are nearly ready, grind 6 to 8 turnings of the pepper mill over them in the oil and stir well. Using the skimmer, lift the potatoes from the oil (with the herbs and garlic—all of them delicious).

Place the potatoes, herbs, and garlic in a basket or deep dish lined with paper, blot the top, transfer to a paper-lined plate, and serve immediately (or keep warm in a 250° F. oven while you make another batch). Serves 2 Tuscans, 3 or 4 Americans.

Note: The oil can be used again to make additional batches of potatoes, but only within a few hours—salt breaks down frying oil. After the first frying, use only half the herbs and salt (but all the garlic), because the oil becomes imbued with their flavors. And make sure the oil remains 1¾ inches deep.

Cesare's herbed potatoes are not classically French fries. They break all the rules. In fact, French fries are not classically French. Belgians point out that true French fries are made by using two frying baths, the first at a lower temperature than the second, just as Alain Passard makes them, and that French cooks did not double-fry their fries until well into this century, long after the Belgians had discovered the principle. Only Americans attribute fries to the French. *The Oxford English Dictionary* dates the name back to 1894, when it appeared in "Tictocq," a short story by the American writer O. Henry, which was published in his humorous weekly, the *Rolling Stone*, just before he fled the country on a charge of bank embezzlement in Austin, Texas. The *OED* should hire my assistant Tara Thomas, who has found another, perhaps earlier, 1894 instance in a recipe for "French fried potatoes" in Dr. N. T. Oliver's cookbook, *Treasured Secrets*, in the New York Public Library.

Neither source treats the name as unusual or exotic, and so it must have been current in speech and perhaps even print, although nobody has found an earlier example. Some people believe that the "French" in "French-fried potatoes" comes from the culinary verb "to french," meaning to cut into thin strips, as in "frenched beans." (This does not explain why we use "frenching" to refer to short-sheeting a bed as a practical joke. The British call it an "apple-pie" bed, for no apparent reason.) The nickname "French fries" first appears in print in 1918, though Graham Greene uses the compromise phrase "French frieds" as late as 1958 in *Our Man from Havana*, which you should read as soon as possible—if you haven't already. There is no record of when "fries" alone appeared.

Neither Dr. N. T. Oliver nor Fannie Farmer, in the first edition of *The Boston Cooking-School Cook Book*, published two years later, uses the double-frying technique, which first appears in an American cookbook in 1906. To understand the virtues of double-frying, cut up a potato into French-fry-sized strips, dry them with paper towels, and fry them at a steady 360 degrees Fahrenheit until they become golden brown. Either the outsides will be tough and dark or the insides will taste and feel undercooked. The reason is that potatoes have a very high "thermal inertia." It takes a long time for heat to penetrate and cook to the center of the potato. And by the time it does, the outside gets overdone. When potatoes are fried twice, the interior gets cooked in the relatively cool first frying of five or more minutes—but before the outside can color and seal. Then the surface is made brown and crisp by plunging the potatoes into very hot oil. The crust quickly becomes impermeable to oil and remains no more than a half millimeter thick.

Cooking the inside means both evaporating a good part of the water (potatoes are 70 percent to 80 percent water) and gelatinizing the starch—causing the hard, microscopic starch granules that line the potato cells to absorb water and swell into puffy, tender, fragile pillows filled with gooey, wet starch. Gelatinization starts when the pieces of potato are heated to about 150 degrees

Fahrenheit and is complete when the very heart of each French fry reaches 170 to 180 degrees.

That's it, in theory at least. Yet every French chef seems to have his or her own special method. The possibilities are endless. What variety of potatoes is best? Should they be peeled and, if so, with a knife or a vegetable peeler? Should they be cut irregularly by hand or into perfect strips with a machine? Should the strips be patted dry with a towel, or washed first, or soaked in ice water, or blanched in boiling water? How many fryings are ideal, in what fat or oil, and at what temperatures? If two fryings are good, would four be better? How much time should elapse between fryings? What kind of salt should you sprinkle on them?

The towering Joël Robuchon, long considered the greatest chef in the Western world, recommends a potato variety called Agria, likes slightly irregular hand-cut shapes, blanches his potato strips in *unsalted boiling water* for two minutes, fries them in peanut oil at 320 degrees Fahrenheit, waits a few minutes, immerses them again at 374 degrees for two minutes, and seasons them "deeply" with fine salt and then with coarse salt, for the crunch of it. He prefers the gray salt of Guerande, from Brittany. Fries may be considered plebeian food in this country, not worthy of a great chef, but in France and Belgium nobody shares our disrespectful attitude. "Ah, les frites!" writes Robuchon. "I know nobody who does not go nuts in front of a plate of crispy French fries."

The great Belgian chef Pierre Wynants likes Bintje potatoes. He washes the potatoes, uses huge amounts of oil, and lets the fries cool for at least a half hour between the two fryings. Ghislaine Arabian, born in Belgium, raised in Lille, and now chef at Ledoyen in Paris, supports a potato called Charlotte de Noirmoulier and the Belgian combination of palm oil and 15 percent beef tallow, quite a low temperature for the first bath, no delay, and then a high temperature for the second.

And a friend in Paris has disclosed to me what he swears is the great Joël Robuchon's personal, simplified home recipe, which achieves what amounts to two fryings (or, really, an infinite number) in one because the potatoes start in cold oil, which is heated gradually but as quickly as possible to 370 degrees Fahrenheit. Commercial frying manuals typically advise you to use large amounts of oil—at least six times the weight of the food to be cooked—so that its temperature will "recover" quickly when cold potatoes are plunged into it. But with Robuchon's home method, heat recovery is not an issue because both potatoes and oil start out cold and are heated together. So Robuchon begins with only enough cold oil to cover the potatoes; little oil makes for faster heating. These fries are much less expensive and much less messy than the classical version. To my knowledge this recipe has not previously been published, anywhere.

4 1 0   This bewildering variety of recipes, the excellence of Cesare Casella's Tuscan fries, the private formula of Joël Robuchon—all these shook me to the core. I began a profound reevaluation of my own French-frying skills and dared to ask the most probing questions of which a French-fry lover is capable: What is a true French fry, and how is it made?

I gathered one hundred pounds of potatoes, ten gallons of peanut oil, four electric deep fryers, and a sheaf of scientific books and papers, and went to work, all the while hoping for the arrival of my horse fat, if Nora Pouillon ever returned from Austria, land of the Lipizzaners. I will not dwell on the details of every experiment. Let us just say that my work with rendered beef fat was the last straw. My wife becomes unaccountably grumpy when our loft reeks like a Burger King and she goes to work with her hair smelling like a steak. Things grew tense between us.

Here are my most stunning findings:

1. I compared several potato varieties cooked the same way. Fries made from starchy Idaho russets were typically the crispest, though often unpleasantly granular inside and with a bitter taste, compared with fries made from large white boiling or all-purpose potatoes, which were more tender, both inside and out, and sweeter tasting. (Boiling potatoes take thirty seconds to a minute longer to fry.) Very waxy, yellow specimens fried dark, soft, and exces-

Easy *Frites*
Attributed to Joël Robuchon

1½ pounds Idaho or boiling potatoes
2 cups peanut oil, at room temperature
Salt

Wash and peel the potatoes, and with a French-fry cutter or a kitchen knife, cut them into long strips with a square cross section about ⅜ inch on a side. Wash them briefly under cold water and dry with a cloth. Put them into a pan about 10 inches in diameter with sides at least 4 inches high. Just cover with peanut oil.

Place the pan over the highest heat. When the oil has exceeded 200° F., it will begin to bubble, first softly and then furiously, and by the time it reaches 350° F., the potatoes will be a deep golden brown and ready to eat. (Make sure that the oil temperature never exceeds 370° F.)

Taste one or two. Drain and blot with paper towels. Salt the *frites* just before serving. Eat with strong Dijon mustard.

sively sweet on the inside, though extremely creamy in texture.

2. I tested several automatic electric fryers—two from DeLonghi, one from T-Fal, and my old Bosch (no longer available in the United States; it required all my cleverness to repair it), plus a manual French stove-top six-quart pan with a frying basket from Bridge Kitchenware in New York City. None of the electric deep fryers had accurate thermostats, but all worked tolerably well when a frying thermometer was immersed in the oil and a sharp eye was kept on the temperature. The DeLonghi Roto-

Fryer, the most expensive, handsome, and solidly made, operates on the crazy principle that putting an angled, motorized basket inside the fryer to rotate the potatoes in and out of the fat not only saves on oil but also produces the crispest surface and lightest texture, which it most surely does not. The thermostat in the cheaper DeLonghi was off by as much as forty degrees Fahrenheit. Its consumer help line was busy for an entire day; I called every thirty seconds for ten hours through the magic of automatic redial. The T-Fal was well enough designed and efficient, and produced fine French fries, though it lacked the power or capacity of either my old Bosch or my stove-top pan and basket, plus thermometer. If I needed an electric deep fryer, I would choose the T-Fal. Otherwise, stick to a large pan and basket.

3. I tested all the brands of microwave French fries I could find in two supermarkets. None was satisfactory. She who invents the perfect microwave French fry will become the richest woman in the world. (Americans pay five billion dollars a year to consume five billion pounds of fries.) Several companies have gone broke in the attempt.

4. I tested all the brands of "oven-fries" I could find. None was better than barely palatable.

5. Frozen French fries come in many shapes and sizes. All have been par-fried in the factory and instruct you to finish them at home by deep-frying, baking, broiling, or even microwaving. Only deep-frying yielded acceptable results. Of all the brands, shapes, and sizes, only Ore-Ida's Shoestrings (about three-sixteenth-inch square when fully cooked, like McDonald's) gave good results; their texture was excellent, their taste less so. No brand was acceptable when cooked in the oven, under the broiler, or in the microwave. They were not French fries.

6. Most American cookbooks have you soak cut-up Idaho potatoes in ice water for at least a half hour, and sometimes overnight. This practice did not produce superior fries; but it does allow you to prepare your potatoes way in advance.

7. Washing the potatoes after cutting them is unnecessary. It does not make for crisper fries, as many recipes claim.

8. Blanching the potato strips—plunging them into boiling water for two minutes or more, as many good French cooks and cookbooks advise—is unnecessary with the starchy potatoes we use in this country or even with all-purpose or boiling potatoes. The goal of blanching is to remove sugar from the surface of the strips, making for lighter-colored fries; to stop enzyme activity in the surface, which would otherwise cause browning as soon as the potato is cut and the formation of unpleasant flavors later; and to gelatinize and seal the starch on the surface, decreasing oil absorption and making for crispier fries with a thicker crust. Waxy, lower-starch potatoes of the kind they use in France may require this assistance, but an Idaho-Burbank does not, unless it has been improperly stored at very low temperatures just above 413 freezing so that lots of sugar has developed in the potato.

9. Raw potato strips will absorb more fat if their surfaces are moist. Dry them carefully.

10. French fries get soggier faster after you have sprinkled salt on them. Salt them only in the last seconds before serving.

11. French chefs disagree about how long you should wait between the first frying and the second. Letting the potatoes cool to room temperature for an hour or two between fryings seems to make Idaho potatoes come out crisper in the end, but has little effect on waxier potatoes.

12. The color of French fries, ranging from golden to darker brown, is not a good indicator that the potatoes are ready. The chief cause of color is the sugar level of the potato, which varies according to how it was stored and what variety it was in the first place. Taste your French fries to tell if they are done.

13. The best combination of times and temperatures is a long, cool frying followed by a short, hot frying at the end, with little waiting in between. This and many of my other findings are consistent with the recipes of both Ghislaine Arabian and Alain Passard. Though they use fancy potatoes and special animal fats, their methods seem to work best even with supermarket tubers and peanut oil. Both learned their fries in Belgium.

Arabian-Passard's Optimum Fries

2 to 3 quarts of peanut oil (or substitute ⅓ to ½ beef tallow)
1 to 1¼ pounds Idaho Russet-Burbank or large white
  boiling potatoes
Salt

Pour the peanut oil into an electric deep fryer or a six-quart stove-top deep-frying pan fitted with a wire basket. Use as much oil as the manual of the electric deep fryer recommends (or up to half the volume of the stove-top version, i.e., three quarts). Using a frying thermometer, bring the oil to 265° F.

Meanwhile, wash and peel the potatoes, and with a French-fry cutter or a kitchen knife, cut them into long strips with a square cross section about ⅜ inch on a side. Discard the smallest and most irregular pieces. You should have between ¾ and 1 pound of potatoes (3 to 4 cups). Use the smaller amount with two quarts of peanut oil and the larger amount with three quarts. Do not wash the potatoes, but dry them carefully in a kitchen towel. Keep them wrapped tightly until the oil is ready.

Put the potatoes into the frying basket and lower it into the oil. Cook over high heat until the oil nears 260° F. again, then lower the heat to maintain that temperature. Stirring often with a long cooking fork, cook for 9 or 10 minutes, until the potatoes are nearly cooked on the inside but are white and somewhat translucent on the outside and have not yet taken on color. Lift the basket and drain the potatoes while the oil reaches 370° F. to 380° F., again over the highest heat. Do not let the oil exceed 380° F.

> Plunge the frying basket back into the oil and fry for about 3 minutes, until the potatoes are deeply golden and crisp. All-purpose or boiling potatoes take about 30 seconds longer to cook.
>
> Lift the frying basket, drain the potatoes for a few moments, invert the basket onto a plate covered with paper towels, blot the top of the pile of fries, and, just before serving, salt them without stinting.

Just in the nick of time Nora Pouillon arrived home from Austria with six pounds of rendered horse fat carried in her suitcase next to her most intimate apparel. My excitement was difficult to restrain. There were seven white plastic containers, each labeled L. GUMPRECHT PFERDEFLEISCHERE. PFERDE-FETT. (Gumprecht is probably the most popular of Vienna's remaining horse-meat sellers, and he occupies stands 58 and 59 at Vienna's Naschmarkt.) Inside each was a white, congealed fat that resembled lard. Nora had glided through customs. One month later she was named 1996 U.S.A. Chef of the Year.

I poured the horse fat into one deep fryer, some home-rendered beef tallow into a second, and peanut oil into a third, and cooked ten batches of French fries, using the Arabian-Passard recipe. The peanut-oil version was good, but the beef- and horse-fat fries were exceptional, especially after I had diluted the animal fats by half with peanut oil. The potatoes were extraordinarily crisp and tasty, and they stayed that way much longer than usual. It is easy to see why McDonald's and the other fast-food chains once cooked their famous fries in beef fat—until the public's concern about cholesterol forced them to change to pure (though dangerously partially hydrogenated) vegetable oil.

Just as I was about to compare and contrast in fulsome and appropriate detail the precise aromas and tastes of horse fat and tallow, the horse fat began prematurely to go rancid and dark. (When frying fat takes on a fishy aroma, it is not yet rancid but is about to become so.) I am afraid that Nora had neglected the fifty pounds of dry ice I had requested to protect my Pferde-Fett on its odyssey from Vienna to Washington to New York City. I apologize.

I have just learned that Alain Dutournier, the excellent Parisian chef from southwest France, cooks his French fries in goose fat. He uses an unusual combination of temperatures: after a first low-temperature frying, you wait two hours, start the second frying at 280 degrees Fahrenheit, and slowly increase the temperature to 392 degrees. The idea is intriguing, and I would like to try it immediately. But my wife has just passed through the kitchen and slipped into bed, leaving me alone, surrounded by four white bubbling-hot electric deep fryers and piles of unpeeled Idaho potatoes. "Smile and the world smiles with you," she said as she disappeared. "Fry and you fry alone."

416

April 1996

Author's Note:

Alain Passard has been awarded a third Michelin star. His horse-fat French fries cannot have been irrelevant to this decision.

When this article appeared, an avid horsewoman organized a campaign against *Vogue* for verbal cruelty to horses. *Vogue* mollified her by publishing, unedited, a letter abusing the author.

I replied: "The United States is the largest horse-meat exporter in the world (as many as 400,000 animals a year are sent to slaughter) because it has the largest recreational horse population. These animals become 'surplus' when horse lovers unnecessarily breed their pets, owners sell their racehorses after only a few years, and recreational riders trade up. Slaughter and export become inevitable when this surplus drives down resale prices below about $600 an animal. The object of Ms. ———'s rage should be the inhumane practices of a good part of the horse-slaughtering industry. And the unwillingness of most horse owners to care for their discarded pets until they die a natural death."

Fish Without Fire

For the past two months I have eaten nothing but microwaved fish. My adventures in bistro cooking are on the back burner— the plump, crisply roasted chickens, the garlic sausage and potatoes browned in goose fat, the sauerkraut braised for hours with pork, apples, onions, and juniper berries. Gone is the week I spent with twenty pounds of Idaho russets and five quarts of heavy cream, trying to recapture the gratiné potatoes we ate last summer in Avignon. Perfect potatoes will have to wait.

It all began some months ago when the most stylish woman I know informed me that my cooking habits were hopelessly out of date. "We," she announced, speaking as always for a fashionable world that the rest of us can imitate but never enter, "have been doing oceans and oceans of microwaved fish. It's lite, it's qwik, it's E-Z, and it's . . ." She searched for the perfect word. "It's fish."

I do not as a rule seek advice about food from thin people, but my friend's words had chastened me. I felt like a vestige of some gladly forgotten age. Worse, I felt like an outsider. It was then that I resolved to eat nothing but microwaved fish until I had learned to love it. But where to start?

Step One: The hardware. Judging from the last five years of *Consumer Reports,* a jungle of features and options awaits the first-time buyer of a microwave oven: cooking power and power consumption, digital readouts, temperature probes, moisture sensors, programmed defrost cycles, programmed roast cycles, programmed combination cycles, and devices like reflective blades, waveguides, and carousels to smooth the irregular energy pattern. All for two or three hundred dollars.

The microwave salesman in the department store sat forlornly amid fifty ovens arrayed on carpeted shelves. He telephoned other salesmen to negotiate his lunch hour. He was unable to explain the range of features, sizes, and power levels or even to remember their names. Doesn't he know he is part of a nationwide revolution in taste, texture, and time management? I relied on *Consumer Reports* and ordered two top-rated microwave ovens, the compact from GE and the giant size from Amana.

Solid facts are hard to come by in this brave new world. The Toynbee of the microwave has yet to set pen to paper, but it is generally agreed that in 1945 or 1946 a radar scientist at Raytheon labs in Massachusetts noticed that a Hershey bar had unaccountably melted in his pocket. If he had remembered that cocoa butter is liquid at 98.6 degrees Fahrenheit, we might all still be living in caves and cooking over peat fires. But our scientist guessed that radar waves had caused the mess in his pocket. He proceeded to pop some corn in a galvanized garbage can and then applied for a patent. There is no record of how the stain was removed.

Since then the garbage can has been reshaped into a metal box, and the FCC has assigned a frequency of 2,450 megahertz (million cycles a second) to microwave cooking, somewhere between marine radar and channel 69 on your UHF television dial. Dividing the speed of light by 2,450 million cycles per second yields a wavelength of about four and three-quarters inches, which is supposed to explain why microwaves penetrate your food by about an inch and a quarter, unlike infrared radiation in conventional cooking with a wavelength only one-fourth as long, which is pretty much absorbed at the surface, where it causes the delicious browning reaction, which microwaves don't.

Microwaving Your Sneakers

Just because you have finally admitted that your microwave oven is useful only for popcorn and reheating leftovers, this is no reason to throw it away. Think up new uses for it. When I read recently that a large appliance manufacturer is developing a microwave clothes dryer and the next day tripped into a puddle in front of my house, I decided to experiment.

Dry Sneakers

1 wet athletic shoe, about 20 ounces, Nike or similar brand
1 full-size microwave oven

Place your shoe on the oven floor, sole up. Set the power level to about one-third for 5 minutes. Repeat, checking each time for hot spots on the shoe. Remove if you find any or when the shoe is almost dry. If you try to get it bone-dry, the rubber parts will bubble up and the instep will smoke and smolder.

December 1988

In both cases, the absorbed energy agitates the food molecules, which we call heat, and the heat is then transferred to the rest of the food by conduction. Infrared waves agitate almost all types of molecules. The books disagree about whether microwaves agitate only polar molecules, principally water, or whether their energy is imparted most effectively to salts and fats. The distinction is crucial to understanding what happens to your dinner in the microwave oven, but I can safely say that the Newton of the microwave has yet to publish his findings.

Sixty percent of American homes have microwave ovens, more than have dishwashers; half of these acquired their ovens since 1984. People in the western states buy them more often than people in the East. Everybody in the West refers to microwave ovens as "nukers" and to cooking food in them as "nuking" it. This metaphor is imprecise because microwave radiation is nonionizing, meaning that it leaves the electron rings in food atoms unaltered. Otherwise your food would emit radiation on your plate and in your stomach.

Step Two: The software. While my ovens were in transit, I assembled a representative pile of twenty current microwave cookbooks, all that I could find with substantial sections on fish. For the most part, these are not books to curl up with on a wintry evening. There are no literary excursions to that perfect little microwave shop near the market in Lyons. The recipes are short and telegraphic with apologies preceding those that require much explanation. The books are unanimous: "Once you have tried microwave-cooking fish, you may never cook it any other way. . . . The fish stays moist and cooks through absolutely evenly." "Fresh fish is so tasty when cooked simply that a sauce may seem unnecessary."

And on and on. Many of these books are tall and thin, like skinny people with no time to read about food. Most were written by home economists with a minor in microwave, appearances on a local television show, or a consulting contract with a microwave manufacturer. Nowhere could I find a book called something like *Cuisine Électromagnétique* by Michel Guerard or Fredy Girardet. Next best is Barbara Kafka's admirable *Microwave Gourmet* (Morrow), which tackles tricky classics like risotto, *confit de canard*, and country pâté and includes an exhaustive dictionary of ingredients, techniques, times, and yields, which alone is worth the price of the book. On a more quotidian level but no less comprehensive is *Mastering Microwave Cookery* by Cone and Snyder, with seventy-five introductory pages of guides, charts, and other sometimes useful information. The lower-end books teach you to create in your own kitchen sombrero party dip, casseroles of tuna and potato chips, fiesta burgers, and shrimp trees, "an attractive Christmas holiday centerpiece" in which peeled micro- 4 2 1 waved shrimp are pinned to a large green plastic cone. I could hardly wait for my ovens to arrive.

Step Three: The shakedown cruise. The minute the GE compact model was delivered I felt a powerful urge to toss everything into its cavity. The bratwurst split after thirty-seven seconds and burst after fifty-eight; a Dove bar was successfully brought to eating temperature in its own little carton; cold coffee reheated less repulsively than usual. In preparation, I had picked up some convenience foods, I think they're called, made just for the microwave. I tried two competing brands of popcorn, which come in individual popping bags. The Orville Redenbacher Natural Flavor won hands down, tender and crisp if much too salty. A prewrapped stack of frozen buttermilk pancakes, which you immerse in your own choice of syrup and breakfast spread before microwaving, disintegrated on the fork, and the side of the box read like a chemistry set.

There were two pounds of leeks and some chicken broth in the refrigerator. What better way to conclude my shakedown cruise than hold a bake-off between my two favorite microwave cookbooks. Their recipes for braised leeks are nearly identical but for cooking times. Barbara Kafka's forty-minute recipe produced a delicious platter of tender leeks swimming in too much liquid, which I drank as a soup after adding a little cream and reheating it in the microwave; the other leeks, ready in half the time, were tough and stringy. Compared with conventional cooking, Kafka had spared me only ten or fifteen minutes of unattended baking and one pot to clean.

This led me to the dirty little secret of microwaving: many dishes take longer in the microwave! The more food you put in, the longer it takes. The magnetron (the vacuum tube that produces microwaves) sends a fixed amount of energy into your oven's cavity, where it bounces off the metal walls until absorbed by food. An entire baron of beef absorbs only a little more energy every second than a little morsel of veal and, consequently, cooks that much more slowly. One baked potato takes five minutes to microwave, two take twice as long, and a dozen almost an hour. In a conventional oven, which circulates hot, dry air around each potato, one takes as long to bake as twelve—about forty-five minutes. Microwaving a twelve-pound turkey requires four and a half hours of cooking and twelve ears of corn fourteen minutes, both considerably longer than with conventional cooking. That's why most microwave recipes serve only one or two people—perfect for today's subnuclear family—and warn you against simplemindedly doubling or tripling the quantities for larger groups.

Step Four: New-wave fish in earnest. Picture the most delicious fish you have ever eaten. I can still taste the spicy, deepfried fingers of speckled trout on a drive through Cajun country, the mountain of tiny grilled fish—without an English name—that we ate, head and all, on the Adriatic coast, the barbecued bluefish at the end of a Long Island summer, the little yellow perch we caught at sunset in Vermont and crisply panfried a few moments later. If this is your idea of goodness, too, use your microwave for melted-cheese sandwiches. It does not panfry or deep-fry acceptably or grill or barbecue at all. It hardly roasts or even toasts, and it only sort of bakes. For dishes you expect to be browned, some recipes make you brush the food with soy sauce

Buying Fish

• Fish should never smell fishy. The skin and gills should smell like fresh seaweed. As time passes, the seaweed smell disappears, then a sour odor develops, followed by the stench of ammonia or sulfur.

• The skin should look lively and iridescent, and the slime (or mucus) should be transparent and bright. As time takes its toll, both slime and skin become less lustrous; finally the mucus grows milky and opaque and the skin's pigmentation becomes dull and, at its worst, mottled and off-color.

• In most species, the eyes should be convex and bulging, with transparent corneas and bright black pupils. Then the cornea changes to opalescent and finally to milky; the pupils become dull black and then gray; and the eyes become slightly sunken, then flat, and finally concave in their center.

• The gills should be brightly colored with no trace of mucus. (Lift the stiff gill cover to see the gills.) As the days draw on, the gills become dull, then discolored and yellowish; clear mucus appears, then becomes opaque and milky.

• The body should feel firm, elastic, and smooth, bouncing back when you press it. As the flesh grows increasingly soft, the scales detach more easily from the skin and the surface becomes wrinkled. Inside, the color along the backbone changes from neutral to slightly pink, then full pink, and finally to red.

Incidentally, the best way to store a whole fish is by keeping it under slowly melting ice, not on top of it (as many reputable fish markets do, though it's next to useless). The melting ice keeps the entire fish at 32° F. and helps wash away bacteria.

423

and paprika or Kitchen Bouquet fluid or, in a stunning number of instances, dehydrated onion soup or dried spaghetti sauce mix. The other recipes try to persuade you not to care.

The one kind of cooking a microwave oven does, and often does quite well, is boiling and its cousins—steaming, poaching, braising, and stewing—and most microwave fish recipes use one of these techniques. So I chose what looked like the best recipes from the best cookbooks in my microwave library and went to work.

The *truite au bleu* did not turn blue and was watery and dull. Bluefish with fresh fennel worked better, if you like steamed bluefish. Fillet of sole amandine was tasteless, decomposed, and swimming in broth, and the almonds had not browned. Whiting *en colère* (biting its own tail) was delicate and moist itself, although the cream sauce never thickened and the parsley was overdone. Swordfish, dry and mushy, lacked taste and, though cooked without liquid, was surrounded by a pool of pungent fish broth; apparently, the flavor of the fish ended up in the dish. Whole trout with lemon butter was quite good but unevenly cooked. Paupiettes of sole and salmon were gray, rubbery, dry, and almost tasteless, the very defects the recipe had railed against in oven-baked paupiettes; possibly I had the timing wrong, but I do not like paupiettes enough to give it a second try. Medallions of salmon were firm and tasty, but much of the taste came from the marinade of mustard, olive oil, and lemon, which was so good that, having grown weary of steamed fish, I broke the rules and grilled a salmon steak smeared with the marinade in my powerful salamander broiler. The results, I regret, were wonderful, better than anything my microwave had produced.

Step Five: The making of a microwave chef. The *Wall Street Journal* reports that 40 percent of the efforts of this country's largest food and flavor company will be devoted in 1988 to making microwavable convenience foods taste like real food. So you can expect to spend much of your time figuring out how to adapt your favorite recipes. Salt in the microwave leaves brown spots on vegetables and leaches out water, withering them. Flour or cornstarch must be used to thicken sauces because shorter cooking times make for less evaporation, and intensity of flavor never develops. Quantities of garlic, ginger, scallions, fresh herbs, alcohol and wine, and spices like coriander and cardamon should be increased because their essential flavors are volatile. Pepper, dry herbs, nutmeg, and cinnamon should be reduced because their flavor has less time to mellow. Pieces of food should be cut into regular shapes (ideally three-inch cubes) and cooked with pieces of the same density, or you can mix smaller high-density pieces with larger low-density ones. Pieces should be arranged in a ring and separated from one another with thicker parts to the outside. By the way, did I warn you not to put recycled paper plates and towels in the oven? They may contain metal particles and cause a nasty fire.

425

Cooking times are very tricky. A recipe will need more or less time in the oven if your baking dish differs in size, shape, or composition from the one the recipe writer used or if the dispersion pattern of energy in your oven differs or if your line voltage varies (common in urban areas) or if you cook more than 3,500 feet above sea level or if your fishmonger has a two-pound sea bass today instead of the one-and-a-half-pounder the recipe calls for. A thirty-second error can ruin your masterpiece.

Cooking time can pose a problem with conventional methods, but then at least we are in closer contact with the food. We feel the heat, watch the surface of the food change in texture, color, and moisture, touch it, smell the changes. One or two microwave cookbooks suggest that you watch the food carefully, but the interior bulb is dim, the door is sealed, the window is small and shielded, and the food is covered with paper towels or waxed paper or steamy plastic wrap that seems to melt into the glass of the sizzling dish.

Undaunted, however, I pursued three favorite fish dishes that should do quite nicely in the microwave.

I sometimes steam flounder with a sweet and spicy sauce for fifteen minutes in a sixteen-inch bamboo steamer set over a large wok filled with boiling water, heat the thick dark red sauce of hoisin, bean paste, soy, garlic, and ginger on a burner, pour it over the fish, and decorate it with slivered scallions. This time I microwaved the fish for seven minutes on a tightly wrapped plate with no liquid other than the *shao-hsing* wine rubbed into the flounder and let it stand while microwaving the sauce. It took three flounders to get it right. The results were more than merely edible, but no matter how I varied the microwave time, the flesh of the flounder never achieved that firm but tender consistency it does in a real steamer. Almost every microwave cookbook writer

marvels at the pool of delicious stock that miraculously forms around a piece of fish cooked without liquid. Some consider this yet another free bonus from the microwave, but any child can tell you that when flavor leaves the fish, the fish loses flavor. Recipes that have you microwave a fillet or whole fish loosely covered with paper towels or waxed paper produce a drier, firmer, but less evenly cooked result than when you seal the dish tightly with plastic wrap. Odd as it sounds, how you cover the fish may be the key to how it comes out.

I can still remember the *loup en papillote* at a restaurant near Antibes. Steam-baked instead of steamed, the whole fish—a type of sea bass—was stuffed with aromatic herbs and vegetables, wrapped in parchment paper, and baked until the paper had browned and puffed and the fish was infused with the perfumes of Provence. In my microwave version the paper remained a ghostly white, but the fish was good. I unsuccessfully tried to concoct a browning liquid from soy and sugar just for the parchment, with the excuse that it would never touch the food. Moral purity disintegrates quickly at 2,450 megahertz.

Finally a scallop mousse microwaved in individual ramekins, unmolded, and surrounded by a *sauce Joinville* made with shrimp and tomatoes, also microwaved: I had the naive idea that custards and timbales would cook to silky perfection in the microwave without scrambling or stiffening. Not true. The waves concentrate on the sides of the dish, leaving the center cool.

In my forthcoming monograph "Microwave: Cult or Culture?" I shall demonstrate that microwave fanatics share a culture—in the anthropological sense of a "trait complex exhibited by a tribe or separate unit of mankind"—that borders on a cult. Its members huddle around the values of progress, speed, health, and freedom from dishwashing. They are prophets of the twenty-first century; we are "unregenerate stove cooks" indulging in the "luxury" of conventional cooking with our archaic equipment. They ignore the fact that progress brought us ultrapasteurized cream and processed-cheese spread, and they ignore recent findings that conventional steaming keeps in as many vitamins as microwaving, which depletes phosphorus, iron, and riboflavin from meat. They are right, though, about dishwashing. Most microwave recipes are mixed, cooked, and served in one glass dish and some on paper plates or towels.

At its best my new microwave oven is a nifty tool to have at hand. Paraphrasing what the great eater A. J. Liebling was fond of saying about his writing, my microwave cooks better than anything that cooks faster and faster than anything that cooks better. In the pantheon of kitchen equipment it stands just below the food processor and just above the pressure cooker. To microwave fanatics, this may sound like faint praise. To my pressure cooker, it is praise enough indeed.

March 1988

Author's Note:
This was the first food piece I ever wrote.

Back of the Box

I spent last week cooking strictly from the back of the box. It all started one fatal evening when my wife came home from work and found me standing in the kitchen, a melting slab of raw bacon in each hand and briny tears of defeat welling up in each eye. Every surface in the kitchen, my clothing, the open pages of a brand-new cookbook—all were covered with slices and shards and strips and scraps and shreds of oozing bacon.

The cookbook was an important and opulent new work of delicious and fanciful modern French food. I had waited several days for a free evening to cook from it. For starters I had chosen a seemingly simple but dreamy-looking potato, cheese, and bacon cake in which layers of thinly sliced potatoes and sprinklings of cheese are all wrapped up in bacon and baked in a hot oven until the potatoes are tender, the cheese melts into them, and the bacon is crisp and crackling.

You begin by slicing six ounces of slab bacon very thinly. Then you line a nine-inch round cake pan with the bacon slices in "spiral fashion" so that their ends drape naturally over the edge of the pan, add the layers of cheese and potatoes, then gather the ends of the bacon to enclose the potatoes.

I know better than trying to slice a slab of bacon at room temperature. It bends and wobbles and won't hold its shape, and the slices come out thick and irregular. But I have a policy of slavishly adhering to another writer's instructions, at least the first time. And I love following orders. Nothing makes me happier than curling up with the ninety-seven-page instruction book for a new VCR or making an elaborate recipe that demands exacting labor over several days or weeks.

It was lucky that I had bought an entire side of bacon because I wasted two pounds of it before managing to extract six ounces of reasonably thin slices. My arm ached, disorder and grease were spreading throughout the kitchen, and the estimated time of arrival for dinner was pushed back to nine o'clock. I moved on to interpret "spiral fashion."

My dictionary says that a spiral begins at the center of a circle and curves out toward the circumference. This is what I tried to make my six ounces of bacon slices do, first flat and then on edge, sometimes starting from the center and sometimes from the rim. Nothing worked. Another hour had passed.

4 2 9

I reinterpreted "spiral fashion" to mean "spoke fashion." Slipping my electronic calculator into a Baggie to protect it from the grease, I determined that a 9-inch potato cake requires 184 square inches of bacon to enclose it—at least twenty-two slices if none of them overlap by more than a millimeter. I resumed slicing. When my hungry wife found me an hour later, everything in the kitchen glistened, and I had lost the ability to speak. My wife read the recipe and shrugged. "This thing will never work," she said. It was the first recipe that had stumped me in fifteen years. It was ten o'clock.

As we cleaned up the kitchen, my voice returned, and we reminisced about those recipes on the back of the box—simple, hearty formulas for good, solid, fail-safe American food—the dips and meat loaves, the quick cakes and no-cook fudge, the casseroles and bakes and instant puddings of our innocent youth. My wife's favorite was her mother's version of Campbell's Tuna Noodle Casserole. Mine was Nabisco's Famous Chocolate Wafer Refrigerator Roll. On special occasions my mother would spread whipped cream on the wide, thin cookies, assemble the layers

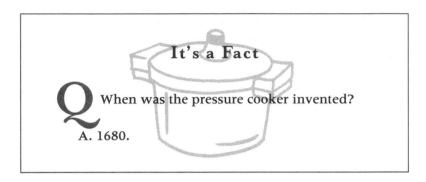

It's a Fact

Q When was the pressure cooker invented?

A. 1680.

into a long log, and chill it until the cookies grew soft and moist, like dark-chocolate cake. When the roll was sliced diagonally, the narrow white and brown stripes formed a festive, elegant pattern. How I longed for those guileless days when whipped cream and chocolate wafers made for gastronomic bliss.

Together my wife and I ravenously read the packages, bottles, and cans on our shelves to find something to cook for dinner. We were not in the mood for Argo Cornstarch Classic Lemon Meringue Pie (which has become the standard American recipe), Quaker's excellent Oatmeal Cookies, Karo Syrup Easy Caramel Popcorn, or any of the five pecan pies on various other packages. The truth is, our kitchen is not well stocked with packaged foods, canned vegetables, frozen chicken parts, or preformed hamburgers. For years I have done my food shopping nearly every day and cooked everything from scratch. In the process, I may have lost touch with the modern American tabletop.

It was eleven o'clock. We ordered in a very large Chinese meal from the place around the corner and did a week of menu planning. To refresh our memories of the classics, we turned to Ceil Dyer's *Best Recipes* (Galahad Books) and Michael McLaughlin's *The Back of the Box Gourmet* (Simon & Schuster). The first has an endless number of recipes; the second is more discriminating, amplifying its recipes with photographs and lore.

The next day, we toured the local supermarkets and returned home with a taxiful of shopping bags. Even before removing our coats, we had fished out an envelope of Lipton's Onion Recipe

Soup Mix and a pint of sour cream, stirred them together, and opened the bag of Ridgies potato chips shown in the serving suggestion on the box of Lipton's. It took us just fifteen seconds to prepare the ur-dip, Lipton's California Dip, purportedly invented by a California homemaker who told Lipton about it in 1963. No mess, no bother, no dishes to clean (we mixed everything in the sour cream's plastic container), and sheer perfection on the palate.

For the next hour we assembled a feast that could have fed a family of ten, while investigating whether Ridgies or smooth potato chips are the ideal vehicle for conveying California Dip from package to mouth. Our main course was Quaker's Prize-Winning Meat Loaf, accompanied by Campbell's Green Bean Bake with Durkee french-fried onions. Our desserts were various and many—Ritz crackers' Mock Apple Pie and Kellogg's never-fail Rice Krispies Marshmallow Squares to begin with—and as we cheerfully rinsed off the tiny number of utensils these recipes required, my wife whipped up her excellent variation on Nestlé's Original Toll House Cookies.

Most gastronomes would agree that the recipe on the cheery yellow bag of Nestlé's Semi-Sweet Toll House Morsels (either the Original Toll House Cookie recipe bought in the 1930s from Ruth Wakefield of the Toll House Inn in Whitman, Massachusetts, or the slightly altered post-1970 version, which Nestlé also calls the Original) has made all other recipes for chocolate-chip cookies superfluous. Everybody fiddles with the Original, but my wife's fiddling is, quite frankly, the best, producing thin and crisp yet chewy treats. I have recently received permission to reprint her formula. Only the quantities have been changed.

4 3 1

1 extra-large egg
1 teaspoon vanilla extract
1²/₃ cups all-purpose flour (measured by the
   scoop-and-level method)

1 teaspoon (scant) baking soda
1 teaspoon salt
1½ cups (3 sticks) softened butter
⅔ cup white granulated sugar
¾ cup firmly packed light brown sugar
¼ cup firmly packed dark brown sugar
2 cups (12-ounce package) chocolate chips
1 cup coarsely chopped walnuts

To make the cookies, follow the mixing and baking instructions on the back of the Nestlé's Semi-Sweet Toll House Morsel bag.

I cannot say that our paradise was without its serpents. Quaker's Prize-Winning Meat Loaf, which predictably substitutes Quaker oats for the usual bread or cracker crumbs, may have won a prize somewhere for oat cookery, but it does not compare with either of our mothers' meat loaves or hypermodern variations like Paul Prudhomme's Cajun recipe in *Louisiana Kitchen* (Morrow). The aggressively dull flavor of the oats becomes distasteful after a few bites. And Quaker's makes you chop a quarter cup of your own onions, which to my mind violates the spirit of convenience cuisine. I was still feeling phobic about intricate knife work.

Campbell's Green Bean Bake is, with the probable exception of Nestlé's Toll House Cookies, the most popular back-of-the-box recipe ever created. You microwave up some frozen green beans and mix them in a casserole with a can of Campbell's condensed cream of mushroom soup, milk, soy sauce, pepper, and half a three-and-a-half-ounce can of French-fried onion rings. Bake for twenty-five minutes, top with the remaining onion rings, and bake for five minutes more, whereupon the onions become golden and crispy.

My wife cannot abide the infinite-shelf-life flavor of canned soup, but the onion rings alone redeem Campbell's Green Bean Bake for me. Therein lies the problem. The only national brand of canned French-fried onion rings is Durkee, and sometime after Campbell invented the recipe, Durkee went and downsized its can to 2.8 ounces, a full 20 percent shrinkage. I suppose there is nothing that Campbell can do about corporate policy at Durkee, but I resented having to buy two cans of Durkee's and waste most of the second. To my taste, 2.8 ounces of canned French-fried onion rings is simply not enough for a proper Green Bean Bake. Three and a half ounces is perfect.

I telephoned Campbell headquarters to complain. Its exemplary spokesman Kevin Lowery quickly mesmerized me with details of the company's side-of-the-can recipe ventures. Every evening in America, one million cans of Campbell's soup are used as an ingredient in dinner, about a third of all the soup they sell. Thursday night is the most popular. Cream of mushroom, introduced in 1934, is still the clear winner. America buys 325 million cans of it every year, 80 percent as a sauce or flavoring in quick main courses and side dishes. Three of the five top-selling supermarket foods are Campbell's soups. Can you guess the other two?*

Six years ago the company published *Campbell's Creative Cooking with Soup*. It has sold two million copies (making it one of the most popular cookbooks of all time) and contains nineteen thousand recipes, each tested three times. Marcella Hazan once told me that Italian cuisine encompasses sixty thousand recipes. How much more rich and abundant is American cookery with its nineteen thousand ways to use condensed soup alone! That's a different recipe every day of the year for fifty-two years, far longer than the life span of the average marriage. And I haven't even told you about *Campbell's 75th Anniversary Cookbook*, published at the beginning of 1991. It sold 750,000 copies the first month. Campbell's research understandably demonstrates that it was they who invented the Classic Tuna Noodle Casserole, their

*Starkist tuna and Kraft macaroni and cheese.

433

second most popular recipe of all time. My own research is silent on the subject.

Mr. Lowery told me that Campbell's vast market surveys have discovered the attributes of the ideal recipe. It must be prepared in thirty minutes or less (including any cooked ingredients within it). It must be a main dish, because homemakers are less willing to try a new recipe for a side dish or a dessert. And it must contain only readily available ingredients, which means that these should not merely be widely displayed on supermarket shelves but, preferably, already be stocked in most people's homes. I found this ideal in sharp and ironic contrast to the recipes I write. Mine take between four hours and four days to prepare, are always for side dishes or desserts, and contain ingredients that you must either send away for or bring back from a trip to Alba or Kyoto.

Campbell's most popular new recipe is Chicken-Broccoli Divan, a casserole of fresh or frozen broccoli, cooked chicken or turkey, and a can of Campbell's condensed cream of broccoli soup, all with a topping of bread crumbs and cheese. "Divan" is a culinary term I have encountered only on the backs of boxes and in traditional American cookbooks like *A Century of Mormon Cookery* and *Joy of Cooking*, and Campbell's had no idea of its source. "Divan" sounds vaguely French, but my old *Larousse Gastronomique* passes from "diuretic" to "dive" without a pause, and among his 5,012 recipes, Escoffier can't be bothered. In *Webster's Second*, "divan" is a Persian and Turkish word for a book of many leaves, a council of state, the room where such a council convenes, a raised cushioned platform upon which its members (or anybody else) can sit or recline, and, especially today, a large couch without a back or sides. On the theory that the meaning of "divan" had somehow expanded to include the delicacies upon which members of the divan feasted while reclining, Levantine style, on the divans, I combed through my classical Turkish and Persian cookbooks. There was not even a morsel named "divan."

At last I discovered that a Divan is a creation of all-American provenance. According to Craig Claiborne, the dish was invented in a New York restaurant of bygone days called Divan Parisien, where poached chicken was laid on a bed of broccoli and covered with hollandaise sauce. Thus "broccoli" in the title of Campbell's recipe is as redundant as its inclusion in the dish is expected. How chicken Divan spread like wildfire into the cookbooks and onto the packages of America's heartland I will never fathom. My etymological research left me too weary to attempt Campbell's Chicken-Broccoli Divan.

The star of our first back-of-the-box meal was Ritz crackers' Mock Apple Pie, which has appeared on the back of the box since the beginning of recorded history and probably forever will. The recipe always sounded like a prank to me, which is why I had never tried it. You line a pie plate with pastry and drop in thirty-six broken Ritz crackers instead of apples. Then you boil up two cups each of sugar and water with a little cream of tartar, add lemon rind and lemon juice, allow the syrup to cool, and pour it over the Ritz crackers. Dot with butter, sprinkle with cinnamon, cover with the top pastry crust, bake for thirty-five minutes, and cool completely.

What emerges is a tasty dessert that cannot easily be distinguished from real apple pie! This has led to a far-reaching and heretical hypothesis: *Cooked* apples have little taste of their own. We identify them by the cinnamon, sugar, and lemon juice with which they are always flavored in American cooking, along with their characteristic mushiness. I fed this pie to a self-styled apple lover. She could not believe that it contained not one apple molecule.

Why anybody would bother to make Ritz crackers' Mock Apple Pie more than once—except for the sheer miracle of it—is another matter entirely. Most of the labor in making a pie is spent on the pastry. Apples cost no more than Ritz crackers, apples are not fattening, and the surgeon general has not yet said that you will die if you eat apples. In her *Fannie Farmer Baking Book* (Knopf), Marion Cunningham includes a version based on soda crackers that, she writes, antedates the Civil War; American pioneers could transport and store sugar and crackers more easily than apples.

As our week of back-of-the-box cooking raced happily on, a new dessert favorite quickly emerged: Milky Way Bar Swirl Cake. A Milky Way bar is the only food I know that is equally delicious frozen, at room temperature, and, as I have now discovered, at 350 degrees. The Milky Way was created in 1923, and it is the best-selling candy bar in the world; everywhere outside the United States it is labeled "Mars Bar," though everywhere it consists of the same malted-milk nougat topped with a layer of caramel, all dipped in milk chocolate. The Mars company is best known for its M & M's recipes. When it first printed a recipe for Party Cookies (really Toll House Cookies with M & M's replacing the semisweet chocolate chips) on the twelve-ounce supermarket package, sales doubled! Less renowned is the eight-page four-color recipe booklet that Mars slipped into its six-pack of full-size Milky Ways in 1986. I have obtained a copy.

The main attraction is Milky Way Bar Swirl Cake, a delicious yellow Bundt cake made from a commercial mix with two Milky Ways swirled inside and another two melted and dripped over the top, where they magically harden into a glossy glaze. The only problem we encountered in making the Swirl Cake was another flagrant case of furtive downsizing. The recipe calls for four 2.23-ounce bars. Milky Ways now on the market weigh 2.15 ounces, a shrinkage of 3.6 percent. Obsessive recipe followers will buy an extra bar, as I did, slice off one-seventh of it, and eat the rest either frozen or at room temperature.

I cannot count the number of boxes of Domino light brown sugar I rotated last week on supermarket shelves in search of the simple and delicious recipe I remember for Butterscotch Nut Ice Cream. Neither of my back-of-the-box anthologies seems to have heard of it. A call to Domino exposed my recollection as only partially correct. A recipe did appear for a brief period, but unlike my adaptation of it, the original employed an ice-cube tray instead of an ice-cream freezer and required the annoying use of a double boiler. When I described my variation to the lady at Domino, she offered to have it reformulated and tested by one of their home economists, which I thought would be fun, though I then med-

Milky Way Bar Swirl Cake (adapted)

4 Milky Way bars (2.23 ounces each), sliced
1 cup plus 2 tablespoons plus 2 teaspoons water
1 package (18½ ounces) pudding-in-the-mix yellow cake mix
⅓ cup (5 tablespoons) melted butter, cooled
3 eggs, at room temperature
2 tablespoons all-purpose flour
Confectioners' sugar
2 tablespoons butter, for the glaze

Stir the slices from two Milky Ways with 2 table-spoons of water in a medium saucepan over medium heat until smooth, and remove from the heat. Meanwhile, generously butter and flour a 12-cup Bundt pan. Using an electric mixer, prepare the cake batter with the ⅓ cup melted butter (even if the package specifies oil), 3 eggs, and 1 cup of water. Scoop out ⅔ cup of the cake batter and stir it, along with the flour, into the melted Milky Ways. Pour the rest of the cake batter into the Bundt pan, and spoon the Milky Way mixture in a ring on the center of the batter, avoiding the sides of the pan. Swirl the batters together with a knife. Bake at 350° F. for 40 minutes and let cool in the pan on a rack for 25 minutes. Invert and unmold the cake and sprinkle lightly with confectioners' sugar.

While the cake is cooling, wipe out the saucepan, add the other two sliced Milky Ways along with 2 tablespoons of butter and 2 teaspoons of water, and stir over medium heat until smooth. Let cool until it reaches the consistency of a glaze and drip it over the cake.

dled with their version, in part because it did not contain enough pecans. I tell you all this so that you can blame me if it does not please you. But it surely will.

Butterscotch Nut Ice Cream

2 eggs
1¼ cups firmly packed Domino light brown sugar
2 cups milk
2 cups heavy cream
2 teaspoons vanilla extract
1 cup shelled pecans, coarsely chopped
2 tablespoons butter
½ teaspoon salt

Lightly whisk the eggs in a 2-quart saucepan and stir in the brown sugar and the milk. Stir constantly over medium heat until the mixture thickens and coats the back of a spoon (180° F. on a candy thermometer). Strain into a bowl, cool to room temperature, add the cream and the vanilla, and chill overnight in the refrigerator.

The next day, toast the pecans in the butter in a large skillet for 5 to 10 minutes over medium heat, stirring often. Toss the pecans with the salt and spread them out on paper towels to drain and cool. Stir the pecans into the ice-cream mixture right before freezing in an ice-cream machine. Makes 1½ quarts.

Packages today are so cluttered with nutritional information, ingredient lists, health claims, and environmental sermons that hardly any room is left for recipes. And the endless list of chemical additives on most packaged foods is enough to send me back to slicing slab bacon at room temperature. Yet food labelers seem able to keep pace with the changing American palate: every yellow winter squash at my vegetable shop has a recipe printed on plastic in English and French and glued to its side. The public is still ceaselessly enthusiastic about back-of-the-box recipes— "multiuse soups" are the fastest-growing sector of Campbell's business. When manufacturers remove a favorite formula from their boxes, as when Domino dropped the butter-cream frosting from its confectioners' sugar, consumers flood them with calls. When Milky Way inexplicably changed the name of its miniature fun size bars to "snack size," and home Milky Way cooks could no longer find the precise product called for in the old recipes, the outcry was so thunderous that Mars was forced to change back the name to "fun size."

439

Just before my back-of-the-box mania went into remission, I resolved to prepare the very first recipe ever printed on the back of an American box. Unearthing it was not as simple as it sounds. Until the Civil War, grocery stores presented and sold their food in bulk—mounds of butter and cheese, bins of sugar and flour, barrels of crackers. (As late as 1928, only 10 percent of all the sugar sold at retail came in packages.) According to Waverley Root, the first machine-made, collapsible, foldable cardboard boxes did not appear until 1879, the achievement of a New York manufacturer named Robert Gair, who had previously produced paper bags (which in their useful square-bottomed incarnation were not invented until 1870). And I was looking for a recipe much older than that.

After a long and winding quest, I finally hit pay dirt. The recipe dates from 1802, and it is, as you might expect, a macaroni-and-cheese casserole.

There was a great vogue for Italian pasta among the upper classes in both France and the United States at the end of the eighteenth century. Most pasta was imported from Sicily by way of London until Lewis Fresnaye, an émigré from the French Revolution, hired some Italian pasta makers and set up shop in Philadelphia. But cookbooks were scarce. The first one originating in this country, *American Cookery . . . By Amelia Simmons, an American Orphan,* was not published until 1796, when the average book cost the equivalent of ninety dollars. So Fresnaye wrapped each bundle of his dried vermicelli and macaroni in a wide sheet of paper printed with recipes for their preparation.

Several years ago Mary Anne Hines of the Philadelphia Library Company discovered one of Fresnaye's broadsides from 1802 in the library's culinary collection, and food historian William Woys Weaver recognized and researched its momentous significance. You can prepare this recipe as easily as if you had found it on the back of a package of Kraft's.

440

Lewis Fresnaye's 1802 Macaroni and Cheese

Take six pints of water and boil it with a sufficiency of salt, when boiling, stir in it one pound of paste [pasta], let it boil [about eight minutes], then strain the water well off, and put the paste in a large dish, mixing therewith six ounces of grated parmisan or other good cheese; then take four ounces of good butter and melt it well in a saucer or small pot, and pour it over the paste while both are warm. It would be an improvement after all is done, to keep the dish a few minutes in a hot oven, till the butter and cheese have well penetrated the paste.

It may be rendered still more delicate by boiling the paste in milk instead of water and put a little gravy of meat, or any other meat sauce thereon.

February 1992

Repairman

How can I ever forget that fresh coconut cake? There were six layers in all, each brushed with coconut-milk syrup and spread with a luscious filling of fresh coconut, butter, and cream. When the layers were stacked on each other, the cake was taller than it was wide, and then the outside was covered with silky vanilla frosting set with crunchy coconut curls. I had stumbled across a generous wedge of it at K-Paul's New York, Paul Prudhomme's onetime northern outpost, and it was the most delicious southern cake any of us had ever tasted. The people at K-Paul's New Orleans headquarters swore that the recipe had already been published in *The Prudhomme Family Cookbook* (Morrow). It looked like a six-hour project.

Thanksgiving arrived, a day when everybody's culinary dreams are meant to be realized, and it seemed the perfect moment to re-create the Prudhomme family's Fresh Coconut Cake and carry it in triumph to a friend's house for a grateful feast. Six hours remained until dinner.

Recalling that I had once struggled for two days with a stubborn coconut before it yielded up its meat for a special ice-cream project of mine, I consulted my vast kitchen library and particularly my two linear feet of kitchen manuals. Among what I estimate to be twenty thousand kitchen tips bound between their covers was lots of advice about the best way to drain, shell, peel, and shred or mince coconut meat. The best method, even including my hand-cranked, ten-dollar grater from southern India, where coconut is as common as salt or pepper, is to put the coconut in a 400-degree oven for fifteen minutes until it cracks all by itself and then peel off the tough brown skin with a vegetable peeler, with occasional assists from a small paring knife honed on my Chef's Choice model 110 sharpener—despite warnings in several kitchen manuals that oven heat will ruin the meat. Elapsed time: nearly two hours for four coconuts.

Everything went smoothly until I got to the cake batter. I combined the sugar and eggs in my electric mixer, added the softened butter, and beat in the milk. It was then that I suddenly began to have trouble breathing—the batter had become completely separated! Firm yellow spheroids the size of small peas floated in a thin translucent greasy soup. Things turned ugly when I increased the speed of the mixer, and the soup began to slosh onto the counter. Dinner was now three hours away, the six layers were not even close to being baked and cooled, I was out of eggs, and the stores were closed.

I turned again to my kitchen collection. The minutes flew by as ten desperate fingers flipped through manuals, cookbook chapters, and magazine articles, searching for "cake batter, separated," "separated cake batter," "batter, cake, separated," and so forth. One of the earliest cookbooks in existence, *De re coquinaria* (ascribed to one or more cooks of ancient Rome named Apicius), devotes its very first chapter to food repair and kitchen tricks. Did you know that you can clear up badly muddied white wine by mixing it with bean meal or the whites of three eggs? And that you can make ordinary Spanish olive oil taste like costly Liburnian oil by adding Cyprian rush, elecampane, and green laurel leaves? But Apicius has nothing to say about curdled coconut cake.

A cookbook from seventeenth-century England includes tricks for "ye boyleing of yellow peese" and a special way "to boyle Spinage green," but nothing about bungled batter.

Dinnertime crept closer. As I stood moodily at the window, I considered following the example of the great Vatel. In April 1671, Vatel was chef to the prince of Condé and had been engaged to organize the visit of King Louis XIV and its climactic dinner for three thousand guests. Madame de Sévigné tells the story in her April 26 letter to Madame de Grignan: Vatel had gone twelve nights without sleep. The king arrived on Thursday; there were "hunting, lanterns, moonlight, a gentle walk, supper served in a spot carpeted with daffodils. [But] there was no roast at one or two tables because of several unexpected guests." Vatel was humiliated. Then the fireworks, which had cost sixteen thousand francs, were a failure owing to fog.

At four the next morning, Vatel rushed madly around, trying to assemble the fish for Friday's dinner. When a supplier erroneously informed him that only two small loads of fish could be found, the great Vatel "went to his room, put his sword up against the door, and ran it through his heart." Just then, great quantities of fish began to arrive.

If I lived above the third floor, I might even now be with the great Vatel. But in the nick of time I came to my senses, drew back from the window, and returned to my kitchen manuals.

Some of them specialize in cleanliness instead of cuisine. They say you can shine copper pots by rubbing them with a paste of flour, vinegar, and salt. (It works only a third as well as copper polish.) Or try baking soda, which was used to clean the inside skin of the Statue of Liberty. A Philippine book of household hints recommends rubbing a halved *calamansi* on your wooden cutting board to remove discoloration. But I cannot find *calamansi* in any dictionary. Is Colgate toothpaste ideal for polishing silverware and gold, as one book suggests? Pick up pieces of shattered glass with a slice of white bread, another book advises, and take your dirty miniblinds to a car wash. (Then what?) According to the Wisk 1995 Cleaning Census, 38 percent of Americans who do laundry at least once a month are very or somewhat worried that home entertaining may ruin their possessions. Dial (800) ASK-WISK for

The Dazey Stripper

It was in 1972 near the Cenote de los Sacrificios at the ruins of Chichén Itzá in the Yucatán—a sacred well or cistern where vestal virgins were sacrificed to the Mayan gods—that I first encountered the automatic fruit and vegetable peeler. After a long trudge under the merciless sun and a cursory glance at the bottomless Cenote, in which not even one vestal virgin could be glimpsed, I saw an old woman sitting nearby on a folding chair behind a shiny steel hand-cranked peeler mounted on a tall wooden stand. For twenty-five cents U.S., she peeled oranges and apples and sold them to thirsty tourists. For an extra twenty-five cents U.S., she let me play with her peeler.

Years later at a dinner party I discovered the Dazey Stripper in my hostess's kitchen while she was busy serving drinks in the living room. I inserted a nearby apple, stood back, and watched in wonder as the Dazey Stripper rapidly and automatically removed the peel in one continuous band. As I also learned, just as my hostess returned to the kitchen, the Dazey Stripper just as rapidly and automatically splatters ripe peaches all over the wall.

That's because the Dazey Stripper was designed to peel *firm* fruits and vegetables. It is a compact, white plastic electric instrument consisting of an oblong platform from which a vertical shaft rises. You place a fruit or vegetable between two spiked plastic holders, raise the cutting blade assembly to the top of the shaft, and let it go. Automatically, the motor starts up, the fruit whirls around, and the cutting blade presses against it, paring an even spiral of skin as it descends. When the blade reaches the bottom, the whirling automatically stops. It works almost every time, even when the fruit is, like a pear, irregular. Watching the Dazey Stripper zest a lemon or an orange, peel a potato, or get an apple ready for a pie has become a source of endless fun and amazement in my household no matter how many times we use it.

445

Dazey Lemon Ice

A good friend of mine who owns one of New York's better restaurants was having trouble with his lemon sorbet. Either in tribute to my prowess at the ice-cream freezer or in desperation, he turned to me for help, and I offered to make five different lemon ices and let him choose. My favorite lemon ices are flavored with the zest—the yellow layer of peel but not the white part, or pith, which is quite bitter. I dreaded the prospect of zesting fifteen lemons with a traditional tool—a vegetable peeler, a zester, or an ordinary grater—because I typically wind up on the verge of exhaustion, my knuckles also zested. The Dazey Stripper was a godsend. The winning recipe:

1¼ cups water
1¼ cups sugar
6–7 lemons
1 orange, juiced

Combine the water and sugar in a 2-quart saucepan. Stir with a wooden spoon over high heat until the mixture comes to a full boil. Pour into a bowl and let cool. Dazey-strip the zest from 3 lemons, chop roughly, and infuse in the cool sugar syrup for 2 hours. Squeeze 1¾ cups of lemon juice (6–7 lemons) and mix into the sugar syrup with the juice of 1 orange. Strain into your ice-cream maker and freeze.

December 1988

advice about cleaning. But not about hideously separated fresh coconut cake batter. I tried.

Dozens of books concentrate on kitchen tricks, tips, *trucs* (French for "tricks"), and *tours de main*. So do the pages of helpful hints in food magazines. Fresh eggs will sink immediately in salted water, but bad eggs will float. (This seems to be true.) Chop onions without tears by wearing goggles, chilling the onion (partially successful), or lighting a candle on the cutting board to burn away the sulfurous gases (small or no benefit). Give gravy a warm, deep color (without ruining its flavor?) by adding instant-coffee powder. Set loaves of bread to rise in your dishwasher (leaving an inch of water in the bottom of the machine from the wash cycle and switching to the dry cycle for a minute or two). For instant whipped cream to garnish desserts, drop dollops (or pipe rosettes) of sweetened whipped cream on a cookie sheet, freeze, transfer to an airtight container, store in the freezer, and remove as you need them fifteen minutes before consuming (a wonderful *truc* that pops up in many sources). Skin hazelnuts by boiling them in water with a teaspoon of baking soda (not a chance). Make it easy to remove whole spices from a soup, stew, or sauce by first putting them in a mesh tea ball. Core and wash lettuces by rapping the bottom on the counter to loosen the core (which can now be pulled out in one piece), inverting, filling the hole with water to rinse out the dirt, and separating the leaves (works well with iceberg).

Keep egg yolks in the refrigerator up to three days by covering them with water (not bad). When you need a small amount of lemon juice, do not cut the fruit in half; just pierce it with a skewer, squeeze out some juice, and then refrigerate the fruit. (A terrific lemon saver. But once, when I squeezed the lemon with excessive force, the entire pointy end flew into my eye.) To cure excessive vomiting, try two teaspoons whiskey, one teaspoon water, and one teaspoon ground cinnamon. (Source: Charlotte,

447

It's a Fact

Q In the days before people had clocks, how did recipes specify cooking times?

A. An Anglo-Norman recipe from the 1200s instructed the reader to cook her chicken for the time it took to walk five or seven leagues (about fifteen or twenty miles), according to Terence Scully's paper "Peculiar Pots in Medieval France." As I have rarely walked five or seven leagues without breaks for lunch and little naps, I am glad to have been born in the age of Swatches.

Michigan, 1909. But what should you do for moderate vomiting?) To remove fat from stock, drop ice cubes into the pot and the fat will cling to them. (You'll need a lot of ice cubes. And remember to remove them before they melt.) When you water hanging plants, cover their bottom with shower caps. When your bread dough is rising, cover the bowl with a shower cap (not the same shower cap).

Put a bay leaf in flour to discourage bugs. Put an unwrapped stick of spearmint gum in flour to discourage bugs. (I have bought a PlenTPak of Doublemint and a bottle of bay leaves and await the results.) A sugar cube in olive oil keeps it from getting rancid. (I feel a little silly, but I'm trying it.) Freezing nuts makes them easier to crack and to extract the meats whole (slightly easier or not at all). Marinating meat does not tenderize it because the marinade does not penetrate very deeply. Add bread to boiling cauliflower or cabbage to inhibit the odor; add rye bread to broccoli. (The effect seems slight.) The combination of butter and oil does not burn as readily as butter alone. (Another source: The butter part of the mixture burns at the same low temperature as it always did.) Open oysters with a screwdriver instead of an oyster knife. Open oysters with a beer-can opener instead of a screwdriver. Open oysters only after freezing them for fifteen minutes. Do not open oysters by smashing them with a hammer. Give frosted cakes that sultry, molten, silky look with a hair dryer.

Alas, my own coconut cake was still in the embryonic, separated-batter stage. The only thing keeping me from starting over was that I had no eggs. I turned to books and charts specializing in the subject of substitutions. For croutons, substitute popcorn. If you run out of frozen strawberries, resort to fresh fruit! For whipped cream, follow this scientifically intriguing suggestion: slowly add baking soda to sour cream until it reaches the desired sweetness as the acidity is neutralized. (When the crisis was over, I tried it. The combination fizzed unpleasantly in my mouth, then made me gag and choke as it reached my throat.) I much preferred mixing a smashed banana with one stiffly beaten egg white plus sugar to taste. This was less an equivalent or facsimile of whipped cream than a fluffy white alternative topping that tastes reasonably good if you don't mind risking salmonella.

Of the thousands of substitutions in my collection, only four referred to eggs. If you need to make cookies and lack eggs (and baking powder and milk), you can try one writer's handy recipe for eggless potato-chip cookies. If you lack whole eggs, simply substitute two yolks plus a tablespoon of water (thanks a million). Grated carrot is a good substitute for eggs in boiled puddings. (I cannot imagine what this means.) The best suggestion of the four was the last: "Snow is an excellent substitute for eggs; two large spoonfuls will supply the place of one egg." Be sure to take the snow from a clean spot.

A happy thought struck me. Why not turn my catastrophic cake into a triumphant innovation?

On August 26, 1837, King Louis-Philippe and Queen Amélie of France were aboard the first train to run from Paris to Saint-Germain. A banquet was planned at the destination, and the menu included fried potatoes. When the train was late, Chef Colinet removed the slices of potatoes from the hot oil. The potatoes shrank and wrinkled, and Colinet considered joining the great Vatel. But later when he plunged the potatoes again into the sizzling oil, the slices magically puffed up into crisp and golden balloons! These *pommes soufflés* were Colinet's greatest triumph. Robert Courtine has called them "the poetry of the potato."

And I have read that fudge was created by mistake in Baltimore in 1886 when somebody overmixed and undercooked a pot of caramel.

And that *tarte Tatin* was discovered when the two unmarried Tatin daughters, in the town of Lamotte-Beuvron, just south of Orléans in France, dropped a pie. (The mechanics of this story make no sense; and a similar *tarte* was already popular throughout the Orléanais.) That Ruth Wakefield invented Toll House Cookies, when, trying to save time in baking chocolate cookies, she added pea-sized morsels of Nestlé's semisweet chocolate directly to her batter instead of melting them first. And that beurre blanc was invented around 1900 when an assistant to the cook of the Marquis de Goulaine left out the egg yolks while making a sauce béarnaise.

I stood staring at my bowl of bungled batter. I poked it with a spoon. I splashed it with a whisk. Not even a tiny triumph appeared. Two fleeting hours stood between me and Thanksgiving dinner.

Most kitchen manuals are full of advice about what you should have done in the first place to avoid fiascoes, failures, and flops (run a knife around the outside of a cheesecake as soon as it is baked or it may crack as it cools and shrinks) rather than how to repair them (hide the cracks with sour cream or sliced fruit). A handful of strategies do work amazingly well. Wilted salad greens perk up nicely when immersed for an hour or overnight in ice water in the refrigerator. Coffee does taste a little less bitter if you put two or three cardamom pods into the pot as the coffee brews. If you transfer burned soup to a clean pot and simmer it for another hour or two, the burned taste often disappears and seems like a deepened level of flavor.

The most popular kitchen tragedy appears to be the oversalted soup, vegetable, or sauce. The solutions fall into two categories. You can add and then discard something starchy (raw potato, beans, or bread crumbs) to absorb the salt. Or you can add brown sugar, parsley, or vinegar to fool the tongue. I have tested them all, and although the absorptive starch method sounded terrific, it failed in all its forms. Oddly enough, parsley and brown sugar work best.

The second most popular is the curdled, broken, or separated sauce (of the butter or egg variety, like hollandaise, mayonnaise, béarnaise, and so forth). Many of the proposed solutions actually work. At the first sign of trouble, remove the pan from the heat and whisk in a few tablespoons of ice water. Or immediately put it into a blender or food processor. If neither works, beat an extra egg yolk with a pinch of dry mustard and very gradually whisk in the curdled sauce. Or vigorously whisk together a little lemon juice and a tablespoon of the curdled hollandaise in a bowl, then gradually beat in the rest. But there were no solutions anywhere, before or after, for separated cake batter. I briefly swelled with pride as I concluded that I was the first person in the one-hundred-thousand-year history of cooking to have experienced this disaster.

Then it struck me. Why not try to repair my cake batter as though it were a curdled sauce! With seventy-five minutes left before dinner, I whirred the greasy, lumpy mixture in the blender in two batches. The result was wonderful—a smooth and shiny golden cream, ready for the addition of flour and baking powder. Into the greased and floured cake pans the batter went, three at a time. An hour later, six layers sat upon the cooling racks, ready to be glazed, filled, stacked, and frosted.

We arrived at dinner an hour late, giving holiday traffic as an excuse, and my fresh coconut cake was greeted with gasps of awe. But when our feast was through, I was depressed about the cake. In taste and texture, it could not have been the cake we had eaten at K-Paul's New York. Nobody asked for seconds.

Just before Christmas, another cake batter cataclysmically separated. I had just learned about Dial-a-Chef at (900) 933-CHEF, which you can call for cooking advice at $2.95 a minute. Speaking quickly, I told Dial-a-Chef about my problem. Just five minutes later they called back with the answer. Don't worry, add the flour and baking soda and proceed. Everything should come together nicely. And it did.

February 1996

451

Big Bird

My second-favorite Thanksgiving dinner took place eighteen years ago inside a midsize maroon rent-a-car. The sun had never shone more brightly than on that Thursday morning as the three of us set off from Manhattan for our friends' farm in upstate New York. But two hours later, in a blinding blizzard made of snowflakes the size of dinner plates, our car involuntarily left the highway and hurtled, headlights first, into a snowdrift big enough to hide a small suburban house. We ransacked the car for a shovel but could find nothing beyond the plum pie, the pumpkin pie, apple pie, two loaves of bread, and the quart of ancient Scotch that were to have been our contribution to the Thanksgiving feast.

Quickly calculating that we had enough gasoline to keep the car's heater running for two weeks, we forsook the ambition of reaching upstate New York and, using the Swiss Army knife and Sierra cups without which we never traveled more than a few feet from our apartment in those days, made quick and thankful work of the pies, bread, and Scotch. A brief nap followed. We awoke to find our snowdrift enfolded in a calm and cloudless evening rich with tow trucks, gas stations, and detailed instructions for driving back to the safety of Manhattan, just in time for a late supper at one of its excellent restaurants.

One happy feature of my second-favorite Thanksgiving dinner is that it was turkeyless. *The Oxford English Dictionary* defines turkey as "a well-known, large gallinaceous bird . . . now valued as a table fowl in all civilized lands." I couldn't disagree more. We eat turkey on Thanksgiving because turkey is an edible symbol, not because it is a valued contender at the table. It stands for the discovery of the foodstuffs of the New World and the brotherhood offered by Native Americans to those who would soon displace them. Edible symbols are rarely gastronomically rewarding, though I did once eat a superb dark-chocolate Eiffel Tower and a swan molded from first-rate chopped liver. If turkeys were not a symbol, we would never eat as many of them as we do. Their meat is nearly always bland and stringy, and their shape is entirely incorrect.

The best part of a roast turkey is its skin. Modern turkey breeders, responding to an apparent demand for more white and less dark meat, have developed a bird consisting mainly of a huge, nearly spherical breast and short, skinny legs and thighs. Yet the breast of the bird is surely its least savory part, and its spherical shape is surely a mistake. Remember what we learned in high school about spheres? Of all geometric figures, the sphere has the lowest ratio of surface to volume; a spherical turkey, therefore, has the lowest ratio of skin to meat. How much more gastronomically delightful would be to breed modern turkey in the shape, say, of a two-foot pizza with little wings and legs at the circumference and two broad surfaces of delicious, crackling, savory, golden-russet skin with very little meat inside!

Even as a symbol, the turkey falls short in at least four ways:

1. The Pilgrims probably did not eat turkey at the first Thanksgiving dinner in 1621. The only firsthand account of the feast, reprinted in the Plimouth Plantation's *Thanksgiving Primer,* does not mention turkey. According to Evan Jones in *American Food* (Overlook), the Pilgrims dined on venison, roast duck, roast goose, clams, eels, corn, beans, wheat and corn breads, leeks, watercress, wild plums, and homemade wine. It is doubtful that the banqueters even had thanksgiving in mind.

2. The Indians did not purposefully feed the Pilgrims or even introduce them to terrific New World foodstuffs in their devastat-

ing first year on these shores. According to Waverley Root and Richard de Rochemont, Native Americans did feed the colonists in Virginia, thus saving their lives, but those in Massachusetts were more suspicious. "It was an Indian habit to stow away caches of long-lasting foods in various places where they might one day be needed; it was the Pilgrims' good luck to stumble on one of these caches, which kept them alive (some of them) over their first terrible winter," they write in *Eating in America*.

3. Even if the Pilgrims did eat turkey at the first "Thanksgiving dinner" in 1621, they surely had tasted much finer turkey back home in England. The turkey, of course, originated not in Turkey but in the New World, where there were several related species; the Mexican version had long been domesticated by the Aztecs when the Spanish conquistadores discovered Mexico in 1518; they brought the Mexican turkey back to Europe, where it was soon raised commercially. In a cookbook of 1615, *The English Hus-wife*, turkey appears nearly as often as chicken; it was surely familiar to the Pilgrims when they arrived here and found the Eastern wild turkey, a species inferior to the domesticated Mexican but a turkey all the same.

Between the time they landed in December of 1620 and their feast nearly a year later, the Pilgrims undoubtedly ate wild turkey, even if they forwent the large gallinaceous fowl at the famous feast itself. Wild game was so plentiful in North America that some writers attribute the success of colonization to its availability. Others believe that the inexhaustible plentitude of wild game, including turkeys, gave rise to the American obsession with meat, which, according to Waverley Root, astonished European visitors for two centuries.

So the turkey really symbolizes unbridled carnivorous behavior and the cardiac problems that that brings. The true meaning of the Thanksgiving menu lies in the garnishes, not in the main course—in the uniquely New World cranberry, pumpkin, sweet potatoes, corn, beans, and other treasures the Europeans found growing here. That's why I consider it a quasi-religious duty to consume a generous range and amount of chocolate on this holiday. You can't give thanks without it.

4. The turkey got its silly name through two or three mistakes. You might guess that the name stemmed from a mistaken belief that Columbus had landed in Asia. You would be wrong. When the Spanish brought the turkey back home only twenty-six years after Columbus's first voyage, Europeans confused it with the guinea fowl, a distinct bird of African origin known to Aristotle and Pliny, and assigned to it the name they already applied to the guinea fowl. For the English, this name was "turkey" because they believed that the African bird had come to Europe through lands controlled by the Turks; now the Aztec bird became a "turkey," too. The Germans called both the old African and new Mexican fowl *kalekuttisch hun*, or "Calcutta hen" (similar to the Dutch *kalkoen*), and the French named it *coq d'inde* or simply *d'inde*, which then became the modern *dinde*—all of these meaning "bird of India." To the Europeans, Turkey and India were more or less in the same neighborhood.

All of this is, of course, a futile exercise in ornithology. The turkey, however imperfect in taste and texture, however sloppy as a national symbol, however misnamed, is gastronomically inevitable, if not on every Thanksgiving then on most of them. The savory and educational garnishes do go quite well with a bland and golden bird; we derive communal pleasure both from splitting up one gigantic object among eight or fifteen people and from eating the same thing as everybody else in the nation; and when properly roasted, the crisp, rendered, intensely flavored skin of a turkey is bested only by that of a roast suckling pig.

And that is why my first-favorite Thanksgiving dinner is a Thompson's Turkey. The problem is that I've never eaten a properly prepared Thompson's Turkey—even though I've followed Thompson's instructions with slavish and obsessive care on several occasions.

Morton Thompson was a newspaperman in the 1930s and 1940s with columns in the *New York Journal* and the *Hollywood*

Citizen-News (though he is more famous for his best-selling novel, *Not as a Stranger,* published in 1954 and later made into a movie). Sometimes Thompson devoted his column to food, and one November in the mid-1930s he gave an elaborate recipe for turkey, one that has often been republished in the years that followed, turning up in pamphlets and in the popular press every ten or fifteen years since his death. You might say that followers of Thompson's Turkey constitute something of a cult (albeit a small and benign cult) whose members differ from the population at large only in their eagerness to expend eight or ten hours of backbreaking labor to prepare an exceptional, a uniquely savory, turkey.

Thompson's Turkey has become such a tradition in one branch of my wife's family that the *Nashville Banner* ran a story twelve years ago about her cousin Bonnie Lloyd (the former Miss Utah); her husband, Bill; their six children, Ivey, Tiffany, Sheffy, Marty, Westy, and Merrilee; and their Thompson's Turkey. It was Bill who first offered me a glimpse of Thompson's Turkey with a torn and tattered article from a 1957 *Gourmet* magazine and a quote from Robert Benchley:

> Several years ago I ate a turkey prepared and roasted by Morton Thompson. I didn't eat the whole turkey, but that wasn't my fault. There were outsiders present who ganged up on me. . . . I will just say that I decided at that time that Morton Thompson was the greatest man since [Brillat-]Savarin, and for all I know, Savarin wasn't as good as Morton Thompson.

To make a Thompson's Turkey, you first mix up Thompson's elaborate stuffing, sew it tightly into a very large turkey, and brown the bird briefly at a very high temperature. Then you paint it with a paste of flour, egg, and onion juice, dry it in the oven, and paint it again, repeating this until the bird is hermetically sealed under a stiff crust. You slowly roast the turkey for five hours, basting it every fifteen minutes. The bird emerges from the oven with a dead black surface from wing to wing. Why would you want to do all this to a turkey? I'll let Morton Thompson explain:

Beneath this burnt, harmless, now worthless shell the bird will be golden and dark brown, succulent, giddy-making with wild aromas, crisp and crunchable and crackling. The meat beneath this crazing panorama of lip-wetting skin will be wet, juice will spurt from it in tiny fountains high as the handle of the fork plunged into it; the meat will be white, crammed with mocking flavor, delirious with things that rush over your palate and are drowned and gone as fast as you can swallow; cut a little of it with a spoon, it will spread on bread as eagerly and readily as soft wurst.

You do not have to be a carver to eat this turkey; speak harshly to it and it will fall apart.

This is the end of it. All but the dressing. No pen, unless it were filled with Thompson's gravy, can describe Thompson's dressing, and there is not paper enough in the world to contain the thoughts and adjectives it would set down, and not marble enough to serve for its monuments.

On the assumption that you will find these words no less seductive than I did, I will give you Thompson's detailed recipe as soon as I have finished telling you about it; I have chosen the 1945 version, the one I slavishly followed, at least on the first attempt.

As the stuffing contains twenty-nine ingredients, it took me three hours to get the bird into the oven, and not only because my spice shelf had fallen out of alphabetical order; nearly every spice I possess found its place in Thompson's stuffing. The completed mixture is reminiscent of no identifiable cuisine; it includes ingredients like crushed pineapple and canned water

---

It's a Fact

Q How strong is the scientifically ideal cooking pot?

A. One thousand newtons. If your pot isn't stronger than 1,000 newtons, it will deform when you drop it. If it is stronger than 1,000 newtons, it will deform your foot when you drop it.

---

chestnuts that daring housewives of fifty years ago put into nearly everything they cooked. And it contains garlic, which was even too daring for most housewives fifty years ago when the American kitchen was still in the thrall of Anglo-German flavor phobias. Made with fresh herbs instead of Thompson's dried, and with several ambiguities in the shopping list properly resolved, this is the most delicious bread stuffing I have ever tasted.

A turkey is the largest creature that most of us will ever cook, twenty pounds of muscle and bone and another five or so of stuffing. Thompson's method asks for too much rotating of the turkey, which quickly becomes a hot, slippery, twenty-five-pound bombshell. It was August when I made my first Thompson's, and although I had all the air conditioners cranked up to maximum to simulate the climate in which the Pilgrims celebrated their first Thanksgiving, I was wearing shorts in the kitchen as I struggled to turn the Thompson's Turkey to and fro. It slipped from my hands and headed in the direction of the open dishwasher. I lunged forward to catch it. In this I was successful, but not before I had pressed both my shins firmly against the red-hot oven rack. Months later I still bear the scars of this roasting injury. All cookbooks should warn you to wear long pants when you roast.

My Thompson's Turkey emerged as Thompson had said it would, a flat, ashen black. When cut into, it did not spurt fountains of juice; and the black coating did not readily peel off to expose acres of ultimate skin. But everything else that Thompson and Benchley said about Thompson's Turkey is absolutely true. The meat of this turkey is the most flavorful and moist that you will ever taste, deeply imbued with the multitudinous perfumes of the stuffing, now mingled and compounded so that none asserts itself over the others. Everyone who has tasted Thompson's Turkey agrees completely. *It may be the only turkey worth consuming for gastronomic as well as symbolic reasons.*

And this almost makes up for the fact that I was able to salvage no more than a few square centimeters of crispy skin from the entire turkey. But not quite. If Thompson himself were alive today, I'm sure he could expand upon his written instructions and set everything right. Cousins Bonnie and Bill, who have cooked Thompson's Turkey ten or fifteen times, seem to have given up on getting a satisfying yield of skin from a Thompson's. But I am not willing to compromise. Until somebody tells me how to cook a Thompson's Turkey with perfect skin, I will rely on a more traditional method of roasting.

"No meat can be well roasted except on a spit turned by a jack, and before a steady clear fire—other methods are no better than baking," wrote Mary Randolph in *The Virginia House-wife* (1824), surely one of the five best cookbooks ever published in this country. (Please buy yourself a copy from the University of South Carolina Press in Columbia; although the book is 168 years old, you can cook right out of it, and the recipes are wonderful.) Having enjoyed spitted birds and mammals turned over and before wood fires throughout northern Italy and parts of France, I know that Mrs. Randolph is correct, and as soon as I get a house with a fireplace, I will write a column about it every month until they stop me.

Just a year ago I bought a new electric Farberware Standard Smokeless Indoor Grill with Rotisserie (after prowling the flea markets in vain for a used Roto-Broiler, an electric rotisserie in a streamlined, chrome-plated cabinet that could be found in every suburban home when I was growing up), and I've achieved magnificent results with four-pound chickens and ducks, especially when I trussed them tightly and compactly and put them as near to the electric coils as I could (and in the case of ducks, pricked their skin all over to let the fat drain). Besides the transitory pleasure of having juicy and crispy birds for dinner anytime I wish, I see myself in training for the day when a real fireplace comes my way.

The Farberware booklet envisions cooking a turkey weighing up to seventeen pounds, and that is the size I tried, with the bird unstuffed and tightly trussed and a roasting time of five hours. Less than one of the five hours had passed when the turkey's wing slipped from under its string and caught on the electric coil, preventing the bird from turning further. Thus fixed, the turkey began to brown rapidly and then to blacken along a stripe from neck to tail; the string holding the legs against the body burned through, and both legs plunged into the glowing coils. It was the stench of charring flesh and the billows of smoke that attracted my attention and drew me back into the kitchen, where for the next hour I struggled with seventeen pounds of hot, greasy flesh and protruding bones as I retied and rebalanced the bird, and plugged the Farberware back into the wall socket. When I returned a half hour later, very little progress was visible because I had, in actual fact, plugged in the blender, whose cord eerily resembled that of the Farberware. I consider my wife a highly cyclical person, like the inconstant moon, and one of her least pleasant cycles occurs around midnight when dinner is still nowhere in sight. But I resisted her terrible pressure to speed the cooking until the strings came loose again in a disastrous thump, whereupon I transferred the bird to a very hot oven. The result was neither pretty to look at nor scrumptious to eat, but I feel that we are that much better prepared for true fireplace cookery.

Mary Randolph would never approve of the endless five-hour cooking time of the Farberware or Thompson's Turkey. In

The Virginia House-wife she recommends *an hour and a quarter* to finish a bird of medium size, presumably around twelve pounds. Her fire must thus have been extremely hot, unless she preferred blood-rare turkey. The reason she refers to roasting at a lower temperature as "no better than baking" is that it allows the bird to steam in its own juices.

Until somebody tells me how to save the skin of a Thompson's Turkey, it is Mrs. Randolph's high-temperature recommendation that I will follow in cooking my edible symbol for Thanksgiving. The easiest and most practical way to do this, I think, is Barbara Kafka's astonishingly simple method, published just a year ago in *Gourmet* (and in her new book, *Party Food* [Morrow]). You put a large turkey into a 500-degree oven, jiggle it every so often to prevent sticking, and take it out less than two hours later. Your kitchen is probably filled with smoke, and the juices have burned in the roasting pan, but the meat is juicy (if bland) and the skin is as crackling and crunchy and intensely flavored as anything you've ever dreamed of. I'll give you the details after the recipe for Thompson's Turkey.

461

Thompson's Turkey

[Except for the sentences in brackets, these are Morton Thompson's own words. His recipe was published numerous times. This version appeared in a collection of his columns entitled *Joe, the Wounded Tennis Player* (Doubleday, Doran and Co., 1945). My invaluable tips and suggested changes appear in brackets.]

The turkey should not be less than sixteen pounds and not more than twenty-two. If it is eighteen pounds or more, buy a hen. You will get more breast. . . . [With today's breeding practices, it is not necessary to insist on a hen, even if your butcher knows what a hen looks like.]

[Remove all loose fat from the inside of the bird and render it by chopping it finely, putting it in a small saucepan with ½ cup of water, bringing to a boil, and simmering until all the water has evaporated and you are left with clear fat and pieces of solids. Reserve the fat for the stuffing, and brown the solids for a treat.]

Rub the bird inside and out with salt and pepper. In a stewpan put the chopped gizzard and the neck and heart, to which add one bay leaf, one teaspoon of paprika, a half teaspoon of coriander, a clove of garlic, four cups of water, and salt to taste. Let this simmer while you go ahead with the dressing. [If you oil the turkey's skin before rubbing it with salt and pepper, you will find that the blackened coating later lifts off almost as easily as Thompson claims!]

Dice [a peeled, cored] apple, [a peeled] orange, [put them] in a bowl and add to this bowl a huge can of crushed pineapple, the grated rind of one half lemon, one can of drained water chestnuts, [and] three table-spoons of chopped preserved ginger. [Try 10 ounces of drained, coarsely chopped water chestnuts and 20 ounces of crushed pineapple.]

In another bowl put two teaspoons of Colman's mustard, two teaspoons of caraway seed, three tea-spoons of celery seed, two teaspoons of poppy seed, two and a half teaspoons of oregano, one well-crushed large bay leaf, one teaspoon black pepper, one half tea-spoon of mace, four tablespoons of well-chopped pars-ley, four or five finely minced cloves of garlic, four cloves minus the heads and well-chopped, one half teaspoon of turmeric, four large, well-chopped onions, six well-chopped stalks of celery, one half teaspoon marjoram, one half teaspoon savory (summer savory if you can get it), and one tablespoon of poultry seasoning. ["Well chopped" means "medium-fine."] Some like sage, some like thyme. Nobody, apparently, objects to poultry seasoning, which, ironically, contains both. Salt to taste. [*I* object to poultry seasoning. And I find the quantity here of ground dried herbs overpowering and acrid. For the poultry seasoning, I substitute 1 tablespoon each of fresh thyme and fresh sage. And I use three times the specified amount of finely chopped fresh oregano, fresh marjoram, and fresh summer savory. A teaspoon of salt should be enough.]

In another bowl dump three packages of bread-crumbs, bought at a bakery. [A pound and a half of fresh bread crumbs seems just right.] Add to this three quarters of a pound of ground veal and one quarter of a pound of ground fresh pork and a quarter of a pound of butter and all the fat (first rendered) you have been able to find and pry loose from the turkey. [I have explained this earlier.] Mix in each bowl the contents of each bowl. When each bowl is well mixed, mix the three of them together. And mix it well. Mix it with your hands. Mix it until your forearms and wrists ache. Then mix it some more. Now toss it enough so that it isn't any longer a doughy mass.

Stuff your turkey, but not too fully. Pretty full, though. Stuff the neck and tie the end. Skewer the bird. Tie the strings. [Sewing up the bird and sewing the wings to the body are better than skewering.] Turn on your oven full force and let it get red-hot. [Do this an hour beforehand—the stuffing should not sit in the turkey while you wait.] Put your bird on the drip pan, or, best of all, breast down in a rack. In a cup make a paste consisting of the yolks of two eggs, a teaspoon of Colman's mustard, a clove of minced garlic, a table-spoon of onion juice (run an onion through your chopper and catch the juice), a half teaspoon of salt, two pinches of cayenne pepper, a teaspoon of lemon juice, and enough sifted flour to make a stiff paste. Take a pastry brush or an ordinary big paintbrush and stand by. [Triple all the quantities for this paste or you'll run out too soon. If you wrap the rack in heavily greased aluminum foil, it will not tear the turkey's skin.]

Put your bird into the red-hot oven. Let it brown all over. Remove the turkey. Turn your oven down to 325 degrees. Now, while the turkey is sizzling hot, paint it completely all over with the paste. Put it back in the oven. The paste will have set in a few minutes. Drag it out again. Paint every nook and cranny of it once more. Put it back in the oven. Keep doing this until you haven't any more paste left.

To the giblet-neck-liver-heart gravy that has been simmering add one cup of cider. [Better to add 3 cups of cider and 1 cup of water.] Don't let it cook any more. Stir it well. Keep it warm on top of the oven. This is your basting fluid. Baste the bird every fifteen minutes! That means you will baste it from twelve to fifteen times. After the bird has cooked about an hour and a half turn it on its stomach, back in the air, and let it cook in that position until the last fifteen minutes, when you restore it to its back again. That is, unless you use a rack. If you use a rack don't turn it on its back until the last half hour.

[I found the multiple rotations that Thompson calls for to be unnecessarily arduous and damaging to the bird. I would modify the previous three paragraphs by browning the bird, breast down, for about 15 minutes and the same time on its back, on a rack opened nearly all the way. Then paint the bird without turning it and leave it on its back for the rest of the roasting time.]

It ought to cook at least four hours and a half to five hours and a half. [Use the shorter time for an 18-pound turkey and the longer for 22. Begin timing when you turn down the oven to 325 degrees. An instant meat thermometer will read about 180 to 185 degrees in the thigh between the leg and body, 170 degrees in the breast, and 160 degrees in the stuffing.]

When you remove it the turkey will be dead black. You will think, "My God! I have ruined it." Be calm. Take a tweezer and pry loose the paste coating. It will come off readily. Beneath this burnt, harmless, now worthless shell the bird will be golden and dark brown, succulent, giddy-making with wild aromas, crisp and crunchable and crackling.

High-Temperature Turkey

[These instructions come from Barbara Kafka's column, "An Opinionated Palate," in the November 1991 *Gourmet*. Her method miraculously roasts a large turkey in under two hours. I have found it most successful with a fifteen-pound turkey, unstuffed and untrussed, in a roasting pan with shallow sides and an oven at 500 degrees. But a friend at *Gourmet* tells me that the method was successfully tested with various sizes and types of turkeys. Again, my own advice appears in brackets.]

The most important thing is to order an unfrozen, untreated bird. Start by removing the packet of innards from the turkey [and make a broth with the neck and gizzards plus some onion and garlic]. Put your oven rack at its lowest level and boost the bake-setting temperature as high as it will go. You might have some smoke in the kitchen, but you will be rewarded by the juiciest, most quickly roasted turkey—with the crispest skin—you have ever made.

I don't use a rack in the roasting pan; the bottom skin is hardly worth bothering about. I don't truss, either. Untrussed, both the white meat and the dark will be properly done at the same time.

Bring the turkey to room temperature. Remove any gobs of fat. Either stuff the cavity or just salt and pepper it and insert a couple of onions. . . . Fifteen-pound turkeys are about an ideal cooking size. If you have a very large family, I would suggest two smaller turkeys rather than one King Kong.

Slide the turkey, legs first, into the oven. After fifteen minutes move the turkey around with a wooden spatula so that it doesn't stick. Repeat moving the bird around every twenty minutes. If the bird seems to be getting too dark before it is cooked, cover it with a tent of aluminum foil. Roast until the thigh joint near the backbone wiggles easily. Remove the turkey from the oven about ten minutes before it is fully cooked. [An instant meat thermometer makes this easier; a wobbly leg joint can sometimes mean overcooked meat. Figure on a temperature of 175 to 180 degrees in the thigh meat, measured deep between the leg and the body, and breast meat between 165 and 170 degrees; these are 5 degrees lower than the usual prescription.]

An unstuffed nine- to ten-pound turkey will take about an hour and fifteen minutes, a twelve-pound bird about five minutes more, a fifteen-pound bird will go up to just under two hours, and a twenty-pound bird takes three hours. If you are stuffing your turkey, add thirty minutes to whichever cooking time applies.

[I found that an unstuffed bird roasted much more evenly; in a stuffed fifteen-pound bird, the dark meat was not done by the time the breast was getting dry. And unlike the meat of a Thompson's Turkey, the flesh of this fast-roasted bird was not imbued with the complex aromas within. Better to make some Thompson's dressing on the side, moisten it with a little broth and cider, and bake at 325 degrees, tightly covered with foil, for two or three hours.]

November 1992

Pies from Paradise

A hundred pies ago, I was sitting at my kitchen table, eating the filling out of yesterday's apple pie, keeping track of the Miss Teen USA Pageant on TV, and waiting for the day's first pie to come out of the oven.

This would be a pie from paradise, an apple pie like none other—for the luscious fruit would be tucked into the most daring and innovative piecrust of a generation, if not of all time. "Some are born great," I murmured happily, playing Malvolio in *Twelfth Night*, "some achieve greatness, and some have greatness thrust upon them."

I had spent weeks reading all the scientific piecrust literature published since 1921 and every recipe I could find, about two hundred in all. My aim was to reinvent American piecrust from the ground up, taking nothing for granted—neither folk techniques, old wives' tales, nor instructions purportedly based on science. And after a long string of near misses (which is why I was eating only the apple filling), I had finally, this evening, figured out a novel, modern way of making the perfect, foolproof American piecrust. It was now browning happily in my oven.

I was under colossal pressure. Marion Cunningham, daunting pie expert and a friend for many years, was coming to town! Beautiful at seventy-three, with a golden gray ponytail and sky-blue eyes, Marion lives in Walnut Creek in northern California.

She is mentor to probably half the bakers in America, through her authorship of the *Fannie Farmer Cookbook* (thirteenth edition), her indispensable *Fannie Farmer Baking Book,* her very successful *The Breakfast Book* (all published by Knopf), and countless magazine and newspaper columns. Marion is the first person I call with questions about American baking. Her patient explanations are usually interrupted by three or four pleas for help on the other line.

Marion is a calmly fanatical believer in simplicity, so I had kept my complex piecrust experiments to myself. When she arrived, I wanted to stun her with a method completely at odds with her own and demonstrate that Walnut Creek rusticity has its limits.

The objective is this: Perfect American piecrust must be seven things at once—flaky, airy, light, tender, crisp, well browned, and good tasting. The tricky ones are flaky, tender, and crisp—because these are independent virtues. Getting flaky, tender, and crisp to happen at the same time in the same pie seems nearly impossible. Yet millions of American women and men in the early 1900s could do it in their sleep, and probably tens of thousands can today. Marion is one of them.

French tart pastry is tender, buttery, and slightly crisp but possesses a compact, sandy texture instead of flaky layers. That's fine for the French, but completely wrong for a fine American piecrust. In this, I think, we are unique among nations. When Jane Austen wrote, "Good apple pies are a considerable part of our domestic happiness," she didn't say, "Flaky, tender, and crisp apple pies." She meant some British predecessor to flaky, tender, and crisp—probably their adaptation of French puff pastry.

Savory pies were invented by the ancient Greeks and imitated by the Romans, who brought pie to Gaul. Years passed. The medieval French were great pie lovers—always meat pies, never fresh fruit—and the Normans took pie along when they conquered Britain in 1066. Huge pies—such as the one containing four and twenty blackbirds—were made with strong, thick crusts (neither tender, crisp, nor flaky) and were used more as containers for cooking and storage. It seems incredible that nobody in the world thought of putting fresh fruit into a piecrust until the English and French did in the early sixteenth century, but there it is. Fruit pie made its first appearance in English literature in 1590 in this seductive line from Robert Greene's *Arcadia:* "Thy breath is like the steame of apple-pyes."

The Pilgrims brought pie recipes and rolling pins on the *Mayflower,* along with apple-tree cuttings. Neither the apple nor most other fruit trees are native to America, and pies of wild berries (the edible varieties were pointed out by the Indians) were the most common in the early years of settlement. Both pie and apples bloomed here like nowhere else in the world. Ralph Waldo Emerson, when questioned about the New England habit of eating pie for breakfast, replied, "What [else] is pie for?" By 1900, in Midwest farming areas, pie was obligatory at least twice a day. And only thirty years ago, pie was America's favorite restaurant dessert, requested by 60 percent of all customers at every meal.

Most piecrust recipes in the first American cookbooks of the late 1700s and early 1800s resemble English formulas for puff pastry, which often included whole eggs or substituted egg whites for water; the dough was repeatedly folded and rolled, with butter added each time. But by the mid-1800s, American recipes appeared that were nearly identical to those we use today. Somehow, in the first half of the 1800s, the classic American piecrust was born and quickly spread throughout the land. I have found nothing to explain how this happened, by whom, or where. I reject the gift-from-an-advanced-alien-civilization hypothesis.

The kitchen timer beeped. I checked the pie and decided to let it brown a few minutes more. I glanced at the television. The poignancy of the bathing-suit competition was over. At this point in the Miss Teen USA Pageant, I had expected a Cherry Pie Contest, my only reason for tuning in to this antiquated and sexist ritual. I watched in vain. Wichita, Kansas, from which the Miss

Teen USA Pageant was broadcast, was once a major world capital of homemade pie. Shouldn't today's teen role models be as adept at pie making as they are at concupiscent display? But now Wichita seems nothing more than the world capital of the Miss Teen USA Pageant. I would happily serve as pie teacher to next year's contestants.

In theory, American piecrust is extremely simple. Most often it follows a three-two-one formula—three parts flour (by weight), two parts shortening, and one part water, plus a little salt and sometimes a little sugar.

Nearly every baker or scientist who writes about pie seems to subscribe to what you might call the Nasty Gluten Theory of Flaky, Tender, Crisp American Piecrust. Wheat flour is mainly starch, plus 7 to 15 percent protein and 10 percent moisture. The two main proteins are glutenin and gliadin. When you stir water into flour, the glutenin and gliadin come alive, connecting with the water and with each other to form gluten, a tough and stretchy substance that, when kneaded or stirred or stretched, forms the elastic network that gives structure to bread, but turns pastry and cakes tough and rubbery.

Piecrust recipes have you go to elaborate lengths to avoid developing gluten. They warn you to use as little water as possible (without water, gluten cannot form); to mix and handle the dough very gently (without manipulation, gluten strands cannot join into networks); to use low-protein pastry flour or all-purpose flour (which has less gliadin and glutenin); and to rest the ball of dough before rolling it out (which relaxes the stretchiness of the gluten, though it also allows the water to reach particles of flour that had remained dry and therefore without gluten).

The ingredient in piecrust that combats gluten is shortening—fat. By coating the little particles of flour, shortening waterproofs the protein, prevents the water from reaching the gliadin and glutenin, and thus makes it impossible for them to combine and form gluten. And if they do combine, shortening keeps the thin strands of gluten apart, stops them from forming sheets and networks that run through the dough, and tenderizes the crust by ensuring that the strands of gluten separate and short. That is why it's called shortening. Or so I've heard.

Pure fats like lard and Crisco have more shortening (tenderizing) power than butter and margarine, which contain 15 per-

Taking Our Measure

Q. How can you tell Americans apart from all other people?

A. By their measuring cups. "Nowhere else but in these United States does an entire nation habitually and almost exclusively measure dry ingredients with a cup," announced Raymond Sokolov, the *Wall Street Journal*'s "Leisure and Arts" page editor, who also wrote for years an indispensable column about food for *Natural History* magazine. There are a few exceptions: Canada, probably Australia, and possibly Iraq, where after decades of British administration some cookbooks specified the Players cigarette tin as a universal unit of measurement which the servants would not steal and could not break.

The rest of the world uses scales to weigh its dry ingredients because scales are vastly more accurate than cups for things like flour, cornstarch, and cocoa. Depending on how densely compacted it is, a pound of flour can fill up as few as three cups or as many as four and a half, which means that Americans almost never bake the same cake twice.

How ever did we get into such a pickle? Sokolov proposes the "Conestoga theory" of cup measurement—that "pioneers and homesteaders heading west did not bother lugging heavy metal scales with their weights." But early American cookbooks call for flour by weight, at least some of the time, and it was not until Fannie Farmer's *Boston Cooking-School Cook Book* of 1896, when most Conestoga wagons were rusting in suburban garages, that cup measurement was universally adopted—on the backward notion that it was more scientific. Marion Cunningham's twelfth edition of Fannie Farmer (1979) gives both cups and grams.

473

cent water and can actually activate the gluten. Soft fats, even vegetable oils, coat the flour particles easily by flowing around them, protecting them all from water but causing other problems. Fats that are solid at room temperature are less effective, unless you first cut them into infinitesimal pieces. Acids attack and weaken the elastic gluten, which is why many people add vinegar to the dough when they make pies.

All of this is aimed at achieving a tender piecrust. But what about flakiness? When you roll out pie dough, the flattened particles of shortening separate the dough into layers. The pieces of fat act as spacers. The larger they are, the wider and longer the layers they produce. Depending on how you cut the fat into the flour, the particles can range from the size of a grain of coarse meal to that of a pea or a small olive.

When piecrust is baked, the solid fats melt, leaving a gap between the layers of dough. The water in the dough begins to turn into steam, puffing the layers of dough apart. And when the dough reaches about 160 degrees Fahrenheit, the piecrust begins to set. Crispiness comes about when enough water has been driven from the dough by the heat of baking.

Lard, the rendered body fat of the pig, has a high melting point and coalesces into especially large crystals when it cools to lower temperatures. That's why lard acts as a terrific spacer between layers of dough. Lard was once widely considered the best fat for making flaky piecrust. Crisco was introduced in 1911 as a lard replacement with a long shelf life. Nowadays, lard has lost some of its popularity because of its pork flavor (which really goes quite well with apples, pears, cherries, and peaches) and widespread nutritional superstitions (even though lard, at 43 percent saturated fat, is less saturated than butter (50 percent), and may come out only a little worse than a vegetable shortening like Crisco, which contains 21 percent saturated fat to begin with and 14 percent transfatty acids when it is hydrogenated to make it solid.

Which brings us back to my kitchen. My object was to get around all of this agonizing about gluten and fat, and to eliminate entirely the need for manual skill. Here is how I made the piecrust about to emerge from the oven: I followed the classic three-two-one formula, using Crisco and medium-protein all-purpose flour—totally ordinary, so far. But it was my technique that would soon astound both the baking world and Marion Cunningham. Using a food processor, I added half the shortening to all the flour and processed it like crazy, for five minutes, until it completely disappeared, coating all the little flour particles and immunizing them against what was to come—water and the threat of gluten. This technique would guarantee the tenderest of piecrusts. Next came all the water, processed briefly until everything began to form into clumps of dough. Finally, the rest of the shortening went in, briefly pulsed to leave it in pieces the size of M & M's. These would form layers when the dough was rolled out. The expected result: perfectly tender, crisp, and flaky pastry.

I turned off the Miss Teen USA Pageant, which was mired in the evening-gown competition, my least favorite part. And then the pie was ready. I allowed it to cool for ten minutes. Most pies, both crust and filling, improve if you let them stand for two hours, until they are only slightly warm. But I needed to know now. I cut out a wedge of crust, lifted it from the apple filling, and took a bite.

It was awful, hard and compact but crumbly when it broke, spotted with black dots, greasy tasting. There wasn't a flake in the entire thing. I had never been further from a perfect piecrust.

When I recovered from my disappointment and panic—Marion would arrive in only two days—I figured out what had gone wrong. By processing half the fat so thoroughly, I had indeed waterproofed all the flour particles and no gluten at all had developed. And as a result, there were no flaky layers for the chunky fat to separate. In furious experimentation over the next forty-eight hours, I realized that the Nasty Gluten Theory pie experts were wrong. You cannot produce a flaky piecrust without gluten! The real objective is not to eliminate gluten entirely but to get the right amount distributed in exactly the right way.

I had figured out nearly everything except how to bake a flaky, tender, and crisp piecrust. In fact, I had proved that a perfect piecrust is theoretically impossible.

I wondered if America's giant food companies had solved the problem. I went out and bought every packaged piecrust I could find: mixes in boxes; frozen pie shells; a refrigerated, prerolled double crust; and several frozen pies. The only nearly acceptable product was the Betty Crocker mix, easy to roll out and yielding a light though mealy crust with inconsequential flakes. But using a mix saves only the three minutes you would spend assembling and measuring the ingredients—you still have to mix and roll out the dough yourself. Pillsbury's refrigerated crust was somewhat tender and flaky, though soft and white instead of crisp and brown, and it had the repulsive, fermented taste of cheap cheese, maybe the fault of sloppy supermarket storage, maybe Pillsbury's fault.

Then Marion Cunningham arrived, at nine o'clock on a sunny Saturday morning, in time for coffee. A gentlewoman

475

even under stress, she tried to seem fascinated with everything I had discovered about gluten and sympathetic to my idea that all these opposing forces make the perfect pie theoretically impossible.

Then she smiled and said, "Let's bake a pie." We walked a few blocks to the Union Square Greenmarket, bought three quarts of bright red sour pie cherries, returned home, and stemmed and pitted them all and prepared a delicious filling. Now for the crust.

Marion measured out two and a quarter cups of bleached, all-purpose flour (Gold Medal or Pillsbury) into a large bowl. She used a metal cup measure, scooped the flour right out of the bag, and with her free hand pressed it lightly into the cup and brushed off the excess. (Why would I mention this? Because cups of flour can range in weight from four to five ounces, depending on how you fill the cup. Measured in Marion's way a cup weighs precisely five ounces, more than most cups of flour do but just what Marion lists on the endpapers of her *Fannie Farmer Baking Book*. It is amazing how many other pie writers warn you to measure your ingredients precisely—a teaspoon of water either way, they say, can ruin your piecrust—but then fail to tell you how they measure their cup of flour or what it should weigh. American home bakers don't weigh their flour; Europeans do. It is a stupendous irony that twelve editions ago the original Fannie Farmer, who aimed at putting home cooking on a scientific basis, was famous for urging the American housewife to measure her flour with level cups and calibrated spoons.)

With her fingers, Marion mixed in a half teaspoon of salt, then measured out three-quarters of a cup of room-temperature Crisco and plopped it onto the flour. She tossed the shortening in the flour, breaking it up into pieces the size of walnuts. All the while she chatted happily. There was none of the grim silence that accompanies my piecrust experiments.

And then she began a hand motion that has became the basis of my own pie making. Reaching to the bottom of the bowl with both hands, Marion scooped up the flour and fat above the rim of the bowl and ran her thumbs over it, against her fingertips, from little finger to index finger. The small pieces of fat and flour slipped between her fingers and back into the bowl and the large pieces tumbled over her index fingers. She repeated this about twenty-five times, until the pieces of fat and flour ranged in size from very coarse meal to grains of rice to green peas to small olives. The irregularity is important, as is the presence of large pieces.

Marion added a half cup of refrigerator-cold water all at once, and stirred it in a spiral pattern with a dinner fork until little clumps began to form. (She recommends adding more water rather than less if you are unsure.) She squeezed together a small handful to see if the dough adhered to itself, which it did, then pressed all the dough firmly together on one side of the bottom of the bowl, split off about half of it with her hands, and immediately rolled it out. She used my huge and very heavy wooden rolling pin with ball-bearing handles, but her touch was light and quick.

Marion had broken nearly every rule of making piecrust. She should have used chilled shortening so that it would not melt into the flour. For the same reason, she should not have used her warm fingers. She should have added vinegar to make the crust more tender, and she should never have stirred in all the water at once, but by tablespoons and then by teaspoons. Consequently, she used much more water than was absolutely necessary and didn't distribute it very well. And she didn't chill the dough or even let it rest before rolling it out. Through the years, Marion had tried all of these safeguards and precautions, yet none seemed to matter much. So she had simplified.

And yet, what emerged from the oven was a perfect cherry pie, or at least a perfect crust—flaky, tender, and crisp. (Something had gone wrong with my filling, and it ran all over the place.) This was the piecrust I needed to master and understand—while Marion was still in New York City.

But a day later, for reasons always unfathomable to me, Marion left New York for northern California—before I was even close. The next two weeks were filled with telephone calls and faxes. Did she hold her hands exactly parallel to the table? Were her fingers curved or straight? Were they separated from each other or tightly closed? And most important, did she pass her thumb back and forth across her fingers each time she scooped up the shortening and flour, or just once? This last question was the subject of three phone calls.

It is Marion's fingers that make the piecrust, not her brain. So every time I called with another question, she would hang up, make a pie or two, or just the crust, carefully observe what her fingers were doing, sometimes take notes, and report back. I held my fingers over the earpiece so that they could hear, too. She baked a dozen extra pies in all. Summer fruit in northern California was at its peak, and nothing went to waste—Marion's friends often drop by, and twice her gardener was rewarded for working hard in the midst of a heat wave. Good piecrust is made by people with cool fingers and a warm heart, the adage says.

At long last, my own hot fingers had learned their lesson. I became proficient, and my crust was tender, flaky, and crisp. After a while, making the dough and rolling it out took only twelve minutes. I timed it. The whole process is much briefer than a trip to the supermarket.

I was committed to Marion's method. But I wondered about Marion's exceedingly generous attitude toward water and her practice of adding it all at once before stirring. She feels that a dry dough will break at the edges as you roll it. These splits can be repaired, but Marion finds that the dough never "bakes out" well.

I will admit to no one that I was annoyed with the perfection of Marion's simple pie dough. But I needed to understand why it worked. And among the scientific papers I read, two helped clear up the mystery. More than that: *they were revelations.*

One, from the *Bakers Digest* in 1967, demonstrated that a flaky crust is produced by a three-way sandwich between layers of flattened lumps of fat that act as spacers, layers of unprotected flour mixed with water to produce gluten, and layers of fat rubbed into flour for tenderness. Plastic (pliable) shortening—such as room-temperature Crisco and slightly chilled lard—is a mixture of solid fat and liquid fat. The liquid part coats the flour; the solid part separates layers!!

The second paper, in the journal *Cereal Chemistry* in 1943, was a corollary of the first. It showed that when you use chilled shortening, the amount of water you add and the way you mix it are critical; but with room-temperature shortening, the kind Marion uses, these factors matter very little! So much for compulsive dough chillers.

This led me to formulate my own recipe by fiddling around with Marion's ingredients in four ways. First, I increased the proportion of shortening so that an amateur baker like me does not have to get things exactly right. With more shortening, you can be sure that enough fat will be rubbed into the flour (for tenderness) while leaving enough over for those all-important, large, irregular lumps. And with the flour well waterproofed, the quantity of water you add becomes less critical. A technical article in the *Bakers Digest* in 1970 showed that raising the proportion of shortening—up to 80 percent of the weight of the flour—increased tenderness without decreasing flakiness at all!

This is a tactic designed for housewives who want a tender piecrust but lack the skill, sneered a male pie expert in a 1952 address to the American Society of Baking Engineers. Being accused of resembling a clumsy housewife does not bother me—I have recently discovered recipes by two very fine pie bakers who use lots of shortening. But when I get better at pie, I may reduce the fat by two tablespoons or so.

Second, I increased everything in Marion's recipe by a third. Most recipes, especially those written by nimble-fingered women, make just enough dough to form a pie if you are perfectly proficient at rolling dough into a very thin, perfect circle. I find this extremely sexist and discriminatory against clumsier males whose cooking genius lies elsewhere. The larger volume I use makes up for messy and irregular rolling and leaves lots of dough at the edges without the need to patch.

Third, I added a little sugar, which many other recipes also include. Marion has no objection to this. My experiments showed that a little sugar in the dough helps the crust brown and adds flavor to counteract the neutral or even slightly bitter taste of Crisco, but that too much sugar gives the crust a sandy texture (like French *sablé* pastry or cookie dough), diminishes flakiness, and is cloyingly sweet.

Fourth, I changed to *unbleached* all-purpose flour, which, because it is higher in protein, is thought to produce a tougher crust. Unbleached flour has a better color and tastes nuttier; with all the shortening I added, the protein was so well coated that toughness was never much of a problem.

My adventures in pie research continued as I tested almost every subsidiary technique recommended by one pie expert or another over the past seventy-three years. In no time at all, every piece of furniture within thirty feet of my oven had been turned into a pie stand. The results:

• Brushing the bottom crust with eggs, yolks, or whites to waterproof it from a liquid filling seems to have no effect.

• Brushing milk over the top crust just before a pie goes into the oven is great for browning.

• Sprinkling sugar over the milk makes for a nice, sweet crunch.

• Greasing the pie plate helps brown the bottom crust and makes it easier to remove pieces of pie.

• Chilling a dough made entirely of Crisco produces an inferior crust with a tight structure compared with room-temperature Crisco, but unchilled lard or butter (they melt at lower temperatures) are nearly impossible to work with.

• When acidic steam rises from a fruit filling, the dough also becomes acidic. Its pH falls. Acidic dough has trouble browning. Adding baking soda was once widely recommended as a way to raise the dough's pH and help it brown. I found that baking soda caused a weird, reddish browning, made for a sandy texture, and left its own identifiable taste.

A recipe finally emerged. It is mainly Marion's, of course, but it is also mine. By following it, you can make a fine piecrust with just your fingers anywhere in the world. And if you find yourself stranded on a desert island without a rolling pin, Marion says, you can use an old wine bottle the waves have washed ashore.

Flaky, Tender, and Crisp: Handmade American Pie

Ingredients for a fruit filling (see step 1 in this recipe and the filling recipes that follow)

3 cups unbleached all-purpose flour (In order of preference, King Arthur, Heckers, Gold Medal, Pillsbury. Measure the flour as Marion did: scoop the flour with a 1-cup measure, press it very lightly into the cup, and level off the excess with the side of your hand. Each cup of flour will weigh 5 ounces or a little more.)

2 teaspoons granulated sugar

1 teaspoon salt

1½ cups shortening (Crisco, butter, lard, or a combination. Crisco works fine; if your kitchen is warm, chill the Crisco for 15 to 30 minutes. For better flavor, substitute 10 tablespoons [1 stick plus 2 tablespoons] cold, unsalted butter for ½ cup of the Crisco. Beat the cold butter with a rolling pin until it is pliable. Home-rendered lard cooled for 3 days—during which time it forms large crystals—and then brought nearly to room temperature is wonderfully savory and makes the flakiest and darkest crust. A lard-and-butter mixture is rich and sweet.)

¾ cup very cold water (a little less if you use butter as part of the
  shortening, because butter contains water)
1 tablespoon additional shortening, for greasing the pie plate
3 tablespoons cold unsalted butter, for the filling
1 tablespoon cold skim or whole milk, for brushing the pie
1 tablespoon granulated sugar, for sprinkling the crust

1. Prepare a fruit filling. You may use one of the recipes that follow this one, or your own. All peeling, pitting, soaking, or cooking should be accomplished before you make the crust. But the final steps—for example, the mixing of apple slices or berries with sugar—must be done at the last minute or the bottom crust will overflow with juices before the top crust has been attached. This can make for a messy pie. If you use one of my recipes for fruit filling, please read it now for instructions on timing.

2. Preheat the oven to 450° F.

3. In a large bowl (say 5- or 6-quart capacity) mix the flour, 2 teaspoons sugar, and salt with your fingers.

4. Drop the shortening onto the flour in the bowl. Toss the pieces to coat them with flour, then quickly break them up into about twelve nuggets the size of small walnuts, again tossing gently to coat, and arrange them on the flour in a rough circle about an inch in from the sides of the bowl.

5. Now "rub" the fat into the flour with your fingers. Do it in two stages.

First, scoop the fingers of both hands down along the sides and bottom of the bowl under the flour, and lift them several inches above the rim of the bowl, with a pile of flour and one large chunk of fat in each. Holding your fingers slightly open, lightly rub your thumbs back and forth across your fingertips, about three times, in order to break up the large chunks of fat into pieces the size of small olives while coating them with flour. Do not smear the fat or blend the flour with the fat; do not press down hard with your thumbs; do not flatten the fat. Roll it between your fingertips. Let the flour and fat fall back into the bowl.

Repeat five times, each time breaking up two of the large nuggets of fat, until all of them are gone.

In the second stage, continue scooping up the flour and fat, each time sweeping your thumbs *only once* across your fingertips, and only in one direction, from little finger to index finger. Be sure to scoop along the bottom of the bowl, then bring your hands high above the bowl. As your thumbs move across your fingertips, the smallest pieces of shortening will slip between your fingers, and the largest pieces will tumble over your index finger. Let whatever flour and fat remains in your hands drop back into the bowl. Everything should fall lightly through the air, as though you were cooling the particles of dough and aerating them. Which you are. Repeat this motion about twenty to twenty-five times.

You are done when the particles of flour-coated fat range in size from coarse meal to grains of rice to peas to small olives. It is important that the fat particles range widely in size. A little flour may remain uncoated.

6. Add ½ cup of the cold water, sprinkling it evenly over the surface of the mixture. Immediately stir the water into the flour with a fork, held vertically, starting at the sides of the bowl, then stirring in smaller and smaller circles toward the center, making sure that the points of the fork sweep the bottom of the bowl. Your motions should be light. After a few stirs, all the flour

should be moistened and the dough gathered into small clumps. If there are too many loose, dry crumbs, add a tablespoon or two of cold water and stir again. Do not overmix. The more thoroughly you have rubbed the shortening into the flour and the more shortening you use, the less water you will need. It is unlikely that you will use the entire ¾ cup.

7. Gather all the dough by pressing it together firmly against one side of the bowl. Break off about half, shape it into a ball with your cool fingertips, not your sweaty palms, and flatten it on the counter into a disk about an inch high. Repeat with the other half of the dough.

8. Grease a 9-inch glass (or dark metal) pie plate with the tablespoon of additional shortening.

9. You may immediately roll out both crusts, or wrap each disk in plastic and refrigerate for 15 to 30 minutes—if this is more convenient or if the kitchen is very warm or if you have used lard and butter as your shortening. If you do refrigerate the dough, it will then require 5 to 10 minutes at room temperature before it becomes malleable; it should not break at the edges when you roll it out.

To roll: On a well-floured surface with a heavy, well-floured rolling pin, roll the larger of the two disks into a rough 13-inch circle, ⅛ inch thick or slightly more. Use a light touch with the rolling pin, placing it on the dough between the center and the near edge and rolling away from you to the far edge, being careful to lift the rolling pin before you flatten the far edge. Roll toward you in the same manner. Turn the dough an eighth or a quarter of the way around, and roll again. You should not compress it downward but stretch it outward. If the dough sticks to the work surface (the first signs are that it fails to stretch freely away from you as you roll it or does not easily pry off when you turn it), run a thin metal spatula under it and flour the surface again. This dough should be easy to work with and require only ten to twelve strokes of the rolling pin. The first few dozen times, your circle of dough may take the shape of an amoeba; just make sure that when you are finished the smallest diameter is 13 inches so that it will fit the pie plate without major patching.

10. Brush any excess flour from the circle of dough (flour can toughen the surface of the crust), fold the circle gently into quarters, and lift it onto the greased pie plate, placing the point of the dough at the center. Unfold the dough into a circle again. Fit it into the pie plate by gently lifting the edges of the dough all around and nudging it (without stretching it) to line the bottom and sides of the plate. Trim the edges all around with a large pair of scissors so that the dough comes just beyond the edge of the rim. If you do not have enough dough in some spots, patch with scraps from other areas, first moistening them with water. This recipe is more ample than most; you will have lots of scraps. If any holes appear on the bottom or along the sides, patch them too, firmly pressing a neat but ample piece of moistened scrap dough over the hole. If the filling leaks through the bottom crust, it will at the very least glue the pie to the dish and burn against the glass. At the worst, the filling may boil under the bottom crust and carry off some of the pie; it once happened to me. Other pie recipes do not tell you this for fear that your hands will shake uncontrollably as you try to patch the dough.

Cover the bottom crust with plastic wrap.

Roll out the other disk of dough into a 13-inch circle and lay it gently over the plastic wrap. Unless the kitchen is cool and the dough is firm, cover with more plastic wrap and refrigerate for 10 to 15 minutes.

11. Meanwhile, finish making the fruit filling—if there is anything left to be done. Then remove the pie plate and dough from the refrigerator and let them come to room temperature for 5 minutes. Remove the plastic and gently fold the top crust into quarters and set aside.

Spoon the filling into the dough-lined pie plate, keeping it away from the rim. Cut the cold butter into thin slices and scatter them over the fruit.

12. Align the point of the folded top crust with the center of the filling and gently unfold it over the filling and the rim. With a large pair of scissors or a knife, uniformly trim the edges of the dough so that it extends a generous ½ inch beyond the edges of the bottom crust, patching where necessary.

Working quickly, fold the ½-inch margin of top-crust dough around and under the edge of the lower crust so that it rests on the rim of the pie plate. With one hand, press lightly to seal, using your other hand to keep the dough even with the edge of the plate.

13. Shape the edges of the dough into a decorative pattern. Here are two easy ones to use when you can't think of anything else.

a. Flatten the pastry all around with the tines of a dinner fork held level with the rim, leaving deep parallel grooves pointing toward the center of the pie. To avoid catching the soft dough each time you lift the fork, tilt the handle of the fork upward first, and then remove the point end.

b. Raise and flute the edge; this will help create a

rampart against the boiling juices. Squeeze the dough on the rim of the pie plate to form a ridge all around about ½ inch high and ¼ inch thick. Be careful not to press your fingers down into the dough against the walls of the pie plate or the crust may become thin and the filling leak profusely in the oven.

Next, shape the ridge into a scalloped edge by placing the tips of your left thumb and index finger on the inside of the ridge, holding them about an inch apart. Place the tip of your right index finger on the outside of the ridge, between the fingertips on the inside. By pressing the fingertips against the dough, you will form a V. Continue all the way around the pie, repeating the same motion, until the entire ridge of dough has been transformed. Then go around again, trying to make the pattern even and regular.

14. Now the pie should be baked without delay; otherwise the fruit juices can make the bottom crust soggy. Lightly brush the milk over the crust. You will probably not need the full tablespoon. Do not allow the milk to puddle in the valleys of the crust; if it does, mop it up with the corner of a folded paper towel.

15. Sprinkle the crust with the granulated sugar.

16. With a small, sharp knife, cut decorative vents into the crust (for example, three V-shapes pointing toward the center of the pie cut along each of three or four radii). Use the knife to open the cuts slightly so that they will not reseal in the oven. You can also make a ¼- or ½-inch circle, square, or triangle in the very center. These vents allow steam to escape, helping to avoid soggy crusts and relieving pressure when the juices begin to overflow. Marion Cunningham does not believe in vents.

17. Set the pie on a baking sheet with raised

edges, and bake immediately in the preheated 450° F. oven until the darkest spots on the crust are very dark brown, about 25 to 40 minutes. Reduce the heat to 375° F. and continue baking until it has been in the oven for a total of about 1 hour, or until the crust is a deep, crisp golden brown. Turn the pie once or twice for even browning. Test the fruit (especially apples or peaches) with a small knife to see that they are fully cooked but not as mushy as applesauce or peach jam. Look through the sides of the glass pie plate to make sure that the bottom crust is browned. (Cover the entire crust or just the fluted edges with aluminum foil if either browns excessively before the filling is cooked.)

A fruit pie does not need to overflow to signal that it is done. Both cornstarch and flour are fully cooked at about 190° F., way below the boiling point. Keeping them above that temperature for, say, 20 minutes, can destroy their thickening power. Baking the pie at too low a temperature encourages overflow before the crust is done. But just a little boil-over gives the pie a nice, homey look.

18. Let the pie cool in its pie plate on a rack for at least 2 hours. If you allow the pie to cool all the way down to room temperature, reheat it slightly at 325° F. for 15 to 20 minutes. Do not refrigerate or cover hermetically. The next day, leftover pie can be reheated successfully at 375° F. for 20 to 25 minutes and allowed to cool for 5 minutes. But twice reheated, the crust may become greasy.

19. Serve with good vanilla ice cream.

20. When your pie has been nearly consumed, go back to step 1 and start again.

Four Fruit Fillings

Apple pie is perfect for fall, after the harvest, when the fruit is at its peak. In later months, taste the apples carefully before putting them into a pie to make sure they are still crisp and full of flavor. At the height of summer you will bake sumptuous fruit pies packed with wild blueberries, peaches, or fresh sour cherries, all picked at their finest hour.

Apple Pie Filling

What I like least about the average apple pie is cinnamon. This filling contains no cinnamon. The only flavorings here are vanilla and lemon juice. The only taste should be pure apple. You can also substitute some well-packed brown sugar for the white sugar to accentuate the slightly caramelized taste of baked apples, which is accentuated by vanilla.

Old recipes from England and America use cloves, mace, nutmeg, orange-flower water, rose water, lemon zest, or brown sugar, but only sometimes cinnamon. The French rarely pair cinnamon with apples. Later American recipes always include cinnamon, as though its rough, gritty, overwhelming flavor were inseparable from the flavor of apples. Try making a mock apple pie (an odd idea from early-nineteenth-century America), using the recipe on the back of a Ritz cracker box, as I did (see page 435); instead of apples, you fill a pie crust with smashed Ritz crackers soaked in sugar syrup, lemon juice, and lots of cinnamon. I tested one on my wife and three friends, and nobody guessed that there were no apples in the pie! Promiscuous use of cinnamon has made us forget the true taste of apples. Now you will remember.

3½ pounds (7 or 8) baking apples (use Gravensteins early in the season when they are less sugary, or Pippins, or Granny Smiths)
1 lemon, cut in half
1¼ cups white granulated sugar (adjusted for extra-tart or extra-sweet apples)
3 tablespoons all-purpose flour
1 teaspoon (scant) pure vanilla extract
¼ teaspoon salt (pie experts, especially from the South, insist that a little salt helps bring out the essential flavor of the fruit; I agree)

1. Before making the piecrust, peel and core the apples, and put them in a large bowl of cold water mixed with the juice of one of the lemon halves.

2. Make the piecrust dough through step 10, page 485. Refrigerate the circles of dough.

3. Immediately remove the apples from their lemon water and dry them. Cut each one into quarters, and then cut each quarter both lengthwise and crosswise into four chunks (yielding 8 to 9 cups), or sixteen chunks for each apple.

4. In a large bowl, toss the apple chunks with all the other filling ingredients and let stand for 10 to 15 minutes. The apples will give off some of their juice and shrink and soften a bit. If you leave the apples much longer, they can become wrinkled and rubbery as they lose too much juice.

5. Resume the main recipe at step 11.

Sour Cherry Filling

This filling makes the classic American cherry pie of song and story. Sour cherries are also known as pie cherries and are in season from about July 1 to mid-August throughout much of the country except the West. They are best in early season—firm, very tart, and bright red. Buy only those with their stems intact. Sour cherries ferment quickly after the stems are removed; this leaves an opening for bacteria and oxygen. Individually frozen sour cherries can make fine pies year-round, but most frozen cherries are shipped only to supermarkets in midwestern states, where cherry pie is king.

491

9 cups fresh sour cherries, stems and pits intact
4½ tablespoons instant tapioca, whirled in a blender until it
*   becomes powder*
2¼ cups sugar (decreased by ¼ to ½ cup if, late in the season,
*   the cherries are particularly sweet for sour cherries)*
1 tablespoon lemon juice, or more if the cherries are sweet
½ teaspoon salt
¼ teaspoon (scant) "pure" or "natural" almond extract

1. At least 2½ hours before you plan to bake the pie, make the cherry filling. Wash, stem, and pit the cherries (you should now have 6 cups), putting them into a non-reactive, 4-quart saucepan. (Williams-Sonoma and the Back to Basics catalog have inexpensive little plastic pitting machines that shorten the labor by at least half. They encourage you to make cherry pies.)

2. Mix all the other ingredients with the cherries, and let the mixture stand for 30 minutes.

3. Bring the cherry mixture to a simmer over medium heat and cook for about 5 minutes, until it thickens.

4. Let the filling cool for 1½ hours or longer, the last 30 minutes in the refrigerator. Warm fillings melt crusts.

5. No more than 20 minutes before the cherry mixture is cool, make the piecrust in the main recipe through step 10, page 485. If you are using Crisco and the weather is cool, there is no need to refrigerate the circles of dough. Pour the cherries and their juice into the bottom crust in step 11.

Peach Filling

4 pounds peaches (about 9 large or 16 medium)
1 lemon, cut in half
½ cup well-packed light brown sugar
½ cup granulated sugar
½ teaspoon salt
1 pinch nutmeg
1 pinch mace
¼ teaspoon (scant) "pure" or "natural" almond extract
3 tablespoons cornstarch
1 tablespoon arrowroot

1. Before making the piecrust, peel the peaches. If you dip each of them in boiling water for 15 seconds, the skins will slip off with the aid of a paring knife. Put them into a large bowl. Toss with the juice of one lemon half to prevent the peaches from browning.

Halve the peaches, remove their pits, and cut each into wedges nearly an inch at their thickest, returning the wedges to the bowl and tossing them with the juice of the remaining lemon half. You should have about 8 cups of peach wedges.

2. Make the piecrust in the main recipe through step 10, page 485.

3. While the dough returns to room temperature, mix all the remaining filling ingredients in a small bowl. Just before pouring the peaches into the bottom crust, toss them with this mixture. Adjust by 2 or 3 tablespoons the amount of both types of sugar if the peaches are especially sweet or especially tart.

Wild Blueberry Filling

Wild blueberries are smaller and more fragile than cultivated blueberries and have a much finer flavor and more interesting texture. A couple of summers ago in the Northeast, they were in season from August 1 to August 28. In a pinch you can use fresh cultivated blueberries or even frozen blueberries. The recipe works fine with raspberries, blackberries, and most others, but strawberries require special treatment. Arrowroot is added to the cornstarch to make the juice shiny and transparent.

6 cups wild blueberries
2 cups sugar
5 tablespoons cornstarch

¹/₂ teaspoon salt
2 tablespoons fresh lemon juice

1. Make the piecrust in the main recipe through step 10, page 485.

2. While the piecrust is in the refrigerator, pick over the blueberries, removing any stems. Wash the fruit delicately and set to drain. Mix the other filling ingredients except for the lemon juice in a small bowl. Blueberry skins contain oxalic acid, which attacks nearly all starch thickeners. Peeling blueberries is an unheard-of task and would wreck their taste and shape. So we must expect irregular success in the thickening process.

3. Resume the main recipe with step 11. Just when the piecrust is ready for the fruit, sprinkle the blueberries with the lemon juice, toss them with the other filling ingredients, and pour them into the prepared piecrust.

November 1995

Index

Page numbers in **bold** type indicate recipes.

503

Permissions Acknowledgments

A Note About the Author

Jeffrey Steingarten trained to become a food writer at Harvard College, Harvard Law School, the Massachusetts Institute of Technology, and the *Harvard Lampoon*. For the past eight years he has been the internationally feared and acclaimed food critic of *Vogue* magazine. Recently he has also become the food correspondent for the on-line magazine *Slate*. For essays in this collection, Mr. Steingarten has won countless awards from the James Beard Foundation and the International Association of Culinary Professionals. On Bastille Day, 1994, the French Republic made him a Chevalier in the Order of Merit for his writing on French gastronomy. As the man who ate everything, Chevalier Steingarten has no favorite food, color, or song. His preferred eating destinations, however, are Memphis, Paris, Alba, Chengdu—and his loft in New York City.

A Note on the Type

This book is set in a typeface called Méridien, a classic roman designed by Adrian Frutiger for the French type foundry Deberny et Peignot in 1957. Adrian Frutiger was born in Interlaken, Switzerland, in 1928 and studied type design there and at the Kunstgewerbeschule in Zurich. In 1953 he moved to Paris, where he joined Deberny et Peignot as a member of the design staff. Méridien, as well as his other typeface of world renown, Univers, was created for the Lumitype photoset machine.

Composed by North Market Street Graphics,
Lancaster, Pennsylvania

Printed and bound by Quebecor Printing,
Martinsburg, West Virginia

Designed by Iris Weinstein